Rearranging the Landscape
of the Gods

Studies of the Weatherhead East Asian Institute
Columbia University

The Weatherhead East Asian Institute is Columbia University's center for research, publication, and teaching on modern and contemporary Asia Pacific regions. The Studies of the Weatherhead East Asian Institute were inaugurated in 1962 to bring to a wider public the results of significant new research on modern and contemporary East Asia.

Rearranging the Landscape of the Gods

The Politics of a Pilgrimage Site in Japan, 1573–1912

Sarah Thal

The University of Chicago Press
Chicago & London

Sarah Thal is assistant professor of history at Rice University.

Title page illustration: The Gold Gate, marking the entrance to the domain of Konpira on the road from Marugame. For complete source information, please see the caption to figure 1.5 on page 20 below.

The University of Chicago Press, Chicago 60637
The University of Chicago Press, Ltd., London
© 2005 by The University of Chicago
All rights reserved. Published 2005
Printed in the United States of America

14 13 12 11 10 09 08 07 06 05   1 2 3 4 5

ISBN: 0-226-79420-2 (cloth)
ISBN: 0-226-79421-0 (paper)

Library of Congress Cataloging-in-Publication Data

Thal, Sarah, 1966—
   Rearranging the landscape of the gods : the politics of a pilgrimage site in Japan,
1573–1912 / Sarah Thal.
      p.   cm.
   Includes bibliographical references and index.
   ISBN 0-226-79420-2 (cloth : alk. paper)—ISBN 0-226-79421-0 (pbk. : alk. paper)
   1. Kotohiragū (Kotohira-chō, Japan)   2. Konpira (Shinto deity)   I. Title.
   BL2225.K652K678 2005
   299.5′6135′095235—dc22
                              2004009967

For my parents,
Norman and Marguerite Long Thal

Contents

Figures

ACKNOWLEDGMENTS

Throughout work on this book, I have been privileged to learn from the generosity of countless people, many of whom appear in the footnotes, but only a fraction of whom can be acknowledged here. Most especially, I would like to thank Carol Gluck, an inspiring mentor and generous friend, whose guidance and encouragement have sustained this project from beginning to end. Richard Sims, Louis Brenner, and Tim Barrett at SOAS, Helen Hardacre at Harvard, and Ryūichi Abe at Columbia provided early encouragement and guidance. Henry Smith, David Howell, James Ketelaar, Elizabeth Blackmar, Janine Sawada, Steve Cantley, and two anonymous readers for the University of Chicago Press gave helpful comments on the manuscript at various stages. Carl Caldwell, Anne Chao, Jamie Forster, Betsy Thal Gephart, David Gray, Ira Gruber, Eva Haverkamp, Chris Hill, Catherine Howard, Anne Klein, Jeff Kripal, Joe Lindley, Hajime Nakatani, Scott O'Bryan, Nanxiu Qian, Richard Smith, Allison Sneider, Gale Stokes, Wada Mitsutoshi, Joel Wolfe, and many, many others provided much-needed encouragement, advice, or assistance. The insights of Angela Zito, Conrad Totman, Norman Thal, and Andrew Bernstein have proven especially helpful.

   I can never express enough appreciation for my mentors in Kōchi, Japan. Yorimitsu Kanji, the late Moriguchi Kōji, and Uchikawa Kiyosuke, as well as the late Sekita Hidesato and Takahashi Shirō, taught me to read the old, handwritten documents and shared with me not only their friendship but also their knowledge and love of local history. Tamura Yasuoki of Kōchi University kindly acted as my sponsor and provided introductions; the staff of Kōchi Prefectural Library and Tosa Shidankai generously opened the stacks and provided a place to work. Ueno Satoko and Nishimura Hiroko traveled with me interviewing fishermen, shipbuilders, and retirees around the Inland Sea. Thanks especially go to Seto Tetsuo and the late Seto Shigeka, who provided a home away from home.

At Kotohira, I am particularly indebted to the late Matsubara Hideaki, archivist of Kotohira Shrine, and the editors of the town history *Chōshi Kotohira,* who generously made available innumerable documents. Hashikata Toshiko, in particular, opened her home to me, providing a local perspective on the business of pilgrimage in the town. Nakao Katsuhide, Ishikawa Nobuaki, and Fujita Hiroshi shared with me highlights of Kagawa prefecture and its religious cultures. Many thanks also go to Hayashi Makoto, Hirota Masaki, Isomae Jun'ichi, Shimazono Susumu, Tamamuro Fumio, and Ōsawa Yasuo, Sadako, and Akiko, who opened many doors to make this study possible.

Special thanks to the following people and institutions for their assistance and/or permission to reproduce original materials: Shinano Itsuki, Takubo Kyōji, and Kaseyama Tomoko of Kotohira Shrine; Matsuoka Hiroyasu of Tawa Archive; Morimoto Shūhei and Shibano Nobuhiko of the Seto Inland Sea Folk History Museum; Ono Yasuo of Kotohira Ezu o Mamoru Kai; Kyūman Museum; Tan'o Yasunori; the National Diet Library; Amy Heinrich of Columbia University's C. V. Starr Library; Kagawa Prefectural Library; and many others. The research and writing were made possible by a Japan Foundation Dissertation Research Fellowship (1995–96) as well as generous funding from several Mosle Research Awards and the Rice University dean of humanities. My great appreciation goes to Madge Huntington at the Weatherhead East Asian Institute of Columbia University, and especially to Alan Thomas and Erik Carlson of the University of Chicago Press, who saw this book into print. Thanks also to Andrea Dunn for the maps and charts, and to Steve Cantley for photographs and much, much more.

My heartfelt appreciation goes to all—whether named here or not—who helped me with this project in any way. They provided enough insight and information, support and enthusiasm for several books. I only hope to express some of that warmth and wealth in the pages that follow.

A Note on Pronunciations, Names, and Dates

Japanese is a polysyllabic language: each syllable is kept distinct, not merged with another. Because there are only five vowel sounds—*a* (ah), *i* (ee), *u* (oo), *e* (eh), and *o* (oh)—pronunciation is very simple. Every syllable ends in a vowel, except for the syllable *n* (nn or mm). Thus, "Konpira" consists of four syllables, "Koh-n-pee-rah," as does "Kotohira," "Koh-toh-hee-rah," and "Ieyasu," "Ee-eh-yah-soo." To the English ear, these can sometimes sound like diphthongs. For instance, "Meiji," or "Meh-ee-jee," can sound like "*May*-jee." Each syllable, however, should be of the same length and emphasis as every other—a good task in rhythmic counting for beginners.

A long vowel, written with a macron, denotes two vowels of the same syllable slurred together. Thus, "Konkōin" becomes "Koh-nn-koh-oh-ee-n," and "Fudō Myōō" becomes "Foo-doh-oh-Myoh-oh-oh-oh." (Pronounced quickly, "Fudō" may sound like a short "foo" just before "dough," in one beat, and "Myōō" with its long *oh*s extending to two.) When two identical vowels appear consecutively, however, they are separated by a short catch, as in the English exclamation "uh-oh." In this way, "Kotooka" becomes "Koh-toh / oh-ka," "Motoori" becomes "Moh-toh / oh-ree," and "Susano'o" becomes "Soo-sah-noh / oh." In these cases, the English speaker may hear a slight emphasis on the second vowel, immediately after the catch.

Following Japanese usage, names are written with the family name first, followed by the given name. A few very prominent leaders are best known by their given names, however, with Toyotomi Hideyoshi frequently called Hideyoshi. In this book, the macrons for common place-names such as Tokyo, Osaka, Honshu, or Hokkaido have been omitted.

All dates in this text have been translated into the Gregorian calendar. Until the Japanese government adopted this calendar in 1873, each year was divided into twelve months of thirty days, with an intercalary month inserted periodically. Years before 1868 were referred to according to era names—for example, "the twelfth year of the Bunka era," that is, 1815. From the Meiji period on, the name of an era coincided with the reign of the current emperor. Thus, the fifth year of Meiji, 1872, corresponded to the fifth year of the Meiji emperor's reign. These Japanese-style dates are maintained in translations and in notes, often abbreviated as Bunka 12 or Meiji 5. With month and day, for instance, Keiō 3.12.28 would correspond to the twenty-eighth day of the twelfth month of the third year of the Keiō era (pronounced "Keh-ee-oh-oh" or "Kay-oh")—22 January 1868.

Introduction

"Not another shrine!"
"More steps?!?"
"Who are all these gods and buddhas?"
"What is Shinto anyway?"

So ring the cries of tired tourists, trudging from historic shrine to art-filled temple to yet another picturesque pilgrimage site as they travel around Japan. While museums, theme parks, and recent architectural feats increasingly vie for visitors' attention, Shinto shrines and Buddhist temples remain the mainstay of tourist itineraries. Historical, cultural, and devotional spaces, they occupy a prominent place in the Japanese landscape. From the perspective of tourists in the twenty-first century, as from the viewpoints of politicians in the twentieth, of pilgrims in the nineteenth, and of imperial historians back to the fourteenth century and even before, Japan can in many ways be called the Land of the Gods (*kami no kuni,* or *shinkoku*).

A major challenge for anyone interested in Japan today is to understand what those gods are, what Shinto (the Way of the Gods) is, and where worship fits in the structures of contemporary Japan. In this industrially advanced, often avowedly secular country, the gods can seem symbols of chauvinistic nationalism, unsullied objects of an innocent nature worship, or quaint, folksy anachronisms, and their shrines modest way stations or prominent tourist attractions. To understand the changing significance of the gods over time—especially from the late sixteenth century, when many new gods appeared, until the early twentieth century, by which time many of the trends evident today had become established—is the goal of this book.

The beings translated here as "gods"—Japanese *kami* or, when combined with other Chinese characters (as in *shintō*), *shin*—are notoriously difficult to define. The most oft quoted writer on the subject, the eighteenth-century literary scholar Motoori Norinaga (1730–1801), himself famously admitted in his magnum opus on the early eighth-century text *Kojiki*, "I do not yet understand the meaning of the term *kami*." Motoori's subsequent definition consisted more of a list of types of kami than a coherent explanation. "Speaking in general," he continued, "it may be said that *kami* signifies, in the first place, the deities of heaven and earth that appear in the ancient records and also the spirits of the shrines where they are worshipped. It is hardly necessary to say that it includes human beings. It also includes such objects as birds, beasts, trees, plants, seas, mountains and so forth. In ancient usage, anything whatsoever which was outside the ordinary, which possessed superior power, or which was awe-inspiring was called *kami*."[1] Consisting of countless named and unnamed beings, enshrined separately and together throughout the Japanese islands, the kami elude generalization, whether in ancient times or today.

Beyond their sheer diversity, why are kami so difficult to define? Four reasons stand out—and each helps explain the rationale for, and structure of, this book.

First, kami have proven difficult to generalize about because of their *particularity*. It is *particular* trees, mountains, foxes, or even humans who come to be regarded as kami, not all of them. They are almost always worshipped in their own distinct places, marked by mountains or trees, shrines or statues. Thus, the kami Amaterasu, although often revered from afar, is inseparable from her shrine at Ise.[2] Similarly, the kami Hachiman at Iwashimizu, though enshrined centuries ago as an outpost of the Hachiman at Usa, nevertheless attracts different worshippers, answers different prayers, and accretes different tales of its exploits. To ignore the specificity of a kami's place—both its geographical location and its social context—thus blinds us to the role of that kami in the thoughts and actions of its worshippers.

This book, therefore, focuses on a single site: Mt. Zōzu (now known as Mt. Kotohira) on Shikoku, the fourth-largest island in Japan. To give a sense of the place at the height of its popularity in the 1850s, chapter 1 draws upon a personal diary to follow a pilgrim to the shrine. The deeply wooded Mt. Zōzu stands prominently in the fertile Sanuki plain. On a clear day today, visitors to the site can look out over rice fields and roads to boats on the Inland Sea and even to the coast of the largest island, Honshu, beyond. In the years before industrial air pollution, when sailors could spot the distinctively shaped mountain from the sea and residents on the plain could gaze up at the forested, foggy slope, Mt. Zōzu apparently exuded an aura of sacred power.

Viewers' interpretation of that power, however, has altered over time. The second difficulty in defining kami, therefore, is *the startling frequency with which they change.* Today, visitors to a shrine are often told that its kami is an ancient deity, recorded in eighth- or twelfth-century texts. Such claims, however, suggesting as they do a timeless being that exists untouched by the vagaries of human affairs, are simply some of the most recent ways in which people have explained and labeled the powers that they sense at the site. Just as the political, social, economic, and intellectual contexts of those powers varied over the years, so too did the ways in which people interpreted them. In Japan, as elsewhere, when worshippers of one deity died out, suffered defeat, or moved away, new residents or occupying victors arrived to claim the powers of its sacred site for themselves, often renaming it in the process. Moreover, as people adopted new ways of looking at the world, they reinterpreted the awesome powers accordingly—placing them in Confucian-influenced histories, in Chinese astrologies or other systems of divination, in Buddhist cosmologies, or, more recently, in humanist, psychological analyses. In many cases, virtually nothing about a sacred site has stayed the same—not its name, its history (which was retold with each transformation), its rituals, its perceived relationship to human beings, or even the type of deity with which it is associated. Any study of sacred sites must therefore look past the seemingly convincing histories told today to understand the many transformations of the gods over time, for it is those changes that shaped the distinctive rituals, reputation, and ambience surrounding each particular god and its shrine.[3]

Interpretations of Mt. Zōzu's power have thus changed dramatically over the years, and most of this book is devoted to chronicling those changes and examining the processes by which they came about. At its most basic level, the book explores how the mountain came to be associated first with the god Konpira, and then with Kotohira, the deity enshrined there today. It also addresses the ways in which both Konpira and Kotohira changed over time, and the broader dynamics of such reinterpretation in general.

Mt. Zōzu gained fame countrywide from the seventeenth to the nineteenth centuries as the site of the miracle-working Konpira Daigongen, attracting hundreds of thousands of pilgrims each year. It grew into one of the most popular pilgrimage destinations of the nineteenth century, compared by writers of the time even to the shrine of Amaterasu at Ise.[4] There is no reliable evidence, however, that people identified the mountain with Konpira before 1573. Instead, architectural and textual evidence, when juxtaposed with broader local and national developments, shows that priests repeatedly altered the identity of Mt. Zōzu's god. They renamed the perceived power of the site to accommodate each new ruler in the area and then altered their interpretations of that god in response to changing political, social, and intellectual trends.

Chapters 2 and 3 chronicle the varied interpretations of the power on Mt. Zōzu up to and including the enshrinement of Konpira and its elaboration as Konpira Daigongen in the late sixteenth century. Typical of sacred sites throughout Japanese history, Mt. Zōzu became an arena for the at times violent encounters of competing rulers and ritual systems. With each change in government, the priests on Mt. Zōzu either moved quickly to ally with the victors or were replaced by the new rulers' appointees, redefining the power of the mountain to legitimize the men who could, with a word, either destroy the shrine or ensure its survival. Thus, after the victory of Tokugawa forces and the establishment of the Tokugawa shogunate in 1600, influential men on the mountain consolidated the support of the Tokugawa-approved lord of the area (*daimyō*), who became a firm devotee of Konpira.

While the first lord donated generously to the shrine, his successors, in contrast, devoted less attention—and less monetary support—to securing the blessings of the gods, turning instead to the ongoing economic and social challenges of administering their domain. In order to ensure their economic, not just political, survival amid the disruptions of a growing market economy, therefore, the priests of Mt. Zōzu cultivated relationships with other increasingly influential groups in the eighteenth-century Tokugawa order: the imperial court, long overshadowed by the shogun, and wealthy commoners. Chapter 4 shows that in doing so, they reshaped their god once again, keeping the name Konpira already approved by the political leaders but either retelling its origins to identify it as a native, imperial kami or adopting new symbols to appeal to potential donors among the growing population of prosperous merchants, shippers, and other businessmen.

Publicized by these new constituencies, Konpira became known and worshipped by people throughout the country. Yet, ironically, as chapter 5 demonstrates, the priests on Mt. Zōzu lost control over the image of the god by virtue of the very popularity they had worked so hard to attain. The number of interpretations of Konpira multiplied, as did the practices associated with it. The cult of Konpira became so widely accepted that, along with the cults of many other popular deities, it became part of the common cultural background of nineteenth-century Japan.

The history of Konpira on Mt. Zōzu thus suggests a general pattern in the transformation of gods not just in Shikoku, but throughout Japan and, indeed, the world. Priests initially work to acquire the approval of rulers and thereby ensure the survival of their god. Then they follow wealth, seeking sponsors for buildings, rituals, and the everyday expenses of continued worship. Finally, if the priests recruit enough followers for the god, worshippers, entrepreneurs, and entertainers make the deity their own, depicting and approaching it in countless personalized ways. Throughout this process, then, because priests respond to the preferences of rulers, donors, writers, and entrepreneurs—indeed, of anyone who speaks of or worships the god—the changing identities and interpretations of deities serve as barometers of political, social, and cultural change.

The third difficulty plaguing efforts at definition is that the gods of Japan not only change into but also *exist in close association with countless other types of powerful beings*—beings not identified by the term *kami,* capacious as it is. Not only do priests and worshippers enshrine many deities at the same site, constructing sacred cosmologies to support each interpretation, but any one spirit of the site (referred to here as a "god") might be envisioned simultaneously as a kami, a buddha, a long-nosed goblin (*tengu*), a dragon, or any of countless other forms, each form overlapping, opposed to or supportive of the others, or even entirely unrelated. For centuries, as evident in this summary of Mt. Zōzu's history, these beings (as identified by priests, scholars, and worshippers) existed in complex relationship to each other. A powerful entity might be defined as a kami yet regarded as a guardian of a buddha, or, defined as a buddha, it might be enshrined to protect a kami. It might be considered a kami that is a manifestation in this world of a Buddhist essence, or less often a buddha appearing as the manifestation of a kami. It might also be portrayed as the vengeful spirit of a dead human being, or so associated with a tengu or animal as to be inseparable from it. Few people saw any contradiction in such multiple interpretations, for they viewed these and many other beings in relation to each other, to humans, and to the everyday world according to an intricate, often overlapping interlacing of related deities.[5]

Such complicated relationships suddenly became problematic early in 1868. Responding to social, economic, and political tensions arising in part from treaties signed by the Tokugawa shogun in 1855 and 1856 that opened ports for trade with the United States, Britain, and other Western powers, a group of southwestern daimyo and samurai, along with allied commoners and members of the imperial court, ousted the Tokugawa from power. They set up instead a new government claiming to "restore" rule to the imperial line in the person of a young sixteen-year-old known to posterity as the Meiji emperor. To legitimize this "Meiji Restoration," a few influential men among the new rulers called upon the support of kami—not as they existed in the common practices of the time, seemingly inseparable from a myriad of buddhas and other spirits imported from across Asia, but as the supposedly purely indigenous deities identified in the early imperial histories by the scholar Motoori Norinaga and his followers. The emperor, these "nativists" emphasized, was descended from the native kami of the sun, Amaterasu, and the land of Japan was created by other kami of the ancient texts. Buddhas from India and other foreign deities only sullied the pure, native gods, and thus the shining rule of the emperor, they insisted; other beings such as tengu were either irrelevant or the confused delusions (later called *meishin,* or "superstitions") of the uneducated populace.

The Meiji nativists defined a sharp distinction between "native" kami and "foreign" buddhas. Beginning in 1868, they enforced a "separation of kami and buddhas" that identified sites of worship either as shrines (*jinja, jingū*) exclusively devoted to ancient, native kami or as temples (*tera,* or, in a combining form, *-ji*) preaching the Buddhist law. They thus split asunder two categories that had previously been intertwined. Moreover, their terminology has persisted until today, forcing everyone who tries to speak or write of the gods to reinforce the separation by referring to "kami," to "buddhas," or to "kami and buddhas," still distinguishing between the two—and to relegate the many tengu, foxes, and other powers of popular faith to the lesser status of "spirits." As the nativists provided legitimization for the Meiji Restoration, then, they revolutionized the religious landscape of Japan, establishing an exclusive, nativist Way of the Gods (*shintō,* literally "Way of the Kami") in conjunction with the new, imperial state.

Chapters 6 and 7 trace on Mt. Zōzu this revolutionary "separation of kami and buddhas" (*shinbutsu bunri*) and the priests' political positioning as they negotiated the uncertainties of the Meiji Restoration.[6] Following the previous pattern, in which his predecessors redefined the god in the early seventeenth century in order to ensure both personal and institutional survival, the tonsured priest of Konpira Daigongen quickly renounced his Buddhist ties and renamed the god Kotohira Ōkami ("Great Kami Kotohira"). In doing so, he avowed exclusive dedication to the Way of the Gods (*shintō*), as defined by the nativists in power. However, the priest of the new Kotohira Shrine sought not only survival under the new regime, but a continuation of the great wealth and prominent status that Konpira Daigongen had enjoyed before 1868. His pursuit of such privileges by cultivating ties to the fledgling imperial state not only brought Kotohira into a new, centralized hierarchy of shrines, but by 1873 committed him and the other priests of Kotohira to the dissemination of nativist teachings designed to combat the influence of

Christianity and support the state. At Kotohira Shrine, as explained in chapter 8, the priests combined this educational agenda of the state with their own efforts to increase donations to the shrine, promoting Kotohira in particular, and by implication Shinto in general, as a model of civilized, educated behavior appropriate to the new, imperial subjects and familiar to the most generous worshippers of the god.

Although it set in place the ideological foundations of the new regime, nativist dominance in the early Meiji government was relatively short-lived. European and American ideas of civilization and progress, as well as the technologies and institutions associated with them, became increasingly influential as the new leaders worked to compete in the world of international commerce, law, and imperialism of which they were now a part. This relationship with the West—especially the translation and dissemination of ideas—gave rise to the fourth, most complicated, difficulty in understanding the gods of Japan: *the problem of applying Western religious concepts to Japanese phenomena.* Including as they do political and intellectual assumptions from nineteenth-century Europe and the United States, the terms "god" and "religion" have shaped the study of religion in Japan and around the world today just as they influenced the development of kami and their worship in late nineteenth- and twentieth-century Japan.[7]

For readers and writers of English and other European languages, ideas of a unitary, omniscient, and omnipotent God (with a capital *G*) dog any attempt to use the word "god" or "deity" to translate *kami*. This concept of God implies a host of assumptions alien to the many, overlapping deities prevalent in Japan. The Western God of the nineteenth century ruled over a bifurcated world, divided between the transcendent and the mundane, the spirit and the body. Yet in Japan, kami, spirits, tengu, and even buddhas were generally thought to exist in the same world as humans. There was little meaningful distinction between natural and supernatural, body and mind, action and intention; and none of the deities, not even the buddhas, embodied an abstract, divine Good against a devil's Evil.[8] This is not to suggest that ideas of a transcendent deity did not exist. In Pure Land Buddhist traditions, for instance, the buddha Amida presided over a Pure Land Paradise far beyond the realm of everyday experience. Yet, for the most part, Japan's gods and spirits, residing in their own particular places, coexisted with humans and with each other in a unitary cosmos. Limited in their abilities, they answered individual pleas more often than they pursued universal agendas. Clearly not "Gods," their role as objects of worship, more powerful than but responsive to humans, nevertheless qualifies them as "gods" (with a lowercase *g*) according to the more inclusive usage now prevalent among anthropologists and scholars of comparative religion. Except when addressing the question of terminology head-on, therefore, in this book the word *kami* will be translated as "god" and alternated, for stylistic reasons, with "deity" and "spirit"—terms that, because of the complex combinations of beings prevalent before 1868, can apply to objects of worship of almost any kind.

While the translation of *kami* into European languages did not prove to be of pressing urgency to Meiji leaders, the translation of "religion" into Japanese did. Formally introduced in the 1850s, when Japan signed the treaties granting Western nations significant trading rights, tariff control, extraterritoriality, and permission for foreign residents to practice their own religion, the Western concept of an overarching term encompassing a variety of spiritual traditions was, if not startlingly new, still relatively unfamiliar.[9] Given that many Westerners doubted whether the Japanese had any religion at all, since they lacked a single, omnipotent creator God in any of their traditions, it should come as no surprise that Japanese translation of the concept did not fully correspond to the understanding of religion in Western societies. The translation that finally emerged for "religion"—*shūkyō* (a Buddhist term for "sectarian teachings")—emphasized religion as doctrine more than as ritual. The significance of this interpretation became evident later, when the Meiji government adopted the principle of "freedom of religious belief" under international and domestic pressure. As government leaders and priests struggled in the 1880s to restructure relations between shrines and the state according to such new constitutional principles, they again redefined both kami and Shinto. In the process, Kotohira and other state-supported shrines became categorized as "not religion"—a matter of ongoing debate even today, long after the disestablishment of state-supported Shinto under the Allied Occupation in 1945.

The separation of state shrines from "religious belief" dramatically influenced activities at Kotohira and beyond. As chapters 9 and 10 show, despite formally transforming the shrine into an "areligious" stage for the support of national progress, the priests of Kotohira, confronted by popular demands for miraculous protection during the Sino-Japanese War of 1894–95, were repeatedly forced to tread the delicate boundary between theology and theater. In the rapid industrialization and development that ensued after 1895, economic concerns overrode all else on the mountain. Even then, however, the status of Kotohira as a state shrine shaped the options available. Chapters 11 and 12 focus on the development of an image of the shrine as a public institution, as the priests of Kotohira sought to return the shrine to profitability after years of fiscal distress and, during the Russo-Japanese War of 1904–5, worked to accommodate the popular demand for military miracles. Around the turn of the century, worshippers, promoters, and, in response, even the priests thus redefined Kotohira and other gods as miraculous protectors of the Japanese nation, sources of a resuscitated "wind of the kami" (*kamikaze*) defending the sacred land.

The role of wartime protection only added to an array of interpretations of the god that had become well established by the early twentieth century. Just as priests and businessmen used the term "public" as a tool to define the shrine, so journalists and other urban, educated writers suggested distinctions between pilgrimage and tourism, faith and science. As chapter 13 demonstrates, however, such contrasts could not stand up. Writers frequently depicted dramatic differences among Western-educated, skeptical, urban tourists; reverent, nationalist, culturally appreciative, rural elites; and superstitious, gullible country bumpkins. But visitors' diaries, donations, and other records betray a much more complex array of attitudes. After all, even the most dedicated skeptic, disinclined to visit the shrine unless to appreciate its art, architecture, or natural treasures, could wonder whether his prayers might yet communicate with some conscious being. Such prejudices and labels, often couched in the language of Western thought, became a part of the image of Kotohira as well, adding to the difficulty of distinguishing religion from culture, Shinto from popular religion, and kami from buddhas and a myriad of other spirits.

All of these difficulties in defining the kami—their site-specific particularity, their repeated transformations over time, their coexistence with countless other beings (sometimes also called kami, sometimes not), and the relatively recent encounter with Western concepts of God, religion, and atheism as well—point to a startling multiplicity in approaches to the gods contingent upon each person's interests and environment, a multiplicity that in turn has created the very diversity of kami that plagues their definition. By focusing on how the varied interests of a vast array of people intersected to shape evolving interpretations of the god(s) of Mt. Zōzu—in particular, how the rising and falling influence of different groups prompted the priests to cater to their demands—*Rearranging the Landscape of the Gods* highlights the politics inherent in portrayals of these powerful beings. For it was by exploiting, and indeed sometimes by creating, political, economic, and intellectual tensions between people that the priests of Mt. Zōzu repeatedly redefined their god and the structures of worship, in the process ensuring their survival and status under constantly changing conditions. That is, on Mt. Zōzu, as around Japan, not only priests but also politicians, pilgrims, entrepreneurs and officials shaped the complex structures of what would become modern Shinto: a purportedly timeless, unchanging, native tradition that in fact emerged from the pressures of the nineteenth and early twentieth centuries. Hidden in plain sight in this newly rearranged landscape of the gods lie the tensions, alliances, and influences that gave shape to the structures of modern Japan—structures that, in many cases, were created around the sites of the gods. The processes of change on Mt. Zōzu thus highlight, in microcosm, the changes in Japan as a whole, as people rearranged the political, social, and cultural landscapes to create those we know today.

Konpira: Site of the Gods

1

The cherry blossoms were in full bloom when Nakahara Suigekka, a well-to-do, rural samurai of the Kurashiki domain, set out on the fifteenth day of the third month of Ansei 5 (28 April 1858) on a pilgrimage of thanksgiving.[1] His destination was the shrine of Konpira on Mt. Zōzu, a site renowned for its wonder-working powers, just across the Inland Sea (figure 1.1). The ailing Nakahara had survived another winter, an outcome he attributed in part to the divine response of Konpira, known for its healing light.[2] As he eagerly tasted the first green vegetables of spring, Nakahara prepared for his trip to give thanks to the god. Not only was the third month an ideal time for pilgrimage—warm enough to enjoy the trip, but before the busy season of spring planting—it was a time especially associated with Konpira and the bustling markets, kabuki plays, and festivals of the shrine. It was this combination of beauty, entertainment, and access to the miraculous powers of a famous deity that drew Nakahara and countless others to Mt. Zōzu and other popular pilgrimage sites.

Rural samurai like Nakahara occupied an anomalous position in the Tokugawa order (1600–1867). Since the late sixteenth century, commoners in Japan had been divided between an administrative, military elite (the samurai) and the majority of peasants, artisans, merchants, and others, who were not permitted to bear arms. The Tokugawa shogun, based in Edo (present-day Tokyo), required that samurai live in the castle town of each domain, close to the seat of their lord, the daimyo, effectively demilitarizing rural areas after centuries of civil war. Over the years, however, the Tokugawa shoguns and the daimyo who

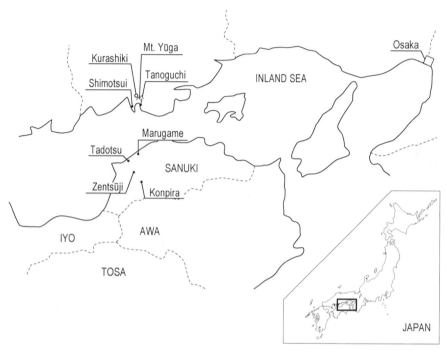

✿ **1.1** From Kurashiki to Konpira: major stops on the route of Nakahara Suigekka (and many other pilgrims) in the spring of 1858.

swore loyalty to them no longer felt such an acute need to pacify militant peasants. Instead, the financial crises of the elite became more pressing. By the nineteenth century, it was commonplace for certain influential rural families to line the pockets of their lords in exchange for honorary samurai status. Nakahara came from one such honorary samurai family. In writing a travel diary of his trip to Konpira, he sought to express the elite, cultural qualities of an ideal, well-cultivated samurai through his discriminating awareness of beauty and art.

The sickly Nakahara had visited Konpira at least once, not too long before his pilgrimage in 1858, perhaps when he offered up the prayer for which he came to give thanks. His travel diary, which he signed with the nom de plume "Drunken Moon and Flowers," describes in flowery language (and the occasional poem) his devotion to the gods and his knowledgeable appreciation of the entertainments and seasonal sights available to him. Nakahara's wealth enabled him to travel in a style that other pilgrims could only envy. During an eighteen-day trip, he spent twenty-one gold *ryō,* the equivalent of one and one-half years' pay for a skilled carpenter working twenty-five days a month.[3] Nakahara's luxurious trip, then, reinforced his privileged economic and cultural position in society.

Renting a boat from a neighbor, Nakahara and a servant first sailed along the coast of the Inland Sea to the harbor of Shimotsui. After a quick visit to worship at Mt. Yūga—a popular complement to Konpira's Mt. Zōzu for many pilgrims—Nakahara and his servant, Shōzō, boarded a regularly scheduled boat and set sail from Tanoguchi that night. Blessed by calm seas, they arrived at Marugame with the morning breeze, alongside hundreds of other pilgrims.

The monumental construction of Marugame port, with the hilltop castle of the Marugame daimyo overlooking the town, formed an impressive sight (figure 1.2). Its grand entrance reminded disembarking passengers of the popularity of Konpira pilgrimage and the authority of the local lord. Marugame, which vied with nearby Tadotsu port for the traffic to Konpira, had dredged its harbor and built stone embankments for the hundreds of passengers disembarking each day. Large stone and metal lanterns at the port not only lit the way for nighttime dockings, but also acknowledged the many donors whose interest in the Konpira pilgrimage made the improvements possible. "When I looked [at the lanterns]," wrote a visitor in 1869, "[I saw that] they were all donations from Edo merchants to Konpira: their enormous size is astonishing."[4]

The lanterns in Marugame—like countless lanterns erected by groups of Konpira worshippers in their own communities, on the road to Konpira, and on Mt. Zōzu itself—not only illuminated shadowed intersections and commemorated donors, but invoked and evoked the power of the deity as well. Lanterns, sometimes associated with the stupas built over Buddhist dead, could serve as sacred markers. Lit each night, they conveyed the prayers of petitioners to the god. The light provided by lanterns could also remind pilgrims of Konpira's wonder-working powers. Certainly, the lanterns of Marugame port—like the miraculous guiding light of Konpira that reportedly appeared to shipwrecked sailors—led foundering ships and their despairing crews through rough and stormy seas to the safety of land. Moreover, in an age without electricity, light often set apart the supernatural or mysterious. Balls of light were thought to surround recently departed souls as they traveled the countryside, and witnesses to the miraculous appearances of Konpira or its amulets often described them as accompanied by a shining brightness. The monumental stone and metal lanterns of Marugame's port thus attested to the popularity and economic influence of Konpira, inseparable from its miraculous powers.

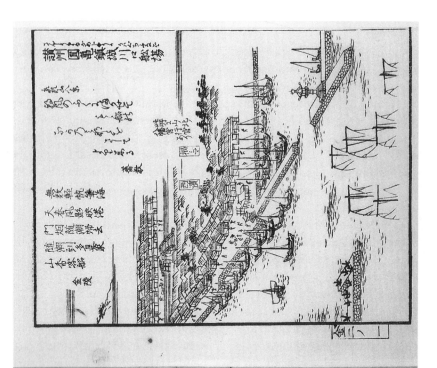

The bustling crowds of Marugame impressed visitors with the sheer number of pilgrims to Konpira. "Although people are always departing and arriving here," Nakahara noted, "especially now, around the third month . . . when the full blossoms of the late cherry have not yet begun to fall . . . old and young, men and women, rich and poor, urbanites and rustics come crowding down the return pilgrimage route." Amid the hubbub, Nakahara hired a horse and guide, joining in the traffic with the sound of the horse's bells and the guide's crooning songs ringing in his ears.

Nakahara rode and his companions trod along a dirt road that wound between the fields of the Sanuki plain. At each intersection, they passed stone markers and lanterns erected by local groups of worshippers to guide pilgrims and point the way to both Konpira and nearby attractions (figure 1.3). Still in Marugame, for instance, a stone signpost pointed to the purported grave site of Tamiya Bōtarō, a young samurai boy featured in the puppet play *A Miracle Tale of Konpira* (*Konpira gorishōki*) who, in answer to his mother's prayers, avenged his dead father with the help of the deity.[5] Farther along the road, lanterns marked the paths to neighboring shrines as well as to Konpira. At one corner, a lantern stood pointing to "Hachiman Shrine" on one side and to "Konpira Daigongen" on the other. Farther on, another lantern simply bore the symbol for gold (*kon*)—the first character of Konpira's name—on the front and "Sannō Gongen," the name of another deity enshrined nearby, on the back.[6] Along this road running amid familiar gods, "there is no pause in the people coming and going," Nakahara remarked.

As Nakahara traveled through the fields, past scattered hamlets and isolated shrines, his destination, Mt. Zōzu, came more clearly into view. Rising out of the fertile Sanuki plain, Mt. Zōzu actually comprised only the southeastern side of an elongated mountain, the bulk of which was known to locals as Mt. Ōsa. While Mt. Ōsa emerged steadily from the plain near Marugame, welcoming local foragers, loggers, and charcoal makers, Mt. Zōzu discouraged such familiarity. The dramatic valleys that punctuated the southeastern side protected the mountain's forests, sheltered its dwindling waterfalls, and—by hindering easy human access—fostered a sense of mystery, seclusion, and supernatural power.[7] With their unusual shape, the highest peaks on the Sanuki plain, Mts. Ōsa and Zōzu (reaching 616 and 524 meters, re-

✽ 1.2 (*opposite*) The port of Marugame: the main gateway to Shikoku for pilgrims to Konpira in the mid-nineteenth century. The spectacular popularity of the Konpira pilgrimage contributed to the growth of Marugame's port out of all proportion to the size and wealth of the domain. The stone embankments and lanterns of Marugame port, with the daimyo's castle behind, formed an impressive sight for arriving pilgrims. (Illustration from Akatsuki Kanenari, *Konpira sankei meisho zue* [Osaka: Sakaiya Sadashichi, 1847]. Courtesy of the C. V. Starr East Asian Library, Columbia University.)

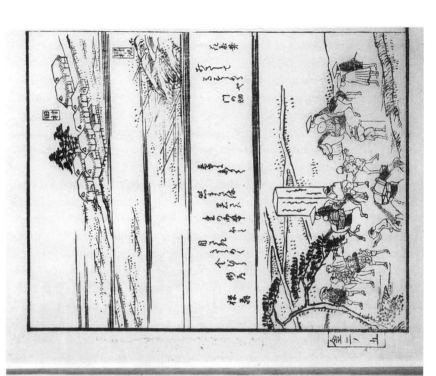

spectively), stood dramatically visible, hiding a powerful god amid the open fields of Sanuki province. "Truly, the shrine of Konpira is as awesome as its reputation," Nakahara remarked. "Its appearance shines upon the world."[8]

Halfway to Mt. Zōzu, Nakahara arrived at a well-traveled intersection at which stood two lanterns, a stone road sign, and a teahouse. The marker pointed travelers to the right to reach Zentsūji, the seventy-fifth temple on the eighty-eight-temple pilgrimage circuit of Shikoku.[9] The pilgrimage route, which circled the island, reputedly followed in the footsteps of the great Shingon Buddhist master Kūkai (774–835), popularly known as Kōbō Daishi, who was born at Zentsūji and meditated on mountains and in caves around the island. White-robed pilgrims of the eighty-eight-temple circuit regularly stopped off to visit Mt. Zōzu, while visitors to Konpira frequently returned to port via the famed Zentsūji as well.

Nakahara passed by the road to Zentsūji, but he stopped to rest at the teahouse nearby. "I had wanted to see the teahouse beauties [*bini,* literally 'beautiful nuns']," he wrote, evoking the Buddhist temple nearby, "and when I first caught sight of the woman who brought out the tea, [I noticed that] her body was lithe and sensuous. Although she may have already seen almost thirty springtimes, [her beauty] was enough to steal away the soul [of whoever saw her]." Playing upon the terminology of the "floating world" of the pleasure quarters that likened such women to Buddhist nuns, Nakahara elevated the encounter to an aesthetic, sensual experience, using the double entendres of poetry:

Kakuwashiki	The beautiful flower
hanasuri koromo	sheds her sweet-smelling,
nuki sutete	blossom-dyed robe—
ukiyo no hoka ni	outside the floating world,
kurozome no sode	a black sleeve.

Refreshed, titillated, and having rhapsodized on one of the cultural tropes of Konpira pilgrimage, Nakahara climbed back on his horse and continued on his way.

After a stop at another teahouse—this time commemorated by a poem on its masses of wisteria blossoms—Nakahara caught sight of the most famous

❀ 1.3 (*opposite*) On the road to Konpira, pilgrims passed stone lanterns and road markers erected by previous pilgrims and nearby villagers. Guides led pilgrims on horses and men begged in loincloths as they traveled between the rice fields. (Illustration from Akatsuki Kanenari, *Konpira sankei meisho zue* [Osaka: Sakaiya Sadashichi, 1847]. Courtesy of the C. V. Starr East Asian Library, Columbia University.)

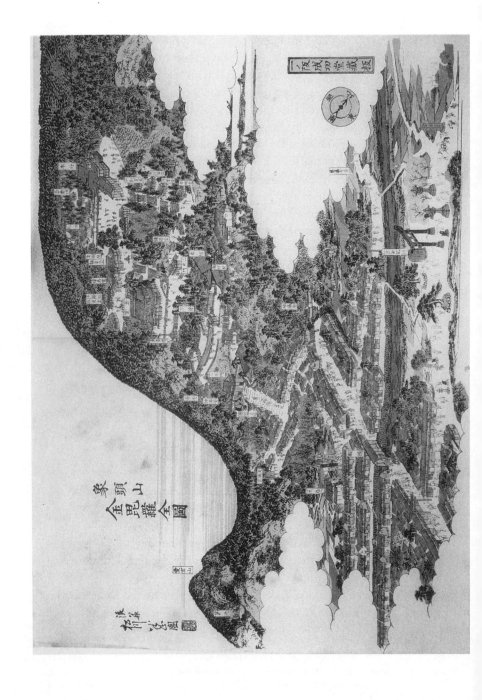

象頭山金毘羅全圖

image of the pilgrimage. Repeated hundreds of times in woodblock prints (figure 1.4), the view of Mt. Zōzu from the Marugame road dramatized both the cultural and the religious character of the site. With a bit of imagination, Mt. Zōzu in this view lived up to its name: it resembled a literal "Mt. Elephant Head." Remarked a traveler in 1869, "The shape of this mountain is truly like the head of an elephant. It has places like a nose and ears, with half of the mountain red dirt, and the back half covered in deep forest." By the mid-nineteenth century, Mt. Ōsa—the mountain of "red dirt"—had been stripped by loggers, laying bare what looked like the naked, wrinkled body of an elephant. With the smaller Mt. Atago as the elephant's trunk on the left, Mt. Zōzu beckoned as a shaded sanctuary: the elephant's head. Inspired by both the fame of the sight and his heart-filled gratitude to the god, Nakahara wrote, "I prostrated myself and prayed to the wonderful peak of the awesome mountain."

Moving onward, Nakahara finally arrived at the Gold Gate (*Kane no Mitorii*), a symbolic gate (*torii*) donated by merchants from Osaka in 1787 (figure 1.5). Flanked by a pair of trees—one pine and one cherry (symbolizing longevity and evanescence, respectively)—and an engraved stone attesting to a miracle of the deity, the Gold Gate marked the entrance to the domain of Konpira, about sixteen kilometers from the port of Marugame. On the right, overlooking teahouses and fields, carpenters were just beginning to build the new Tall Lantern, a twenty-eight-meter-high stone and wooden lantern, paid for by the donations of hundreds of pilgrims and patterned after the famous lantern of Sumiyoshi Shrine near Osaka, to be lit every night, visible to boats in the Inland Sea. Despite the construction, it was once again the women and the scenery that caught Nakahara's eye. "The brothels look out over the fields," he remarked, and with a hint of literary eroticism added, "and there is no need to mention the prospect of the elegant beauty of luxuriant flowers."

Nakahara and his entourage continued on to the Sayabashi, one of the few covered bridges in Japan and a distinctive landmark of Konpira (figure 1.6). Carrying pilgrims over the Kanakura River, the bridge served as a portal into Uchimachi, the center of town, and the entertainment district, Kinzanji, nearby. "We passed through the Sayabashi and found ourselves caught up in the flowering Uchimachi [district]," wrote Nakahara. "The sounds of shamisen, drums, and flutes seem to float over both the eaves of the brothels and

❀ 1.4 (*opposite*) Repeated in countless woodblock prints sold to pilgrims as souvenirs, the view of Mt. Zōzu as Mt. Elephant Head became the most well known image of the site. The dark head of the elephant (Mt. Zōzu) stands in the center, the wrinkled body of the elephant (Mt. Ōsa) on the right, and the elephant's trunk (the small hill known as Mt. Atago) on the left. (*Zōzusan Konpira zenzu* [Ichinosaka Seikōdō, undated]. Courtesy of Kotohira Ezu o Mamoru Kai.)

❀ 1.5 The Gold Gate marked the entrance to the domain of Konpira on the road from Marugame. The gate, with the stone carving of a miracle tale nearby, and the two trees (a pine and a cherry, symbolizing longevity and evanescence, respectively) became a shorthand visual symbol of Mt. Zōzu and Konpira as a whole. (Illustration from Akatsuki Kanenari, *Konpira sankei meisho zue* [Osaka: Sakaiya Sadashichi, 1847]. Courtesy of C. V. Starr East Asian Library, Columbia University.)

the great earth as a whole. The hearts and minds of even traveling saints, or the most devoted of people, would be captivated. The cares of the world are torn away: I feel as if I have entered the [legendary] realm of the hermits." The center of Konpira truly seemed a world apart. Brothels and inns crowding against each other, the voices of women in the doorways calling out for customers, and the crowds of people jostling in the streets all testified to the popularity of the site. The excitement of adventure set Konpira apart from the

⊛ **1.6** The Sayabashi, a covered bridge over the Kanakura River, served as a portal into the center of town. Peddlers displayed their wares under its protective roof, profiting from the pilgrimage traffic. (Illustration from Akatsuki Kanenari, *Konpira sankei meisho zue* [Osaka: Sakaiya Sadashichi, 1847]. Courtesy of C. V. Starr East Asian Library, Columbia University.)

quiet villages of the countryside or the regulated neighborhoods of castle towns.

Having arrived at his destination, Nakahara, still weak from his illness, sent his servant, Shōzō, up the mountain to perform on his behalf a "naked" pilgrimage—a type of worship considered particularly efficacious because the relative nakedness of the pilgrim (wearing only a loincloth) demonstrated the humility of the petitioner before the god. Meanwhile, as Shōzō climbed hundreds of stone steps to the shrine, Nakahara settled in at one of the larger, more luxurious inns, the Yoshimaya. After a short nap and a bath, Nakahara was ready for a bite to eat, but "since I still hadn't performed the pilgrimage, I observed the taboos [of Konpira] and avoided seafood, ordering only a small meal." Conveniently, Nakahara did not consider the restrictions of pilgrimage to extend to relations with women, for "at exactly that time, Kura—the woman who had been my regular [entertainer] before—heard that I was spending the day, and unexpectedly came to my room." Nakahara ended up hiring two more women to dance for him until nightfall, then kept Kura in his room until the following morning. Pleasure and purification merged in the freedom of Konpira's inns and entertainment districts.

The next day, Nakahara readied himself to fulfill the stated purpose of his trip. "I straightened my kimono and summoned Shōzō, then took along a young man from the teahouse and left to perform the pilgrimage." Nakahara, however, did not feel well. After a few steps, he hired a palanquin to carry him up the mountain, past more inns and candy and souvenir shops. The palanquin bearers stopped at the main gate to the sacred precincts, the Niōmon, beyond which all visitors were required to walk. Nakahara, to express his grateful dedication to the god, progressed barefoot.

The Niōmon—a large wooden gate with a protective Buddhist deity (*niō*) on either side of the entrance and a framed, wooden sign above announcing Mt. Zōzu—marked a divide between the sanctified mountain of the god and the noisy world of commerce below. As soon as visitors passed under the roof of the imposing gate, they entered the sudden, protected peacefulness of a new world. The muted sounds that passed faintly through the gate only accentuated the otherworldly calm created by the mass of cherry trees that lined each side of a broad, smoothly paved path leading far ahead, an area known as the Sakuranobaba (figure 1.7). Hidden behind the trees on the right stood four small subtemples, which Nakahara, like most visitors, ignored in favor of the glorious cherry blossoms, impressive stone lanterns, and stone balustrades.

The detailed inscriptions on the lanterns provided ample entertainment for visitors as they enjoyed the airy scene. Perhaps Nakahara paused by one of a pair of lanterns donated by members of a shipping group from Awa province in 1779 (figure 1.8).[11] Labeled prominently with the trademark of the group, and carved with the shapes of the moon and sun to let the light emerge, the lanterns advertised their donors, provided light, and offered up continual prayers to the god of Mt. Zōzu. Farther down the path, Nakahara might have stopped again to try to decipher some of the ninety-three names on a two-and-one-half-meter-tall lantern donated by merchants from Shinano province in 1818.[12] The lines of donated lanterns, labeled with trade-

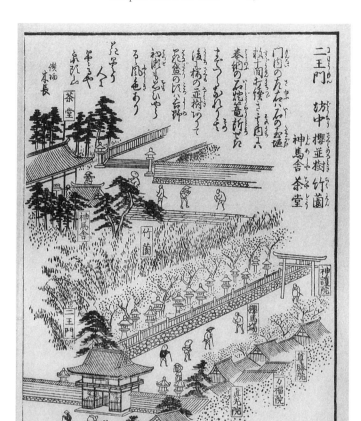

✿ 1.7 The Sakuranobaba, a broad walkway beyond the Niōmon (Gate of Two Guardian Kings) lined with cherry trees, led pilgrims past small subtemples on the right (Shinkōin, Manpukuin, Sonshōin, and Shingoin) and a stone fence and lanterns donated by worshippers on the left. At the upper left of the image stand a teahouse at which pilgrims could rest and a small shelter for a wooden horse donated by the first Matsudaira lord of the Takamatsu domain. (Illustration from Akatsuki Kanenari, *Konpira sankei meisho zue* [Osaka: Sakaiya Sadashichi, 1847]. Courtesy of C. V. Starr East Asian Library, Columbia University.)

marks, places, and dates and filled with thousands of names, emphasized the connection of Mt. Zōzu to the prayers and pocketbooks of individuals and groups from farming and fishing communities, cities, and villages, spanning not only the islands but the years as well. The scenery of the Sakuranobaba invoked on Mt. Zōzu a seemingly timeless combination of natural beauty and widespread faith.

❀ **1.8** One of a pair of stone lanterns along the Sakuranobaba donated by members of a shipping group from Awa Province in 1779. The trademark of the group prominently displayed on the front served both to both symbolize the donors' unity and to advertise their business, while the carved sun and moon insignia—and the lantern itself—evoked the shining light associated with the god. (Photo by Steve Cantley, with the permission of Kotohira Shrine.)

The intricate layout of monuments, trees, stairways, and buildings on Mt. Zōzu has fascinated scholars of architecture and spatial perception for years. The twists and turns of the upward path, the play of light and shadow, the architectural interest of small shrines beckoning through shaded walkways—all have been studied to understand how the landscape so effectively pulls visitors upward and inward to a mysterious, hidden "interior" (*oku*).[13] Indeed, the entire mountain was presented to visitors as a series of symbolic layers: visible and invisible, accessible below and raised to distant heights above. These dynamics replicated the visual and spatial structures of Tokugawa-era politics, in which the shogun, the emperor, a daimyo, or any exalted figure was elevated on a dais and often hidden from the view of the lowly altogether. Differences in height and distance relative to either political or sacred power ritually marked the social differentials of the actors involved, whether when a poor peasant bowed down on the dirt floor of an entryway below the raised tatami mats where the village headman sat, or when a worshipper prostrated himself on the wooden walkways below the elevated sanctuary where priests performed rituals, itself below the raised and hidden altar of the god. Thus, the pilgrim at the bottom of the mountain found himself drawn to the power at the top, a power that became more accessible, the closer one approached. Despite this emphasis on proximity, however, the most revered images on the mountain responded to the prayers of worshippers without ever granting humans the privilege of seeing them. Inequality enforced through ritual, spatial, and visual distinctions thus enhanced the perceived power of the gods, as it did the power of human beings. Permanently hidden from view, the invisibility of the spirits most intimately associated with Mt. Zōzu placed them in the position of the highest, most unknowable power.

Where Nakahara stood in the lower reaches of the sacred precincts, in contrast, all was visible, with only hints of hidden attractions beckoning visitors higher up, toward the interior. Past the flat stretch of the Sakuranobaba, the ailing Nakahara and other pilgrims would have started up some shallow stone steps, drawn on first by a sunny stop for tea near a small hall housing a life-size statue of a wooden horse—an offering from the first daimyo of the Takamatsu domain. After a rest, he would have been ready to tackle the first long stretch of stairs, leading past a small shrine to Mt. Atago on the left, to another hall and a five-story pagoda on the right. Pausing to catch his breath, Nakahara may have wandered over to the pagoda, wondering—like hundreds of others—why some eighteenth-century man had donated a temple gong so large that it could never be hung, only propped against the wall of the building.[14]

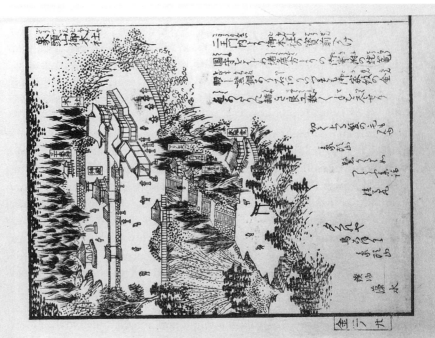

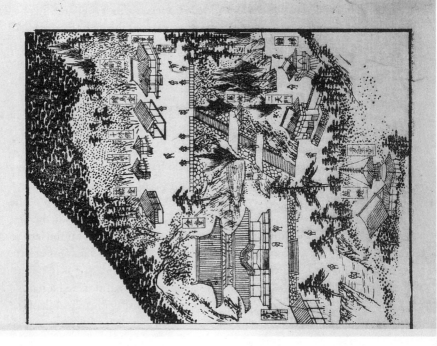

Nakahara finally climbed up to emerge on a broad, sunny plateau in front of the huge, imposing Gold Hall (figure 1.9). Still focused on reaching the top, however, he saved the Gold Hall for later. Turning to the right, past more lanterns, he came to another wooden gate, the Nitenmon, housing the two fierce Buddhist guardian kings (*niten*) of the north and east. Passing through, he would have noticed that one of the pillars expanded instead of shrinking in size as it rose from the ground to the roof, earning the structure the popular epithet of Upside-Down Gate. Beyond the gate, suddenly plunged into a dark silence, Nakahara would have waited for his eyes to adjust, then found himself closed in between the steep slope on his left, a wooden bell tower on his right, a line of stone lanterns in front, and the overhanging trees above. Guided by the dark, shaded pathway towards his left, Nakahara passed under a stone torii and across a stone bridge to arrive—still in the dark—at a small prayer hall enshrining the first of many statues of Fudō Myōō, the fierce deity to whom many esoteric (that is, secretly transmitted) rituals were performed on the mountain.

After the restfulness of this wooded passageway, Nakahara could see on his left the final hurdle: long flights of shaded stairs leading up to the sunshine and the beckoning roof of the main shrine. Leaning on the stone handrails alongside the steps—and perhaps pausing to catch his breath and read the names of donors carved into the supports—the tired Nakahara would have climbed the precariously steep stairway, passing between several matching pairs of intricately carved lanterns bearing the crest of the Takamatsu lord. Between the lanterns on the right, at each of three landings, stood small altars to the protective deities of the mountain: the Gyōja Hall, to the revered early ascetic En no Ozunu, often considered the founder of the *shugendo* sect of mountain worship; the Daigyōji shrine, to another protector of the mountain; and the altar of Bishamonten, Buddhist protector of the north.

At the top of the steps, thrown off balance by the steepness of the climb and his sudden emergence into bright sunlight, Nakahara came face to face with his ultimate destination: the main shrine of Konpira. "The shrine is

❀ **1.9** (*opposite*) As visitors walked through the upper precincts of Mt. Zōzu, they were surrounded not only by the gods (in their shrines) but also by reminders of the power of the domainal lords (as represented by the impressive lanterns and other donations bearing their names and family crests). Following the path to the right, visitors approached ever closer to the powerful deity Konpira, entering through the Nitenmon, or Upside-Down Gate (*lower right corner of left panel*) and passing several smaller shrines until they climbed the steep steps to emerge at last on the sunlit plateau of the main shrine above. On the return route is the imposing Gold Hall (*far left of left panel*). (Illustration from Akatsuki Kanenari, *Konpira sankei meisho zue* [Osaka: Sakaiya Sadashichi, 1847]. Courtesy of C. V. Starr East Asian Library, Columbia University.)

awesome," Nakahara wrote, "and I prostrated myself and prayed, offering thanks." After a dramatic ascent, approaching ever closer to the mighty god, Nakahara had finally arrived.

To say that Nakahara had arrived, however, suggests that the power of the mountain was located in a single place, or that that place was accessible. Neither was the case. When Nakahara prostrated himself at the main shrine, he did not climb the steps to the altar area itself, nor could he see the image of Konpira Daigongen, for, as befitting a fierce and powerful deity, it was hidden from view. Instead, Nakahara and other worshippers tossed their coins into an offering box in an antechamber a few levels below the altar, separated by height and distance from the deity, with the space in between used by priests for rituals. Indeed, for the closest possible contact with Konpira Daigongen, Nakahara would have had to continue on to the prayer hall to the left of the main shrine, purchase a large wooden talisman, and wait for a priest to emerge from the sanctuary to bless him with a golden wand. Even this proxy access, however, did not necessarily connect worshippers to the site of power itself. Konpira not only appeared in his carved representation but resided in a cave above and behind the main shrine, hidden from view lest the god, angry at being disturbed, unleash its wrath on the unwary, as it reputedly had upon an unlucky priest three centuries before. The powerful Konpira Daigongen was thus protected by layers of restriction and representation. Located above and beyond the site of worshippers' prayers, enshrined as an image behind the altar of the priests, then hidden beyond even the image in a cave closed to all human contact, Konpira Daigongen and its miraculous powers were enhanced by the tantalizing proximity, yet distance, of the god.

Worshippers could experience a similarly simultaneous proximity and distance for themselves, as well. At a stone railing to the right of the main shrine, they could look out northward over the fields of the Sanuki plain and watch the tiny pilgrims and horses plodding along the road far below (figure 1.10). Beyond, they could see the ports of Marugame and Tadotsu, the white sails of boats on the Inland Sea, several small islands, and the hills of mainland Honshu beyond.

On the mountain itself, more altars stood nearby to attract attention. Even after Nakahara worshipped at the main shrine, his prayers were far from over. "I prostrated myself before each of the branch shrines," he wrote, attesting to his dedication not just to Konpira but to the many gods associated with it. First, near the back of the main shrine and the cave of Konpira behind it, Nakahara probably visited the Shrine of the Thirty Deities, protectors of the Buddhist law. Then, he may have worshipped the figures enshrined in the storehouse for Buddhist texts (*sūtras*): an image of the historical Buddha,

名にされ治の上より いくるる浦の りなやらん 立りつ

隆祐

ぞろ二八すて

ぶどうろうか名場の

の見海ぞてんへて絶景

撮庭篠八束五褶岳あ

る鋭の山とそなわ九逸

牡甲礫底の富士と岩す

ことて一至二尺てと

まこ海上の名を浦く郷

辺よりの北の方と眺望そ

弁殿の傍わる玉運り

⊛ **1.10** Looking out over the stone railing around the plateau on which stood the main shrine, pilgrims could enjoy a rare perspective on their surroundings, gazing down upon the fields of the Sanuki Plain, with its "Little Fuji," and spotting the white sails of boats in the Inland Sea and even the coastline of Honshu beyond. (Illustration from Akatsuki Kanenari, *Konpira sankei meisho zue* [Osaka: Sakaiya Sadashichi, 1847]. Courtesy of C. V. Starr East Asian Library, Columbia University.)

Śākyamuni, to whom the teachings in the sutras were attributed, as well as statues of his attendants and representative disciples.

Nakahara would have definitely stopped to worship at the hall of Kannon (Avalokiteśvara), where an image of the Buddhist embodiment of compassion, said to have been carved by Kōbō Daishi himself, was enshrined, surrounded by images of its thirty-three different manifestations. Votive plaques crowded around the walls attested to the importance of the Kannon Hall, second in size only to the main shrine on this upper plateau. With his interest in art and literature, Nakahara might have risen from his prayers to admire a large painting of a horse by an artist of the Kano school or the painting of the Gion festival donated by the daimyo of Tosa, a large domain beyond the mountains on the other side of Shikoku. All of these were visible because, unlike at the main shrine, worshippers were allowed to enter the Kannon Hall to pray. In contrast to the fierce and awe-inspiring Konpira Daigongen, the compassionate Kannon allowed its image to be made visible to the public periodically, when the curtains were opened (*kaichō*) every thirty-three years to display the statue. Worshippers were even permitted to spend the night in the Kannon Hall—a privilege of which many supplicants took advantage, eager for access to the powers of the mountain at midnight, the most potent time of prayer.[15]

Behind the Kannon Hall stood a shrine to Kongōbō, the deified form of a seventeenth-century priest of Mt. Zōzu. Although in Nakahara's time the wooden statue of Kongōbō was hidden, the image had been temporarily displayed at least once. According to rumors, about a decade before Nakahara's visit, when the image was to be shown to the public for three days as part of the 250th anniversary of Kongōbō's enlightenment, the statue protested. As soon as priests opened the doors on a beautiful, sunny day, the image summoned threatening clouds and caused a sudden, violent thunderstorm. After three hours, according to the tale, the priests closed the doors to the image, whereupon the weather immediately cleared.[16] Such stories reinforced the reputation of Kongōbō, like Konpira, as a fierce, protective deity, simultaneously heightening its aura of awe-inspiring power.

The many visitors to Mt. Zōzu revered Kongōbō in particular because of his connections to the magical rituals of mountain worship. The image showed the priest in the form of a tengu: a beak-nosed, winged, and goblin-like creature thought to live in the mountains and often associated with ascetic practioners of shugendo, a tradition of mountain meditation strongly influenced by esoteric Buddhism (figure 1.11). Tales of the tengu Kongōbō's aversion to being seen reinforced assumptions not only that weather, especially thunder and rain, was controlled by the gods, but also that the strongest

❀ **1.11** Kongōbō: the spirit of Yūsei, a seventeenth-century priest of Mt. Zōzu, in the form of a *tengu* (a beak-nosed, winged, and goblinlike creature). In this illustration from a miracle tale, the tengu Kongōbō, carrying his distinctive fan and sword, and wearing the small hat and robe that mark him as an esoteric Buddhist mountain ascetic, rescues a small child. (From *Zōzusan Konpira Daigongen Reigenki,* undated. With permission of Matsuoka Hiroyasu, Tawa Archive.)

powers were fierce and wild. The ascetic turned tengu thus became part of the animal-like wildness of the mountains, powerful yet uncontrolled, appeased only through the observance of taboos and proper ritual.

Kongōbō, Konpira, Fudō Myōō, and the other most powerful deities of Mt. Zōzu stood outside the periphery of exoteric Buddhism—that is, they did not appear in the relatively accessible teachings attributed to Śākyamuni. Instead, they appeared in the complicated, secretly transmitted texts and rituals of esoteric Buddhism, which revealed and manipulated the hidden workings of the cosmos according to teachings brought to Japan by Kōbō Daishi in the ninth century.[17] Fierce guardians and deified humans, on Mt. Zōzu these awesome esoteric deities overshadowed the gentler exoteric buddhas such as Kannon, demonstrating their overwhelming might in violent storms and dramatic disasters. These were beings with the power to hurt, but, when properly worshipped, they could also help. The miraculous reputation of Mt. Zōzu relied on their intervention in the human world.

A popular cult of Kongōbō flourished on Mt. Zōzu. Wooden masks of tengu donated by worshippers hung around the hall. With their long noses, red-painted skin, bulging eyeballs, and sometimes even bushy eyebrows made of human hair, the masks gave a visible face to the hidden image. Indeed, the tengu masks, carried by traveling ascetics to towns and villages throughout the country, provided the only anthropomorphic face of the mountain's magical power.

Hundreds of individual offerings crowded the area from the altar of Kongōbō to the halls of offerings nearby. Worshippers donated *ema,* literally "picture horses"—votive plaques that expressed thanks or petitions to the gods—so named because in centuries past, living horses, statues, or painted images, or even paintings and models of other objects or scenes, were offered in prayer.[18] Thus, in the Ema Hall, amid painted scenes of sickrooms and gamblers, among anchors and ship models, each visitor could find some curiosity to catch his or her eye. For the author Jippensha Ikku, the distinctive offerings in the Ema Hall, as well as particular taboos associated with Konpira, helped set the stage for the Konpira installment of his long-running travel comedy, *Hizakurige,* in 1810:

> People with all sorts of petitions send "Konpira kegs" from long distances with offerings of sanctified rice wine [saké]. They put the saké in a keg and set it adrift on the waves; it will eventually arrive at Mt. Zōzu. If a sailor retrieves one [from the sea] and drinks some of the sacred wine, it tastes absolutely delicious. This is because the saké has been gently rolled by the waves. If, after he finishes drinking it, he does not refill the keg with saké, he will suffer retribution [from the god].

Pilgrims to this mountain should refrain from eating crab for fifty days, river fish and garlic for thirty-five days, and sea salt for thirty days. If they eat it by mistake, then it is said that they will be struck [by divine retribution] aboard ship [on their way to the shrine]. Since long ago, there have been no problems on the boats of Konpira pilgrims. This is proof of the god's powers.

In front of the shrine can be seen many ema. . . . When ship captains are in danger of losing their lives, if they cut off their hair and make a vow to this deity [Konpira], it is said that they will always be saved. Therefore, they offer up their hair so that future generations will not forget the benevolence of the god.[19]

Around the time Nakahara came to the site in the 1850s, a writer of illustrated gazetteers, Akatsuki Kanenari, noted the preponderance of tengu masks and paintings of storm-tossed ships in his *Famous Sites of the Konpira Pilgrimage.*[20] And a traveling swordsman who visited the shrine in 1855 found his own items of interest there, remarking that "many of the donations come from several daimyo. Among them is a long sword engraved with the name of Kawanishi Yūnosuke, donated when he went to Edo to study swordsmanship at age seventeen."[21] Each visitor thus interpreted the donations for him- or herself, adding to the personalized meaning of the entire worship experience. Before leaving the Ema Hall, the ailing Nakahara—like hundreds of pilgrims before him—surely stopped to rub the belly of a conveniently situated bronze statue of a horse, following the long-standing tradition that it would heal an illness in the same part of his own body: in this case, Nakahara's apparent digestive problem.

If Nakahara truly worshipped at each of the shrines on the mountaintop, he then continued on to worship at two more altars on the plateau: a hall to Amida, the buddha of the Pure Land Paradise, and one to Kujaku Myōō, an esoteric guardian king associated with the bringing of rain. On the way down, he returned alongside the massive Gold Hall, where, because of his illness, he certainly stopped, for it enshrined an image of the buddha Medicine Master, Yakushi. Nakahara thus completed his pilgrimage after praying at the altars of both esoteric and exoteric deities. He could have worshipped Amida, Yakushi, and Kannon almost anywhere in Japan. But, more important, Nakahara had bowed to Kongōbō and Konpira Daigongen—the hidden powers particular to Mt. Zōzu, who had answered his prayers and those of countless others.

After his obeisances, Nakahara returned to his inn, admiring the flowers and commenting on pilgrims along the way. But for many worshippers there remained a crucial stop. Just before returning to the Sakuranobaba, they entered the precincts of the head subtemple, Konkōin. There, at a window on

✾ 1.12 This 160.2-cm-tall image of Fudō Myōō, with his sword of enlightenment and saving rope, stood over Konkōin's popular fire (*goma*) ceremony, in which priests offered up wooden slats bearing the prayers of petitioners. (Photo by Steve Cantley, with the permission of Kotohira Shrine.)

the right, they could purchase talismans and amulets commemorating one of Konkōin's claims to fame: the esoteric fire ritual (*goma*). The powerful fire of the goma ceremony burned constantly at the Goma Hall, night and day, throughout the year. There, priests fed the prayers of petitioners, inscribed on pieces of wood, into the flames at the foot of a fierce, smoke-blackened image of Fudō Myōō. Faintly visible in the shadows of the Goma Hall, the Fudō, with one bulging eyeball staring balefully out into space and the other eye half closed, presided over the fire with his sword of enlightenment raised to cut through delusion and a rope in his hand to save people from ignorance (figure 1.12). The fierce imagery of Fudō's sharp sword was repeated in the wooden talismans that worshippers could purchase, either at Konkōin or above, near the main shrine, to commemorate their prayers. In the 1840s and 1850s, pilgrims could buy a full-size talisman (101.7 cm tall by 16.3 cm wide) for twelve and one-half silver *monme* or three gold *shu*, about four days' worth of a carpenter's wages, with a smaller talisman available for half the price.[22] Pointed, with the mantric seed syllable of Fudō Myōō painted in Sanskrit at the top, each talisman announced "the offering of the Fudō Myōō goma ritual for two nights and three days, praying for maritime safety," or "household safety," or "flourishing trade." On each side of the main inscription was written the year, month, and "lucky day" of the ritual, and the granter of the talisman: Mt. Zōzu Konkōin. Even the esoteric goma ceremony, however, had its hidden counterpart. The priest of Tamon'in, a subtemple outside the main gates in the town of Konpira, apparently offered a competing "hidden" goma ritual, for which he issued smaller wooden talismans and paper amulets with images of Fudō Myōō inside, labeled from "Konpira Tamon'in."[23] Despite Konkōin's dominance, therefore, it held no monopoly on the rituals of Konpira's power.

With their talismans wrapped in oil paper, or their paper amulets carefully tucked into amulet boxes or folds of their clothing, pilgrims finally descended the rest of the way down the mountain. They returned once again to the noise and enticements of the town below, heading toward the brothels, playhouses, and gambling spots of the Kinzanji district. After an afternoon or night of entertainment, they would continue on, perhaps to visit the birthplace of Kōbō Daishi at Zentsūji or the reputed "inner temple" of Konpira Daigongen at Hashikuraji in neighboring Awa province, before heading back to Marugame and the boat trip home.

Through their visits to Mt. Zōzu and ascent of the mountain, Nakahara and his fellow pilgrims to Konpira physically and ritually experienced many of the unspoken assumptions of their mid-nineteenth-century world. First, the act of pilgrimage reinforced their convictions that the powers of the gods were located in specific places. These powers could be contacted in many different ways. On Mt. Zōzu, pilgrims could address their petitions to Konpira Daigongen, to Kongōbō, to Kannon, or to Fudō Myōō. They could fast, walk barefoot, stay overnight, or just toss a coin in an offering box. There was no single religious authority on the mountain to dictate appropriate behavior, so each worshipper prayed according to models provided by family, neighbors, or popular publications. The multiplicity of gods, buildings, rituals, and offerings on the mountain subtly confirmed the great variety of religious traditions that together merged to shape relations with the gods.

Second, the thousands of donations displayed on Mt. Zōzu confirmed the common assumption that the gods of such sacred places actively intervened in the human world. As the practice of pilgrimage and the inscriptions on lanterns and other donations attested, such intervention was influenced by the date, place, and actions of petitioners. The different deities were thought to be most accessible to prayer on certain "days of connection" (*ennichi*), in Konpira's case the tenth day of each month and especially the tenth day of the third and tenth months. Nakahara and others observed dietary taboos, abstaining from crab or other forms of seafood in preparation for pilgrimage or prayer. They offered distinctive ema, cut their hair, sent kegs of saké, and marked their donations with names, dates, and locations to ensure that the god could find them again. The myriad offerings and forms of prayer took shape according to an elaborate logic of contact through which the gods affected human activity.

Third, these miraculous interventions of the gods were intimately connected to the economic realities of the everyday world. Worshippers prayed for prosperity in trade, for the safety of ships and cargo, for large catches of fish, for bountiful harvests, and for the stability and health of their households.[24] Monetary offerings and purchases of amulets stood at the core of ritual prayer. Moreover, the act of pilgrimage itself was impossible without the myriad economic transactions of hiring boats and paying for inns. Visits to brothels, gambling dens, theaters, and souvenir shops formed an integral part of the experience of pilgrimage. The songs of geisha, the noisy entertainment districts, and the shouting crowds vying for amulets within the sacred precincts of the mountain vividly demonstrated that the unruliness of consumerism was part and parcel of the worship of the gods.[25]

Fourth, the physical dynamics of the trip closer and closer to the hidden power of Mt. Zōzu—from the port of Marugame to the mountain, from the bottom to the top, from light through shadow to an even brighter light—allowed pilgrims to transcend the hierarchy of the world while yet confirming both its existence and its relevance. Worshippers' relationships to the gods replicated their relationships to lords, administrators, and family members in other parts of their lives, visually confirming their place in the broader social, economic, and political hierarchies of the mid-nineteenth century. Nevertheless, by climbing beyond the lords' lanterns and approaching ever closer to the god at the top, pilgrims could, for a while, rise above the structures of their everyday lives before returning to them once again.[26] Whether admiring the splendor of lanterns donated by shipping guilds or purchasing amulets for each member of their worship groups at home, riding on horseback past pilgrims struggling on foot or emulating the amorous exploits of literary heroes, worshippers located themselves within a social and political hierarchy made manifest in ritual and physical form.

Expressed on Mt. Zōzu, the hierarchical relations, humanized sacredness, and active intervention of the multiplicity of gods all appeared to be natural and permanent characteristics of the world. Only superficially altered by the ever-changing seasons, the gods—like the mountain and the social and political order they portrayed—would, it seemed, always be there. Moreover, it seemed that they always had. The very physicality of pilgrimage and its focus on that symbol of permanence, the mountain, imparted an aura of unchanging naturalness to the social, political, and economic orders they expressed. It was this apparent stability of the gods within rapidly changing surroundings that enhanced the fame of the mountain deity and attested to what countless people referred to as the "amazing efficacy of its miracles."[27]

Of Gods and Rulers
(to 1587)

2

Despite the stability suggested by its moss-covered stones, both Mt. Zōzu and its cult of Konpira Daigongen were, in fact, the products of centuries of change. Over the years, priests gave form to the powers perceived on the mountain by identifying gods to worship and obtaining images to enshrine. They secured funding from sponsors, then hired carpenters, purchased materials, and designed buildings and the ceremonies to perform in them. The men of Mt. Zōzu did not retire to solitary meditation. Instead, they built a growing institution to relate the powers of the mountain to human affairs. Therefore, their ideas and concerns, their economic resources and political necessities all contributed to the shaping of the site and its gods. Because of these human considerations, caves, pathways, buildings, and images—that is, records of years of worship on Mt. Zōzu—offer tantalizing hints of violent, even fatal struggles that shaped the broader religious and political history of the area. Warlord fought with warlord, and priest fought with priest, each wielding the ideas and institutions of rival ritual systems in their support. Thus, successive structures of worship on Mt. Zōzu, as elsewhere, attest to successive structures of rule.

The complex history of Japan and its gods made available for worship innumerable forms and combinations of deities, each advocated by different groups and their leaders. Since the earliest recorded times, rulers have allied with gods, seeking their favor to answer changing political needs. One of the first written commentaries on Japan—included in a Chinese imperial history of the third century—records the female ruler of a settlement who claimed magical powers, apparently

communing with an unnamed god.[1] By the time Korean scribes recorded the
first histories in Japan four centuries later (that is, the earliest histories still extant today), much had changed. Waves of immigrants from the mainland,
primarily fleeing the wars in and around the Korean peninsula, had brought
with them not only writing but also the ideas, rituals, and other technologies
prevalent in their former homes. However, the importance of rulers' ties to
the gods remained. Heads of lineages and communities throughout the islands claimed special access to powerful kami through priesthood, divine descent, or both. Powerful leaders in the plains around present-day Nara commissioned two histories, the *Kojiki* and *Nihon Shoki,* to solidify their claims to
legitimacy through narrations of the past, placing them in a sacred lineage of
rulers (later called emperors) descended from a sun goddess, Amaterasu, and
before her from the creators of the world. The immigrant writers of these histories compiled stories of the defeat and assimilation of various kami
throughout the islands into a cosmology headed by Amaterasu, thereby
recording the defeat and assumed assimilation of the gods' followers as well.
In their hands, the history of the gods stood for the history of politics, with
the scribes' version of those events relating each lineage or community to the
rulers in Nara.

These texts from the early eighth century depict a complex mixture of sacred and magical traditions that had already emerged from the interactions of
residents of the islands, new and old. By then, people were increasingly interpreting the kami within the all-embracing structures of continental thought
and practice: a mixture of Daoist, Confucian, and Buddhist traditions as well
as less well documented practices such as spirit possession, mountain asceticism, and magic. All of these traditions shared a sense of the unity of the cosmos, whether expressed in Daoist ideas of yin and yang or magical powers,
Confucian emphases on the proper hierarchy of heaven, man, and earth, or
Buddhist evocations of enlightenment. Since the workings of stars, animals,
and humans—as well as unseen deities and demons—were thought to influence each other, meteor showers or other omens in the heavens portended
important changes in the realms of earth (e.g., earthquakes) or humans (e.g.,
a dynastic change). The actions of humans, such as meditation or the performance of particularly efficacious rituals, could influence the workings of the
cosmos as well. All things in the cosmos, seen or unseen, existed in relation to
one another.

The eighth-century histories provide hints about how rulers used different elements of this mixture to legitimate themselves. In particular, they suggest how the three most recent rulers—Tenchi, Tenmu, and Jitō—developed
the ideological structures of "imperial" rule, juxtaposing ideas of the relation-

ship between kami and rulers with the major traditions from the continent. It was around this time, it seems, that imperial ideologues created the sun goddess, Amaterasu (literally "Illuminating Heaven"), to evoke the powerful associations of heaven and the sun in Korean and Chinese thought.[2] Tenchi further associated himself with Confucian teachings, claiming the mandate of heaven for his rule and that of his descendants. His brother Tenmu, who defeated Tenchi's successor in a bloody civil war, added sponsorship of Buddhism—in particular, the Golden Light Sutra (*Konkōmyō saishōō kyō;* Sanskrit *Suvarṇa-prabhāsa-uttama-sūtra*). And Tenmu's consort, Jitō, who ruled as emperor after Tenmu's death and oversaw the completion of the *Kojiki* in 720, claimed the mantle of a Daoist sovereign (*tennō,* "heavenly sovereign," the Japanese term now translated as "emperor").[3]

Over the ensuing centuries, Confucian and Daoist ideas evolved into widely accepted assumptions undergirding the political and intellectual order: they became unremarkable supports for the hierarchy of imperial bureaucracy and accepted principles of divination and medicine. But the teachings of Buddhism arrived with ties to an existing, international organization of priests and temples as well as a distinct symbolism found in sculpture, painting, and architecture. Buddhism maintained a separate identity that would influence, and indeed dominate, interpretations of kami and their worship for centuries to come.

The teachings of the Enlightened One (Sanskrit *Buddha*) are attributed to "the sage of the Śākya people" (*Śākyamuni*) in northern India who lived in the sixth and fifth centuries before the common era. According to the earliest scriptures (Sanskrit *sūtras*), written several generations after his death, the teachings of the historical Buddha, Śākyamuni, focused on helping people escape from the endless cycle of suffering, sickness, death, and rebirth. Such escape could be attained through meditation: realizing the transient, illusory nature of this world and focusing instead on that which does not change, enlightenment.

In the ensuing centuries, followers of Śākyamuni expanded the reach of his teachings, gaining support for their rites and monasteries by appealing to leaders throughout India. In many cases, these rulers, and their communities, already worshipped their own deities. In a long and complicated process that won millions of converts, proponents of the Buddhist law, such as the authors of the Lotus Sutra (*Myōhō rengekyō;* Sanskrit *Saddharma-puṇḍarīka-sūtra*) and other scriptures, transformed Śākyamuni from an insightful human into a manifestation of universal enlightenment. They created multiple buddhas, one for each universe, including the Medicine Master (Japanese *Yakushi*) of the Land of Emerald, or Infinite Light (Japanese *Amida*), the buddha of the

Western Pure Land. They added countless "knowers of enlightenment" (Sanskrit *bodhisattvas*) to help others reach enlightenment or buddhahood, most notably Avalokiteśvara, the compassionate One Who Observes the Sounds of the World (Japanese *Kannon*). Instead of following the rigorous meditative practices of Śākyamuni, or as aids in their pursuit of such meditative perfection, people could pray to or meditate upon these buddhas and bodhisattvas in order to receive their help.

As Buddhist teachings spread through India and Central Asia, priests and writers of sutras worked to accommodate the deities of each locality and community. They transformed countless gods and goddesses into Buddhist guardian deities, telling how the gods of local mountains and communities vowed to protect the Buddhist teachings or, in some cases, converted to them. These lesser deities included demons (*yaksha*) such as the demon king or general Khumbīra (Japanese *Konpira*), a fierce, crocodile-like god associated with a mountain in northern India, who purportedly led thousands of his followers to listen to the Buddha preach. In the Golden Light Sutra, the yaksha general Khumbīra leads five hundred other yaksha alongside several such generals and a multitude of other deities who "protect those who hear this sutra."[4] In other sutras he appears as the guardian of Śākyamuni, as the first of twelve generals who accompany the Medicine Master, or even, in a later, Daoist-influenced sutra written in China, as a great dragon form—synonymous with the universe—into which Śākyamuni converts himself in order to preach to the people and teach them how to obtain supernatural powers.[5] The Buddhist sutras, like the Japanese imperial histories several centuries later, incorporated countless local deities into a larger, more coherent narrative—this time of the spread of Buddhist, not imperial, law.

On their journey from India through Central Asia to China, Korea, and Japan, proponents of Buddhism worked to secure the favor of rulers not just by presenting them with attractive gods but by proving the worth of the new religion in more mundane affairs as well. In China, from at least the fourth century on, monks gained the support of rulers by demonstrating the magical efficacy of Buddhism in rainmaking, medicine, and divination on the battlefield.[6] Official support made possible the subsequent establishment of monasteries and temples, where priests expounded upon the practical benefits of rites and sponsorship and studied techniques of meditation and enlightenment as well as the complex cosmology of buddhas, bodhisattvas, gods, demons, and guardians that now surrounded them.

The formal introduction of Buddhism to Japan likewise relied on the reputation of the new religion for effective support of the ruler. Although some immigrants doubtless brought teachings and rituals to the islands before that time, the *Nihon Shoki* records that in the middle of the sixth century, the king of the Korean state of Paekche sent a copper and gold image of Śākyamuni Buddha, along with several sutras, to the ruler of Japan. In the accompanying memorial, he praised the usefulness of the new religion, writing, "Imagine a man in possession of treasures to his heart's content, so that he might satisfy all his wishes in proportion as he used them. Thus it is with the treasure of this wonderful doctrine. Every prayer is fulfilled and naught is wanting."[7] While this first overture came to nothing, members of the imperial court soon adopted Buddhist deities, texts, and rituals because of the benefits for their personal welfare and ability to govern. They became enamored of the ideal of a Buddhist king (Sanskrit *cakravartin*) expounded in the Golden Light Sutra and especially the sutra's promises that myriad deities would "protect [such a] king and his people, give them peace and freedom from suffering, prolong their lives, and fill them with glory."[8] Emperors soon sponsored Buddhism in general and, from at least the eighth century on, an elaborate annual recitation of the Golden Light Sutra in particular.

In the late eighth century, a young Japanese man from Shikoku traveled to the capital to study. There, the twenty-four-year-old Kūkai encountered Buddhist texts that seemed to shed light on his meditative experiences in the mountains of home.[9] In 804, at the age of thirty, Kūkai won a spot on an imperial mission to China. After studying with Buddhist masters there, he brought back to Japan the secretly transmitted ritual teachings of esoteric Buddhism: the importance of ritual performance, particularly the use of mantras, mudras (gestures), and mandalas (visual meditative aids) to help realize one's unity with the enlightened nature of the entire cosmos—one's already existing, essential enlightenment. With the support of the emperor, Kūkai (later known as Kōbō Daishi) established a monastic center of scholarship on Mt. Kōya, where his teachings on the performance and interpretation of efficacious rituals developed into the Shingon (True Word) denomination of Japanese Buddhism. Kūkai's esoteric teachings, with their emphasis on efficacy, drew students from other schools of Buddhism. The Tendai lineage, in particular, became known for its combination of exoteric (text-based) scholarship and esoteric (secret) transmissions of rites. The esoteric teachings of meditation and ritual likewise found fertile ground among ascetics who meditated on mountains throughout Japan as they sought to obtain supernatural powers of healing, rainmaking, and the like and to use those powers for the benefit of petitioners in their communities. In this way, esoteric Buddhism became closely tied to the developing traditions of mountain asceticism (shugendo).

In 835, Kūkai used his ritual expertise to translate the Golden Light Sutra, long revered for its promise of protection for the ruler, into a magically efficacious ritual performance, the Mishuhō, thenceforth staged annually inside the imperial palace. The seven-day-long ritual effectively confirmed the role of the emperor as a Buddhist king, granting him the powers of the wish-fulfilling jewel, identified in Kūkai's writings with the relic of Śākyamuni, with an attendant of the Cosmic Buddha, and with the wisdom of enlightenment itself. The rites included an esoteric fire ceremony (Japanese *goma*; Sanskrit *homa*) as well as offerings to the Five Wrathful Deities led by Fudō Myōō, conferring the powers of those deities upon the sponsor of the ritual. The Mishuhō was thus designed to ensure both the fulfillment of the sutra's promises for the protection of the ruler and the centrality of esoteric ritual in the imperial court.[10]

During the ensuing years, esoteric rituals and teachings—including the use of ritual to convey to various deities their worshippers' prayers for protection, safety, or other worldly benefits—developed not just in Kūkai's Shingon school but in the influential Tendai denomination as well, eventually coming to pervade religious thought and action throughout Japan. By the eleventh century, emperors and ruling aristocrats buttressed their authority not so much through ritual enactment of the Golden Light Sutra, although such rituals continued at court, as through appeals to the Lotus Sutra, which promised that countless bodhisattvas, guardian demons, and other beings would protect supporters or sponsors of the sutra far beyond the imperial elite.[11] The Lotus Sutra, with its emphasis on the transcendence of the Buddha and the help of the Medicine Master Yakushi and the compassionate bodhisattva Kannon, suggested that anyone could attain buddhahood. Even a woman could become a buddha, as demonstrated in the sutra's tale of the daughter of the Dragon King who, upon offering a wonderful jewel to the Buddha, achieves sudden enlightenment.[12]

Such inclusiveness contributed to the growing popularity of the Lotus Sutra and its imagery. While mountain ascetics (*shugenja*) and Tendai practitioners incorporated the deities of the Lotus Sutra into esoteric fire ceremonies,[13] other priests of the Tendai denomination focused more on lecture and debate than on offerings and empowerment. They developed the Hokke Hakkō—eight lectures on the Lotus Sutra, conducted over four days—as a showy spectacle that established its sponsor as a devout, virtuous leader and displayed his vast economic, social, and political power.[14] Because of the promises included in the Lotus Sutra, however, the Hokke Hakkō, too, was performed for its reputed effectiveness in averting misfortune or guaranteeing protection. The competing ritual systems of the Golden Light Sutra and

Lotus Sutra—whether the fire ceremony of Buddhist rulership dedicated to the Cosmic Buddha and Fudō Myōō in one, or sermons and the prayers of individuals dedicated to Śākyamuni or the bodhisattva Kannon in the other—thus came to share a focus on worldly benefit. Partaking of a shared universe of gods and symbols, in which Kannon could appear holding the wish-fulfilling jewel, for instance, they nevertheless provided alternative structures for the support of rulers by the priests who sought their favor.[15]

Indeed, the work of a priest entailed politics as much as prayer. As envisioned by worshippers throughout the land, the gods most accessible to human petitions inhabited particular sites—whether mountains or caves, buildings or carved images.[16] To worship such a deity required access to its site of enshrinement and, for priests, control over the site as well. In order to secure the worship of his god, therefore—not to mention his livelihood—a priest needed either to become ruler of his own territory, with the military and economic wherewithal to protect his domain, or to obtain the sponsorship, protection, and recognition of a more powerful lord. Moreover, because worship focused on particular sites perceived to host mysterious power, a priest could often face competition from rivals—those who interpreted the sacred presence according to a different school, sutra, or meditative tradition and identified it, accordingly, with a different deity. Faced with both the religious and institutional need to control the site, priests who lived side by side frequently vied among themselves, promoting their own rituals or doctrinal interpretations in order to gain sponsorship at the expense of their rivals. Such struggles for institutional control and, in a world at war, priestly survival, of necessity were framed in religious language—the naming of the sacred powers, their depiction in images, their worship in rites. Given the limited resources available, such priestly competition frequently turned fierce, resulting on Mt. Zōzu, at least, in accusations of assassination attempts and, at least once, in death.

The landscape of the gods—so deceptively tranquil—thus records in its edifices the politics of humans. From the earliest recorded history of Mt. Zōzu in the thirteenth century, through the upheavals leading to the victory of the Tokugawa forces in 1600, the military threats and political transitions in northwestern Shikoku and in Japan as a whole prompted priests repeatedly to reinterpret the powers of the mountain for their own survival. Drawing upon the complementary and competing ritual systems of the Golden Light Sutra and the Lotus Sutra, fire rituals and lecture ceremonies, successive priests shifted the meanings and even the identities of the gods on Mt. Zōzu, eventually enshrining the demon king Konpira on the mountain in Shikoku.

Mt. Zōzu before Konpira

Mountains in Japan have long been associated with sacred powers, whether as abodes of the dead, sites of meditation, sources of life-giving water, or homes of powerful gods or spirits.[17] Long before it appeared in written texts, Mt. Zōzu presumably functioned in all of these ways, rising dramatically from the flat Sanuki plain, with its steep valleys, flowing waterfalls, deeply shaded forests, and secluded caves.

The earliest references to the wooded hillside that eventually came to be known as Mt. Zōzu attest to the location of the site amid several coexisting ritual structures, each affiliated with a political sponsor among the military, aristocratic, and religious rulers of a disunited land. The mountain first appeared in texts in the early thirteenth century, when it stood within the Komatsu estate (shōen), an area owned in absentia either by the aristocratic Kujō family or by a shrine or temple to which the Kujō had donated the governing and income rights of the estate.[18] According to the diary of Dōhan (1184–1252), a priest who visited the mountain in 1248, there stood at the base of the mountain, amidst a "small grove of pine trees," a hermitage called Shōmyōin. There a priest recited the name of the buddha (nenbutsu), calling on Amida Buddha so that those buried in the graveyards on the mountain would be reborn in Amida's Pure Land after death.[19] Such recitation practice, focused on Amida and his attendant Kannon (the same compassionate Kannon found in the Lotus Sutra), had spread widely in Sanuki province since Hōnen (1133–1212), the great advocate of the nenbutsu, had lived in exile on the Komatsu estate under the protection of Kujō Kanezane three decades before.[20] It therefore seems possible that the Kujō family provided the funds to construct and staff the small hermitage, thereby enjoying the peace of mind, the practical benefits, and the virtuous reputation thought to accrue to sponsors of Buddhist practice.

The priest Dōhan, however, was not affiliated with the Pure Land practices that would soon become a third major form of Buddhism in Japan. Instead, he had been sent from the esoteric, Shingon Buddhist center of Mt. Kōya to live for a while at Zentsūji, the birthplace of the Shingon founder, Kūkai.[21] Having already traveled the ri (not quite four kilometers) from Zentsūji to the mountain, Dōhan climbed up past the hermitage Shōmyōin to Takidera, literally "Waterfall Temple." He remarked that Takidera faced east toward the site where a "dragon" resided, and that the main hall enshrined a "buddha with a thousand arms": Kannon, the bodhisattva of compassion, thought by many to be the daughter of the dragon king.[22] Around

Takidera, wrote Dōhan, lay "the foundation stones of an old temple," perhaps one dedicated to the "dragon" itself, who not only could provide much-needed rain to the dry plains of Sanuki province, but also in popular lore possessed a wish-fulfilling jewel with which it could help other beings.[23] In any case, both "Waterfall Temple" and the site of the "dragon" suggested an emphasis on securing the power of the mountain to ensure moisture, successful harvests, and other benefits. Moreover, Kannon, the dragon (identified with the Great Kami Miwa), and waterfalls (in the form of Seiryō Gongen or Kiyotaki Myōjin, literally "the deity of Pure Waterfalls," guardian kami of the great Shingon temple Daigoji), water, and healing were being linked together in the worship of kami at the great Shingon centers of Dōhan's time.[24] By the early thirteenth century, then, the mountain hosted at least two Buddhist institutions—Shōmyōin and Takidera—each linked in some way to a powerful estate holder in the area: the Kujō aristocratic family or the Shingon Mt. Kōya.

The complex, overlapping systems that combined kami, buddhas, dragons, and other spirits on Mt. Zōzu were characteristic of the worship of the gods in medieval Japan.[25] By the thirteenth century, scholars and priests had merged the cosmology of the sutras with the landmarks of Japan. Interpreters identified the protective Indian gods (Sanskrit *deva,* translated into Japanese as *kami*)—who guarded sites in the sutras—with gods (kami), sites, and shrines in the Japanese islands, utilizing these associations to support the rulers as well.[26] Thus, both the dragon king and Kannon, of the Lotus Sutra, were linked to Mt. Zōzu. And priests and scholars in the Lotus-influenced traditions of Tendai and Nichiren (Hokke) Buddhism, as well as Yoshida (Yuiitsu) Shinto, associated the Thirty (Indian) Protecting Deities said to guard the Lotus Sutra not only with the kami of thirty prominent shrines around the capital, but also with each of the thirty days of the month, thirty guardians of the imperial palace, and the like.[27] Many of the local kami so associated hence bore the name *gongen* or "manifestation," signifying their identity as the local appearance (*gongen*) of an originally Buddhist form (*honji*)—that is, a deity in the human world with enlightened buddhahood as its essence. Indeed, as seen in the linking of the early Takidera on Mt. Zōzu with the dragon, the bodhisattva Kannon, and the god of Pure Waterfalls—such manifestations opened the doors not only to one-on-one identifications but also to complicated networks of related associations, tying together not only kami and buddhas, but also dragons, culture heroes, and mythical beings.[28] By Dōhan's time such combinations had already become well-established elements of the sacred landscape of Japan.

A generation after Dōhan's visit, an unprecedented event threw estates on

Shikoku and throughout western Japan into turmoil. In 1268, Khubilai Khan, leader of the Mongol armies then invading Sung China, sent a messenger to the shogunal government in Kamakura demanding the surrender of Japan. In response, the regent to the shogun called on the administrators of estates in western Japan to strengthen their defenses. Rulers and residents in Shikoku, Kyushu, and western Honshu therefore feared invasion and sought the help of the gods in their preparation against attack.[29] A charismatic Buddhist ritualist, Nichiren (1222–82), took advantage of these concerns at court to promote exclusive worship of the Lotus Sutra as protection against the Mongol threat. One of Nichiren's followers in Shikoku, the lord Akiyama Yasutada, established shrines to the Thirty Deities thought to protect the Lotus Sutra (Sanjūbanjin) in seven villages that he controlled during his tenure in Sanuki from 1278 to 1288.[30] Whether sponsored by Akiyama or by his followers, one such shrine to the Thirty Deities was built on Mt. Zōzu, and a four-day ritual of lectures on the Lotus Sutra (Hokke Hakkō) was established, presumably for protection against invasion as well as for the benefit of the deceased. In any event, when the Mongol forces arrived in Kyushu 1274 and 1281, they were successfully repulsed during the violent typhoon season.[31]

When sources next mentioned Mt. Zōzu, almost three hundred years later, in the late sixteenth century, the site had been transformed into a landscape of the Lotus Sutra. The Hokke Hakkō had become an annual festival held in the tenth month of each year. The Thirty Protective Deities were revered as guardians of a temple called Matsuoji, sharing the name of a temple at the Lotus Sutra–centered Tendai headquarters on Mt. Hiei. Worship on Mt. Zōzu apparently focused on the main image, an eleven-headed Kannon, the bodhisattva of compassion, whose response to human prayer is praised in an entire chapter of the Lotus Sutra.[32] And, whether because of a variation upon place names in the sutras, or simply because it looked like an elephant, the mountain became known as Mt. Elephant Head, or Mt. Zōzu.

It was within this Lotus landscape, amid the widespread military upheavals that eventually brought the Tokugawa shoguns to power, that yet another deity was enshrined on the mountain. During the 1560s and early 1570s, the warlord Chōsokabe Motochika (1538–99) brought the large province of Tosa on the southwest side of Shikoku under his rule. As refugees fleeing from his forces spread the news, lesser lords in Sanuki, Iyo, and Awa provinces began to suspect that Chōsokabe's ambitions ranged beyond Tosa, perhaps to the rest of Shikoku. In this context, a priest named Yūga, apparently the nephew of the lord of nearby Nishi Nagao castle, built a shrine to "the king Konpira, who is also a kami" on Mt. Zōzu in 1573. It is only this inscription, later found on a small wooden placard originally placed on the ridgebeam of the small shrine to commemorate its construction, that records the first appearance of the deity Konpira (Khumbīra) on the mountain.[33]

Scattered evidence suggests that Konpira may have been gaining prominence around Japan in the last decades of the sixteenth century. In the Lotus traditions, for instance, the Hokke priest Nisshū (1532–94) named Konpira, along with Indra, Brahma, and the Four Heavenly Kings, as important deities (Sanskrit *deva;* Japanese *kami*) of Buddhism in India.[34] His interpretations influenced not only fellow priests in the Nichiren school of Buddhism but contemporary ritualists of Yoshida Shinto as well.

However, the dedicatory ridge placard of the new shrine made clear that the installment of Konpira on Mt. Zōzu did not occur within the Tendai, Nichiren, or Yoshida Shinto traditions associated with the Thirty Protecting Deities. Instead, its enshrinement drew upon esoteric Shingon rites focused on the Golden Light Sutra, one of the sutras in which the protective general Konpira appears. The placard records that the shrine to Konpira on Mt. Zōzu was built by Yūga, the *bettō* (administrative priest) of the subtemple Konkōin—literally "the subtemple of the Golden Light." The enshrinement ceremony consisted of rituals from the esoteric Shingon tradition performed by a priest from a subtemple on Mt. Kōya with a history of scholarship on the role of kami—that is, both Indian and local gods—in Shingon Buddhism.[35] Moreover, through the use of the name Yūga, the priest announced his affiliation with the Shingon institutions in the area: he adopted as the first character of his name part of the name of Yūhan (1270–1352), a renowned Shingon priest and scholar credited with the revival of Kūkai's birthplace, Zentsūji, who more than two centuries before had retired for a while to Shōmyōin at the foot of Mt. Zōzu.[36]

In the face of imminent invasion, then, this time from the warlord Chōsokabe across the mountains of Shikoku instead of from Mongol forces across the Japan Sea, Yūga and his lordly sponsor enshrined alongside the Thirty Deities of the Lotus Sutra a powerful, protective god from the esoteric Buddhist pantheon, a general of the gods associated with both the ideal of Buddhist kingship and Shingon palace rituals empowering and legitimizing the Japanese imperial house. The fierce Indian protector of Buddhism—the "king and kami" Konpira—was thus first enshrined on Mt. Zōzu to protect against the threatening armies of the Tosa warlord in 1573.

The Tosa Invasion

The fears of Yūga, the Nagao family, and other residents of Sanuki province proved well founded. While the warlords Oda Nobunaga and Toyotomi

Hideyoshi consolidated large parts of Honshu under their control, Chōsokabe led his forces across the mountains of central Shikoku in 1576 to embark on the conquest of the rest of the island. The Tosa warlord defeated the strongholds of various small lords, including the priest Yūga's sponsor's castle at Nishi Nagao. As Chōsokabe continued on toward Mt. Zōzu, Yūga fled before the invading forces, taking with him the written records and treasures of the temple Matsuoji and the "subtemple of the Golden Light," Konkōin (and thereby accounting for the almost three-hundred-year gap in the history of the mountain).[37] When Chōsokabe Motochika arrived at Mt. Zōzu, the priest of Konkōin and Konpira had departed (figure 2.1).

As Chōsokabe completed his final victories on the island, he turned his attention to Matsuoji on Mt. Zōzu. In Yūga's absence, the Tosa warlord installed his own priests on the mountain, ensuring that the rituals there would be performed according to traditions that had already supported his rule at home. In 1583, Chōsokabe paid for the rebuilding of the shrine to the Thirty Deities under the ritual leadership not of a Lotus priest, but of Yūi, a practitioner of esoteric mountain asceticism (shugendo) from the peaks of Tosa.[38]

While it is unclear exactly what form Yūi's particular shugendo practice took in the late sixteenth century, the tradition of shugendo in general involved a combination of austerities, meditation, and rituals designed to endow practitioners (shugenja) with superhuman powers accessible only in the mountains. Shugendo, an organized religious tradition since about the ninth century, drew heavily on the rites and logic of Shingon Buddhism—especially the idea that it is possible to become enlightened in this very body through identification with an enlightened deity. Thus, shugenja meditated in caves, traveled throughout mountains, performed fire ceremonies (goma), wore short swords, and carried ropes in their efforts to identify with the Buddhist deity Fudō Myōō and thereby realize their essential enlightenment.[39] Doubtless Yūi, called to Mt. Zōzu by his lord Chōsokabe, brought most, if not all, of these practices with him.

Exploiting the powers imputed to the sacred mountain, the warlord from Tosa set himself up as the Buddhist ruler of all Shikoku. In 1584, calling himself King Mahābrahman (Japanese *Daibontennō*)—and thereby, according to esoteric commentaries, ostensibly king of Japan—Chōsokabe funded the construction of an entry gate for Matsuoji.[40] Yūgon, another shugenja from

❀ **2.1** (*opposite*) Rulers and priests, 1573–1600. During these years, priests relied heavily upon rulers for sponsorship, and rulers relied on priests for rituals of legitimation and blessing. As a result, either a new ruler (such as the invading Tosa warlord Chōsokabe) installed his own priests or the priests promoted deities (such as Konpira) in order to appeal to incoming lords loyal to emerging rulers on the mainland of Honshu.

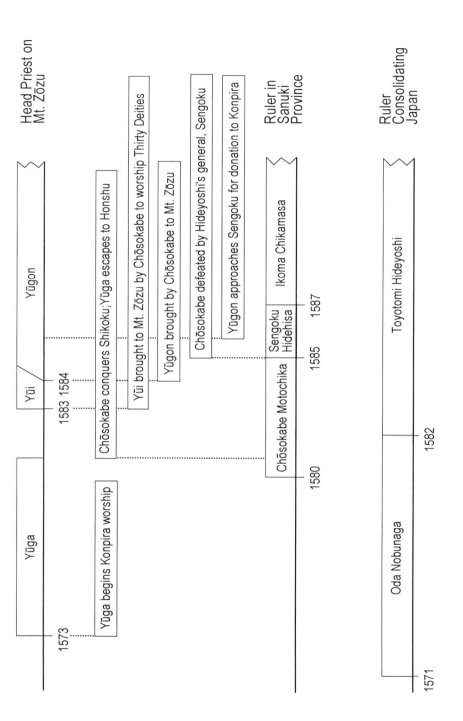

Head Priest on Mt. Zōzu

Yūga | Yūi | Yūgon

1573 — Yūga begins Konpira worship

1583 1584

Chōsokabe conquers Shikoku; Yūga escapes to Honshu

Yūi brought to Mt. Zōzu by Chōsokabe to worship Thirty Deities

Yūgon brought by Chōsokabe to Mt. Zōzu

Chōsokabe defeated by Hideyoshi's general, Sengoku

Yūgon approaches Sengoku for donation to Konpira

Ruler in Sanuki Province

Chōsokabe Motochika | Sengoku Hidehisa | Ikoma Chikamasa

1580 | 1585 | 1587

Ruler Consolidating Japan

Oda Nobunaga | Toyotomi Hideyoshi

1571 | 1582

Tosa, moved to Matsuoji to supervise the ritual installation of Chōsokabe's entry gate and take up the position of head priest. Thus, with the help of Yūi and Yūgon (both of whom followed Yūga's practice of adopting the first character of the Shingon priest Yūhan's name), Chōsokabe associated himself with the powerful Mt. Zōzu, pronounced himself a Buddhist king, and transformed the Thirty Deities into protectors of his own regime. He also displaced Konpira, the protective deity that had been installed by Yūga and his Nagao sponsors against the Tosa warlord's invasion. At the same time, Chōsokabe staffed Matsuoji with his own people: shugendo practitioners from his native Tosa—men who owed their new positions to the warlord's generosity. There is no indication that Chōsokabe ever recognized the shrine to Konpira. His attention focused instead on the Shrine to the Thirty Deities and Matsuoji as a whole, transforming them into centers for shugendo rites in support of his ambitious rule.

The Return of Konpira

Within months of his construction of the Matsuoji gate, however, Chōsokabe's grand ambitions collapsed. Toyotomi Hideyoshi's forces invaded Shikoku from Honshu in the spring of 1585, defeated Chōsokabe, and confined him to Tosa. To replace Chōsokabe and consolidate his victory, Hideyoshi appointed as lord of Sanuki province Sengoku Hidehisa (1552–1614), one of the generals who had led the attack on the island. The result was a change, once again, of the gods on Mt. Zōzu.

Sengoku immediately acted to consolidate his authority as lord of Sanuki. Because temples and shrines had frequently governed their own territories with armed forces during the years of decentralized rule, Sengoku sent notices to prominent institutions in the province, including "Matsuoji in Komatsu estate," announcing that it was illegal to maintain military forces or foment unrest.[41]

Skillfully riding the new political wave, Chōsokabe's appointee, Yūgon, quickly moved to reassure Sengoku of his shift in loyalty. He maintained shugendo rituals on the mountain, but instead of espousing the Thirty Deities of the Lotus Sutra sponsored by Chōsokabe and reenshrined by Yūi, he drew Sengoku's attention to the benefits available to a ruler who sponsored Buddhism in the form of Konpira and, apparently, the Golden Light Sutra. Two months after Sengoku's initial warning to Matsuoji, the new lord of Sanuki donated ten *koku* worth of land (theoretically yielding enough rice to feed ten people each year) to "Konpira," the deity that Yūga had originally installed in opposition to the now vanquished Chōsokabe. During the following year, Sengoku gave additional land to Konpira and other major shrines and temples in the province.[42] After virtually disappearing from view during Chōsokabe's two-year tenure in the area, the shrine to Konpira founded by Yūga in 1573 had suddenly been revived. The shugenja Yūgon, himself appointed by Chōsokabe, had, with Sengoku Hidehisa, reinstated Konpira, now as a protective deity associated with the new lord. He dramatically severed the ties of the mountain to the Tosa warlord but continued shugendo rituals, now under the aegis of the protector of Buddhist rulers in the Golden Light Sutra: Konpira.

Just as Chōsokabe and Sengoku allied themselves with different deities and ritual traditions in their struggles for military and political power, so too the priests on Mt. Zōzu used the gods on the mountain to jockey for influence among themselves. No sources remain to tell of any priest of the Thirty Deities at this time, but as soon as Yūga, safe in hiding across the Inland Sea in the port city of Sakai, learned that Sengoku had replaced Chōsokabe, he tried to return and take up his earlier position as head priest of the subtemple Konkōin.[43] Yūgon, however, proved a formidable opponent. Perhaps the Tosa shugenja solicited donations from Sengoku in the name of Konpira in order to preempt Yūga's bid for power based on the Konpira shrine. Whatever the case, Sengoku confirmed Yūgon as head priest of Konkōin, and Yūga, the original priest of the shrine to Konpira, was not permitted to return.

When in 1587 Toyotomi Hideyoshi removed Sengoku Hidehisa and appointed Ikoma Chikamasa (1526–1603) as lord of Sanuki in his place, Konkōin (that is, Yūgon) received another fifty koku of land in three installments from the new lord, once explicitly as a donation to Konpira.[44] While Yūga fumed in Sakai, then, Yūgon successfully associated himself with both Konpira and the patronage of the ruling lords. From this time on, Konpira remained central to the shugendo-shaped rituals of the sacred mountain. Because Ikoma Chikamasa and his descendants remained in control of Sanuki even after Tokugawa Ieyasu's regime displaced that of Hideyoshi, and because successive years of peace kept the Tokugawa in power, no dramatic change in the ruling mandate occurred. Therefore, there was no need for the rulers to replace the gods of a previous rival.

The gods on the mountain thus reflected the politics of the time. Priests of rival deities on Mt. Zōzu, as elsewhere in Japan (and, indeed, throughout the world), gained and lost influence through their alliances with influential sponsors. In times of violent political change, as in the late sixteenth century, the most crucial such sponsors were the rulers: men who could either destroy the mountain temples or provide generous support. In order to ensure the survival and status of themselves, their heirs, and their gods, therefore, rival ritualists invoked the esoteric ceremonies of rule to secure the benefits of lordly recognition. Dedicated to different gods and different rites of worship, they vied to prove the efficacy of their own traditions for legitimizing, protecting, and enhancing the governing ability of the ruling lord.[45]

Konpira, Kongōbō, and the Establishment of the Tokugawa Order (1600–1675)

3

From 1585 on, the rulers of Sanuki province supported the shrine to Konpira on Mt. Zōzu. Without a broader income base and without a coherent identity attractive to worshippers, however, Konpira's priests would be forced to rely indefinitely upon the whim of the ruler alone. Aware of these problems, they worked to secure their dominance on the mountain, to gain control over a taxable population, and to develop a distinctive and powerful identity for their site. Negotiating amid the complicated pressures of the first several decades of the seventeenth century—as the Tokugawa shoguns came to power, consolidated their control over the countryside, and established the guiding principles of their government—the priests of Konpira created the institutional and symbolic structures that would shape the god and its cult for centuries to come.

Yūgon and his successors created Konpira in these years while contending with persistent rivals. The priests of Konpira, the Thirty Deities, Shōmyōin, and other temples or hermitages on the mountain competed with each other for dominance, fighting to enhance the prosperity and autonomy of their own spheres of influence. Each celibate priest worked to secure the continuation and welfare of his institution for future generations, thereby ensuring his lasting influence within a priestly, instead of a genetic, lineage. It was therefore by engaging in the inevitable institutional struggles that priests could establish what they saw as the best form of worship for years to come. Only the victors, after all, would be able to maintain the shrines and their rituals, allowing future generations to remember and worship their god in the manner they believed appropriate.

In the early seventeenth century, the priests of the god Konpira, in particular, successfully positioned themselves politically, ritually, and economically in relation to both wealthy rulers and rivals on the mountain, thereby establishing the long-term survival of Konpira on Mt. Zōzu and the hereditary security of their administrative base, Konkōin. In doing so, they responded and contributed to the intellectual, social, and political structures of the time. With Konpira as their focus, the priests of Konkōin would secure a small domain based on support of the god and shape the mountain precincts to enhance the prestige not only of Konpira, but also of themselves and their lordly sponsors. They would combine the legitimating symbols and rituals of countless past regimes to secure the administrative order of Sanuki province in Tokugawa Japan.

Building a Sacred Domain

By the time of his death in 1600—the year of Tokugawa Ieyasu's decisive victory at the Battle of Sekigahara—the shugenja Yūgon had forged a profitable alliance with the Ikoma lords of Sanuki focused on the rituals of Konpira. His successor Yūsei (head priest, 1600–1613), a pivotal figure in the history of the Konpira cult, capitalized further upon this political connection. Born as the eldest son of a trusted vassal of the Ikoma, Yūsei arrived on the mountain well positioned to prevail upon the Ikoma family.[1] It was perhaps due to this connection that the second Ikoma lord, within months of Yūsei's succession to the head priestship, allowed people from other provinces to move into a new village at the foot of Mt. Zōzu tax free and donated more than seventy-three additional koku of land to Konkōin.[2] Whatever the case, Yūsei, as had Yūgon, supported the Ikoma lords' political consolidation of Sanuki province, allying the protective powers of Konpira with the authority of his Ikoma sponsors and receiving from the lord in return the foundation of his own power base in land and people.

But Yūsei did more than simply continue Yūgon's policies. While he prominently acknowledged his debt to the Tosa shugenja—referring to himself as Igonbō, borrowing characters from the names of both Yūi and Yūgon—Yūsei built up the mountain as a sophisticated center of Shingon ritual. Educated in the tradition of Kūkai, Yūsei studied on Mt. Kōya, copied esoteric Buddhist texts, and wrote treatises on Shingon teachings. He even served as titular head of a subtemple on Mt. Kōya during his tenure at Konpira.[3] On Mt. Zozu, he effectively reproduced, now in support of the lord of

Sanuki, the imperial rituals of the Golden Light Sutra (the Mishuhō) that had fallen into disuse at court almost two centuries before.

To do so, Yūsei, with the support of the Ikoma lords, transformed the ritual landscape of Mt. Zōzu. In 1601, when Ikoma Kazumasa rebuilt the Shrine of the Thirty Deities, Yūsei oversaw the enshrinement of sacred protectors for the mountain from the Shingon mandalas: Marishiten (Sanskrit *Marīci*), protector of the sun and moon, and Bishamonten (Sanskrit *Vaiśravana*), guardian king of the north. Three years later, perhaps encouraged by a growing interest in the Mishuhō on Mt. Kōya (a trend that would culminate in the revival of the Mishuhō in the imperial court in 1623),[4] Yūsei oversaw construction of a hall for fire ceremonies dedicated to Fudō Myōō, leader in the Mishuhō of the Five Wrathful Deities, who brandishes his sword of wisdom in order to save sentient beings from the fires of ignorance.[5] With his carving the next year of an image of Kannon holding a wish-fulfilling jewel, Yūsei completed the essential elements of the Mishuhō landscape, for Kūkai, in his promotion of the ritual, had deemed the jewel to be central, calling it "the wisdom of enlightenment that grants all wishes" and attributing to it the "Golden Light" of the sutra's title.[6] Moreover, by depicting this jewel in the hands of Kannon—the popular bodhisattva of the Lotus Sutra and attendant of Amida in his Pure Land Paradise—Yūsei skillfully merged the symbols of three Buddhist traditions, each with adherents in Sanuki province. He depicted Mt. Zōzu, and the rites of Konkōin, within the overlapping systems of local devotion.

The next year, in 1606, Yūsei confirmed his dedication to Shingon rituals of esoteric shugendo, carving a statue of himself as a winged, beaked manifestation of Fudō Myōō.[7] That is, he depicted himself as a tengu: a magical creature who lived in the mountains, associated in the popular mind, as well as in ritual, with the supernatural powers of adept shugenja. Thus, through the carving and enshrinement of selected images from 1601 to 1606, Yūsei transformed Mt. Zōzu into a center of miraculous powers to be conferred through esoteric rites on the sponsor of its goma rituals—in this case, the Ikoma lord. In effect, copying the strategy of Kūkai in the ninth century and the ambitions of ritualists on Mt. Kōya in his own time, he elevated himself, as an esoteric specialist and practitioner endowed with magical powers, above the sponsoring lord. He placed himself in a position to confer upon the Ikoma lords the sacred powers of a Buddhist ruler.[8]

Yūsei used this new position of symbolic power along with his ties to the Ikoma to raise his subtemple Konkōin to dominance on the mountain as the effective head of Matsuoji. First, he arranged for the demise of the other institutions on and around Mt. Zōzu. Yūsei engineered the departure of at least three priests, including one called Shōmyōji (probably a nenbutsu practitioner at the ole Shōmyōin), a "southern priest" within Matsuoji, and the influential priest of the Shrine to the Thirty Deities. With the support of the Ikoma lord, Yūsei then confiscated the wealth of their institutions.[9] During his ensuing tenure, the renowned shugenja attracted several students who established shugendo subtemples of their own on the mountain. In effect, Yūsei replaced his rivals with his disciples. He skillfully deployed ritual structures and political ties to raise his own subtemple, Konkōin, to a position of undisputed superiority on the mountain.

As Konkōin, under Yūsei's leadership, gained control on an increasingly influential Mt. Zōzu, succession to the office of head priest beckoned as an attractive option for well-born young men in the area. Unlikely to become head of his natal family, a younger son without promising prospects of adoption into another lineage could hope instead for entry into the secret transmissions and ritual lineage of a successful temple. Yūsei's relatives—in particular, Yūsei's brother's wife's family—therefore turned their attention to the growing prominence of Konkōin. Drawing upon their ties of blood, marriage, and vassalage to both Yūsei and the Ikoma lords, the Yamashita family of western Saita, ten kilometers southwest of Mt. Zōzu, gained control of Konkōin, eventually securing the celibate, ritual lineage as a hereditary post for younger Yamashita sons.

The political ties of the Yamashita family came to shape the fate of Mt. Zōzu. The Yamashita family of samurai had arrived in Saita during the upheavals of the 1570s, taking as brides the daughters of their new lord and helping to administer the area on his behalf. It is unclear with whom the Yamashita sided during Chōsokabe's invasion, but when the first Ikoma lord arrived, he conferred 200 koku worth of land upon the head of the family in return for his work as administrator of the village. A Yamashita daughter, Onatsu, served as concubine of the second Ikoma lord, Kazumasa; their son then became the second-highest vassal of his half brother, the third lord, Masatoshi.[10] Thus, when Onatsu's nephew entered the priesthood and succeeded Yūsei as head priest of Konkōin in 1613, he could immediately call upon the support of his well-connected relatives. Indeed, shortly after the rise to office of Onatsu's nephew, Yūgen (head priest, 1613–45), Masatoshi gave the largest donation yet to Konpira. When the fourth Ikoma lord, Takatoshi, came to power in 1621 while still a child, Yūgen's relatives arranged an additional donation of 100 koku to the god. Konkōin, as the base of the Konpira cult, thus came to reap income from 330 koku of land in three neighboring villages and the growing community of Konpira itself, by far the most land of all religious sites under the Ikoma, and enough to support the development of both the village and a larger ritual complex on the mountain.[11] Yūgen had effectively parlayed his familial relationships into long-term institutional support from the lord of Sanuki province.

Yūgen and his successors—the younger sons of the Yamashita family, who employed their relatives as advisers and administrators on Mt. Zōzu—continued to exploit not only personal relations but also the ritual traditions established by Yūsei to secure authority for the Yamashita lineage over a semi-autonomous domain based at Konpira. In the process, they added new meanings to the Indian god. In 1614, the year after Yūsei's death, Yūgen enshrined the carved wooden image of Yūsei as a tengu version of Fudō Myōō. An inscription on the statue conferred upon Yūsei a new name, Kongōbō (literally "Diamond Priest"), evoking the adamantine wisdom of Fudō Myōō. "The image of the *shamon* Kongōbō entered into the Way of the Tengu," declared the label, apparently predated to the tenth month of 1606, clearly identifying Kongōbō as "the great monk Yūsei, reviver of this mountain."[12] Yūgen thus enshrined his predecessor (and his uncle's brother) as a protective deity, in effect positioning him as an ancestral god and founder of Konkōin's lineage as well. By enshrining the deceased Yūsei in 1614, just as the shogun Tokugawa Iemitsu would enshrine the first Tokugawa shogun, Ieyasu, after his death the following year, Yūgen effectively positioned the priest-tengu as the founder of a priestly lineage on the mountain to be carried on by the Yamashita sons.[13] Yūgen's acceptance in 1615 of a donated copy of the Golden Light Sutra and his receipt of Shingon rank in 1621 suggest that he continued Yūsei's ritual legacy as well.

Capitalizing upon personal ties and strengthened by the ritual and economic support of the Ikoma rulers, Yūsei and his successor Yūgen secured a landed, economic base for Konkōin. By 1630, the sacred domain of Konpira—sanctified as well by the powerful image of its tengu "reviver," Kongōbō—was well on its way to developing into an estate of its own.

Konpira in the Structures of the Tokugawa Order

During the first decades of the seventeenth century, Yūsei, Yūgen, and their assistants focused their attentions on building a stronghold on Mt. Zōzu with the permission and support of the lords of Sanuki. From the 1630s on, however, events dramatically revealed that the political structures of Sanuki existed within a broader, more intrusive framework than in centuries before: what had been virtually autonomous estates became incorporated into a larger system of hereditary domains subject to the oversight and, to some extent, the standardizing regulations of the Tokugawa shoguns. As the priests of

Mt. Zōzu turned to work within this broader context, they once again redefined the nuances of their site, shifting emphasis from the conferral of power upon a Buddhist world ruler to magical fulfillment of wishes less obviously linked to domination. They redefined Konpira less as a source of political legitimacy that could potentially compete with Tokugawa rulers than as a font of more diverse miraculous powers compatible with the new political structures.

During Tokugawa Ieyasu's rise to undisputed dominance—his victory at Sekigahara in 1600, his investiture as shogun in 1603, and his elimination of Toyotomi Hideyoshi's heir in 1615—the Ikoma lords merely shifted their avowed allegiance in order to stay in power in Sanuki. Tokugawa Ieyasu and his son, intent upon securing all of Japan, tolerated such nominal loyalty. However, when the third Tokugawa shogun, Iemitsu, succeeded to office in 1623, he worked to ensure that such lords came more directly under his control. As the first shogun without personal experience in battle, Iemitsu sought to consolidate and institutionalize shogunal dominance by confirming his grandfather's military subordination of possible rivals through legal and administrative means. In 1635, Iemitsu began a campaign to prevent both domainal lords and religious institutions from developing or maintaining sufficient autonomy to challenge shogunal authority. He therefore required that all daimyo spend alternate years in attendance on his court in Edo, leaving their consorts and heirs permanently hostage in the eastern capital. At the same time, he intensified control of religious institutions and their estates. These domainal and religious policies together drew Mt. Zōzu into the expanding structures of Tokugawa organization. The priests henceforth elaborated upon the cult of Konpira, Kongōbō (Yūsei), and Fudō Myōō within the hierarchies of Tokugawa control.

Iemitsu's religious policies pushed Yūgen and his supporters into a formal affiliation with the official leaders of Shingon Buddhism. In 1635, Iemitsu clarified the temple-branch system, which required temples and shrines throughout the country to affiliate with a recognized denomination, submitting to the leadership of a head temple approved by the Tokugawa shogunate.[14] For Yūgen, this meant confirming his ties to the Shingon denomination, from which both he and Yūsei had received the tonsure. Konkōin would now rely upon the Shingon hierarchy for privileges.

The temple-branch system necessitated the cultivation of aristocratic ties, priestly titles, and the status they brought. High Buddhist office had long been intimately tied to courtly rank: each upper-level Buddhist officeholder was required to obtain the corresponding imperial rank. As a result, ambitious priests sought out aristocratic connections, securing rank through adoption into prominent families—an arrangement that benefited both the aspiring priest and, because of the gifts involved, the cash-strapped aristocracy. Because tonsured imperial princes and upper aristocrats (*monzeki*) presided over the head temples of the Shingon denomination and determined the offices therein, cultivation of courtly connections proved particularly important for Konkōin. While no record of an aristocratic adoption of Yūgen remains, the priest did approach one of the most powerful monzeki-led branches of the Shingon sect, receiving in 1637 the priestly rank of *shōnin* (which required that he also hold the fifth rank of the aristocracy) by decree of the monzeki of Kyoto's Daikakuji temple.[15] This is the first indication in the extant records on Mt. Zōzu of a formal affiliation with Daikakuji, whose monzeki—doubtless for substantial compensation—continued to grant similar rank to later priests of Konkōin.[16] Tokugawa Iemitsu's policy therefore drew the temple on Mt. Zōzu into a hierarchical system of control under the supervision of members of the imperial court.

Iemitsu also forged more direct ties between priests and the shogunate by conferring upon selected institutions letters with red seals (*shuinjō*). Such red seal letters not only recognized the institutions' rights to income from existing land holdings. They also placed priests in positions analagous to minor lords': through an agreement with the shogun (albeit sometimes mediated by a more influential sponsor), the priest of a red seal domain enjoyed the right to rule within his shogunally recognized territory. Holders of the red seals, like other lords, were required to perform a modified form of alternate attendance. Each successive holder—that is, each new priest of the temple or shrine—traveled to Edo to renew the red seal upon his own succession to office and the succession of each new shogun.[17] Through these systems of privileges, confirmations, and grants, Tokugawa Iemitsu strengthened the network of loyalties and responsibilities that tied both daimyo and prestigious religious institutions to shogunal authority.

To take advantage of this system, Yūgen quickly sought to receive a red seal through the mediation of the Ikoma lord.[18] However, before his efforts bore fruit, the authority of the Tokugawa shogunate became startlingly and disruptively clear. In response to complaints from within Sanuki province, Iemitsu removed the fourth Ikoma lord for incompetence and sentenced to death the men who had usurped the daimyo's authority. The shogun then split the plain of Sanuki into two, awarding the new Marugame domain in the west (approximately 50,000 koku) to a vassal in 1641, and in 1642 granting the larger Takamatsu domain (approximately 120,000 koku) and its castle in eastern Sanuki to Matsudaira Yorishige (1622–95), oldest son of the lord of the Mito domain, a branch family of the Tokugawa.[19] With this move, Iemitsu brought the province more closely under his control. By placing the strategic ports and fertile plains of Sanuki under the control of a loyal vassal and a relative, respectively, and by splitting the lucrative land into two domains, he reduced the likelihood of a single, large ruler's emerging to challenge his heirs. In the process, the shogun set in place a new political configuration within which the priests of Konkōin were forced to work if they hoped to maintain, let alone improve upon, the advances they had already made. Since Mt. Zōzu now fell within the borders of the new Takamatsu domain, Yūgen and his successors turned their attention to their new lord, Matsudaira Yorishige.[20]

When Yorishige arrived in Shikoku in 1642, he quickly turned his attention to religious affairs, ensuring the support of influential priests for his rule and, through them, demonstrating his symbolic support of the Tokugawa regime. In 1645, he began negotiations with the Tokugawa shogunate on behalf of the priests of three temples and shrines, including Konpira, to obtain for them red seal status.[21] On Mt. Zōzu, doubtless as part of this endeavor, Yorishige rebuilt the shrine to the Thirty Deities—emphasizing Mt. Zōzu's affinity with the Tendai-derived system of Buddhist kami worship (Sannō Ichijitsu Shintō) according to which Iemitsu had recently enshrined the founder of the Tokugawa shogunate at Nikkō Tōshōgū. Indeed, Lotus-influenced rituals seemed ascendant on the national scene. With the death later in 1645 of the resourceful Yūgen, the time seemed ripe on Mt. Zōzu for the dominance of the shrine to the Thirty Deities, whose priests, now returned to the mountain, began mobilizing support for their cause.

But the priests of the Thirty Deities reckoned without the resources and experience of the Yamashita family. When Yūgen's nephew, Yūten, succeeded to the head priestship of Konkōin in 1645, he petitioned the Takamatsu lord to take his younger brother as a vassal, thereby forging ties between the Yamashita, Konkōin, and the new lord.[22]

Subsequently, with the active support of the Takamatsu lord and the relative autonomy conferred by Konkōin's receipt of its first shogunal red seal in 1648, Yūten transformed the landscape of Mt. Zōzu and the village at its foot. Through a series of prominent donations, Yūten and the lord Yorishige worked in close alliance to once again reduce the influence of the Shrine of the Thirty Deities. Confirming Mt. Zōzu as a center of esoteric, shugendo ritual under the control of men from the Yamashita family, they built it into an impressive site befitting the powers of its gods.

From the beginning, Yūten (head priest, 1645–66, d. 1675) clearly sought to create a large-scale religious complex that would elaborate upon the priest-tengu Yūsei's vision of esoteric power. In 1648, the same year that Konpira Gongen received the red seal letter confirming its income of 330 koku, Yūten completed a massive construction project, changing the overall layout of the mountain.[23] (See figures 3.1 and 3.2.) By adding twists and turns in the path up to the main shrine, he enhanced the mystery of the site and expanded the space available to build new altars on the various plateaus. He established a new traffic pattern for potentially large numbers of pilgrims, dividing the approach to the main shrine into two paths: one up and one down. And he diverted attention away from the four shugendo subtemples staffed by the heirs of Yūsei's disciples, creating the spacious Sakuranobaba to lead visitors straight to Konkōin. These activities laid the foundation for the contruction of a large, impressive complex. They also exacerbated relations with the priests of the Shrine of the Thirty Deities, who, with their supporters, appealed to the Takamatsu authorities against the rising dominance of Konkōin on the mountain.

Such appeals, however, faced increasing obstacles, because the Takamatsu lord's involvement with Yūten on Mt. Zōzu increased exponentially after Konkōin's receipt of the red seal in 1648. It seems that, having secured the seal from the shogun, the lord Yorishige turned his back on the affinities of the Thirty Deities to the Tendai cult of Tokugawa Ieyasu at Tōshōgū. Instead, Yorishige focused on Konpira. The pattern of his donations and the changes that they wrought in the landscape of Mt. Zōzu suggest that he supported the god for both political and personal reasons.

First, Yorishige's involvement demonstrated his awareness of the local politics of religious sponsorship. In 1650, he donated to Mt. Zōzu an image of Amida, the buddha of the Pure Land. He thereby tied the mountain directly to the larger landscape of Pure Land Buddhism: the Takamatsu Matsudaira's family sect and, since the time of Hōnen, a tradition with strong roots in Sanuki. To Konpira, as to other kami in the area, Yorishige also donated a sacred horse. The following year, he donated a small stable and wooden horse to go in it. These gifts resembled his donations to other temples and shrines throughout his domain, suggesting a general policy of religious support and Pure Land Buddhist affiliation that would be well accepted by residents of Sanuki.

To demonstrate his political dominance, Yorishige also drew upon the esoteric Buddhist symbolism so powerful in the area around Zentsūji. From 1649 to 1651, he rebuilt the main gate to the precincts as an impressive Niōmon (Gate of the Two Guardian Kings), eclipsing the presence of Chōsokabe on the mountain by doubling in size the Tosa warlord's gate, now relegated to a subsidiary, peripheral position farther up the mountain. In 1654, Yorishige further enhanced his prestige and that of the mountain com-

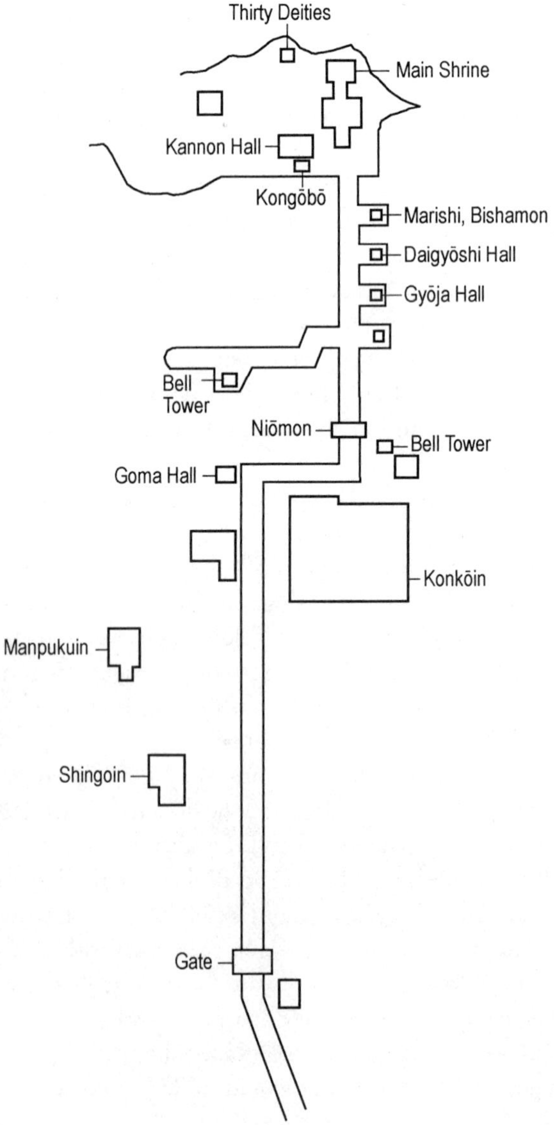
Thirty Deities
Main Shrine
Kannon Hall
Kongōbō
Marishi, Bishamon
Daigyōshi Hall
Gyōja Hall
Bell
Tower
Niōmon
Bell Tower
Goma Hall
Konkōin
Manpukuin
Shingoin
Gate

❀ 3.1 Layout of the precincts of Mt. Zōzu, 1644–47. The subtemples Manpukuin and Shingoin stand to the left of the main pathway; Chōsokabe's gate, the Niōmon, marks the entrance to the inner precincts. (Diagram modified from Ōsaki Teiichi, "Kotohiragū no enkaku," in *Konpira shomin shinkō shiryōshū*, vol. 1 [Kotohira: Kotohiragū Shamusho, 1992], 20. With the permission of Kotohira Shrine.)

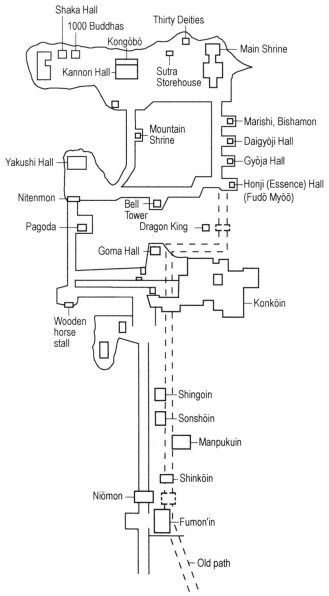

Shaka Hall
1000 Buddhas
Kongōbō
Thirty Deities
Main Shrine
Kannon Hall
Sutra
Storehouse
Mountain
Shrine
Marishi, Bishamon
Daigyōji Hall
Gyōja Hall
Yakushi Hall
Honji (Essence) Hall
(Fudō Myōō)
Nitenmon
Bell
Tower
Pagoda
Dragon King
Goma Hall
Konkōin
Wooden
horse
stall
Shingoin
Sonshōin
Manpukuin
Shinkōin
Niōmon
Fumon'in
Old path

⊛ **3.2** Layout of the precincts of Mt. Zōzu, 1704, after the priest Yūten embarked on a major construction project with the help of Matsudaira Yorishige, the first lord of Takamatsu. This project produced the broad Sakuranobaba, focusing attention on an enlarged Konkōin while shifting the path away from the smaller subtemples. It highlighted the donations of the Takamatsu lord (the new Niōmon and the wooden horse, for instance) while relegating Chōsokabe's gate to a subsidiary position (as the Nitenmon) and enlarged the complex with additional shrines and buildings, making it worthy of its new designation as a site of imperial worship and exclusive shrine. The dotted lines show the route of the previous path. (Diagram modified from Ōsaki Teiichi, "Kotohiragū no enkaku," in *Konpira shomin shinkō shiryōshū*, vol. 1 [Kotohira: Kotohiragū Shamusho, 1992], 20. With the permission of Kotohira Shrine.)

plex by donating two plaques written in the calligraphy of an imperial prince: one with the inscription "Mt. Zōzu," the other with "Matsuoji."[24] Yūten, as befitted his emphasis on the shugendo aspect of the cult, chose to hang the plaque bearing the name "Mt. Zōzu" on the gate, unmistakably emphasizing the centrality of the mountain.

Matsudaira Yorishige's second agenda became evident in 1655 and 1656: a personal involvement with the deity, conceived as a fierce and powerful blend of Konpira, Kongōbō, and Fudō Myōō. Yorishige's association with Mt. Zōzu from this time on showed a level of intensity unparalleled in his relations with other religious sites. In 1656, he penned the earliest extant origin tale (*engi*) of Konpira on Mt. Zōzu; then he continued to donate new buildings in support of Yūten's renovation of the mountain.

Yorishige's attention during this time seems to have focused on the miraculous feats of Konpira. As early as 1643, the year after Yorishige arrived as lord of Takamatsu, Konpira reputedly saved his overseer of ships from shipwreck in the Genkai Straits between Kyushu and Korea.[25] A collection of miracle tales published more than a century later suggests an even more direct connection between the miracles of the god and the lord of the Takamatsu domain. The *Zōzusan Konpira Daigongen Reigenki* relates that Konpira protected Yorishige in the course of some of his most dangerous duties. When Yorishige—wearing an amulet of Konpira Daigongen—was watching the testing of a new cannon, the tale states without giving a date, he allegedly found himself miraculously pulled to safety at the very moment that the cannon exploded.[26] In later years, at least, writers clearly attributed Yorishige's close connection with Konpira and its miracles to a very personal faith.

Doubtless, Yorishige wrote his origin story of Konpira Daigongen in close consultation with Yūten (if, indeed, he did not simply rewrite Yūten's own version). It fitted closely with Yūten's broader agenda on the mountain in the mid- and late 1650s, heightening the prominence, miraculous reputation, and hidden power of Konpira. In 1655, as part of his campaign to increase the mountain's stature, Yūten had replaced the small image of Fudō Myōō that stood in the Goma Hall with a larger, more imposing image said to have been carved by Kūkai's nephew, who also grew up not far from Mt. Zōzu: the esoteric Tendai priest, Enchin (Chishō Daishi, 814–91). The next year, Matsudaira Yorishige presented his origin tale to the god, establishing in written, historical form the hidden power of Konpira and its relation to Fudō Myōō while positioning himself as both sponsor and beneficiary of Konpira's miraculous powers.

Yorishige's origin tale, the *Sanshūji Zōzusan engi* (*Origins of Mt. Zōzu of the Sanuki Region*) consists of four sections: establishing the ties of the site first to India and the historical Buddha; second, to the Indian god Konpira, who, settled on Mt. Zōzu, struck down those who dared to look upon it; third, to Fudō Myōō, who, implicitly as Yūsei, carved an image of himself; and fourth, to En no Ozunu, the great seventh-century ascetic and legendary founder of shugendo in Japan, who purportedly recognized the god and its power on the mountain. The tale begins by explaining why, on the sacred Mt. Zōzu, only eight ri away from the lord's castle in Takamatsu, the main shrine of the avatar (*gongen*) faced east—because, three hundred years ago, after the Buddha's entry into nirvana, the deity Konpira (*Konpira kami*), protector of Vulture Peak, left India with some of the buddha's relics, arrived on this mountain, and secluded itself in meditation in a cave. Later, when a priest (*shamon*) Yūhen sought to view the body of the god (*shintai*) directly, he was struck down by its power, and his corpse appeared on the nearby cliff of Hashiarai, his left hand shaped in a mudra and his right hand holding a sword. Having hinted at a sacred connection, the tale goes on to identify these mysteries and the deity on the mountain with Fudō Myōō, evoking the rock of wisdom upon which the wrathful deity stands, using his sword to cut through ignorance and his rope to bind up the demons of evil:

> The original form of the avatar is an incarnation of Fudō Myōō. The hat on its head is [Fudō's] jeweled crown of the five wisdoms. The cave in the cliff is Fudō's rock of wisdom. Its left hand holds a rosary: this is [Fudō's] rope. Its right hand holds a cypress fan: this is [Fudō's] sword. On both sides are attendants, Gigaku and Gigei. It is said that they are Kongara [Sanskrit *Kimkara*] and Seitaka [Sanskrit *Cetaka*]. It is said that this august form which is worshipped by us now was made by the avatar itself.[27]

With this tale, Yorishige merged the identities of Konpira, Fudō Myōō, and the self-carved image of Yūsei in a narrative intended to demonstrate the miraculous powers of the Great Avatar Konpira (Konpira Daigongen) on Mt. Zōzu. The god itself came from India, carrying the remains of the buddha, and its powers at this site were recognized by people throughout history. Most dramatically, Konpira had demonstrated its fierce, amazing powers by enforcing its hidden status in an event still evident in the existence not just of the sacred cave but of another landmark nearby—Hashiarai, a site immortalized by an artist retained by Yorishige in a set called "Twelve Scenes of Mt. Zōzu," painted between 1658 and 1660.[28]

In the origin tale and other donations, then, Yorishige focused on the overwhelming power of Konpira as both the tengu Kongōbō (Yūsei) and Fudō Myōō. Yet by eschewing any reference to Konkōin, Buddhist kingship, or the Golden Light Sutra and identifying Konpira instead with Vulture

Peak, the renowned site of the Buddha's preaching in the Lotus and other sutras, Yorishige tied the meaning of the god to the broadest of Buddhist contexts. He thus maintained the symbolism of the imperial Mishuhō rituals
while distancing the wish-fulfilling magic of the relics and the god from direct suggestions of political empowerment. Indeed, these strategies proved
very effective, for in years to come, Yorishige's description of the god appeared
virtually verbatim in later texts. The noted poet Okanishi Ichū (1639–1711),
for instance, copied segments of the text almost word for word in 1682; a nō
play written in 1690 reiterated the identification of Fudō; and in a local history written in the 1740s, the only change merely identified Konpira with an
additional bodhisattva of wisdom.[29] With parts of Yorishige's text reappear-
ing well into the nineteenth century, the Takamatsu lord's identification of
the god as the shugendo deity Fudō Myōō clearly shaped ideas of Konpira for
generations to come.

Yorishige's and Yūten's subsequent modifications to the mountain served
mainly to enhance the architectural impact of the site, adding subsidiary
buildings while subtly reinforcing the wish-fulfilling associations of the complex. The Takamatsu lord donated a sutra storehouse, several pairs of stone
lanterns, and a five-story pagoda (symbolically enshrining the relics of the
Buddha) patterned after the one on Mt. Kōya, as well as a small shrine to the
Dragon King.

Yorishige also used legal measures to ensure the continuing dominance of
Konkōin and the Yamashita family on the mountain. With the Takamatsu
lord's backing, the retired Yūten secured unquestioned dominance for his
successors on the mountain when the shogunate's overseer of temples and
shrines resolved a challenge brought by the priests of the Shrine of the Thirty
Deities. The overseer sentenced Yūten's rivals to death for insubordination.
According to his judgment, they had challenged the authority of the priest of
Konkōin, who, as holder of the shogunal red seal, ruled the mountain and the
village at its foot. The two priests and their seven children were beheaded in
1670 on the border of the Konpira and Takamatsu domains.[30]

The Takamatsu lord soon confirmed not just the primacy of Konkōin,
but also its role as a hereditary institution. In 1672, Yorishige oversaw written
confirmation that the head priestship of Konkōin would remain in the hands
of the Yamashita family in perpetuity.[31] By the time of Yorishige's retirement
in 1673 and Yūten's death in 1675, therefore, the combined cult of Konpira,
Kongōbō, and Fudō Myōō had been firmly established in an impressive complex on Mt. Zōzu. The status of Konpira as a distinct, Yamashita-controlled
domain had been assured.

Through a close alliance with the daimyo of the Takamatsu domain, the priests of Mt. Zōzu carved out for themselves a position of relative autonomy within the Tokugawa system. Politically, they governed their own population, yielding to Takamatsu's authority only in criminal court matters and in relations with the shogun.[32] Within the religious structures of the time, Konkōin answered to monzeki of the Shingon denomination. With the help of these allies, the priests of Konkōin developed a landscape and legends on Mt. Zōzu that emphasized the punitive and wish-fulfilling powers of the mountain: the fierce guardian Fudō Myōō, as both the tengu Kongōbō and the deity Konpira, stood hidden and powerful, ready to reward and punish its human worshippers. The priests of Konkōin, like their Takamatsu sponsor, invoked the now "ancient," fierce powers of an Indian protector of Buddhism to legitimize their right to rule. They portrayed the god they found on Mt. Zōzu—that is, the identity they ascribed to the powers that they and others perceived at the site—in terms that they and their contemporaries found familiar, potent, and convincing: the history of the Buddha, the protection of Fudō Myōō, and the mysterious powers of a shugenja turned tengu. In the struggle to perpetuate that interpretation, the priests of Mt. Zōzu used every advantage they could find.

It was thus in close relation to the politics of lords that the powers of Konpira on Mt. Zōzu were first established. As rulers changed, the gods proliferated, with rival priests invoking competing ritual systems to secure the benefits of lordly recognition. The result was a cultic center on Mt. Zōzu that reflected years of political, and thus ritual, change. Images of Konpira, Kannon, and Amida each hid a tale of conquest or legitimation. The Thirty Deities, deprived of their priests, endured in the annual festival of Konpira on the tenth day of the tenth month: the former date of the Hokke Hakkō. And the priest Yūsei, the retrospectively identified founder of the Yamashita line at Konkōin, lived on in the form of the tengu Kongōbō, embodiment of wisdom, magical powers, and the fierce Fudō Myōō. By the late seventeenth century, firmly established amid the hierarchical religious and political structures of the Tokugawa regime, the site of Konpira had accumulated layer upon layer of meaning, evoking complex rituals of rulership and miraculous benefit in support of the priests, of the Takamatsu domain, and of the Tokugawa order.

God of the Market
(1688–1760)

4

By the end of the seventeenth century, the supporters of Konpira on Mt. Zōzu had established the dominance of the fierce tengu and incarnation of Fudō Myōō on the mountain. During the next several decades, however, the priests on Mt. Zōzu and people throughout western Japan faced new challenges, as the political settlement of the midseventeenth century gave way to the impressive economic growth and, with that growth, social diversification of the Genroku and Kyōho eras (1688–1735). Priests and rulers, as well as ambitious administrators, businessmen, and aristocrats, were forced to forge new alliances in order to secure the wealth or status that had heretofore been available through more clear-cut military loyalties and political hierarchies. It was as a focus for these connections—whether through the symbolism of the god, the accessibility of the site, or the cultural patronage of the priests—that Konpira attracted a growing following. Interpreted by each in his or her own way, Konpira could gather support from a variety of social groups, building first a local, then a regional, and eventually a national following.

In the late seventeenth and early eighteenth centuries, Konpira stood poised at the intersection of political and economic forces that would both give shape to its constituencies and enable its spectacular development. Politically, the priests occupied an interstitial position in the Tokugawa order. Rulers of Mt. Zōzu and the village of Konpira at its foot, they swore fealty directly to the Tokugawa shogun and received income from land in four neighboring, shogunate-owned villages but relied upon the lord of the Takamatsu domain for intercession in Edo

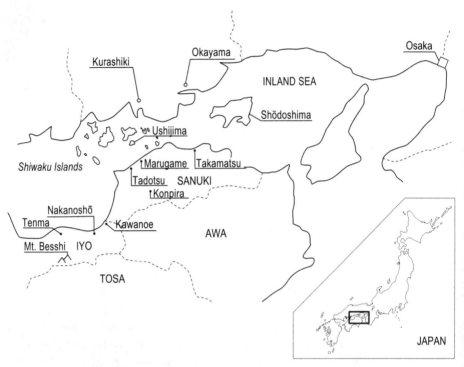

⊛ 4.1 Significant sites in Konpira-related networks, ca. 1700. Mt. Zōzu's location between domainal boundaries and along the Inland Sea, a crucial shipping corridor in the increasingly mercantile economy of the late seventeenth and eighteenth centuries, helped the priests develop profitable relationships not only with several sponsoring daimyo but also with merchants, entrepreneurs, village headmen, shippers, and other emerging productive elites. This relationship with an educated, propertied elite would prove crucial to the prosperity and growth of the site in the ensuing centuries.

and judicial decisions at home. They thus negotiated regularly not only with the domainal authorities of Takamatsu, but also with the shogunal intendant (*daikan*) in nearby Kawanoe, as well as the lords of the Marugame and, in neighboring Iyo province, Saijō domains (figure 4.1). Konkōin also depended upon members of the imperial court: because of the temple-branch system, the priests required confirmation of their status from the monzeki-led temples of the Shingon denomination. Konpira thus stood tied to the three major political institutions of the Tokugawa regime: the shogunate, the domains, and the imperial court. This position would prove useful in the years to come.

On Mt. Zōzu, the priests also occupied a promising geographic place at the crossroads of the growing market economy. Economic change was closely related to the structures of Tokugawa rule. By requiring lords to maintain year-round establishments in Edo while spending alternate years in their home domains and in the shogun's capital, the alternate attendance system built an instant market for goods and services and ensured frequent travel on the roads and waterways. The resulting movements provided an indispensable impetus to the growth of the market economy and the dissemination of cultural trends throughout the country. Economic and social networks proliferated, owing not only to the improvement of the famous Tokaido and other highways, but even more to dramatic changes in shipping structures and techniques that allowed an increase in trade throughout the islands. Osaka, in particular, developed as the great market of the shogunate, as ships carrying tribute rice and other goods converged upon the shogunate's primary port in the Inland Sea.

Growing trade fostered fierce competition—among priests and daimyo seeking prosperity for their domains, among producers and merchants seeking lucrative contracts, among religious rivals seeking the donations and prayer commissions of would-be worshippers. The god Konpira became both resource and benefactor, as people sought to build and capitalize upon the pilgrimage at the same time that they prayed to the god for health and wealth. Amid these market forces, Mt. Zōzu grew from a center of local trade to become an important link among the emerging entrepreneurial elites of western Japan. By the mid-eighteenth century, Konkōin's priests would obtain national recognition and economic security as the imperially sponsored, exclusive site of a redefined Konpira. The object of prayers from people across the social and economic spectrum, Konpira became for many a god of money, symbolically as well as miraculously powerful in the increasingly fierce competition of a market-oriented age.

For Local Development

The growing power of the market quickly made itself felt in the tiny domain of Konpira. As the Tokugawa shoguns appointed or confirmed hereditary rulers in each domain, such as the Matsudaira in Takamatsu or the priests of Konkōin in Konpira, they set boundaries on their jurisdictions, thereby limiting the rulers' opportunities to obtain more land. Thus, daimyo and priests seeking to increase their revenues or ensure the prosperity of a growing peacetime population were forced to look beyond subsistence agriculture for a solution. In this context, the powers of Mt. Zōzu held out great promise: if promoted effectively, the mountain could attract the traffic and expenditures of worshippers from throughout the region, benefiting the businesses and, therefore, the priestly rulers of Konpira. Through promotions and personal connections, the priests of Konkōin encouraged the attention of commoners and neighboring daimyo, drawing them in, whether emotionally or financially, to a growing local economy tied to pilgrimage to Mt. Zōzu.

The priests of Konpira, like priests of other would-be pilgrimage sites, simultaneously developed the attractions of both the god and the town to boost the economic viability of the sacred domain. Three times a year—in the third, sixth, and tenth months—they hosted markets in the town to coincide with rituals on the mountain. Early in the seventeenth century, Konkōin had sponsored sumō wrestling matches, then theatrical performances, to raise money for the temple. Due to these early promotions, Konpira remained one of the few places in the country with a theater well into the eighteenth century. Drawn by the opportunities available during festival and market months, both performers and theatergoers flocked to the town.[1]

Entertainments thus proved greatly attractive, whether sponsored by Konkōin or provided by local entrepreneurs. In 1653, three years before Matsudaira Yorishige wrote his origin tale laying the historical groundwork for pilgrimage to the site, Konkōin issued its first recorded attempt to restrict unofficial entertainments, announcing regulations on the renting of rooms and, in accordance with shogunate policy, placing a ban on gambling. Crowds evidently continued to gather, for Konkōin issued a similar ban on gambling again in 1666, explicitly extending the ban to include prostitution in 1689.[2] Thus, from early on, Konpira's development as an attractive site of worship proceeded in tandem with the popularity of its markets and entertainments. In a phenomenon common to pilgrimage sites in Japan and around the world, Mt. Zōzu and its gods grew amid a bustling pilgrimage economy of entertainments and commerce: performances, prostitution, and gambling proved as integral to the growth of the site as amulets and worship.[3]

The priests of Konkōin catered to such demand for entertainment in order to raise both the income and the status of the sacred domain. In 1688, Yūei (head priest, 1666–91) and his advisers significantly increased the lavishness of the annual festival and procession of Konpira on the tenth day of the tenth month, raising the annual donations collected from nearby villages for the ritual and featuring village leaders in a grand ritual parade.[4] For Yūei's successor Yūzan (head priest, 1691–1736), the hustle and bustle of the town were as important to the well-being of the god and the domain as were the quiet precincts on the mountain. Some time around 1700, following the precedent of other domainal lords, he commissioned two large, six-paneled folding screens from a painter of the Kano school.[5] Depicting the shrine and the town of Konpira at the time of the festival of the tenth month, the gilded screens devote particular attention to the procession of village representatives as well as details of shopfronts, kabuki performances, and throngs of people. Along the roads of the town, for instance, appear purveyors of used clothing, lacquerware, and noodles. In inns and their gardens, women sit at mirrors, arranging their hair. The Kinzanji district bustles with at least five kabuki and puppet theaters, each crowded with spectators. In contrast, the mountain is serene and wooded, with the Hashiarai pond made famous in Matsudaira's tale of the god secluded in silence on the far left panel. The general impression given of Genroku-era Konpira is thus of a religious center overseeing the hustle and bustle of a small, but active town: an oasis of entertainment profiting from the promotional policies of Konpira, in contrast to the more regulated domains of Marugame and Takamatsu nearby.

Such proximity of prayer sites and pleasure quarters was by no means distinctive to Konpira. Indeed, in many ways, Yūzan seems to have modeled his promotion of Konpira on the Asakusa area of Edo: the site of the famous Asakusa temple (Sensōji), near which the great pleasure quarters of Yoshiwara had been moved in 1657.[6] In the ensuing years, the area of Sensōji and Yoshiwara developed into a prosperous playground for Edo's samurai and merchant men, complete with souvenir shops, sideshows, restaurants, performers, gift stores, brothels, and—not least—the religious displays and attractions of the temple.[7]

During the early years of his tenure, Yūzan modeled the attractions of Konpira after the thriving pleasure quarters of Edo not only in entertainment but in worship as well. In 1699, he sought to capitalize upon the growing popularity of the bodhisattva Kannon. For centuries, worshippers had focused on the bodhisattva of compassion mentioned in the Lotus Sutra both on its own and as an attendant of Amida, the buddha of the Pure Land, making it one of the most popular deities in Japan. Politically, then, Kannon united the Pure Land traditions of the Takamatsu lords with the Lotus Sutra faith still evident in Mt. Zōzu's now unattended Shrine of the Thirty Deities.

More important for Yūzan, however, was Kannon's growing renown as the object of a lucrative popular cult. In 1647, crowds of people had converged upon the Asakusa temple in Edo, marking the rise of the Asakusa Kannon as an important focus of popular worship in the shogun's capital. In 1654, Asakusa held its first kaichō—a grand display of the sacred image, held approximately every thirty-three years thereafter—to raise money for the temple. In 1676, the Ishiyama temple in Ōmi province raised money by sending its image of Kannon to Edo for display.[8] Following suit, Yūzan held the first Kannon kaichō on Mt. Zōzu in 1699, revealing a newly carved image of the bodhisattva in the existing Kannon Hall. Following the traditions of Kannon, the priests of Konkōin continued this tradition approximately every thirty-three years thereafter. In this way, as in their sponsorship of entertainments, the priests of Konkōin built in provincial Konpira a miniature center of prayer, entertainment, and commerce akin to the attractions of the shogun's capital.

Between the markets, entertainments, and celebrations of Kannon, the growing numbers of visitors—and their money—contributed to the wellbeing of the townspeople of Konpira, who sold meals, rented rooms, and provided additional services to the crowds. The proceeds of the pilgrimage business also paid for the priests' official visits to Edo, for expenses associated with their alliance building in Edo and Kyoto, and for the conspicuous displays of consumption on Mt. Zōzu designed to bolster the prestige and authority of Konkōin for the people it ruled at home and for visitors from elsewhere in Japan. Yūzan's strategies of pilgrimage promotion had started to succeed.

The lords of neighboring domains also worked to foster the god, its pilgrimage, and the resulting business in the region. As noted in chapter 3, one of the first—and certainly the most influential—donors to Konkōin and Konpira Daigongen was Matsudaira Yorishige, daimyo of the Takamatsu domain. In cooperation with Yūten and the Yamashita family, Matsudaira shaped much of Mt. Zōzu before his retirement in 1673. His successors continued their involvement with the site and the deity, offering swords, rice, sutras, and impressive stone lanterns over the years.[9] From around 1734, when a relative of the Yamashita family rose to the office of Takamatsu elder (*karō*), a pattern developed in which the Takamatsu lords treated Konpira as a guardian deity of domainal prosperity. They sent representatives to receive amulets on the eleventh day of each new year, to make offerings for a plentiful harvest at the end of the year, and to give thanks for healings, safe births, and other blessings in between.[10] By 1752, the Takamatsu lords had enshrined the Great Avatar Konpira in their mansion in Osaka; in 1793 they built a shrine in their new mansion in Edo as well.[11]

The reasons for the Takamatsu daimyo's involvement were clear. Before 1648, Mt. Zōzu occupied a prominent place in his domain both topographically (on the highest mountain in the Sanuki plain) and politically, as a focal point of the activities of his predecessors: first the Tosa invader Chōsokabe Motochika, then the Ikoma lords, and finally the founder of the Takamatsu domain, Matsudaira Yorishige. The institutions of Konpira thus legitimized, protected, and enhanced the prestige of the Takamatsu lords. The ties between Konkōin and its Matsudaira sponsors, then, were strong and longstanding.

Yet Konpira Daigongen did not become identified solely with the Takamatsu lord and domain. Indeed, the priests of Konkōin skillfully exploited the interstices of the Tokugawa order, beginning with domainal boundaries. Most notably, they balanced the attentions of the Takamatsu lord, eight ri away, with the lords of Marugame in their castle, only three ri from Mt. Zōzu. The Kyōgoku lords of Marugame focused most of their religious expenditures on Zentsūji, only one and one-half ri from Mt. Zōzu but squarely within their domain. Yet the port town of Marugame had reputedly developed economic ties to Mt. Zōzu even before the arrival of the Kyōgoku lords. According to local legend, some time around 1633, when Marugame still functioned as the seat of the Ikoma lords in western Sanuki, Yūgen (head priest, 1613–45), apparently seeking to promote the tengu Kongōbō by evoking the fan that he held, proposed the production of persimmon-wood fans as souvenirs. The manufacture of such fans flourished in Marugame, growing under the Kyōgoku lords into one of the most profitable enterprises of the domain.[12] In part because of such economic ties, and surely for more personal reasons as well, the Kyōgoku lords of Marugame worshipped at Mt. Zōzu alongside Zentsūji. As early as 1679, when the lords moved their mansion in Edo from Mita to outside the Toranomon gate of the shogun's castle, they transferred the small shrine of Konpira to Toranomon at the same time.[13] Such ties between Marugame and Konpira only intensified after a relative of the Yamashita family rose to the office of senior inspector (ōmetsuke) in Marugame in 1738.[14]

Even more than the Marugame lords, however, the Kyōgoku lords of Tadotsu—a smaller, branch domain split off from Marugame in 1694—were actively involved with Mt. Zōzu. Tadotsu, a port like Marugame only three ri from the mountain, stood to gain economically from growth in traffic in the area. Moreover, the Tadotsu lord—who did not actually live in Tadotsu until 1827 but stayed in Marugame—may have either felt a more personal relationship to Konpira or thought that donations to the deity distinguished him from his more powerful Marugame relative. Whatever the case, beginning with a stone lantern in 1712, donations from the lords of Tadotsu significantly outnumbered those from Marugame. Every lord but the second donated a pair of lanterns to the god, as well as sutras, hangings, and—in the case of the fourth lord—a votive plaque drawn in his own hand.[15]

The Kyōgoku lords of both Marugame and Tadotsu sent representatives on pilgrimage to Konpira regularly, in the first, fifth, and tenth months. They offered prayers before departing on their journeys to Edo. These lords, like the lords of Takamatsu, apparently viewed Konpira Daigongen as a powerful local guardian, good for guaranteeing prosperity as well as safety upon their journeys.

The Matsudaira and Kyōgoku families, then, became committed supporters of Konpira Daigongen shortly after their arrival in Shikoku. They carried Konpira with them to Osaka and Edo, where they enshrined the deity at their mansions. They supported the development of the pilgrimage to Mt. Zōzu, facilitating traffic through the three ports of Takamatsu, Marugame, and Tadotsu, thereby fostering custom for boat operators, innkeepers, fanmakers, and other businesses in Konpira and their own domains. In effect, their support of Konkōin worked for the mutual benefit of all parties, weaving the sacred domain of Konpira—outside the formal boundaries of any of the three larger domains—into an expanding network of personal, economic, and ritual relationships.

God of the Inland Sea

During the years around 1700, Konpira became part of a growing web of relationships spreading not only into nearby domains but also across the Inland Sea and beyond. Under the Tokugawa regime, domains throughout the Japanese islands grew increasingly tied to the markets of Osaka, whether to deliver rice and goods to the shogunate's warehouses or to take advantage of the currency exchanges and commodity markets of the burgeoning trading center.

For centuries, the best route to Osaka from western Japan lay through the Inland Sea. Sailors and ships from the Shiwaku Islands, just off Marugame, had built great shipping enterprises based upon this route, carrying trade goods and military forces throughout East and Southeast Asia as well as within Japan. In the 1630s, however, the third Tokugawa shogun, Iemitsu, cracked down on foreign trade as part of his effort to consolidate shogunal power. He banned the Japanese, and thus the Shiwaku shippers, from either going abroad or building the large ships necessary for foreign travel. By limiting foreign merchants' access to Japanese markets, as well, he ensured that the shogun could both control imports and exports and secure the profits from them. Having banned both Christianity and Portuguese traders entirely, owing to Portuguese support of a Christian-influenced rebellion against the shogunate in 1637, Iemitsu limited foreign trade to Nagasaki, where only Dutch and Chinese merchants could reside; he also delegated control over the limited trade with the far north, Korea, and the Ryūkyū Islands to the daimyo closest to each area. Iemitsu thus set in place an economic policy that not only bolstered Tokugawa control but also turned merchants' attention inward for the next two hundred years. As a result, domestic trade blossomed, aided by the establishment of a western maritime route, with safe, strategic harbors, from Edo and Osaka through the Inland Sea, around Honshu, and up the Japan Sea coast to northern Japan. The new route thus encouraged trade, and the Inland Sea became the main corridor connecting the people and the economies of northern, western, and central Japan.

Standing within view of that increasingly busy waterway, Mt. Zōzu attracted the attention of merchants, shippers, and sailors. It is unclear for how long such seafarers had prayed to the oddly shaped mountain or for how long or to what extent they associated Konpira specifically with their protection.[16] In any case—whether through the promotion of the Marugame and Tadotsu lords, or because of a longer tradition of worship among sailors and shippers—people with business along the Inland Sea frequently turned their attention to the god on Mt. Zōzu. Indeed, the earliest records of donations by people from beyond Takamatsu, Marugame, and Tadotsu highlight the status of Konpira in the changing economic, and therefore social and political, dynamics of the Inland Sea, Japan, and East Asia in the years around 1700.

The discovery in Shikoku of what became one of the largest copper mines in Japan—indeed, in all of East Asia—drew Konpira into a network of administrators, merchants, and entrepreneurs that extended from the markets and metalworks of Osaka, to the mine in Shikoku, and on to the Chinese merchant community in Nagasaki. In the mid-1680s, as Chinese merchants brought unprecedented amounts of goods to Japan to trade in the wake of peace on the continent, the Tokugawa shogunate sought to develop exports of its own in order to prevent the draining of silver from the country.[17] Around the same time, some enterprising miners discovered copper on Mt. Besshi in the mountains of Iyo province, a little more than fifty kilometers from Mt. Zōzu. In 1691, the shogunal intendant in Kawanoe entrusted management of the Besshi copper mine to Izumiya Yoshizaemon of the Osaka merchant and copper-smelting Sumitomo family, who at the time managed a copper mine across the Inland Sea in Okayama.[18] The Besshi copper mine quickly turned a profit, and its spectacular productivity during the next decades brought trade and prosperity to the nearby port of Tenma, through which all of the rice, materials, and manpower from Osaka came to the mine (figure 4.1).[19]

It was amid this sudden prosperity, in the tenth month of 1694, that the village group headman (*ōjōya*) in Tenma, Terao Ujiharu, erected a stone lantern to Konpira in Nōda village, on the road from the port of Marugame to Mt. Zōzu.[20] Three years later, in 1697, amid several disasters, including a fire at the mine that killed 132 people, Izumiya Yoshizaemon, "holder of Besshi copper mine," in conjunction with "external investors" in the mine donated a pair of bronze lanterns to "Mt. Zōzu Matsuoji."[21] The six-sided lanterns, standing more than three meters tall near the main shrine, impressively displayed the character for gold as well as images of dragons and a finial in the shape of a flame (figure 4.2). In 1706, the Tenma headman Terao and his sons donated a smaller bronze lantern, with the character for gold likewise prominently displayed.[22] Around the same time, the Terao men donated yet another lantern that prominently featured the character for gold, this time inside a circle.[23]

Why the gold? The character for gold or metal (*kon*) was used as the first character of, and therefore as a shorthand expression for, Konpira. By inscribing it on lanterns, donors dedicated their offerings specifically to the god of Mt. Zōzu. Since the character also appeared in *Kon*gōbō and *Kon*kōin, it could signify—depending upon the interpretation of either the donor of the lantern or its viewers—not only Konpira but also the magical powers of the tengu on the mountain, or the authority of the head priest, ruler of Konpira domain. Beginning with these early lanterns donated by the investors in and village headmen around Besshi copper mine, the character for gold appears inscribed in a circle, perhaps invoking the round copper coins minted by the Tokugawa shogunate from the seventeenth century on. It was in this context of copper and trade, at the very least, that this "encircled gold" symbol (*marukin*) first appeared, before its later adoption as the official seal of Konkōin and one of the most visible markers of Konpira worship in general.

In this developing role as a god of money and mining, Konpira gained a following among the Chinese merchants in the copper trade. In 1706, the priests of Konkōin officially approved the request of a shugenja in Nagasaki for an official enshrinement of Konpira Gongen. The small shrine, located at the foot of a prominent mountain that was apparently used as a navigational marker by sailors coming in to port, attracted the worship of Chinese merchants and sailors who carried Besshi's copper and other goods to and from China.[24] The god, like the economy of the shogunate and the Inland Sea, thus shared in a world that extended beyond Japan. In later years, guidebooks and travelogues would highlight donations to Konpira from Chinese and Ryukyuan merchants as evidence of the far-reaching powers of the mountain deity.[25]

The remarkable prosperity at Besshi could not last forever, however, and in the second and third decades of the eighteenth century, production began to taper off. Yet, even if not so prominently displayed, connections between the mining entrepreneurs and Konpira remained, as shown by the mine manager Izumiya Yoshizaemon's donation in thanks to the shrine for receipt of a small amulet in 1713.[26] These ongoing donations and the symbol for gold hint at a deeper connection of these men to Mt. Zōzu. Both Izumiya and the headman Terao must have made the pilgrimage to the mountain many times,

❀ 4.2 One of a pair of bronze lanterns donated in 1697 by Izumiya Yoshizaemon, manager for the Sumitomo mercantile house of the Besshi copper mine in nearby Iyo province, one of the largest copper mines in the world at that time. This lantern, as well as lanterns donated in the early 1700s by the village headmen of Tenma village and of Nakanoshō, suggests the importance of Mt. Zōzu in the lives of an emerging managerial and productive elite in the eighteenth century. Note the prominent symbol for gold (*kon*)—the first character of *Kon*pira, *Kon*kōin, and *Kon*gōbō—on the underside of the lantern in the center of the photo. Slightly above the eye level of visitors, this gold symbol would have been especially noticeable. (Photograph by Steve Cantley, with the permission of Kotohira Shrine.)

praying for the protective powers of the deity to come to bear on their monumental project. Moreover, it was the profits of the copper mine—and the domestic and international trade that provided them—that made the men their fortunes.[27] The mines and the trade—indeed, the money evoked by the encircled gold symbol used to represent the god—enriched the headman and the copper-mining merchant, enabling them to commemorate their worship of Konpira on a par with the worship of domainal lords: through the construction of expensive and impressive lanterns that would survive over countless generations.

The involvement of another village group headman with Konpira highlights the development of a second regional network of wealthy commoners around the god and its shrine. On an auspicious day in the third month of 1696 (Genroku 9), the year before the Besshi investors' donation, Sakagami Hanbei Masayasu (1653–1730), the headman of Nakanoshō village in the Saijō domain—in the same district as Terao—offered an elaborate bronze lantern to "Konpira Daigongen." Even taller than the mine investors' offering, from its six-sided limestone base to the peak of the flame on its top, Sakagami's donation is the oldest lantern, other than daimyo donations, still extant on Mt. Zōzu.[28]

Why did the headman of Nakanoshō, thirty-odd kilometers away, donate one of the most ornate and largest lanterns to Konpira? In addition to Sakagami's personal turn to religious sponsorship—apparently occasioned in 1693 by the death of two sisters, his mother, and his father within only two years and evident in his donations to several temples after his retirement from the office of village headman around the same time—there seem to be three reasons. First, the Shingon Konpira fit nicely within the religious framework of Sakagami's personal faith. It was apparently because of his experience during a visit to the Shingon center of Mt. Kōya that Sakagami made his first significant religious donation in 1693, offering a large gong to his local Shingon temple to pray for the enlightenment of his deceased relatives.[29] Konkōin on Mt. Zōzu, likewise affiliated with the Shingon denomination, thus fit into a Kōya-centered sensitivity.

Second, the association of Konpira with both merchants in the Inland Sea and the lords of the Takamatsu and Marugame domains linked the site with some of Sakagami's everyday concerns. During his time as village group headman, from 1678 until 1693, Sakagami was sent to Osaka by his lord (the daimyo of the Saijō domain) to oversee the transfer of the domain's annual rice tribute to the shogunate storehouse, to arrange the sale of surplus rice, and to obtain loans. As he carried out these duties, Sakagami built up a successful record at the commodity exchanges in Osaka and amassed a personal fortune, eventually extending his own loans to the Saijō lord as well as to the lords of the nearby Imabari domain, Marugame, and Takamatsu.[30] It is easy to imagine, then, that Sakagami's ties to his lordly borrowers might have been maintained in part during regular visits to Mt. Zōzu, where he could pray for his own and his family's welfare to a god that these lords worshipped as well.

A final clue comes from a gift that Sakagami gave to the priests of Konkōin when he donated the lantern in 1696: *Sudare,* a collection of poetry edited by the wealthy headman. Offered as a donation to "the kami and buddhas of Iyo and Sanuki," the collection included verses from poets in Yoshino, Nara, Wakaura, and other sites along the route of Sakagami's travels.[31] Sakagami's interest in both writing and collecting poems, which he then donated to temples and shrines, helped secure his status among his peers.

The practice of writing poetry seemed tailor-made to traveling businessmen like Sakagami. Classic models of poetry writing—whether Chinese or Japanese, by the traveling Buddhist priest Saigyō (1118–90) or the more recent son of a samurai, Matsuo Bashō (1644–94)—placed the act of poetic composition within a framework of travel and the appreciation of famous scenes. By Sakagami's time, the formal poetic styles of the aristocracy had been increasingly challenged by writers outside the imperial court. Scholars, samurai, and especially merchants developed more informal and iconoclastic poetic styles within the tradition of comic linked verse (*haikai*), which eventually gave way to short, independent verses—what is known today as the seventeen-syllable *haiku*.[32] By the time that Sakagami compiled *Sudare* in 1696, merchants and wealthy peasants around the countryside had adopted poetic noms de plume and joined a growing network of poets linked by traveling teachers, book lending, and poetic compilations. Sakagami himself adopted the literary name Senchō, sponsored visits by poetry teachers, and published three edited volumes of haikai before his death in 1730.

Shrines and temples frequently served as the arenas for poetic composition, especially of the linked verse, haikai. Both professional and amateur poets composed verses when meeting for festivals or poetry gatherings at the sacred, scenic sites; they also frequently offered their poetic compilations to the presiding deities.[33] Given the prominence of religious sites in this poetic, cultural circle, then, the early efforts of Konkōin's priests to sponsor poetic and artistic compositions—such as Yūten's commissioning of two sets of scrolls depicting "twelve sites of Mt. Zōzu," painted by Kano school artists with poems by the heads of the Hayashi school, and calligraphy by a renowned nō chanter—can be seen as the active cultivation of this growing group of influential men.[34]

Thus, the village group headman and rice trader Sakagami joined and cultivated a wide-ranging literary network of merchants and priests, producers and scholars in western Japan. Sakagami, through his activities, helped the priests of Konkōin turn Konpira into a prominent site on that cultural circuit. In addition to his offerings in 1696, Sakagami urged the priests to invite a prominent musician to perform on Mt. Zōzu in 1711. He donated a Chinese-style gilded pagoda to the temple in 1714, donated another pagoda in 1715, and visited again in 1718.[35] The priests of Konkōin clearly cultivated the attentions of Sakagami, for they recorded their own gifts sent to him in return. Through the actions of people like Sakagami and the promotions of the Konkōin priests, then, Mt. Zōzu became part of the cultural landscape of the commoner elites. It became the type of place where village group headmen—as well as other men who were permitted to wear a family crest on their formal jackets (*haori*) and other elite badges of status—came to worship, to appreciate culture, and to meet with their business partners and social equals.

Such social networks would not have been possible without the dramatic changes in shipping and transport that occurred during the years around 1700—changes that were reflected in yet another group of early, prominent donors to Konpira. The sea lanes through the Inland Sea were central to the Tokugawa economy, and the ship captains and sailors of the Shiwaku Islands in many ways ruled the seas during the late seventeenth century. In those years, the shogunate hired Shiwaku shippers no longer to carry war materiel but to transport rice from the scattered shogunate-owned lands to Osaka. Many of the shippers employed by the shogunate lived on the island of Ushijima, home to Maruo Gosaemon, owner of the most and largest ships (more than eight hundred koku in capacity) in the Shiwaku Islands. The size, number, and superior construction of the Maruo house's vessels helped them enjoy unprecedented prosperity as the shogunal shippers from the 1660s until the early 1700s, during which time they helped develop the official western shipping route from Osaka around Honshu to northern Japan.[36] It was, perhaps, in thanks for this good fortune that thirty ship captains of the Maruo house donated two bronze hanging lanterns to Konpira in 1715.[37]

Around the turn of the century, however, Shiwaku shipbuilding and navigation techniques spread throughout the country, spawning significant competition. In the 1720s, the shogunate turned for the first time to shipping middlemen (*ton'ya*) in Edo to hire ships to transport the rice. Over the following years, the Shiwaku shippers lost their special rights to the shogunate's rice shipping and became only one—although still among the most prominent—of many shippers in the business.[38] It was in this context that Maruo

Gosaemon donated a large votive plaque to the god in 1724, followed by enough lumber to build a reception hall (*settaisho*) in 1729.[39] It seems that, like the merchant and mine manager Izumiya, the shippers of the Maruo house offered their thanks to Konpira during times of prosperity, then petitioned the god again as they faced a decline in their fortunes. Nothing in the context of the donations suggests whether the Maruo shippers viewed Konpira as a special guardian of sailors or simply as a nearby, influential deity. In any event, their donations—whether lanterns or votive plaques—served to advertise their business on the mountain in a time when employment increasingly depended on securing new, contractual customers instead of relying on old loyalties and monopolies.[40] The offerings also functioned as statements of identity, silently asserting that shippers like Maruo belonged alongside other wealthy, responsible men among the most prominent donors to the shrine.

Lanterns, votive plaques and other offerings also functioned as prayers to the god for safety at sea. As one scholar and samurai who visited the site wrote in 1722, Konpira—not as the Indian yaksha general, but as the tengu Kongōbō instead—had clearly become renowned for its maritime miracles: "In Sanuki on Mt. Zōzu, [people] pray to Konpira kami. Its image, sitting about three *shaku* [feet] tall, is in the form of a priest with a fierce visage. It wears the same hat that shugenja wear today and holds a fan made of feathers in its hand. This is a far cry from the image of Yakushi's twelve generals! . . . In the middle of the night, when ships' crews are lost on the sea lanes, when they think on this god and pray to reach shore, a ball of light never fails to appear. If they go in its direction, there will be no shipwreck."[41] In the early eighteenth century, then, popular lore associated the amazing powers of the mountain with both the tengu Kongōbō and a mysterious light, reflected perhaps in the lanterns donated by wealthy worshippers to the shrine.

The changes in shipping that brought sailors and ship captains to Konpira brought more politically prominent visitors as well. Mt. Zōzu grew as part of the itinerary of daimyo and their representatives, who traveled through the Inland Sea on their way to or from Edo. In 1708 and 1711, the lord of the Hamada domain in Iwami province, a domain on the Japan Sea that prospered after the 1672 opening of the western maritime route, became one of the first daimyo to send a representative to the mountain from beyond Takamatsu, Marugame, and Tadotsu.[42] The lord of Okayama, across the Inland Sea from Takamatsu, soon joined in, and from 1720 on, the number of daimyo offerings listed in Konkōin's records increased significantly. Representatives of lords from the western edges of the Inland Sea, from Kyushu and Honshu near the Shimonoseki Straits, dominated the official worshippers on Mt. Zōzu until about 1749. By the peak of daimyo offerings in the 1780s and

1790s, when Konkōin recorded up to thirteen representatives of daimyo arriving in a single year, they generally arrived from further east—from the Kii Peninsula on the eastern edge of the Inland Sea or inland as far as Kōzuke, northwest of Edo.[43] By the middle of the eighteenth century, visits by daimyo and their representatives, as well as the enshrinements of Konpira in the mansions of the Marugame and Takamatsu lords in Edo, combined with the actions of traveling merchants, shippers, and producers to introduce Konpira to more and more people throughout the country.

Konpira and the Imperial Court

As the popularity of Konpira grew, so too did the number of ways in which people imagined the god. Whereas rulers had earlier seen Konpira as a symbol of legitimacy or a granter of peace, daimyo, shippers, and entrepreneurs around 1700 saw in the deity a god of economic success, literary culture, and protection at sea. The priests of Mt. Zōzu supported this multiplication of the god's attributes while promoting their own visions of the deity, complete with supporting histories, rituals, and symbolism. The result was the establishment in the eighteenth century of a second image of Konpira more suited to emerging Confucian and Shinto intellectual trends. In lieu of the shugendo-style image of Konpira as both the tengu Kongōbō and the Buddhist spirit Fudō Myōō, set forth by Yūten and the Takamatsu lord in the century before, Yūzan in the eighteenth century promoted the identification of Konpira with a kami found in the ancient imperial histories. While this second image failed to gain the popularity of the first, it grew increasingly influential among scholarly elites as the priests of Konkōin used this historical, imperial affiliation as an entrée into the politics of the imperial court and the literary culture of the rural elites. The dual identity that resulted—that is, the increasing ambiguity of the god—made possible the growth of Konpira into a prominent pilgrimage center both officially recognized by the emperor and worshipped by countless people throughout Japan.

Since the time of Yūten in the mid-seventeenth century, there had apparently existed a growing tension on Mt. Zōzu between the ascetic shugendo worship of Konpira as the fiery Fudō Myōō and more sedate, scholarly approaches to the god, whether in Shingon or literary studies.[44] The relationship between shugendo and scholarship was not necessarily antagonistic. Shugenja tended to focus primarily on ritual performance—most notably rigorous meditation and the three-day-long goma ceremony, during which petitioners' prayers were brought to the gods. Scholars, in contrast, tended to study texts in order to understand why the rites worked and how to improve them; in doing so, they made new connections between the gods of the sutras and the kami of Japan, between the teachings of Kūkai and those of his contemporary, Saichō (766–822, the founder of the Tendai sect), as well as information gleaned from other texts and legends. Clearly shugendo and scholarly concerns overlapped, as seen on Mt. Zōzu in the active shugendo agenda of Yūsei (Kongōbō), perhaps the most renowned scholar in Konkōin's history.

Nevertheless, as the priests of Konkōin became increasingly accustomed to the privileges of domain administration, the rigors of shugendo asceticism apparently grew less attractive. Yūsei had secluded himself in meditation, and the shugenja Yūgen and Yūten built the cult of Konpira upon Yūsei's shugendo prowess. Indeed, in part to combat claims by Zentsūji that Konpira was a branch temple of the nearby Shingon temple, Yūten encouraged the arrival of at least nine additional shugendo practitioners, thereby emphasizing a heritage of mountain asceticism that clearly set Mt. Zōzu apart from Zentsūji on the Sanuki plain.[45] Despite this sponsorship, however, the importance of shugendo for the priests of Konkōin declined. It was during Yūten's retirement and the priesthood of Yūei that Konkōin began to distance itself from the rigorous ascetic practices of active shugendo, apparently delegating management of shugendo affairs on the mountain to Tamon'in, a shugendo subtemple outside the gates of Matsuoji that had been established by a disciple of Yūsei.[46]

By the time of Yūei's successor, Yūzan, in the late seventeenth and early eighteenth centuries, the number of shugenja on Mt. Zōzu had dwindled. The men who practiced on the mountain under Yūten had died; their heirs now lived in the town with little connection to the mountain practices.[47] Likewise, for Yūzan as well, shugendo rites and symbolism apparently had faded in importance. Yūzan was apparently the first priest of Konkōin, for instance, who did not wear as part of his garb a modified sword of Fudō Myōō, the symbol of the shugenja.[48] Instead, he focused on scholarship, commissioning annotations of texts, drawing Shingon mandalas, and assisting in Shingon rites to the kami. His efforts in Shingon circles paid off, for in 1709 he was raised to a higher Buddhist rank and was granted the privilege of entry into the emperor's presence. From soon thereafter, however, while still allowing for the worship of the kami by Shingon rites, Yūzan reinterpreted the powers of the mountain within a context far distant from the rigors and rites of shugendo. He espoused, instead, an interpretation of Konpira tied not to Buddhist sutras but to Japanese histories, as mediated by the Shinto and Confucian ideas increasingly prominent at the time.

The study of the kami, in Shingon and in other traditions, had long focused on the early eighth-century imperial history, the *Nihon Shoki*. Written primarily in Chinese, the *Nihon Shoki* proved more accessible to scholars over the centuries than did the *Kojiki,* the other imperial history from around the same time but recorded in a confusing mix of Japanese and Chinese. Over the years, therefore, the *Nihon Shoki*—originally written to legitimate the dominance of the imperial house—served as an important source for scholars interested in local gods. The *Nihon Shoki* also proved invaluable to people interested in local history—a focus encouraged by the spread in the seventeenth century of Confucian education, with its emphasis on studying the models of the past. Thus, in communities throughout Japan, priests, scholars, and aspiring literary elites devoted increased attention to history in general and to the *Nihon Shoki* in particular. The result was a growing familiarity with this ancient imperial history, especially its early chapters on the Age of the Gods, which affected scholarly interpretations of the deities throughout Japan.

This focus on local history both drew upon and reinforced the development of a distinctively Japanese Shinto. For centuries, study of and worship according to the Way of the Kami—that is, Shinto—had been an integral part of Buddhist practice, not a separate entity.[49] Ever since the introduction of Buddhism, priests and scholars had been interested in the relationship of the native gods of Japan (kami) to the Buddhist law. Drawing upon the myriad sutras as well as a variety of linguistic, symbolic, and political associations, they identified Indian deva with kami and kami with deva—all as locally manifested guardians of Buddhism in Japan. For most priests, such identifications provided reassurance that local helpers would ensure the extension of Buddhist enlightenment and thus salvation to all. Yet, for an increasing number of kami specialists in the fifteenth century, the kami—not the buddhas and enlightenment—became the primary focus.[50]

One innovative and ambitious priest, Yoshida Kanetomo (1435–1511) of the Urabe family of kami ritualists attached to the imperial court, made the case for the primacy of the kami with particular force and effect. He argued, for instance, that the kami named in the ancient texts appeared both in and outside Japan, but had mistakenly been interpreted elsewhere in Buddhist terms. Thus, he asserted, seemingly Indian, Buddhist deities were actually native, Japanese kami.[51] Among his copious writings, Kanetomo included a reference to Konpira. In a passage on the historical Buddha, Śākyamuni, for instance, Kanetomo suggested that when "Śākyamuni revered twelve deities for Heaven and Earth" in India, he in effect worshipped kami from Japan. "[Śākyamuni] revered the kami Konpira, who is among these twelve kami, as a guardian deity of the spirit mountain," Kanetomo wrote. "The kami Konpira is Miwa Daimyōjin of Japan, as Dengyō Daishi [Saichō] reported when he came back to Japan."[52] Identifying the Great Kami Miwa as the original form of the Indian mountain deity Khumbīra, then, Yoshida Kanetomo added to his argument for the primacy of Japan's local kami over Buddhist gods—and, thus, for the primacy of his own teachings of the "One and Only Way of the Kami" (Yuiitsu Shintō) over Buddhist teachings.

By the end of the seventeenth century, Yoshida's school of Shinto had secured important privileges in the Tokugawa regime. Official Tokugawa ideology from the 1630s on emphasized Confucian teachings of loyalty and filial piety—an effective support of the hierarchical, hereditary order. Confucian scholars, focused on history and administration, found the emphasis on native kami attractive. Not only did it provide an alternative to Buddhism, but a focus on local kami, as found in the *Nihon Shoki* and other texts, also merged well with the Confucian emphasis on learning from the models of the past—albeit in this case Japanese, not Chinese, history. Hayashi Razan (1583–1657), for example, whose interpretations of Confucian texts became orthodox doctrine under the Tokugawa, developed his own Way of the Kami, using it to encourage Confucian morality and philosophy in Japan.

The result was both the increasing prominence of kami-focused, Shinto proponents and the blending in their teachings of Shinto and Confucian ideas. By the late seventeenth century, the Yoshida house of Shinto priests had translated its prominence in kami rituals into an official position under the Tokugawa bakufu: priests of smaller kami shrines around the country could not claim priestly qualifications without official investiture by the Yoshida house. In the late seventeenth century, the teachings of Yoshikawa Koretaru (1616–94), heir to the Yoshida lineage, attracted the attention of influential daimyo and prominent Confucians, including Yamazaki Ansai (1618–82), whose own Shinto teachings (Suika Shinto) combined Yoshikawa's interpretations of the kami with a Confucian emphasis on loyalty to insist, above all, on loyalty to the emperor as the descendant of the sun goddess Amaterasu.[53]

Proponents of the resulting intellectual mix of Yoshida Shinto and Confucian morality elaborated upon their ideas in the context of Japanese history, in the process redefining many of the kami of the islands. In some cases, local historians took up the kami-focused research agenda, as in the case of the priest of a kami in Sanuki who—drawing upon Yoshida's attributions to Saichō—identified Konpira in 1677 not only as the Great Kami Miwa but also as the related Ōmononushi: a snake-shaped kami in the *Nihon Shoki* who, when worshipped correctly, ensured the well-being of Amaterasu's descendants.[54] Around the same time, Yoshikawa Koretaru further elaborated on the identity of Konpira in an analysis of the first chapters of the *Nihon Shoki* intended to demonstrate in part the primacy of the kami Susano'o. He asserted that Susano'o traveled to the Korean kingdom of Shilla (Japanese *Shiragi*), to China, and to India only to be reintroduced to Japan by the Tendai priest Enchin in the ninth century as Shiragi Myōjin (the kami of Shilla). Likewise, asserted Yoshikawa, Saichō and Kūkai taught that Susano'o and the kami Ōnamuchi (another name for Ōmononushi) appeared on Vulture Peak in India as the guardian deities Matara and Konpira respectively; the two priests then reintroduced them to Japan as Kiyotaki Myōjin and Hie Ōmiya Gongen.[55] Yoshikawa, drawing upon texts and legends from generations before him, thus drew upon the authority of some of Japan's greatest Buddhist figures to identify a constellation of deities with Susano'o and, in the process, with Konpira. His references—to Ōnamuchi, Susano'o, Shiragi Myōjin, and Kiyotaki Myōjin—would repeatedly appear in later descriptions of Konpira.

Yoshikawa's interpretation spread through the influence of his colleague Yamazaki Ansai, whom Yoshikawa initiated into the secret teachings of the Yoshida school. Some of Yamazaki's students participated in one of the greatest scholarly undertakings of the time: the compilation of the *Great History of Japan* (*Dai Nihonshi*) under the lords of the Mito domain, beginning in 1657. Like Yamazaki Ansai's teachings, the *Dai Nihonshi* emphasized the Confucian idea of "rectification of names," and thus clarification of loyalties, especially to the imperial house.

The growing influence of Yoshikawa's interpretation of the *Nihon Shoki*, the spread of Yamazaki's teachings, and the ongoing Mito history project shaped the intellectual context in which Yūzan formulated his new interpretation of Konpira on Mt. Zōzu in the early eighteenth century. The priest of Konkōin, after all, worked in close collaboration with the officials of the Takamatsu domain, a domain founded by Matsudaira Yorishige, the eldest son of the first Mito lord, whose son then became the next lord of Mito. The third lord of Takamatsu then gave his own eldest son to his uncle to become the fourth lord of the Mito domain.[56] Such intimate ties between Takamatsu and Mito encouraged a sharing of both ideas and people. Moreover, as Yūzan worked to obtain favors from the Tokugawa shogunate, he was doubtless aware of the status of the Yoshikawa house as the formally acknowledged officials of Shinto in the bakufu. Given their growing influence, the Yoshikawa and Suika Shinto interpretations of the gods based on the *Nihon Shoki* must have seemed increasingly plausible to Yūzan and his peers.

It should come as no surprise, then, that in the second decade of the eighteenth century, Yūzan began promoting Konpira as a native Japanese kami. In 1711, he gave away one of Konkōin's images of Fudō Myōō to the shugendo subtemple Tamon'in, leaving the fierce guardian presiding over only the fiery altar of the goma ritual, which had long since proven its miracle-working powers not only to the priests but to worshippers as well. The next year, Yūzan ordered a sacred kami-style palanquin (*mikoshi*) built for the annual procession in the tenth month of 1712, apparently for the first time.[57] While accepting donations and worship in the name of Konpira Daigongen (the kami Konpira as a manifestation of a Buddhist essence), Yūzan increasingly promoted the essence of the deity as a native, Japanese god. In 1719, he commissioned a new origin tale and history to replace Matsudaira Yorishige's identification of the Indian god with Fudō Myōō. The new text, "Record of the Shrine to Konpira Kami on Mt. Zōzu in Naka District, Sanuki Province" ("Sanukishū Nakagun Zōzusan Konpira Shinshi Ki")—written by a Confucian scholar in the employ of the Takamatsu lord—never mentioned the name of Konpira at all, except in the title. Identifying the god of Mt. Zōzu as Ōnamuchi, the new text brought the Indian deva Konpira, heretofore interpreted in the Shingon shugendo idiom of Fudō Myōō and the tengu, into the cosmology of kami named in the ancient imperial histories.[58]

This did not mean, however, that Yūzan turned his back entirely on the shugendo tradition of Mt. Zōzu. Instead, he and the Confucian author of the text focused on the most crucial aspect of the cult—the miraculous powers of the mountain—translating that into the Shinto idiom of the intellectual elite of their time. In an oblique stab at the Shingon temple of Zentsūji nearby, the text begins with a clear statement on the power of the mountain. "Kami do not reside in places that lack spirit [*rei*]. Wherever kami do reside, those places necessarily have spirit. For this reason, plains, fields, towns, and noisy areas are not residences of the kami. Without fail, kami live instead amid deeply wooded peaks and valleys to which no humans or smoke rise and to which no horses or paths lead."[59] Although the text never mentions the practices of mountain worship, even in its accompanying history, it prefaces the entire narrative with a focus on the mysterious landscape of the mountain, continuing with the identification of Mt. Zōzu's kami as Ōnamuchi and immediately emphasizing the fame and powers of the kami at this site. Those who pray for status, wealth, long life, work, or healing, states the text, inevitably receive it. "Therefore, people come from near and far, from those above to those below, to revere and petition it."[60] The text thus reinforces and extols all claims made for Mt. Zōzu and its powers while resituating the mountain within the Confucian Shinto context of the time. The new identity of the god as a kami named in the *Nihon Shoki* thus coincided nicely with Yūzan's efforts to appeal to the growing numbers of influential, educated administrators and merchants in Japan—from headmen like Sakagami Senchō, who read ancient texts as part of their study of poetry, to the Confucian Shintoists in and around the shogunate, in influential domains, and in Takamatsu, as well.

The new emphasis signaled a change in priorities on Mt. Zōzu. The rewritten origin tale excised Yūsei from the narrative of the deity, avoided any suggestion of Kongōbō, tengu, or Fudō Myōō, and in an accompanying history relegated Yūsei and his "sacred powers" (*shin'i*) to the realm of the distant past, even before the arrival of Chōsokabe on the mountain.[61] While Yūzan ensured that Konkōin continued to perform the popular and lucrative goma rituals to Fudō Myōō, he reduced the prominence of the fierce Buddhist guardian elsewhere on the mountain. By 1719, then, Yūzan had reinterpreted the shugendo cult of Konpira on Mt. Zōzu, directing worship, at least in theory, to a manifestation of an ancient Japanese deity.

Whether because of Yūzan's discouragement of overt Buddhist shugendo on the mountain or simply because of the growing popularity of Konpira and its pilgrimage, shugenja and other ritualists challenged the identification of Konpira with the kami Ōnamuchi. Staging kaichō of Konpira independently of Konkōin in towns and cities throughout the country, they insisted upon the shugendo version of Konpira worship, often identifying the god explicitly with Fudō Myōō.[62] These independent kaichō, from which Konkōin received no income and over which it had no control, came at an inauspicious time for the priests on Mt. Zōzu. A fiscal crisis among the shogun and daimyo in the 1720s and 1730s reduced the reliability of income from lordly donations. Moreover, both the lord of Takamatsu and the Shingon temples on Mt. Kōya demanded that Konkōin contribute forced loans to assist them in their financial straits.[63] Confronted with these financial pressures, the priests of Konkōin became particularly sensitive to what they regarded as the increasing competition of the rival displays of the god.

A possible solution, however, was in sight. During the Kyōhō era (1716–35), doubtless in its own effort to secure income from wealthy religious institutions, the Tokugawa shogunate began cracking down on "false" kaichō and other religious fund-raising activities. That is, the shogunate labeled "false" the activities of people and institutions who did not cultivate close relations with the shogunate and perform prayer rituals on its behalf.[64] For the priests of Konkōin, who had already—along with many other temples around the country—received a shogunal petition for prayer in 1709 to protect the shogun from smallpox, this policy suggested new possibilities. In 1721, 1730, 1732, 1738, and throughout the 1740s and 1750s, Yūzan and his successor Yūben exploited the new shogunal policy, calling upon the Takamatsu overseer of temples and shrines to intervene with the shogunate in order to stop the "false" kaichō of competitors in Edo, Osaka, and Kyoto, as well as Bingo province.[65] These repeated lawsuits, however, served only as stopgap measures; as their repetition made clear, lawsuits alone could not secure a permanent solution to the problem.

While the priests could appeal to the shogunate each time for the suppression of individual incidents of "false" kaichō incidents, in the long run, an effective monopoly could effectively be granted only by the imperial court. The emperor and his court, while peripheral to most of the political dynamics of the Tokugawa system, did in fact play an important formal role in the social and political hierarchy. It was the emperor, with the approval of the shogunate, who granted rank, whether in bureaucratic office or among the aristocracy. Without the imprimatur granted by imperial rank, a Buddhist could not rise to the highest levels of the Buddhist priesthood, nor could a daimyo obtain the aristocratic titles that helped determine social hierarchies in the capital. In the same way, shrines and temples favored by the imperial court as sites for imperial prayer (*chokugansho*) gained renown from this recognition and status as sponsors of "genuine" kaichō, thus reaping both economic and social benefits.

Yūzan's successor, Yūben (priest, 1737–60), pushed actively for the privileges of imperial favor. In 1736, during the last months of Yūzan's life, the imperial court requested prayers performed around the country to protect the young emperor, Sakuramachi, from an outbreak of smallpox in the capital. Yūzan's adoptive kin, the Ōgimachi family, from whom came the consort of the third Takamatsu lord, apparently arranged for Konpira to be included on the list.[66] From the imperial viewpoint, this was not considered a significant innovation. However, after Yūben succeeded to the priestship of Konkōin later that year, he soon seized upon the opportunity to achieve closer, more formal ties, turning the single prayer order of 1736 into an occasion for continued communication with the court.

Yūben built upon his connections to take advantage of the structures of the imperial court. In large part, imperial policy was shaped by the *sekkanke*: the five most important aristocratic houses, including the Kujō, from whom imperial regents were drawn and who controlled the administration of the court. Using the aristocratic connections of his older brother, who had been adopted by a lesser aristocratic family under the Kujō clan, Yūben began to send thank-you gifts to the court for having ordered prayers from Konpira.[67] With continued support from the influential Kujō, these gifts—sent along with the records of prayers after each large festival on Mt. Zōzu—increased the profile of Konkōin at court. Within three years, Yūben won independence for Konkōin from the Shingon head temples; from 1739 on, all head priests of Konkōin would receive their Buddhist rank through direct imperial

appointment.[68] This independence freed the priests from the fiscal requirements of the Shingon sect while tying them more closely to the imperial court
and sekkanke, whose tonsured members would henceforth confirm the Shingon priestship of Konkōin directly. From this time on, Yūben—and all his
successors—would become adopted into one of the lesser houses under the
Kujō family, an arrangement that brought influence to Konkōin and gifts
from the increasingly wealthy temple to the influential sekkanke house.[69]

These connections to the Kujō dependents drew Konkōin into the world
of the lesser aristocrats in Kyoto—many of whom became caught up in the
1740s and 1750s in the Suika Shinto theories of Yamazaki Ansai. Around
that time, the teachings of Takenouchi Shikibu (1712–67), a charismatic
proponent of Suika Shinto, gained popularity among the lesser aristocrats.[70]
Aided by the mediation of the caretaker of the Takamatsu lord's mansion in
Edo as well as several lesser aristocrats—some known either then or later for
their ties to loyalist Suika Shinto supporters—Yūben and the Kujō continued
to push for privileges. In 1743, Konkōin not only received further orders for
prayers from the Kujō family, but was also entrusted with the task of immo-
lating ritual paper castoffs from imperial purification rituals. And, after yet
another decade in which imperial princes, sekkanke, and lesser aristocrats repeatedly commissioned prayers and requested talismans, Konpira Daigongen
received a formal imperial request for prayers in 1753, at the same time that
Yūben received the highest Buddhist rank, *hōin*.[71] The 1719 origin tale commissioned by Yūzan had no doubt proven of great help to Yūben as he worked
to capitalize upon his ties to the aristocracy. By aligning Mt. Zōzu with imperial kami and the traditions of Suika Shinto based on the *Nihon Shoki,* Yūben
appealed to the lesser aristocrats' sense of their imperial duty as outlined by
Takenouchi Shikibu.

The imperial request for prayers, however, did not explicitly identify
Konpira as a chokugansho. Yūben and the Kujō consequently pushed for
clarification on this point. In 1760, the young emperor Momozono (r.
1747–62)—who had shown great enthusiasm for Suika Shinto study of the
Nihon Shoki—decreed, with approval from the sekkanke and the bakufu,
that "Konpira Daigongen is the one shrine of Sanuki province; there are no
others. How much more so, then, because of our reverent belief, should it be
a site for imperial prayer."[72] Not only did the emperor explicitly call Konpira
a chokugansho, but he also effectively guaranteed a monopoly over the name
and image of the deity Konpira, conferring upon Konkōin the legal status
with which to combat any competition from others seeking to profit from the
popular deity. Other temples and shrines around the country were thence-

forth required to receive permission from the priests on Mt. Zōzu to enshrine or use the name of Konpira.[73]

The strategies of Yūzan and Yūben had succeeded. Konkōin's receipt of imperial favor stifled much of its competition: the priests of Konkōin would not confront significant rivals again until the 1830s. Through their alignment with rising aristocratic and, eventually, imperial interest in the *Nihon Shoki,* the priests of Konkōin secured imperial protection in an increasingly competitive world.

Yet the shugendo image of Konpira as a manifestation of Fudō Myōō and the tengu Kongōbō did not disappear. Shugenja evicted from Mt. Zōzu, as well as other ritualists and promoters, carried their interpretation of the god throughout western Japan, publicizing it in village after village, kaichō after kaichō. Indeed, for the general public, it was the tengu image of Kongōbō that cleared the way for yet another identity of the god, ironically linking it to the imperial house as well. However, by identifying Konpira Daigongen with the vengeful spirit of the twelfth-century retired emperor, Sutoku, popular proponents tied the deity not to the staid origins of the imperial house but to its violent and, at times, grotesque history.

As commemorated in the popular war tale, *Hōgen Monogatari,* Sutoku (1119–64; r. 1123–41) set off the Hōgen War of 1156 when he allied with a samurai house in an attempt to put his son on the throne. Sutoku's side lost, and he was exiled to Sanuki province. There he died and, according to the tale, became a demonlike tengu, copying sutras in blood and vowing to punish the imperial house. This tale of blood and revenge titillated audiences in the eighteenth century, gaining popularity in the wake of *Chūshingura* and similar plays of heroism and retribution. In 1756, shortly before Mt. Zōzu acquired the imperial privilege of an "exclusive shrine," the second Takeda Izumo, head of the prominent puppet-play-writing family in Edo and author of the blockbuster play *Kanadehon Chūshingura,* penned a new work in commemoration of the six hundredth anniversary of the Hōgen War. Identifying Sutoku with the increasingly popular tengu of Mt. Zōzu, he dramatized the connection in *The Sanuki Legend of the Retired Emperor Sutoku, the Original Source of Konpira* (*Konpira gohonji Sutokuin Sanuki denki*).[74] Other reiterations of this identification followed, with several well-received tales of Sutokuin keeping identification of the two tengu alive.[75]

In the end, then, Yūzan's promotion of Konpira as a Japanese kami and his discouragement of shugendo on Mt. Zōzu helped him achieve his goal of promoting the pilgrimage to Konpira—but in a way that nobody could have imagined. His actions encouraged displaced shugenja to spread the worship of Konpira as the tengu Kongōbō, fostering a popular image that playwrights and authors took up to link the tengu of Mt. Zōzu with the other tengu of Sanuki, the retired emperor Sutoku. At the same time, however, Yūzan's identification of Konpira as the manifestation of the kami Ōnamuchi, so important in the *Nihon Shoki* and Suika Shinto interpretations, helped him win support among the lesser aristocrats in Kyoto and, eventually, from the young emperor Momozono himself.

While the divergent interpretations of the god appealed to different groups of people, between them they fueled the popularity of Konpira as a whole. The ambiguity of the god allowed it to appeal to headman-poets and shippers, to mining magnates and aristocrats, to theatergoers and gamblers. Moreover, the ambiguity of the encircled gold insignia, which could stand for Konkōin, Konpira, Kongōbō, and even money at the same time, further promoted the popularity of the site in the increasingly diverse and market-oriented age of the eighteenth century.

It was fitting that the symbol of money should be so inextricable from the identities of the god, for the national cult of Konpira grew, in large part, through the workings of market forces. Using and fueling the growing cult, the priests of Konkōin, along with neighboring daimyo, encouraged local service business and souvenir manufacture in part as attempts to regulate domainal trade balances in an increasingly mercantilist environment. The wealthiest commoner elites—local administrators and successful businessmen—adopted Mt. Zōzu as an arena in which to develop and demonstrate their positions in the networks of influence, while petitioning the god for the security and prosperity that underlay their status above their poorer neighbors. And, just as domainal lords elsewhere were enforcing monopolies and monopsonies within their domains in their attempts to solve their fiscal problems, the priests of Konkōin used their connections at court to claim a monopoly on Konpira throughout all of the Japanese islands—a stunning success for the rulers of a tiny domain. Through the overlapping and uncoordinated efforts of the priests on Mt. Zōzu, of wealthy worshippers, of displaced shugenja, of playwrights, and of anyone who spoke of the deity to anyone else, Konpira grew—with its multiple identities—to command the attention of ambitious entrepreneurs and many others throughout Japan.

Culture of the Gods
(1744–1867)

5

Konpira rose to prominence with the expansion of the market economy and the social stratification that ensued. Yet the priests' successful promotion of Konpira faith came at a price. By the early 1800s, the men on Mt. Zōzu had lost control over perceptions of the god. As the cult of Konpira flourished in Edo, supported by a burgeoning world of print and performance, the worship of Konpira became part of a mass culture of gods, miracles, and pilgrimage that shaped the thoughts and behaviors of people in nineteenth-century Japan—a culture to which the priests of Konpira could only contribute, not one they could control. The miracles of, and pilgrimage to, Konpira formed a prominent part of this ubiquitous culture of the gods—a culture not dominated by any single deity. Riding the wave of popular worship, Konpira grew into a nationwide attraction, drawing upon the faith and donations of people from throughout Japan.

While the priests of Konpira worked with educated elites to propagate literary and artistic interpretations of their god, the mass of worshippers focused instead on the efficacy of the deity. They prayed for health and wealth, safety and protection. Through both prayer and pilgrimage, they sought to ensure a strong connection to the powerful god, in hopes of receiving a favorable, miraculous response. Thus grew a culture of pilgrimage, as people converged on the sites of Konpira and other gods in order to ensure the greatest response to their petitions.

This growing popular culture of gods, miracles, and pilgrimage only intensified amid the pressures of the nineteenth century. Fiscal pressures and social tensions fueled competition and burdened workers, who turned to the gods even more for relief and recreation. With coins in short supply—especially among peasants increasingly forced into supplementary work to make ends meet, or among urban workers and merchants waiting for delayed payments from impoverished samurai—prayers to a god of money seemed very attractive, especially when coupled with a respite from work and the opportunity to travel. Added to these everyday tensions came the threatening presence and troubling rumors of foreign ships along the coasts of Japan. With little or no voice in their government, commoners and lower-ranking samurai turned to the ever-changing gods with prayers and petitions. Unable and unwilling to rely on the efficacy of a government already in crisis, they called instead upon the efficacy of the gods so eloquently portrayed in the tales, performances, woodblock prints, and popular legends of the time. Thus grew, for instance, the reputation of Konpira as a tengu—for tengu represented in popular lore adept, almost magical beings with supernatural powers to both reward and torment people.

By the 1850s, then, the worship of Konpira had become part of a general culture of pilgrimage, part of the accepted background that shaped practices at home and experiences on the road and that informed popular and scholarly responses to the growing tensions of the time. Konpira grew beyond the control of its priests, who from the mid-eighteenth century on focused instead on establishing and maintaining their exclusive right to the god, thereby supporting and profiting from the pilgrims who came to Mt. Zōzu.

Growth of a Culture

The development of a widespread pilgrimage culture in the nineteenth century both relied upon and enabled the growth of economic networks of consumption, advertising, and offerings—transactions in which the gods were thought to play an active role as providers of benefits in exchange for offerings and prayer. The growth of such networks thus contributed to the development of an economy, a society, and ultimately a multifaceted culture in which the gods played an integral part.

In the early eighteenth century, the sponsorship of increasingly influential entrepreneurs had helped spread the cult of Konpira beyond the confines of its immediate vicinity. Investors in copper mines, village headmen cum poets cum rice dealers, ship captains and sailors of the Inland Sea—all widened the network of believers in the god. It was through the proliferation in the following decades of a myriad of such networks—in person and in print, each enabling the further exchange of money, goods, and services—that Konpira became part of an unquestioned culture for untold numbers of people not only in western Japan, but also in Edo and the country as a whole. Encouraged by entrepreneurs in the pilgrimage business and in the media, the cult of Konpira grew throughout the 1700s and early 1800s, eventually forming a prominent part of popular nineteenth-century culture.

From the 1740s on, businessmen throughout western Japan not only worshipped Konpira but also made more, and larger, donations to the site. Because of the expense involved in commissioning and donating a monument—usually a stone lantern—the effort often provided an occasion to consolidate ties through a joint project. In 1742, for instance, a group of shopowners from Hiroshima, Echigo, and Osaka joined together to erect a pair of two-and-one-half-meter-tall stone lanterns on Mt. Zōzu, doubtless giving a substantial monetary donation to Konkōin at the same time.[1] These donors were followed in subsequent years by growing numbers of merchants, landowners, and saké brewers, papermakers, or other small producers, often pooling their resources in groups called *kō* (usually translated as "confraternities") to make substantial offerings.

The number of lanterns and other items donated to Konpira by such commoners increased in large part through the mediating efforts of men whose primary business involved Mt. Zōzu. In 1744, the popularity of Konpira among the residents in and around Osaka and Kyoto had grown enough that the operator of a boat inn in Osaka, Tadaya Shin'emon, formerly a resident of Sanuki province himself, asked for and received permission from Konkōin to publicize his and his partners' services as providers of "Konpira pilgrimage boats."[2] This marks the beginning of Konkōin's licensing of businesses to use the name of Konpira and, eventually, its symbol of encircled gold—thereby increasing the visibility of Konpira while asserting the priests' right to approve pilgrimage-related enterprises. Soon, Tadaya, his partners, and his competitors vied with each other to publicize their services. In the process, they publicized and promoted the pilgrimage to Konpira as well.

Tadaya and his peers sought out and encouraged donations to Mt. Zōzu. A pair of stone lanterns donated in 1745 by 235 members of an "Osaka kō"—shopowners from Osaka, and one from Marugame—acknowledges Tadaya and several other Osaka boat-operator families as facilitators of the transaction between the donors and Konkōin.[3] In the 1750s, Tadaya solicited individual donations from an unrecorded number of people, recruited under the auspices of a "Ten Thousand Person Confraternity," Manninkō, to commission and donate a pair of three-foot-tall bronze guardian dogs (*komainu*) to the shrine.[4] He thus clearly used his position to encourage donations from current and prospective customers and, in doing so, thanked the priests and the god for the profits he accrued from the pilgrimage.

Tadaya and his partners provided important publicity for the shrine as they advertised their services not only in person but also in print. In 1769, for instance, Tadaya paid for the publication of a set of miracle tales of the shrine.[5] In 1774, he and two partners also published one of the earliest prints in which Konpira appears: "A Seaborne Pilgrimage Guide to Konpira in Sanuki and Miyajima in Aki."[6] Prominently featuring the "Konpira Pilgrimage Boat Inns" of Tadaya and his partners at the top, followed by the names of affiliated inns and souvenir sellers, as well as recommended souvenirs for sale in Marugame and Konpira, the prints provided an abbreviated guide to ports en route from Osaka to Marugame, then on to Miyajima and Hiroshima farther west. Tadaya and his heirs continued to publish prints and arrange for donations in the ensuing years; in 1787, for instance, Tadaya helped make the arrangements for a donor to sponsor a hall for votive plaques on the mountain.[7] Other "Konpira boat inns," "Konpira boat-departure sites," inns, and souvenir sellers acted similarly as go-betweens for donations and as publishers of guidebooks or tale collections, publicizing both their own enterprises and Konpira in the ensuing years (figure 5.1).[8] The cult of Konpira, like the cults of myriad deities throughout Japan, was thus spread and supported by the owners of affiliated businesses as they used the deity to recruit customers.[9]

The Konpira boats connected not only the residents of Osaka and Kyoto to Shikoku, but travelers from Edo as well. From the 1790s on, during a series of epidemics, people in the shogun's capital turned to a variety of miracle-working deities for protection. Prominent among them was Konpira, to whom both the shogunate and the imperial court had already appealed for the healing of smallpox. In Edo, the branch shrine of Konpira in the Marugame lords' Toranomon mansion proved particularly popular. Open to the public on the tenth day of every month, the Toranomon Konpira attracted countless worshippers, spreading the fame of the god of Mt. Zōzu among the townspeople of Edo while raising money through donations for both Konkōin and the Marugame lords.[10]

The growing print culture, centered in Edo in the nineteenth century, added fuel to the popular fervor for Konpira. Lending libraries made available literary travelogues of authors and poets who had visited Konpira. Collections of miracle tales penned by people with connections to Konpira began

❀ 5.1 (*opposite*) Prints such as this one advertising the Konpira boat operator Hiranoya (*lower right*) publicized pilgrimage to Konpira and the route to the mountain by sea: from Osaka, around Murotsu and Tanoguchi, arriving at the port of Marugame in order to reach Konpira on Mt. Zōzu at lower left. (Kagessai Hōjū, untitled print [Naniwa: Hiranoya Sakichi, undated]. Courtesy of Kotohira Ezu o Mamoru Kai.)

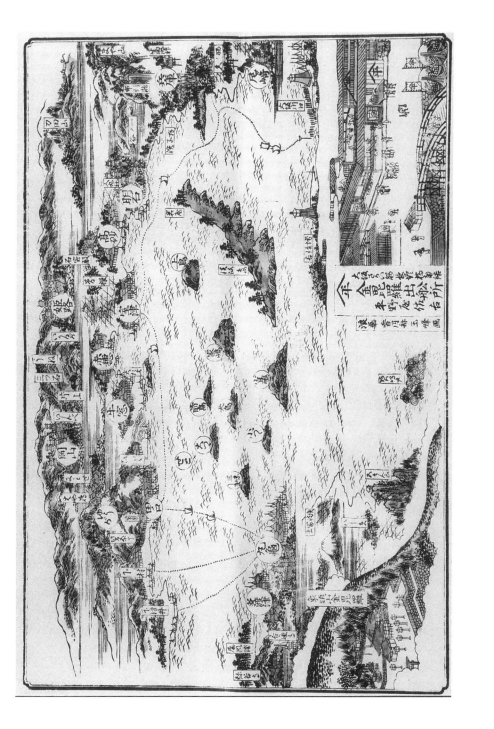

to circulate, as did growing numbers of illustrated travel guides that, in relating distinctive miracles and offerings to the shrine, further suggested its powers and efficacy. By the early 1800s, pilgrimage to Konpira began to rival pilgrimage to Ise, with as many as half of the pilgrims to Ise continuing on to visit Konpira, and large numbers traveling to Konpira from western Japan as well.[11]

For many people, pilgrimage to Konpira was inextricable from appeals to its healing and protective powers. The advertisements at the back of a collection of miracle stories published in Marugame in 1819 illustrate the reputation of the god for healing remedies and its intimate, popular identification with the tengu Kongōbō. Among souvenirs from the pilgrimage available at Marugame, the advertisements listed not only fans (associated with Kongōbō), oil, and miso, but also patent medicines such as "Mt. Zōzu Kongōbō's renowned Konjinmaru" and "Konshōtan (made with the miraculous water of Mt. Zō[zu], an amazing medicine for abdominal pain and convulsions)." The names of both medicines capitalized upon the connotations of Konpira's symbol and the character for gold: *kon*. In the town of Konpira itself, even more items were available for sale: sweet bean treats, candy, mushrooms, noodles, golden ginger, "amulet threads for the prevention of water and fire disasters," amulet boxes for the amulets of Konpira Daigongen, as well as a variety of medicines, including "the undreamed-of divine blessings [medicinal] powder of Mt. Zōzu," and "Gold Spirit medicine" (Konreitan), among others.[12] In an age when many people suffered from syphilis, trachoma, and other disabling diseases, such patent medicines—as well as the possibility of healing from prayer—seemed to promise that Konpira, Kongōbō, and the waters and other properties of the sacred mountain could ease insurmountable burdens, if only people donated to the gods or made purchases from purveyors.

The growth of Konpira faith thus paralleled the growth of its pilgrimage, promoted by those business owners (including the priests) who could profit from it. In fact, growth of the pilgrimage to Konpira seems to have relied as much on business owners as it did on priests officially affiliated with the site. At Konpira, unlike at Ise, Ōyama, and other famous sites, innkeepers (as far as we know) did not act as ritual guides (or *oshi*). They did, however, play a crucial role in popularizing the pilgrimage, often traveling around the country to recruit regular customers.[13] Clearly, then, the famed attractions of the site developed in a way that was inextricable from the economics of the region. Pilgrimage, and the service industry that supported it, was integral to the growing market economy of Tokugawa Japan.

Approaching the God

Throughout the first half of the nineteenth century, pilgrimage to Konpira and other sites of supernatural power became ever more popular. As a culture of pilgrimage spread in both urban and rural areas, a variety of practices became known as distinctive to Konpira worship, most with little or no encouragement from the priests on Mt. Zōzu. Instead, theatrical productions, publications, and word of mouth shaped the expectations of worshippers while they were still at home and then influenced their practice and experience of pilgrimage on the road.

Konpira rose to prominence at a time of increased mobility, and the vernacular, illustrated literature of travel fueled the popularity of the pilgrimage and the deity. Most prominent among these travel writings was the comedic tale by Jippensha Ikku, *Hizakurige,* which narrated the adventures of two protagonists, Yaji and Kita, as they meandered along the Tokaido highway, sharing uproarious adventures and falling afoul of the many dialects of the areas through which they passed.[14] As a result of the outstanding success of this first tale, Ikku published several further installments, beginning in 1810 with the tale of Yaji and Kita's pilgrimage to Konpira.

Konpira Hizakurige combined the fierce miracles of the deity with the physical pleasures of pilgrimage in memorable images that shaped pilgrims' ideas of Konpira for more than a century. Praising the "clear miracles" of the "deity whose divine powers and mysterious deeds extend throughout Japan and China," Ikku told a tale focused on common vows to Konpira to abstain from saké, on prayers to the god for rescue from shipwreck, and on petitions for relief from that scourge of the pleasure quarters, syphilis. As Yaji and Kita sailed through the Inland Sea, visiting brothels and suffering from seasickness, they witnessed the blessings of the deity and experienced "divine retribution . . . swifter than an arrow, more immediate than a bullet." Yaji in particular, who rashly promised to quit drinking in his terror at sea but then imbibed anyway, was tormented by the god until the completion of the pilgrimage.[15] The connections between pleasure, pilgrimage, and godly retribution provided a fertile ground for humor in this most popular comedy.

At Konpira itself, the merging of prayer and prostitution had become so central to the pilgrimage business that the priests of Konkōin finally gave up after more than a century of exhortations against the sex trade. After repeated pronouncements banning the practice of prostitution during the seventeenth and eighteenth centuries, Konkōin finally conceded in 1824 that "since many pilgrims come into [the town], there would be suffering if there were no prostitutes." The priests therefore established a set of rules that all owners of prostitution-related businesses were required to sign, regulating the clothing and movements of prostitutes, forbidding the employment of local women as prostitutes, and permitting brothel owners to run seasonal theaters for profit.[16] In later years, brothel owners and innkeepers collected *hanegin,* percentages taken from the fees charged by prostitutes and geisha, to fund the construction of a permanent kabuki theater to attract pilgrims.[17] Shogunal and Takamatsu domain officials in the ensuing decades repeatedly attempted to halt prostitution in Konpira, but Konkōin—which, because of its shogunal red seal, ruled the small domain—permitted it to flourish for the prosperity of the town.[18]

While the priests permitted the sex trade because of its economic value, they became increasingly concerned with its effect on residents. In 1829, the head priest of Konkōin decreed that all plays and prostitution be limited to the Kinzanji area, behind the inns of Uchimachi. Thus, it was primarily Kinzanji that resounded with the noise and frivolity of revelers, particularly during the three market seasons in the third, sixth, and tenth months of every year. Not only brothels, but also a lottery and kabuki playhouses attracted the crowds. Established by Konkōin in 1825 at the behest of the aristocratic Kujō family of Kyoto, the lottery raised money for sutra readings (and for Konkōin and the Kujō) while drawing pilgrims and gamblers to the town.[19] Although kabuki and puppet plays had also drawn audiences for decades, the actors had performed in temporary theaters moved and rebuilt each season. It was through the tax on the regulated prostitutes' services that brothel owners and innkeepers constructed the first permanent kabuki theater in 1835. Owing to the pressure of pilgrims' demands, Kinzanji had become a permanent site of pleasure and profligacy, open year-round to visitors from throughout the land.

From the 1820s to the 1850s, pilgrimage to Konpira reached its peak. Worshippers in hundreds of communities formed groups to pray to Konpira and save money for pilgrimages and donations, building lanterns and small shrines to the god in villages and on mountainsides throughout Japan. Indeed, worship of the famous deity was in many ways based on the physical presence of Konpira in each community. Small shrines to the god were scattered around the country, some as guardian shrines within temple precincts, others as independent structures on wooded hills or in seaports. Supported by local legend, these sites underscored histories of local relationships with the deity that often showed little connection to the shrine on Mt. Zōzu. One shrine in Nishigahō, a village in the mountains of present-day Kōchi prefecture, for instance, claims origins in the sixteenth century, when a villager saw a strange light and heard a strange sound on the mountain; a traveling diviner later determined that the mysterious presence was Konpira Daigongen. To-day local residents point out a tree, a stone lantern erected in 1821, and a group of fallen stones that once presumably housed a small shrine to mark where the villager had stood.[20] In 1822, the year after residents of Nishigahō built their lantern, the people of Hirose in present-day Shimane prefecture, on the other side of Japan, also enshrined Konpira in their community.[21] In countless communities throughout Japan, the popularity of Konpira in the 1820s prompted people to enshrine or revive the presence of the deity in their local landscapes.

In addition to shrines, "Konpira lanterns" stood as physical reminders of the deity's presence and protection, whether at crossroads, on roadsides, in fields, on piers, at the borders of villages, or in the middle of towns. Some-times carved and dated, at other times consisting merely of rough-hewn stone, the Konpira lanterns served as a focal point of Konpira worship. Resi-dents lit the lanterns on Konpira's festival days or even every night, providing outdoor light for gatherings in the age before electricity.

Aided by the seeming permanence of the mountains and stones that bore the name Konpira, local traditions of Konpira worship could seem timeless, extending back for generations before living memory. Tales of older people who had gone to Konpira in their youth, diaries left by educated travelers, even the lanterns themselves testified to the importance of Konpira worship for the ancestors of village residents. A lantern inscribed with the name of someone's grandfather, thirty years before, or undated, erected out of stone apparently untouched by human hands, exuded a sense of age and apparent naturalness that lent authority to local traditions. In this way, local worship practices were linked to physical markers, reminders of the independent reli-gious authority that the community derived from the accumulated practices of generations of its residents.[22]

Informed by the traditions and practices of countless communities, Kon-pira worship took a variety of forms not dictated by any single authority. If one man lit a candle at home, made a vow, and experienced a miracle, he and eventually his friends and neighbors would probably incorporate candle lighting as a central practice in their worship of the deity. If, as in the popular kabuki play *Konpira Gorishōki*, a mother and son avenged the father's death after countless pilgrimages and repeated cold-water ablutions at the shrine, viewers of the play might also be inspired to pray while dousing themselves with water when they were truly in need.

Spread through unofficial channels, a few common practices, such as the erection of lanterns, the receipt of amulets or talismans, and an emphasis on pilgrimage, came to characterize most Konpira worship around the country, although these, too, differed slightly from place to place. In some villages, lanterns carried inscriptions to Konpira or the encircled gold insignia; elsewhere, they were unmarked, known by local legend as memorials to Konpira. Worshippers throughout Japan valued talismans from the shrine on Mt. Zōzu, for they brought the power of the deity directly into their homes. Yet some insisted that large wooden amulets were more effective than paper ones; others recommended swallowing an amulet or its ashes; and in the mid-nineteenth and early twentieth centuries, people in Kyushu and northeastern Japan considered it important to enclose the amulet in a shrinelike paulownia box to protect it on the trip home.[23]

Throughout the country, pilgrimage—the act of approaching as close as possible to the most powerful site of the deity—was considered important, but people differed on which Konpira shrine was most powerful for particular requests, whether pilgrimage was as effective when performed by a community representative or family member instead of by oneself, or whether it was more effective when planned with neighbors or undertaken on the spur of the moment. People also differed on what actions at the shrine itself were most effective: whether a sincere pilgrim should go up and down the long steps one hundred times, walk barefoot, stay on the mountain overnight, offer coins, wrap the coins in paper, or do any of countless other things.[24] These regional, community, and personal variations highlight the magical purpose of Konpira worship in popular practice. Far from adhering to a canonical format of ritual or prayer, worshippers did whatever they considered most effective in an effort to secure practical benefits. The diversity of worship practices was united by a common purpose: to petition for divine favor and intervention in the world.

The search for practical benefit was most often a private endeavor. People prayed for their own welfare and that of their families. As records from the goma ritual on Mt. Zōzu attest, some of the most common prayer requests throughout the nineteenth century (and still common today) included petitions for "household safety," "prosperity in trade," "healing" and the like (figure 5.2).[25] While many people gave offerings that referred to personal aspirations only in oblique terms, asking for "fulfillment of a desire," for instance, some depicted their hopes much more concretely. Letters, testimonials, and votive plaques left at the shrine attest to prayers of a very personal nature, as gamblers and drinkers prayed for the willpower to break a bad habit and childless couples begged for offspring. Whether to protect one's worldly goods, heal a child, or guarantee an insect-free crop, prayer for worldly benefits was the most common reason that people communicated with Konpira, as with other popular deities.[26]

household safety	prosperity of one's descendants
fulfillment of the five grains	prosperity in trade
good luck forever	fulfillment of desire
fulfillment of desires	aversion of evil difficulties
fulfillment of the heart's desire	aversion of disasters
safety in the temple	safety in the subtemple
prosperity in making saké	aversion of disaster
safety and long life	village safety
reduction of water in the manor	safety of the kō
safety in the district	safety on the boat
maritime safety	safety on sea and land
healing of this illness	safety on rough seas
healing of smallpox	fulfillment of the great wish
prosperity in making vinegar	safety on the mountain
ending of the epidemic	military fortune forever
dispersal of the enemy	safe birth and healing
benefit from gentle rain	aversion of theft
aversion of great disasters	

❀ **5.2** This list of requests for prayers for the goma fire ceremony at Konkōin on 29 February 1852 (Kaei 5.4.18) demonstrates the popular interest in practical benefits. (Zōzusan Konkōin, "Gokitō on-toku," recorded in "Konotabi goma fuda tsuki ichimai hanshū ni ainari narabini ganbō kakitsukitō iri," Kaei 5.4.18, in *Kotohiragū shiryō,* ed. Kotohiragū, vol. 32.)

Often the content of a person's prayer grew out of his or her occupation. The patronage of the ship captains, sailors, and traders of the Inland Sea, for instance, promoted Konpira as a guardian of the sea. Boats braved not only the vagaries of the market but the ever-present danger of the sea as well. With shallow bottoms and sharply turned prows, Japanese-style boats were susceptible to being overturned or capsized in the unpredictable storms that plagued the shipping routes. Owners, captains, and crews therefore prayed for safety in the miracle-oriented paradigm of nineteenth-century worship. Such petitioning took several forms. Some boat owners gave large monetary donations to the shrine while boat builders made detailed models of their vessels, setting them before the attention of Konpira and other gods. When boats encountered danger at sea, crew members often prayed fervently to the deity, then donated ema or anchors in thanks for salvation (figure 5.3).[27]

Konpira became the guardian not just of seaborne trade but of all mar-

itime pursuits. Members of fishing and whaling fleets prayed to the deity for bountiful catches, sometimes commissioning spectacular ema for their cause. Inscriptions on lanterns, fences, and other offerings to Konpira show that residents of fishing and coastal villages constituted many of the shrine's devoted followers. One man, reminiscing in 1907 of his childhood in a fishing family on the island of Sado in the Japan Sea, recalled how his mother calmed him on stormy nights with stories of "Konpirasama of Sanuki," to whose shrine thirty or forty people from the village went on pilgrimage each year.[28] Stone monuments on Cape Omaezaki in Shizuoka prefecture commemorate pilgrimages by boat crews from the area throughout the century after 1846.[29]

Konpira's image as the guardian of sailors undergirded its broader association with manufacture and trade. In the nineteenth century, almost all long-distance trade involved ships and the dangers of the sea. Thus, not only the sailors themselves but also prosperous farmers and fishermen—now branching out into saké and soy sauce brewing, papermaking, and other pursuits reliant on trade—filled the grounds of the shrine with offerings. These rural elites, known in the historical literature as "wealthy peasants" (*gōnō*) or, later, "rural notables" (*chihō meibōka*), constituted a crucial group of economic, administrative, and cultural leaders scattered throughout the countryside.[30] As entrepreneurs, village officials, poets, letter writers, and, of course, major donors, these rural elites formed the backbone of the popularity, and especially the wealth, of Konpira in the nineteenth century.

Records and monuments, both at the shrine and in villages around the country, bear out the connection of such rural elites to shipping and, thus, to Konpira. Wooden talismans carried home from Mt. Zōzu by the Minami family of Yasuda village in Tosa, for example, reflect a shift in the household's occupation: from shipping in the 1840s and 1850s, when talismans from Konkōin commemorate prayers for "maritime safety," to saké brewing in the 1860s, when the talismans record prayers for "household safety" or "prosperity in saké brewing" instead.[31] Elsewhere, as wealthy landowners began producing and selling coal, soy sauce, and other items on a larger scale than before, they and their neighbors built Konpira lanterns in communities across the land.[32]

Since people identified with their neighbors and peers, such offerings and prayers could be both personal and communal. Often, prayers for one person

---

❁ 5.3 (*opposite*) Sailors, fishers, and terrified passengers offered votive plaques, thanking Konpira for their survival. This ema was donated much later than the period described in chapter 5, in 1900. (Photo by Steve Cantley, with the permission of Kotohira Shrine.)

included of necessity prayers for everyone. This was especially true in agricultural communities, with petitions for rain. Often, prayers for one person included of necessity prayers for everyone. This was the case with petitions for rain (*amagoi*). Whole villages near Konpira congregated during times of drought and sent relay runners to light a torch at the shrine. The runners would then bring the sacred fire and, it was hoped, rain back to the fields.[33]

Even when worshippers wanted to procure divine favors of a personal nature, economic necessity often forced them to rely on communal resources to do so. Although some well-to-do people, such as the rural samurai Nakahara (whom we followed up the mountain in chapter 1) and a few other members of the rural elite, were able to finance their own pilgrimages,[34] most people in the nineteenth century could not afford the expense of pilgrimage on their own. The financial burdens of travel dictated that would-be pilgrims who lived more than a day's journey from Konpira save money for the trip.

The most common solution to this economic problem was to form a confraternity, or kō—not to make expensive donations but to fund the trip itself. Residents of a village interested in visiting Konpira would form a group of up to twenty households, each of which would make a small monthly contribution so that after a certain period of time, two or three members of the kō, picked by rotation or lottery, would be able to go on pilgrimage as representatives of the group. Many kō operated in cycles—one cycle operating until all members had gone on pilgrimage with the financial support of the group. After the completion of a cycle, new members could join or old members drop out, and a new cycle would begin.[35] Some Konpira kō, usually relatively close to the shrine, saved money in order for the entire membership to go on pilgrimage together.

In rural communities, especially, kō functioned as far more than groups that saved for pilgrimage; they often played a major role in social life. Konpira kō existed amid a patchwork of kō and community groups whose overlapping memberships met on designated evenings of each month, setting a rhythm for the social lives of residents that measured time in relation to the gods. With a calendar of thirty-day months, without weekends or sabbaths, people organized special occasions of rest and entertainment around the "connection days," or ennichi, of the gods, days when prayers to the deity were considered most effective. Thus, Konpira kō would meet on the tenth day of each month, Kannon kō on the seventeenth, and Tenjin kō on the twenty-fifth. Each kō focused attention on a different deity, located in a different direction. Moreover, by helping to fund pilgrimages, kō offered one of the only politically and socially recognized reasons for which people could leave their home district.[36] By going on pilgrimage, they could escape from

everyday routines and enjoy themselves away from home while still performing a recognized community service: bringing the favor of the gods back into
the community through amulets and other tokens of the trip. Because travel
was theoretically prohibited for commoners except when officially on pilgrimage, village residents often increased their knowledge of the wider world
in the context of the gods. In pilgrimage diaries, for instance, travelers frequently commented on the appearance of new battlements erected for defense, on the devastation caused by floods or riots, or on the impressive
beauty of famous buildings seen en route—all amid references to shrines,
temples, and the purchase of amulets. The effect was that prayer and pilgrimage shaped images of the Japanese islands for countless people.

This kind of popular, divinized mapping of both land and time may be
seen in a simple survey of the nine most prominent pilgrimage kō in one harbor community in western Honshu in the mid-nineteenth century. In Nagasaki, a village of about one hundred households on a peninsula jutting into
the Inland Sea (not to be confused with the major international port of Nagasaki in Kyushu), pilgrimage kō tied the rhythms of community social life to
a variety of nearby and distant landmarks (figure 5.4). Nearest to home, kō
linked their members to the shugendo and esoteric Buddhist traditions of
Shikoku and the Inland Sea. A Daishi kō, named after Kōbō Daishi (Kūkai),
met on the twenty-first day of each month, sending representatives to the
seven closest temples of the eighty-eight-temple Shikoku pilgrimage, across
the sea near Matsuyama. The Ishizuchi kō sent pilgrims to Mt. Ishizuchi, the
renowned shugendo mountain in Shikoku, while the Gyōja (literally "ascetic
practitioner") kō met twice a year, sending members to Mt. Ōmine. Each
year, the Konpira kō borrowed a boat to take all members on pilgrimage to
Mt. Zōzu. In the other direction, toward the Japan Sea, members of various kō
undertook the thirty-three-temple pilgrimage of Kannon of the Western provinces and traveled to the shrines to Tenjin in Ōfu and Dazaifu, to Izumo
Taisha, and—for people with trachoma and other eye diseases common in the
days before modern hygienic techniques—to Ichibatake Yakushi. Finally, the
Ohimachi assocation greeted the dawn three times a year, hiring an officiant
of the local kami shrine to purify their houses and sending pilgrims to Ise
Shrine.[37] In other parts of the country, similar configurations of kō tied communities to the times and places of local, regional, and more distant gods.

Kō also shaped the symbolic and social context in which people related to
the gods. Since membership was voluntary, they brought different members
of the community together. Some kō were formed by immediate neighbors in
village hamlets, others by people of similar age and sex, others (like the Ichibatake kō above) by people with shared concerns such as illness, still others by

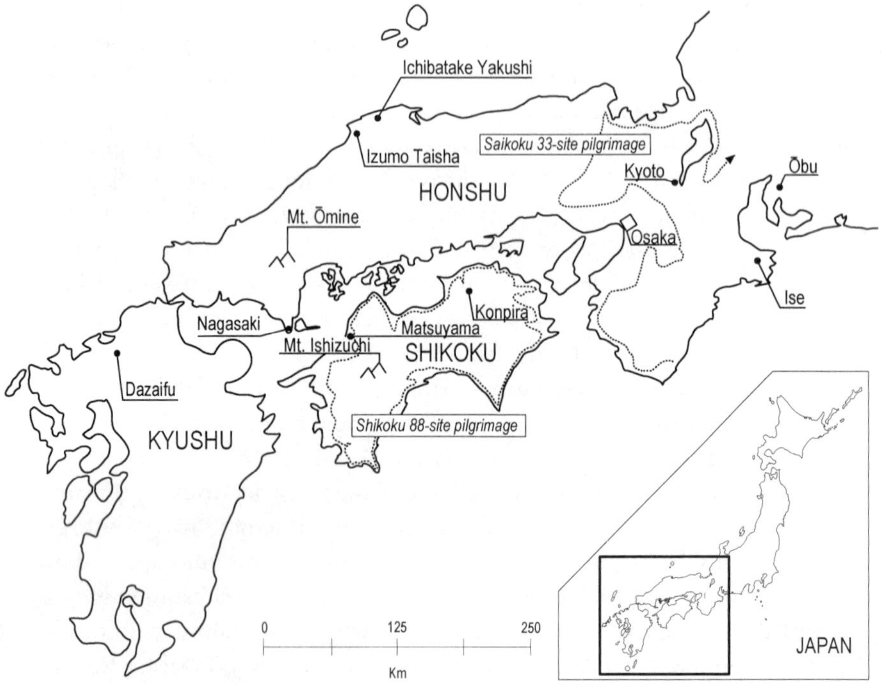

5.4 Destinations of pilgrimage kō active in the village of Nagasaki in the mid-nineteenth century. The monthly meetings and periodic pilgrimages of such kō structured both time and space for people in communities throughout Japan. (Map constructed from information in Miyamoto Tsuneichi, *Ise sangū,* Tabi no minzoku to rekishi 5 [Tokyo: Yasaka Shobō, 1987], 142–44.)

people of similar socioeconomic levels. Each member of a kō held a responsibility to the group as a whole. In addition to the monetary donation required each month, each household took turns hosting the kō meeting. Members also performed ongoing duties. Many Konpira kō built lanterns to the god; the host of the month was responsible for lighting it each evening.

Members of Konpira kō gathered at the host's house on the tenth day of each month to hold a short prayer ceremony. Prayer styles varied widely from group to group, often shaped by traveling mountain ascetics who may have encouraged their establishment, or by charismatic leaders such as Kino, the leader of a Konpira kō in the castle town of Nagoya, who, possessed by Konpira in 1802, preached a moral discipline focused on salvation that became the core of a new religion, Nyoraikyō.[38] Some kō owned treasured ritual objects such as golden purification wands, large conch shell horns, room-sized wooden rosaries, or a hanging scroll representing the deity. Worship could range from bowing in front of the scroll while calling on the name of Konpira, to sitting in a circle holding a large rosary while reciting the Heart Sutra, to blowing the horn and listening to the leader preach. In many cases, kō worshipped in front of a paper or wooden amulet enshrined in a special box, in a portable shrine, or on a small platform: it was the duty of each successive pilgrim of the group to replace this amulet with a new one from the shrine.[39]

Yet kō meetings consisted of more than prayer and duty. They were fun, too. In many rural households, night work—such as making straw sandals or repairing nets—occupied almost every evening. Families eagerly anticipated the monthly meeting of the kō as a respite from their usual chores. As one mother and son reminisced in 1997 about the meetings of their local Konpira kō on the island of Shōdoshima in the 1930s: "It was the old equivalent of a party [*mukashi no paatii*]. . . . Everyone came: families, kids. . . . I looked forward to it because we would eat [red rice]."[40] In communities where people worked hard day and night, any evening off to socialize with friends and neighbors became a welcome event.

Kō pilgrimage was considered an important social responsibility. Representatives, entrusted with money to donate on behalf of the kō, brought back amulets for the kō and kō members. Fellow members saw them off on their trip and welcomed them back in the same way. In a village in present-day Kōchi prefecture, for instance, a Konpira lantern stands at the outer boundary of the community, marking the place where people said goodbye to relatives and friends setting off on a trip or welcomed them back from their pilgrimage with a party, songs, and festivities. Pilgrims' diaries from throughout the nineteenth century record that they would often spend the final night of their trip within only a short distance of home in order to send word ahead of their arrival. Community members then took the day off work and gathered at the edge of the village to welcome the returning pilgrims, hear their stories of the trip, and receive the amulets and souvenirs brought home by the travelers. Depending on local tradition, this welcoming-home ceremony could often include a trip to the local shrine or the construction of a special hut for celebration.[41]

Pilgrimage kō thus constituted Konpira pilgrimage as both social responsibility and communally sanctioned vacation. As long as the representative pilgrims took the donations and prayers of the kō to the shrine and brought back the desired amulets or talismans, they were free to enjoy their trip however they liked. Pilgrimage to Konpira and other sites usually occurred during the seasonal downtimes of farming or fishing work—in the depths of winter and, in agricultural communities, after the spring planting and before harvest.[42] At those times, pilgrims could entrust their affairs to neighbors and relatives and enjoy anywhere from three days to two months away from the pressures of community life.

Indeed, the sense of escape often formed an integral part of the pilgrimage.[43] In some communities, running away for pilgrimage (*nukemairi*) without telling other people (and therefore using personal funds) was considered more effective for prayer. In others, pilgrimage to Konpira served as a rite of passage into adulthood, or a honeymoon given to newlyweds as a chance to get away.

While inextricably shaped by attitudes at home, pilgrimage to Konpira also served as an escape from the restrictions of everyday propriety. Attracted by the relative anonymity of the pilgrimage town, lovers frequently escaped their families or spouses by going on "pilgrimage" to Konpira, sometimes for a month or even longer. Vacationing men found the gambling and pleasure quarters of Kinzanji at Konpira integral to the pilgrimage, with entertainers at Konpira's inns and brothels constituting one of the main attractions. Trained in Edo traditions of song, dance, and costume, the prostitutes and geisha of Konpira were available for hire by the hour or the night at the inns in town.[44] Worship itself was also surrounded with a sense of abandon. On major festival days at the shrine, drunken revelers not only participated in the processions and reeled noisily about the streets, but also poured into the shrine grounds to buy amulets and pray. The popularity of the shrine, occasioned by the perceived miraculous powers of Konpira, translated into a bustling, at times chaotic revelry as hundreds of thousands of people visited the mountain to pray, pay, and play at the site of the deity.[45]

In the end, though, no matter how unrelated to everyday life the trip may have felt, pilgrims were repeatedly reminded of their commitment to the community.[46] Not only kō members, but even those who had set off on their own were expected to return bearing amulets and prints as presents for the people at home. As one man recalled of his pilgrimage to Konpira with friends in 1873, "After [returning home], we chose a day, distributed talismans and amulets of the gods and buddhas as souvenirs to relatives and acquaintances, and held a welcome-home party [literally a party to take off the leg-wrappings worn on a long trip]. This party wasn't any special ceremony; we just gathered together the people we had dealings with, celebrated our safety on such a long trip, gave thanks for the blessings of the gods and buddhas, and exchanged stories of the trip and of what happened while we were gone."[47] Thus, pilgrims related stories of Mt. Zōzu and their travels, adding to the lore of miracles and adventures in Jippensha Ikku's *Hizakurige,* gazetteers, and theatrical performances. As pilgrims told of their encounters with people of other regions, sharing anecdotes and impressions of places far away, they helped create the ties that bound together a nationwide culture.[48] But it was not just a sense of shared identity that emerged—it was an identity linked to the gods. The faith in Konpira's miracles that spread from sailors and shippers to townspeople and farmers, from Ezo in the north to the Ryūkyūs in the south, helped shape a shared world of gods, miracles, and pilgrimage in the nineteenth century.

Explaining the God

During the early 1800s, stories of the miraculous powers of the gods in general, and Konpira in particular, became so ubiquitous in popular culture that scholars took note, seeking to account for them in learned treatises. The most prominent such scholar was Hirata Atsutane (1776–1843), the self-proclaimed successor to the nativist Motoori Norinaga.[49] While other thinkers set out economic and social solutions to the intensifying crises of the time—which included famine, epidemics, economic instability, and the appearance of foreign ships along the coasts—Hirata found both the cause of and the answer to contemporary disasters in the world of the gods. In his explanations, Hirata brought together rulers' long-standing political emphasis on propitiatory worship and Motoori Norinaga's identification of the native kami with the powers of creation to form a new theory of worship designed to rescue the entire country from catastrophe. Hirata's prolific works built on his interest in ancient Japanese texts and such supernatural phenomena as ghosts and tengu to set forth a comprehensive national agenda. He redefined worship, the gods, and the entire cosmological structure in order to solve the problems of his day without reliance on the "foreign" knowledge that he condemned.[50]

Hirata posited an extensive hierarchy of native kami presiding over all Japanese, with each person under the jurisdiction of his local deity. At the apex of this hierarchy stood the deity Ōkuninushi, creator of the land and ruler over the hidden world of the gods. This identification of Ōkuninushi as ruler of the gods drew directly upon Motoori Norinaga's interpretation of the myths recorded in the *Kojiki* and *Nihon Shoki*. According to the myths, Ōkuninushi ceded control of the Land of Reed Plains (Japan) to the imperial grandson of the sun goddess Amaterasu. He ensured the obedience of all the gods to this agreement in exchange for a shrine at which he would be worshipped in Izumo. Motoori compiled several versions of the myths to conclude that Ōkuninushi was therefore worthy of the greatest worship: "This deity called Ōkuninushi is the deity of the Great Shrine of Izumo. In the beginning, he created everything under the heavens. He leads the myriads of kami. According to the promise [to cede the land to Amaterasu], he is the deity who rules over all hidden things in the world. Therefore, he is a deity whom all people, whether of high station or low, must reverently worship."[51] In other words, Ōkuninushi had once ruled everything both seen and unseen. Therefore, when he ceded the visible world to the imperial line descended from Amaterasu, he retained control of the invisible world.

Elaborating upon Motoori's identification, Hirata asserted that Ōkuninushi monitored the intents and actions of all people from his position in the invisible world of the gods. He ruled over people not only while they were alive but before and after death as well.[52] In Hirata's analysis, the myriad deities led by Ōkuninushi formed a territorial hierarchy, with each kami overseeing the spiritual welfare of a village or region and reporting to Ōkuninushi on the activities of the inhabitants. For Hirata, the hierarchy led by Ōkuninushi was a crucial element in maintenance of the social order: all people would worship at their local shrines, public rituals would appease the gods at the regional shrines, and imperial rites would be performed at the imperial shrine. This pyramid of public worship would ensure the good will of all gods and especially the greatest of them, Ōkuninushi.

But the nationwide popularity of Konpira and its pilgrimage, which cut across geographical and social boundaries, disrupted Hirata's theory of neatly arranged worship duties. Hirata wrote his works in early nineteenth-century Edo, a city where countless people worshipped at the Toranomon Konpira, took months off work to go on pilgrimage to Mt. Zōzu, and even reportedly sent their dogs as proxies when they could not afford the trip themselves.[53] Thus, he was clearly aware of the disruptive drawing power of Konpira's miraculous reputation. Always interested in evidence of unseen powers, Hirata sought to explain the miracles of Konpira Daigongen by disclosing the hidden identity of the Buddhist avatar as a native kami.

In *Tamadasuki,* published in 1833, Hirata identified the "true" kami behind Konpira, highlighting the anomalous position of the deity on Mt. Zōzu in his hierarchy of the gods. To do so, he used one of the many tales of Konpira's miraculous powers then being related in Edo.[54] According to Hirata, there was a stonemason's apprentice who suffered from a severe case of syphilis. The man prayed to Konpira, vowing to abstain from his beloved saké in return for a cure. After months of abstinence and good health, the man began to drink and dance in the festival of his local kami. Before noon, he was afflicted with a high fever and began to cower before a vision that only he could see: Konpira had appeared. Attended by strong, demonlike attendants, the deity of Mt. Zōzu berated the apprentice for breaking his vow and ordered his attendants to break each of the apprentice's fingers and toes. Before they could act, however, the man's local kami arrived and accused Konpira of meddling in his relationship with his parishioner. The two gods stood, glaring daggers at one another, until a third deity, Inari, to whom the man had occasionally prayed for bodily safety, arrived to arrange a truce: Inari would suffer the bulk of the physical harm intended for the man, who would then appease Konpira by performing a pilgrimage to Mt. Zōzu. The miracle tale as Hirata reported it points out an exception to Hirata's theory of the overriding primacy of the local deity-parishioner bond: while a local deity could usually protect a worshipper from another god's wrath, Konpira was so strong that a stalemate ensued until appeasement was arranged. In explaining this anomaly, Hirata described the "true" identity of Konpira Daigongen.

In Hirata's cosmology, there were only two types of beings that could demonstrate the strength shown by Konpira in this confrontation, and the foreign (because Buddhist) deity Konpira Daigongen was not one of them. Drawing on the evidence of Konpira's miraculous strength, Hirata selected two of the many existing theories of Konpira's identity to explain the strength of the popular deity. In the process, he associated Konpira, possibly the most widely worshipped god of the time, with the most powerful beings of his own cosmology. First, citing a "secret text of the true transmission of Konkōin" that no scholar has ever identified, Hirata repeated the assertion of Yoshikawa Koretaru and others that Konpira was actually the kami Ōmononushi, confused with the Buddhist deity Konpira because of a similarity of form. Here, Hirata was apparently referring to the association of both Konpira and Ōmononushi with rain-bringing reptiles such as dragons, snakes, and crocodiles. By identifying Konpira with Ōmononushi—another name for Ōkuninushi, ruler of all the gods and the hidden world in Hirata's cosmology—Hirata explained the strength of Konpira in the confrontation with the local deity and aligned the power of the most famous miracle-working deity of his time with the apex of his pantheon.

Second, Hirata continued his analysis to confirm the popular identification of Konpira and the twelfth-century emperor Sutoku. Citing a similarity of the specifics of Konpira's revenge and the modus operandi of the vengeful spirit of that emperor—specifically the infliction of burning fevers and the accompaniment of both Sutoku and Konpira by strong, muscular attendants—Hirata asserted that part of Emperor Sutoku's spirit was jointly worshipped with Ōmononushi under the name of Konpira.

Hirata went so far as to repeat that identification in a later addendum to *Tamadasuki* devoted almost entirely to the importance of worshipping and appeasing the spirit of Sutoku in order to obtain respite from the ills of the time.[55] In this addendum, Hirata asserted that Sutoku's imperial spirit was furious at being burdened with the "dirty, Sanskrit name" of "Konpira." He therefore insisted that use of the Indian name be stopped and the joint deity henceforth be called by its "true" name: the Great Deity of Kotohira (Kotohira no Ōkami).[56] Here, Hirata added his own twist, coining a new name, "Kotohira," written with characters that evoked the rituals and myths of the ancient kami: *koto* (a stringed instrument often used to entertain the kami) and *hira* (a flat place, or peace). In this series of moves, Hirata insisted upon the "native" identity of the deity of Mt. Zōzu, both as the creator kami Ōkuninushi and as the most powerful imperial spirit. He proposed that by correcting the degenerate, Buddhist-influenced neglect of the true kami, the people of Japan could avert all famines, droughts, political tensions, and foreign threats. The wonder-working god of Mt. Zōzu—for Hirata as for the thousands of pilgrims who worshipped it each year—could be a powerful force amid the problems of the time.

Indeed, whether they speculated on the "true" identity of Konpira or not—and most people did not—almost everyone agreed that the most important quality of Konpira and other deities was their responsiveness to prayers. On pilgrimage and at home, in print and in performance, worshippers sought the protection of the gods and their miracles. The dramatic rescues recounted on paper, in stone, on stage, and in conversation formed an integral part of the popular culture of the nineteenth century.

Tengu, Kami, and the End of the Tokugawa Shogunate

This culture of gods and miracles shaped both popular and political responses to the deepening crises of the 1850s and 1860s. By the mid-nineteenth century, the political balance of the Tokugawa order—among shogun, daimyo, and imperial court—had changed. In the seventeenth century, the Tokugawa shoguns had enjoyed unparalleled influence due to their recent military victories, extensive domains, and control over mines and foreign trade. With the growth of the market economy, however, the shogunate lost its position of overwhelming dominance, weakened not only by the reduced productivity of its mines and the dwindling profits from a restricted foreign trade, but also by repeated peasant uprisings, famines, and other challenges to shogunal governance. Incursions by foreign ships—sometimes including as many as five a year from England, France, Russia, or the United States—further strained the authority of the shogunate. After long maintaining a strict, exclusionary policy, bakufu leaders found themselves unable to mount a credible defense when shipwrecked whalers seeking coal and supplies gave way to smoking, black gunships demanding treaties and trade.

After Admiral Matthew Perry's arrival in 1853 with an ultimatum for the shogun—to sign a treaty with the United States and open ports for trade—the ensuing debate dramatically highlighted the new balance of power in Japan, with an indecisive shogun and his advisers consulting both major daimyo and the imperial court. The shogunate signed treaties first with the United States, then with other European powers, opening ports to foreign trade and residents, granting to foreigners the right of extraterritoriality, and signing away control over tariffs. In doing so, it incurred the wrath of people terrified of invasion and gave a powerful weapon to its rivals among the daimyo and around the court. The opening of the ports thus fanned into flame a growing antiforeignism that, interpreted in the powerful culture of the gods and their miracles, became fused with both the powerful image of tengu and Hirata's exclusivist emphasis on "native" kami. In the hands of the imperial court, loyalist activists, and Hirata-school nativists throughout the land, the miracle-working tengu and other gods became effective supports for an emperor-centered movement that would not only bring down the Tokugawa shogunate in the Meiji Restoration of 1868 but also revolutionize attitudes toward the gods—including Konpira—throughout Japan.

As evident in the history of Mt. Zōzu, the winged tengu had long been associated with the magical powers of mountain ascetics. In Shikoku, interest in Konpira as one such tengu revived in the nineteenth century as a result of renewed competition for the profits of Konpira worship. The shugenja of Hashikuraji in nearby Awa province, in particular, promoted this image as they tried, after a hiatus of several decades, to circumvent Konkōin's profitable "exclusive shrine" monopoly on the god. In 1835, the priests of Hashikuraji proclaimed their site the "inner temple" (*okunoin*) of Konpira and staged a kaichō of Konpira Daigongen in the village of Nōda—one of the bakufu-owned villages that provided income to Konkōin. In 1844 and 1845, Konkōin sued Hashikuraji for publishing a "false" origin tale and selling "false" amulets, and in 1851 for staging another "false" kaichō—all prominently featuring shugendo rites. These activities of Hashikuraji clearly exerted an important influence on Mt. Zōzu, for this intensification of tengu popularity appeared in donations at the shrine. A bronze lantern donated by a saké brewer in 1848 and inscribed with prayers for healing and saké production, for instance, not only displayed the encircled gold insignia of Konpira but also several images of the feathered fan held by the tengu Kongōbō (figure 5.5).[57]

With Perry's arrival and the signing of the unequal treaties, tengu soon took on more political meanings, as antiforeign loyalists began mobilizing the image of the mountain spirits for their cause. As early as 1855, in the Mito domain, an antiforeign, proimperial faction of the domainal government

❋ 5.5 Bronze lantern donated by a saké brewer in 1848, displaying both the encircled gold symbol (near the top) and the feathered fan held by the tengu Kongōbō (partially visible in the latticework). Inscriptions include prayers for healing and saké production. (Photo by Steve Cantley, with the permission of Kotohira Shrine.)

adopted the name Tengutō (Tengu Party).[58] In 1857, as part of a more concerted use of ritual and the conferral of titles to boost imperial prestige, Emperor Kōmei (r. 1847–66) suddenly granted Konkōin's seventeenth-century
priest-cum-tengu, Yūsei-Kongōbō, the highest rank in the Buddhist hierarchy, *daisōjō* (great archbishop), thereby conferring imperial legitimacy on the
cult of Mt. Zōzu's tengu.[59] Three years later, the priests of Konkōin staged an
impressive kaichō in honor of Kongōbō, building upon that recognition. As
a consequence, several woodblock prints of Mt. Zōzu appeared that boasted
the image of the tengu or its fan, framing a reminder that the mountain had
been designated both an imperial prayer site (*chokugansho*) and the "Exclusive Shrine [of Konpira] in Japan" (figure 5.6).[60] The wonder-working god of
Mt. Zōzu had been linked once again to its powerful tengu, now in alliance
with the imperial court in the struggle against the West.

The vengeful spirit of Emperor Sutoku also shared in this tengu craze, fueled both by its identification as a powerful tengu and by Hirata's connection
of its proper worship to the welfare of the imperial house. By 1866, Emperor
Kōmei was issuing calls to reenshrine Emperor Sutoku's spirit in Kyoto, apparently seeking to appease the powerful spirit in order to protect the court
from epidemics, attacks, and the arrival of the foreigners.

The nativist studies of Hirata Atsutane and others not only laid the
groundwork for renewed worship of Sutoku but also provided a textual rationale for the more general mobilization of tengu against foreign invasion. By
1866, at least one nativist scholar was making the connection between tengu
and protection against barbarians, quoting the first reference to tengu, found
in the *Nihon Shoki,* in which the purported seventh-century emperor Jōmei
saw a shooting star on an expedition to defeat the barbarians in the east. "But
that is not a shooting star," the emperor supposedly said, "that is a *tengu*" (literally a "heavenly fox").[61] An interest in tengu originally fostered by shugenja
thus gained political and scholarly support: nativists, loyalists, and indeed
Emperor Kōmei himself deployed the wild, violent reputation of the tengu in
popular culture within a nativist, imperial, and antiforeign context, skillfully
promoting their cause in connection with a revered object of popular worship.

While a few nativists looked for tengu in the ancient texts, they more often focused on Hirata's broader theories of gods and worship. Throughout
the nineteenth century, Hirata's ideas spread not only at court but among a
growing network of educated proponents around the country. Indeed, the
eventual influence in political circles of Hirata's cosmology and his accompanying program of worship derived in large part from its popularity in the
countryside. While some nativist scholars from outlying regions brought

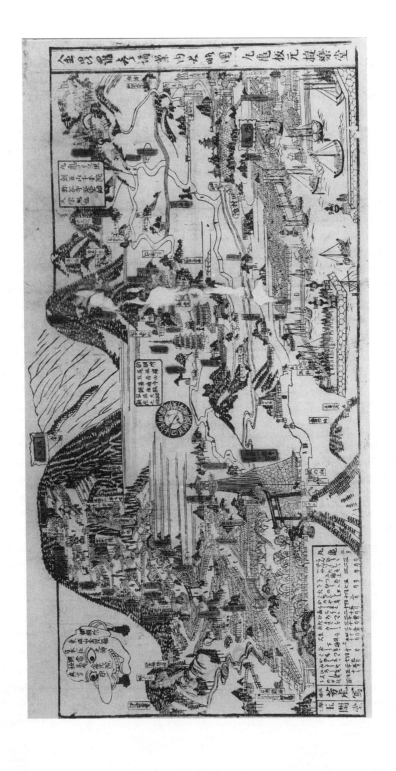

their convictions to the capital, others worked to spread and implement their ideas at home. In Sanuki province, Hirata's theories arrived at Konpira in the 1850s, then spread through formal and informal cultural networks among the hereditary priests and nativist scholars of the Takamatsu domain. The geographical location of Mt. Zōzu amid several unrelated domains assisted in the flourishing of these intellectual developments. While scholars in Takamatsu remained committed to the Confucianism of the Mito school and the more literary pursuits of Motoori Norinaga's nativism, the men of Mt. Zōzu, less integrated into official domainal circles of learning, imported the competing ideas of Hirata Atsutane from neighboring Iyo province.[62]

One of the first recorded adherents of Hirata's thought in Sanuki was the head of the influential Yamashita family at Konpira, Yamashita Moriyoshi, who joined the official Hirata school in Edo, the Ibukinoya, in 1854.[63] Yamashita Moriyoshi maintained ties to family members in the Uwajima domain of nearby Iyo province. It was he who arranged for the younger son of the Uwajima branch of the Yamashita family to be adopted first by the Konpira Yamashitas, then by the aristocratic Amaroji house in Kyoto; the young man then took the Buddhist tonsure at age eleven, became the protégé of the administrative priest of Konkōin, and succeeded to the position of Konkōin head priest in 1857 as the eighteen-year-old priest Yūjō.[64] Yamashita's exposure and commitment to the thought of Hirata Atsutane may have been facilitated by his Iyo connections. The leading first-generation Hirata disciples Yano Harumichi, author of the 1867 proposal for the revival of the ancient Department of Divinity, and Hirata Kanetane, the adopted official heir of Hirata Atsutane and head of the Ibukinoya after Hirata's death in 1843, both came from Niiya, a small but prosperous domain near Uwajima.[65] Yamashita, highly respected locally for his cultural attainments and influential position at Konpira, used his contacts to spread the writings and discuss the ideas of Hirata.[66]

The diary of one prominent nativist scholar in Sanuki, Matsuoka Mitsugi, the hereditary priest of Tawa Hachiman Shrine near Takamatsu and

---

❀ 5.6 (*opposite*) Woodblock print depicting the route from the bustling port of Marugame (*lower right corner*), past Zentsūji with its famous five-story pagoda (*middle*), to Konpira (*left*). Depicting the Tall Lantern beside the torii at the entrance to the town of Konpira, this print can be dated between 1857 and 1868. Its inclusion of the tengu mask in the upper left, framing the announcement that Mt. Zōzu's Konpira is an imperial prayer site and an exclusive shrine, is indicative of the heightened popularity of the image of tengu on Mt. Zōzu and around Japan in the years following the shogunate's opening of ports to foreign trade in 1854. (Haga Tora, *Konpira sankei annai dairyakuzu* [Marugame: Yūrakudō, undated]. Courtesy of the Seto Inland Sea Folk History Museum.)

later a longtime priest on Mt. Zōzu, illustrates the way in which Yamashita Moriyoshi and his cultural network brought new people into contact with Hirata's ideas. Matsuoka, locally renowned for his artistic ability and erudition, was often called upon to identify the artists of scrolls held by prominent families. Shortly after beginning his diary in 1864, he recorded how he inspected a scroll that had been brought to him by a student of Hirata and then entered into "a very long conversation about the Great Man" of the Ibukinoya, that is, Hirata.[67] While working on a commission to make drawings of the treasures of Konkōin between 1862 and 1866, Matsuoka frequently spoke with and borrowed books from Yamashita Moriyoshi, also discussing Hirata's ideas. Matsuoka became a member of the Ibukinoya in 1865 through the introduction of Yamashita Moriyoshi and in turn, during the next six months, sponsored two more of his colleagues and students to join the Ibukinoya.[68] This spurt of inductions into the Ibukinoya reflects the exponential growth of the school after Hirata Atsutane's death, in 1843. Under the leadership of Hirata's adopted son, Kanetane, the school grew from 553 members in that year to at least 1,330 in 1863, and more thereafter.[69]

Yet Matsuoka's diary shows that membership in the Ibukinoya, especially applied for from afar as Matsuoka had done, although confirming an avid interest in nativist scholarship, did not signify full commitment to all of Hirata's teachings. Indeed, while Matsuoka seems to have found particular arguments in Hirata's works compelling before joining the school, he maintained a distance from certain of Hirata's teachings even after his induction into the Ibukinoya.[70] Instead of confirming an unquestioning acceptance of the school's teachings, membership in this formal academic circle seemed more valuable in helping rural intellectuals such as Matsuoka secure access to texts in an age without libraries and public editions. It also provided him with connections in Edo that would lead to later career advancement.

While Matsuoka did not adopt all of Hirata's ideas even after joining the Ibukinoya, he was influenced by Yamashita Moriyoshi's more profound commitment—especially Moriyoshi's high evaluation of Ōkuninushi and the identification of Konpira with that kami. In 1864, for instance, Matsuoka drew an image of Ōkuninushi requested by Yamashita.[71] Shortly after Matsuoka's entry into the Ibukinoya and after one of his visits to Yamashita in 1865, Matsuoka composed a poem about Mt. Zōzu that linked it to the creation of the land by Ōnamuchi (yet another name for Ōkuninushi). He then, for the first time, recorded in his diary a reference to the supposedly indigenous identity of Konpira Daigongen. "It is said," Matsuoka wrote, "that the Daigongen enshrined on this mountain is the kami Ōkuninushi."[72] Comments throughout his diary make it clear that Matsuoka's training—like that of other Sanuki nativists, mainly in the textual tradition of the Motoori school—shaped his relationship to Ōkuninushi and Hirata's ideas. The importance of Hirata's identification of Konpira and Ōkuninushi for Matsuoka and other elites in the Takamatsu domain therefore lay less in Hirata's idiosyncratic portrayal of Ōkuninushi as an omniscient, judging ruler than in his reemphasis of the role of Ōkuninushi in the classic texts identified by Motoori: that is, Ōkuninushi as creator of the land and ruler of the hidden world of the kami.

It was not until 1867 that hints of Hirata's sharp distinction between native deities and foreign, Buddhist, influence appeared in Matsuoka's diary, despite Matsuoka's prominent position in local nativist studies. At a time when the large southwestern domains of Satsuma and Chōshū had already forsaken antiforeignism, engaging in trade and pursuing Western knowledge to support their alliance against the Tokugawa shogunate, nativists argued ever more fervently against foreign influence, agitating for the "pure" native worship of Hirata's gods. For Matsuoka, this emphasis on exclusively native kami, distinct from their Buddhist interpretation, seems to have arisen not directly from Hirata's writings, but indirectly through his involvement in the Jingikō, a group of local notables who espoused the "pure" Shinto of Hirata's nativism.[73] While hitherto Matsuoka had always referred to the institution on Mt. Zōzu as Konpira Daigongen, he first referred to it as Konpira Jingū (Konpira Shrine) after visiting the mountain with other members of the Jingikō in April 1867.[74] From this time on, Matsuoka deliberately eschewed the Buddhist title of Daigongen, referring to the institution not as a temple (*tera* or *in*) but as a shrine to a native kami (*kami no yashiro, jinja,* or *jingū*)—clearly heeding Hirata's exhortation to banish Buddhist terminology from the site. It was through academic or cultural groups such as the Ibukinoya and the Jingikō, then, that Hirata's ideas and influence grew among the educated men of Sanuki, encouraging an adamant antiforeignism focused on the sites of the gods.[75]

Despite the growing influence of Hirata's ideas among Yamashita Moriyoshi and his friends, however, the dissemination of them in the Takamatsu domain, where the lord was closely linked to the Mito school and the shogunate, remained limited to a small segment of the scholarly and cultural elite.[76] Although Yamashita Moriyoshi was an influential administrator on Mt. Zōzu, he did not wear clerical robes. His nephew, the Konkōin head priest Yūjō, and the other ritualists on the mountain apparently did not share Moriyoshi's commitment to nativism: they continued to worship Konpira Daigongen with Shingon rituals regardless of Hirata's insistence on the true, "native" identity of the deity. The fire of the esoteric goma ceremony continued to blacken the feet of the Buddhist guardian image, Fudō, and the large, pointed wooden talismans that commemorated the ceremony continued to attract donations from worshippers eager for contact with the miraculous power of Konpira. An exhibition (kaichō) of the image of Kannon and the statue of the priest-tengu Kongōbō in 1860 drew huge crowds, estimated at thirty or forty thousand people in a single month,[77] demonstrating the continuing importance of both buddhas and tengu on the mountain.

As the leaders of the southwestern Satsuma and Chōshū domains and their allies declared a new government, replacing the Tokugawa in early 1868, the powers of the tengu and Emperor Sutoku still held sway. In spring of that year, Matsuoka reported hearing of a man in Bitchū province (present-day Okayama prefecture) who had been possessed by the spirit of Sutoku, although this time in the form of a Shinto kami.[78] In autumn of the same year, only days after his enthronement, the Meiji emperor carried out his father's last wishes: he ordered the recalling of Emperor Sutoku's banished spirit from Shikoku and its reenshrinement with all honors in the capital itself.[79]

During the loyalist campaign against the Tokugawa shogunate and the early days of the new Meiji regime, both tengu and kami thus rose to the forefront of what remained a complex, overlapping cosmology of miraculous spirits. On Mt. Zōzu, visitors continued to depict the masks of tengu on votive tablets, and people around the country still referred to the deity as Konpira Daigongen. For the vast majority of people, Konpira Daigongen was no more and no less than a powerful and responsive deity, worshipped and petitioned through a mix of any symbols, rituals, or language that seemed effective. After the Meiji Restoration in 1868, however, nativists in the capital and in the countryside would work not only to redefine Konpira but also to reshape the popular culture of the gods. The nativists' efforts, and the actions of priests and worshippers in response, would permanently transform the landscape of the gods throughout Japan.

From Konpira to Kotohira
(1868–1869)

6

Since this autumn, in places throughout Japan, there have been reports that amulets from various provinces have fallen from the sky, including amulets and talismans from [our Mt. Zōzu], wooden statues of kami and buddhas, and even . . . human beings! This is truly a strange situation.

In the sacred domain [of Konpira] as well, on the twenty-fifth day of the eleventh month [20 December 1867], Ise amulets fell at the grain merchant's house in Uchimachi. Since then, amulets not just from Ise but from Konpira too have fallen at various places, as have wooden talismans. By the twenty-eighth day of the last month [22 January 1868], they had fallen at more than fifty houses. . . . At each of those houses, many people gathered and held parties where they celebrated with saké. Then they changed into strange costumes and danced like madmen. Large crowds gathered both on and below the mountain. There have been reports that the same thing happened in nearby provinces and districts.

Since around the middle of the twelfth month, there have been a huge number of these pilgrimages that people call *okagemairi*. Every day, [the town of Konpira] is noisy and crowded, as it is during the festival of the tenth month. This is a situation unseen in previous generations. On the evening of the twenty-second of the twelfth month [16 January 1868], at my house as well, three amulets fell on the northern roof: a wooden talisman of Konpira, a talisman of Kyoto's Gion shrine, and an amulet of Asakusa Kannon in the Eastern Capital. We immediately offered up prayers, prepared sacred saké, and the like. From that night, for the next three days, we celebrated with boisterous dancing.[1]

During the last months of 1867 and the beginning of 1868, as loyalist and Tokugawa forces clashed on the battlefield, administrators of

Konkōin, like the one quoted above, recorded that thousands of people descended on Konpira to celebrate miraculous showers of amulets. The unprecedented rush kept priests busy making, blessing, and selling additional amulets to the pilgrims.

On 8 February 1868, however, the arrival of a runner in Konpira from the lord of the Takamatsu domain banished all other concerns from the administrators' minds. Because of the Takamatsu lord's ties to the Tokugawa house, his Kyoto and Osaka mansions had been confiscated by imperial command, said the runner; the amulet-selling branches of Konpira Daigongen had therefore been closed as well.[2] Thus arrived at Mt. Zōzu the first news of the demise of the old order and its consequences for institutions such as Konpira associated with the shogunate. Soon, the impact of the Meiji coup struck closer to home. Within three days, six hundred soldiers from the domain of Tosa, part of the winning imperial, loyalist coalition, moved into Takamatsu; less than a week later, representatives of the Tosa forces entered the village of Konpira.

In the first months of 1868, the town of Konpira, its residents, its priests, and the god itself thus became caught up in a change of political control that would have far-reaching consequences. On 3 January 1868, a coalition of anti-Tokugawa forces seized control of the imperial palace in Kyoto and announced the end of the Tokugawa shogunate. Combining the political acumen, international experience, and military forces of three large southwestern domains—Satsuma, Chōshū, and Tosa—with the social status, ideological rhetoric, and even religious zeal of select imperial courtiers and nativist activists, the new leaders of what became the Meiji government quickly worked to secure their power.

Thus, in early 1868, after more than two hundred years of peace and stability, Konpira once again faced an invading military force, and once again the troops were from Tosa. As part of the victorious loyalist coalition, Tosa forces, especially the Tosa-led navy (the Kaientai), led the winning forces in Shikoku. Because the Takamatsu domain had fought on behalf of the shogunal forces, an imperial order instructed Tosa to invade.[3] After Takamatsu capitulated without a fight, Kaientai leaders from Tosa moved on to consolidate control over all shogunate lands within Shikoku—territories that, because of the red seal grant, included the income lands of Konkōin.[4] Despite the priests' attempts to prove their jurisdiction and buy leniency by displaying official documents and donating thousands of gold ryō to the occupiers, Konkōin lost control of its shogunate-granted territory to Tosa in March 1868.[5] Konpira's lands—which had included rights to the income of four neighboring villages as well as outright control over the town of Konpira, Mt.

Zōzu, and outposts in the major cities—were thus reduced to Mt. Zōzu and the small town at its foot. Moreover, an occupying military force stood poised to take over the town below, further restricting the jurisdiction of Konkōin to the mountain precincts of the temple itself. In the face of such disinheritance, the priests and administrators on Mt. Zōzu turned to the challenge of ensuring their property, wealth, and social standing—not to mention their survival—through affiliation with the newly ascendant imperial government.

This political, military, and economic upheaval around Mt. Zōzu, as throughout Japan, brought with it an epochal intellectual transformation. For, as the new leaders sought acceptance of their nativist-justified rule, they simultaneously required the repudiation not only of the previous, Tokugawa regime, but of the very patterns of belief that had supported it. In short, they encouraged the conversion of Konpira and other combinatory gods to exclusively nativist kami. Whereas, in previous decades, the kami Konpira had existed within a combination of overlapping intellectual and ritual frameworks—esoteric Buddhism, shugendo, kami worship, Suika Shinto, and folk practices among them—now the state sought to define an exclusive Way of the Kami. During the first year of Meiji, then, as the priests of Konpira Daigongen negotiated within a changing morass of political and economic realities, they also maneuvered among rapidly changing—and, indeed, hardening—definitions of religious traditions. Long having operated within both Buddhist and Shinto idioms, neither of which stood distinctly apart, the priests of Konpira, as they redefined their god once again, helped draw a new boundary between "foreign" buddhas and "native" kami. Out of combinatory, inclusive, esoteric worship, they and their peers around the country forged a newly separate, exclusive, and imperial Way of the Kami: they began the long process of creating modern Shinto.

Ambiguity and Exclusivism

The first inkling of this religious agenda became apparent on Mt. Zōzu within weeks of Tosa's occupation of Konpira. With the new imperial government seeking to displace not only the shogun but also the gods of the Tokugawa regime, the survival strategies of Konkōin would soon require more than legal evidence and bribery: in the nineteenth century, as in the sixteenth and seventeenth, a change of rulers would necessitate a change of gods as well.

On 5 April 1868, the increasingly confident national leaders embarked on a series of changes in policy that would fundamentally alter the relationship of worship to the state. First, they declared an intimate link between worship of kami and the imperial state. The agenda of the nativists triumphed as the new leaders declared that they would "restore the system of unity of rites and rule (*saisei itchi*)" and revive the ancient Office of Rites (Jingikan). Accordingly, shrines to kami would no longer be subject to the private authority of the shogunate-approved Yoshida school; they would instead be brought under the jurisdiction of the Office of Rites. Hereditary succession would cease: all priests of kami would be attached to the Office of Rites and would henceforth require approval from the ministry for changes in rank and other actions.[6] While Konpira Daigongen, affiliated as it was with a Shingon Buddhist denomination, was not immediately affected, the new leaders had announced the most recent ideological preference of the state. The battle lines of sacred legitimization had been drawn.

Soon, however, it became clear that the new government did not espouse merely a new emphasis on kami instead of buddhas. Instead, erasing entire fields of practice, the rulers attacked the very combinatory nature of worship that had characterized the prayers and petitions not only of the Tokugawa family (including, for instance, the enshrinement of Tokugawa Ieyasu at Nikkō as Tōshō Daigongen) but of the majority of people for the last thousand years. No longer would they recognize kami—in the form of avatars—as existing within a Buddhist framework. Instead, following the interpretation of Hirata Atsutane and other nativists, they designated kami as exclusively "native" gods.

This attack appeared in a series of edicts dubbed the "separation of kami and buddhas" (*shinbutsu bunri*). The first edict, on 9 April 1868, proclaimed that no combinatory priests (*bettō* or *shasō*) could serve at shrines of the kami: they must shed their Buddhist robes, turn in their Buddhist ranks, and await new appointment as officially recognized priests of the now exclusively Shinto kami. On 20 April, the status of Konpira came explicitly into question with the second "separation" edict, which forbade both reference to kami using Buddhist titles like *gongen* (avatar or manifestation of a buddha), as in Konpira Daigongen, and the enshrining of Buddhist images in kami institutions.[7] Priests at sites of kami or gongen were ordered to renounce their Buddhist identity. In effect, all sites of kami worship, in whatever form, were to be reconfigured as "shrines" (*kami no yashiro, jinja*) to "indigenous" deities using the supposedly pure, ancient nomenclature and ritual approved by nativist scholars. At the same time, all sites of deities deemed "Buddhist"—shrines to the buddhas Śākyamuni or Amida, for instance, or to the bodhisattva Kannon—would be stripped of subsidiary shrines to kami, thereby becoming exclusive "temples" (*tera, -ji*) of the foreign religion.

If Buddhism, according to nativists, posed such a threat of contamination, then why did the government allow it to exist? The main reason was expediency: Buddhist deities and institutions commanded the devotion of vast numbers of people, and Buddhist priests performed almost all funerary rituals throughout Japan. Yet a split within nativist ranks also played a part. Just as two groups of Buddhists had vied to provide the ideological and ritual framework for the Tokugawa shogunate in the seventeenth century, so now two factions of nativists competed to shape the intellectual and symbolic order of the Meiji regime. Followers of the Hirata school, such as Hirata Kanetane and Yano Harumichi, envisioned purified shrines and sanctified government in the service of the gods. By April 1868, however, Hirata and Yano had been ousted from their positions in the Office of Rites; they no longer shaped state policy toward kami and shrines. Instead, the former daimyo of the Tsuwano domain and his leading nativist scholar, Fukuba Bisei, dominated the scene. The samurai Fukuba, a student of Ōkuni Takamasa (who himself had once studied under Hirata Atsutane), focused more on the visible world of politics than on the hidden world of the gods. Under the leadership of Fukuba and his lord from 1869 to 1872—first in the Office of Rites, then in the Department of Divinity, and finally in the Ministry of Doctrine—the ritual policies of the state would focus not on eradicating Buddhism but instead on exalting the emperor, Amaterasu, and the sacred legitimacy of the imperial line.[8] According to these advocates of the Ōkuni school of nativism, as long as Buddhist priests and institutions contributed to the stability of the emperor-centered Meiji regime, respecting the supremacy of the "pure, native" kami of the ancient texts and their association with the imperial house, then a separate Buddhism, distinct from nativist Shinto, fulfilled an important role. Nevertheless, under nativist supervision, even the most prominent, now unequivocally Buddhist, priests and institutions would be banned from privileged status in the Meiji order for their affiliation with the "foreign" deities dominant during years of shogunal rule.

The leaders of the new ruling clique thus created a set of standards to which the priests of Konpira and other combinatory institutions would be forced to conform if the loyalists successfully stayed in power. As part of their demand for unequivocal, exclusivist dedication to the new government, the Meiji rulers required an absolute distinction between kami and buddhas. What the separation edicts portrayed as merely a matter of ritual required, in effect, an explicit repudiation of the previous political and religious order: the enshrinement of "purified" kami signaled adherence to the new government alone.

The rulers thus translated their political claims of imperial jurisdiction over all of Japan into exclusivist ritual claims governing all sites of worship. In doing so, they attacked the ambiguities of both the multiple allegiances of the shogunal order and the all-encompassing intricacies of esoteric Buddhist practices and teachings. They attacked the ambiguity that allowed priests of protective kami to coexist with priests of larger, more powerful temples in the same combinatory institutions, and priests of protective buddhas to serve likewise at the shrines of prominent kami—all within a shared, Buddhist framework. The new rulers especially attacked the ambiguity that, in many ways, brought so many people together at pilgrimage sites such as Mt. Zōzu. Until 1868, worshippers could come to the god whether they envisioned it as a tengu, a kami, a gongen, or a combination of all three. The buildings, priests, and rites at the site carefully supported all three interpretations. After 1868, while in fact many people continued to interpret the god in these multiple ways, the new rulers initiated a battle between exclusivist nativism and ambiguous esotericism. The outcome of that battle would rely in large part on the response of the priests of those institutions, who frequently used the new, national initiatives to further more personal agendas closer to home.

At many sacred sites, priests embraced the government's strong distinction between "native" kami and "foreign" buddhas. Several Shinto and nativist priests of shrines to protective kami, hitherto subservient to the more powerful Buddhist temples within whose precincts they worked, seized the opportunity to avenge centuries of perceived subjugation: they and their allies declared their entire site a shrine to a native kami, burned Buddhist images, and even chased their Buddhist competitors out of the sacred precincts.[9] In an attempt to rally against such attacks, the nativists' victims increasingly identified themselves as exclusively Buddhist, facilitating the government's effort to draw a line between what had hitherto been interrelated parts of an integrated, esoteric ritual order.[10]

While, elsewhere, rival ritualists wielded kami against buddhas in a contest for control, on Mt. Zōzu such rivals struggled to define the main focal point of all the priests' attentions: Konpira. Not only the head subtemple, Konkōin, but its administrative subtemples as well performed rituals to the avatar, albeit sometimes, as at the subtemple Tamon'in, with more emphasis on its shugendo affiliation with the esoteric Fudō Myōō. It is unclear to what extent the priests of these administrative subtemples, especially Tamon'in and Fumon'in, threatened Konkōin's dominance on Mt. Zōzu in the final years of Tokugawa rule. Ensuing events provide hints of substantial divisions between some of these subtemple priests and Konkōin that later manifested themselves in a struggle for power over the god and its site.[11] But the apparent solidity of Konkōin's hold on administrative affairs in 1868 suggests that the primary context of the institutional struggles prompted by the separation edicts was less internal than external. In the early years of the Meiji period, any tension between Konkōin and the other subtemples on Mt. Zōzu remained secondary to the strategic maneuvers of Konkōin that shaped the future of the mountain complex as a whole.

At Konpira, three groups waged a struggle for control: Konkōin; the new central government, in particular the Office of Rites and its successors; and the military and civil government of the Tosa occupiers. During the first few years of the Meiji period, Konkōin's head priest—Yamashita Moriyoshi's nephew Yūjō—politicked frantically in the capital among court, nativist and government circles. He worked toward two ends: first, to ensure his own continued control over the mountain and its profits; and second, to ensure the wealth of the mountain by confirming its imperial status under the new order. Unfortunately, these economic and political imperatives came into conflict. The wealth of the pilgrimage relied in many ways on the ambiguity of the god, yet politics required exclusivism. In the ensuing months and years, Yūjō fought—first in vain and, finally, with some success—to combine both.

Yūjō first reacted to the separation edicts by attempting to forestall any change at all, by buying an exception to the new laws through large donations to the new government's coffers and, it seems, by reasserting the convenient ambiguity of Konpira Daigongen as both a kami and a gongen.[12] Such equivocation, however, was no longer feasible in the political context of the times. Yūjō was forced to choose between two options: a commitment to his existing Buddhist affiliation that would place Konpira at odds with prevailing nativist trends in the central government, making the site unlikely to receive favorable treatment from the government and possibly stripping him of his home and livelihood, or a conversion to the exclusive worship of nativist kami, through which advancement under the new regime would become possible.

Caught between news of violent attacks on prominent Buddhist and combinatory institutions elsewhere and the nativist urgings of his uncle, Yamashita Moriyoshi, as well as those of his adoptive family at court, the twenty-eight-year-old Yūjō quickly concluded that only his formal conversion to nativist rites and identity would allow the continuation of Konpira's profitable association with the state. Later Buddhist accounts, seeking to portray his capitulation as the result of trickery or personal weakness instead of logically reasoned intention, asserted that Yūjō was harangued, forced to eat meat, and lectured on the imminent destruction of all temples until he caved in.[13] Whatever the details of the case, Yūjō's concern for institutional survival and prestige triumphed over his commitment to the Buddhist pantheon. The young priest apparently could not envision his role at a Konpira severed from both imperial favor and the Tokugawa-granted income lands that his predecessors had obtained two centuries before.

For similar reasons of survival and status, other priests at combinatory sites throughout Japan likewise chose to adopt rites to the nativist kami, though few as quickly as Yūjō. Indeed, in this wider context, Yūjō's conversion was not as drastic as it seemed. Although the priests of Konkōin, including Yūjō, had distanced themselves from shugendo practices for years, Konpira was still affiliated with an officially recognized shugendo lineage. Focusing as they did on prayer and practice, and only tangentially concerned with the details of Buddhist doctrine, many mountain ascetics at sites designated as shrines to the kami adopted Shinto robes and office in 1868 and 1869. Indeed, the headquarters of the Tōzan shugendo lineage went so far in the tenth month of 1868 (four months after Yūjō's dilemma) as to instruct its members who served at shrines nationwide to adopt a Shinto identity, five years before shugendo was outlawed and its lineages forced to affiliate with Buddhist denominations.

When Yūjō submitted his formal response to the separation edicts on 2 August 1868, then, he redefined Konpira and himself in exclusive, nativist terms. At the same time, he requested confirmation of the special status of both. Catering to the nativists and imperial loyalists then in charge of religious affairs in the capital, Yūjō borrowed from Hirata Atsutane's *Tamadasuki* to identify Konpira as the kami Kotohira: a joint enshrinement of the deity Ōmononushi (Ōkuninushi) and the spirit of the retired emperor Sutoku on Mt. Kotohira (not Mt. Zōzu).[14] Yūjō did, however, make one very significant alteration—in effect, a claim for the continuation of profitable ambiguity. Although committed to pronouncing the true name of the deity as "Kotohira," he changed Hirata's writing of the name so that it approximated as closely as possible the writing of "Konpira." Thus, not only did the written name of the god retain the initial character for gold, which symbolized money and, when placed within a circle, formed the official seal of Konkōin, but also, when written vertically with its characters pressed close together, the new name would look like a simplified variation of the name Konpira (figure 6.1). While Yūjō obtained government approval of a new name for the shrine, Kotohiragū (Kotohira Shrine), in popular usage both deity and shrine continued to be called variations of Konpira or Konpira Daigongen and are still so called today.[15]

Upon identifying Konpira as a nativist kami, Yūjō of necessity shed his Buddhist robes and took a secular name, Kotooka Hirotsune. In doing so, he retained the Chinese characters of his Buddhist name, Yūjō, read now in "native" pronunciation as "Hirotsune," and adopted as his family name, Kotooka, a toponym for Konpira associated with the hypothetical status of the mountain as an imperial mausoleum.[16] Yūjō (hereafter referred to as Koa.

b.

c.

d.

❀ **6.1** The ambiguity of Kotooka Hirotsune's proposed orthography for "Kotohira" is clear when the original writing of "Konpira" (*b*) is placed alongside Kotooka's proposed "Kotohira" (*d*). The version in the middle (*c*) frequently appeared on woodblock prints in the Meiji era, compressing *d* to look like an abbreviated form of *b*, thereby encouraging people to read "Kotohira" as the original "Konpira." All of these orthographies, unlike the original "Kotohira" proposed by Hirata Atsutane, retain the character for gold integral to the encircled gold symbol of the site (*a*).

tooka) further emphasized to the Office of Rites the purportedly Shinto nature of observances on the mountain (especially the use of the portable shrine instituted under the influence of Suika Shinto in 1712), the long-standing role of the deity in praying for the safety and prosperity of the realm, and his own personal donation in 1868 of ten thousand ryō to the new government to defray the military expenses of the Restoration. In return, he requested imperial reiteration of Konpira's status as a "shrine for imperial prayer" (*choku-sai no yashiro*) and his own appointment as head priest (*daigūji*).[17] In this way, Kotooka attempted both to confirm his own control over the mountain under the new regime and to renew the shrine's profitable institutional ties with the central government. Without committing to any substantial changes in practice on the mountain, he acceded to the nativist naming required by the state, while preserving old ambiguities in ritual and, indeed, creating new ambiguities in writing. Acknowledging the exclusive claims of the new regime, the priest of the renamed Kotohira Shrine nevertheless hedged his bets, working to maintain the attractions that formed the basis of pilgrimage and, thus, the wealth of the shrine.

A Civil Government

While Kotooka negotiated in the capital, events at home threatened his position from a different quarter. Three weeks after Kotooka changed his name, on 20 August 1868 (Keiō 4.7.3), Tosa administrators moved into Konpira, set up office in the middle of town, and declared the town to be under Tosa control.[18] Despite Kotooka's efforts, therefore, not only had the newly converted priest lost Konkōin's income lands to the invaders, but Tosa forces had wrested away control of Konpira town as well, leaving Kotooka, formerly the primary authority in the area, in charge of only the mountain precincts.

The troops of Tosa, representing the new central leaders, set in motion at Konpira a drastic diminution in religious authority, which characterized the seizure of power by the fledgling government throughout the early years of Meiji. As the new leaders established new structures of civil administration, they stripped shrines and temples of all but their innermost precincts. In doing so, they legally transformed Konpira, like other towns, from a domain of the gods, ruled by the priests, to an administrative jurisdiction like all others, with priests simply staffing a shrine in its midst. Thus, as Kotooka bowed to nativist pressure in order to maintain his domain, that very domain shrank dramatically; overrun by the political and fiscal needs of the new government, the authority of priests over their populations gave way to an increasingly regularized, national civil administration.

In 1868, however, such nationwide coordination remained in the future. Indeed, although Tosa was nominally acting on behalf of the imperial government (occupying a role akin to the former shogunate), both the troops themselves and the people of Konpira saw the occupiers as forces of the Tosa domain, not of the emperor. Leaders of the Tosa forces referred occasionally to their mandate from the imperial government, but in Konpira, as elsewhere in Sanuki province, they issued all proclamations from "the Tosa domain" or "the Tosa occupying headquarters."[19] The retainers of Konkōin likewise referred to occupying administrators as Tosa officials, rarely if ever as representatives of or proxies for the emperor.[20]

This emphasis on Tosa in lieu of the imperial government reflected the di-

vided jurisdictions of the Tokugawa order, in which the lord of each domain—whether civil or religious—ruled his own people on his own land, albeit within a general framework shared by all. Because of this structure, the
coalition that overthrew the Tokugawa shogunate was less a united, centralized force than a loosely affiliated group of virtually independent domains.
Their troops had acted independently during the military campaign and continued to do so during the aftermath and consolidation of the victory. Moreover, in the large domain of Tosa, at least, much of the "national" consciousness of the Tokugawa period focused not on the larger archipelago but on
domains and provinces.[21] Although the occupiers of Takamatsu and Konpira
may indeed have been dedicated imperial loyalists, they enjoyed official rank
within Tosa and identified themselves with the source of their intimidating
power, the Tosa domain.

In Konpira, the very real threat that the occupiers posed to the administrative power of Konkōin was compounded in the eyes of residents by historical resonances with the legend of that early Tosa warlord, Chōsokabe
Motochika. Like Chōsokabe in the 1580s, Tosa troops in 1868 held at least
nominal control of the entire island of Shikoku—even though this time
through an imperial mandate to control lands loyal to the shogunate instead
of through unilateral invasion directly from Tosa. By the early nineteenth
century, storytellers had reinterpreted the legacy of the Tosa warlord to advertise the profitable, miraculous powers of the deity while warning rulers
against interfering with the power of Konpira's priests. First appearing in
print in the early nineteenth-century travel guide *Konpirasan meisho zue,*
where it was recorded as local legend, the dramatically elaborated story was
afterward repeated in numerous guidebooks and collections of miracle tales:

> Long ago, when Chōsokabe Motochika, the lord of Tosa, invaded and destroyed the
> province [of Sanuki], he intended to burn down [Mt. Zōzu] as well. When he set fire to
> the main gate, though, a strange thing happened. Suddenly, a great wind blew up, and
> from the top of the mountain, a horde of hornets descended upon the warriors and
> stung them. From the great general on down, no one was able to proceed a single step.
> At this, Motochika was immediately overcome with remorse. He made a vow to level the
> ground and build the Nitenmon gate in a single night. Since this was done so quickly,
> however, the carpenters and builders made a mistake, erecting one pillar of the gate up-
> side down. From that time on, the gate has been called the Gate of the Upside-Down
> Tree [Sakaki no Mon].[22]

The drama of the story of Chōsokabe's gate effectively recast the Tosa warlord
as an enemy of the deity, transforming the gate from the symbol of a power-

ful rival of mainland control into evidence of violent occupation met by the revenge and triumph of a wrathful deity in the form of a swarm of hornets. Thus, the actions of the Tosa occupiers in 1868, magnified by the legend of the disrespectful Chōsokabe before them, seemed a dramatic assault, showing little or no reverence for the deity and focusing more on civil control and administration. Although not setting out to destroy the mountain entirely, the Tosa troops did enforce the stripping of income lands from Konkōin and encroached upon the other basis of the shrine's political status—its control over the town.

Led by Yagi Hikosaburō, a prominent officer of the recently disbanded Tosa navy, the Tosa occupiers consistently undermined the authority of Konkōin and aimed to disrupt the local hereditary status order. An enthusiastic promoter of the idea of government by merit, the loyalist Yagi instituted reforms even before orders were issued from the capital. Thus, two of Yagi's first actions were to consult townspeople about administrative policy and budgets and to set out a petition box for residents to submit their ideas for the new town leadership.[23] Both of these actions blatantly challenged the governing and tax-collecting authority of Konkōin. Yagi's radical policies continued in direct contradiction to the status politics espoused by the priests, breaking the symbolic and, indeed, political dominance of the hereditary families of village officials. Even before such policies issued from the new, Meiji rulers, Yagi and his officers banned the wearing of swords and permitted the use of surnames by all residents (not just the elites); they hired townspeople as patrol officers and gave all people in the town a chance at public office.[24]

Under Yagi, control of the town shifted away from Konkōin and its hereditary allies into the hands of businessmen and civil administrators. This transfer of power became clear in the management of the tax on prostitution income. Before 1868, Konkōin collected a tax on the income of the town's many teahouses, where female entertainers and prostitutes worked, placing the money in a reserve fund meant to supplement budgetary shortfalls or to sponsor theatrical entertainments designed to attract pilgrims. When the town of Konpira passed into Tosa's control, Yagi confiscated this fund, asserting that its five thousand ryō belonged to the town, not the shrine. Based on consultation with representatives from the town, he used this money for repair of small local shrines and temples below Mt. Zōzu, as well as for dikes, roads, bridges, and—whether as a matter of sound economic policy or, as the shrine asserted, as a side effect of profligate carousing—the promotion of the entertainment businesses.[25] From this time on, representatives of the townspeople and eventually the brothel owners who provided the funds decided jointly on their use. No longer did the mountain administrators determine plans for the prosperity of the town. Strategies for promotion of tourism and the like ultimately became a matter for an independent town government to decide.

As a consequence, at the same time that the identity and status of Kotooka and his subordinates were threatened at court, their administrative control and tax-collecting power were challenged by the Tosa occupation at home. This lent further impetus to Kotooka's political efforts in the capital. He redoubled his attempts to cultivate ties with the central government and obtain confirmation of his control over both the shrine and the town. Yet, while Kotooka sought to maintain his old civil, as well as religious, authority, the new Meiji leaders were more interested in bringing all land and taxes under central control. Moreover, they worked to increase government influence not just over land and population, but over the shrine as well. It was unlikely that the leaders of the fledgling imperial government would relinquish any of their newfound power to a former Buddhist priest such as Kotooka.

Kotooka, like the many others who knew only the Tokugawa-era political order of autonomous domains, failed to predict the centralizing juggernaut that would characterize the new government. He therefore worked repeatedly to prove his dedication to the new regime in an attempt to regain the status, and therefore the autonomy, that he and his institution had previously enjoyed. Concentrating in turn on the shrine, on his own official rank, and on his jurisdiction, Kotooka pursued a strategy that, under the previous regime, should have ensured his autonomy. Over the early months and years of Meiji, however, the leaders of the new imperial order significantly modified the structures of the Tokugawa regime, time after time rewarding Kotooka's efforts with unintended consequences. The quest for status, successful in name, would not save Kotooka and Kotohira Shrine from state intervention; on the contrary, it would increasingly subordinate them to the centralizing state.

Oblivious to the ironies of the future, however, Kotooka—now presiding over a shrine to a native creator deity and imperial spirit—renewed his attempts to retain, or regain, Konpira's earlier, privileged position. By relabeling the mountain complex a shrine to a kami (*jinja*) in August 1868, Kotooka thought he had succeeded in securing at least part of his previous authority under the protection of the central government, since the declaration of unity of rites and rule (*saisei itchi*) had placed all shrines under the jurisdiction of the Office of Rites. By the time Tosa troops established themselves in Konpira, however, state policy had changed: all shrines would now fall under the control of their local domains and prefectures—in Konpira's case, Tosa. Exceptions to this rule would be granted only to imperial worship shrines (*chokusaisha*).[26] On 28 September 1868, then, Kotooka focused more narrowly on the shrine, postponing the struggle for jurisdiction over the town. He reiterated his earlier petition that Kotohira Shrine be designated an imperial worship shrine.[27] One month later, the Office of Rites accepted Kotooka's request and permitted the shrine to erect a large sign proclaiming its imperial status.[28] It was through Kotooka's successful campaign, then, that Kotohira was brought to the attention and placed under the control of the Office of Rites, becoming one of the first shrines incorporated into the ritual policies of the central government.[29]

Kotooka's successful petition for the shrine did not necessarily translate into success for himself. Under the Meiji regime, as under the Tokugawa, higher-level priests received their rank only upon confirmation by the government. Thus, at the same time that he waged his campaign to raise the status of Kotohira Shrine, Kotooka pursued a variety of strategies in an attempt to obtain the title of head priest (*daigūji*) as well. He appealed to government nativists by joining the official Hirata school and giving funds to support the publication of Hirata Atsutane's *Koshiden*.[30] He submitted petitions emphasizing both Kotohira's enshrinement of the retired emperor Sutoku and his own former high Buddhist rank.[31] He paid visits to aristocratic relatives in Kyoto who arranged his initiation into the sacerdotal Shinto Shirakawa lineage.[32] In Kyoto, he also studied ritual at the Kasuga Shrine, learning the music and dance traditions of Shinto worship.[33] As a result of his imperial connections and advancement within the world of Shinto ritual, Kotooka received a court status to replace his Buddhist rank and was appointed *shamushoku* (shrine officer) of Kotohira Shrine by the Office of Rites on 1 November 1868, less than a year after the Meiji coup. Although he did not hold the top position at the shrine, no one was appointed to take office above him at Kotohira for the following four years. Kotooka repeatedly petitioned for advancement to a higher rank, donating thousands of additional ryō to the government and continuing his Shinto training, but he was not promoted.[34] Instead, the Office of Rites restated its decision that Kotooka and the officials below him at Kotohira fell under its control.[35]

Kotooka's concerns over the loss to Tosa of his civil authority—whether pertaining to town government, tax collection, or the appointment of civil administrators (jobs heretofore held by hereditary employees loyal to Kotooka)—only intensified his pursuit of close ties with the central government. They also prompted him to undertake a limited, but proactive, conversion to Shinto ritual and nomenclature at the shrine. As Tosa control over the village of Konpira tightened, Kotooka attempted to parlay the new impe-

rial status of the shrine into permission for him to return home and personally take over government of the village from Tosa officials. In the first of two
petitions submitted to the official in charge of shrine affairs (*jingiyaku*) on 5
December 1868 (Meiji 1.10.22), Kotooka summarized the administrative
situation as follows: "After their appointment [by the new government] to
pacify the shogunal lands in Iyo and Sanuki, Yagi Hikosaburō, Katsurai Hay-
ata, and six or seven other men from Tosa, calling themselves the Kaientai,
came to the kami's domain of Konpira to pacify it. They have established a
military station, overseen the government of the people, and managed the actions of the townspeople and officials." Because of this, he continued, Kotooka requested permission to return home.[36] In the second petition, reiterating the imperially sanctioned status of the shrine, Kotooka committed
himself to establishing new, nativist, Shinto-style rituals and in return sought
permission to control personally "the promotion and dismissal of the laicized
men and all employees, not to mention the government of farmers and merchants and tax collection in the kami's domain."[37]

Kotooka's petitions backfired. In early 1869, after the town and surrounding area had come firmly under the civil authority of Tosa, Kotooka was
finally permitted to return to Sanuki to resume active control, but only of the
circumscribed religious sphere of the mountain itself. He was, however, still
held to his commitment to execute a full conversion of the site.[38] Through
the pressure of the Tosa occupation, Kotooka had been driven into ever further acceptance of nativist, Shinto rhetoric, nevertheless losing the domain
over which he had ruled. Indeed, the military strength of the new regime
helped wrest away the authority of all priests—whether "Shinto" or "Buddhist"—confiscating their sacred domains and confining them to reduced
shrine precincts within larger civil jurisdictions. Not only had "Shinto" been
separated from "Buddhism," but the gods in general had been physically and
legally fenced off from the realm of everyday life.

Translation to Shinto

From the day of his name change and retirement from the Buddhist priesthood, Kotooka dedicated himself to making an outward show of commitment to nativist Shinto for the benefit of powerholders in the capital. Significantly, however, he avoided making irrevocable changes on the mountain
itself, leaving open the possibility of returning to previous, combinatory
practices. Instead of restructuring worship and the gods entirely—a move
that might have been expected in a concerted effort to wipe out combinatory
worship—Kotooka simply translated the names of deities from a Buddhist

idiom into a nativist one. In doing so, as he had with the characters of the god's name, he preserved the content of the pilgrimage site for worshippers to interpret as they pleased. Thus, the former Ten Thousand Lights Hall partway up the steps was renamed for the creator kami of fire (Homusubi no Mikoto), the old sutra storehouse became an archive, and the former Gyōja Hall, commemorating the archetypal mountain ascetic, En no Ozunu (also known as En no Gyōja), was renamed Great Peak Shrine (Ōmine Yashiro).

Other changes were more significant. The imposing Gold Hall (Kondō), splendidly built from 1812 to 1845 to house an image of the buddha Yakushi, was renamed the Dawn Shrine (Asahi Yashiro); its image of the Medicine Master gave way to the three imperially connected kami of Ise, Hachiman, and Kasuga. Likewise, Kotooka removed the bell from the bell tower just inside Chōsokabe's Upside-Down Gate. He designated the now bare platform as a place to worship Ise Shrine, the pinnacle of imperial worship, from afar. He renamed the two small shrines on the approach closest to the main shrine, as well as the deities enshrined within them, to reflect the order of the classic myths: first came the ultimate creator deity of Motoori's interpretation of the *Kojiki,* Takami Musubi no Kami; then, at the top, came the Eternity Shrine (Tokiwa Jinja), dedicated to Izanagi and Izanami, the two deities credited with creating the Japanese archipelago. Finally, in the main shrine, Kotooka identified the Great Kami Kotohira as a joint enshrinement of Ōmononushi, the creator deity and lord of all things mysterious and unseen, and the powerful, threatening spirit of Emperor Sutoku.[39]

It is unclear whether these early changes went beyond the paper they were written on. The shrine publicized the new names in printed guides and illustrations, available for display to men in the capital and a few public readers, but there is no evidence that they were so labeled on the site. Neither did the new publications provide any explanations of the new names or deities: several early Meiji prints merely erased the old names and inserted the new ones.[40] More tangible changes were slower to arrive. At the time he announced the new shrine names to the government in 1868, Kotooka promised to replace the Buddhist guardian images in the main front gate with Shinto kami.[41] Yet at least four months after the ostensible change, the statues remained the same as before.[42]

By April 1869, Kotooka's pursuit of Shinto credentials committed him to the implementation of more concrete alterations. When he was finally permitted to resume active control of Kotohira Shrine, Kotooka brought with him to the mountain a Hirata-school ritualist and member of the Shirakawa Shinto sacerdotal lineage, Furukawa Mitsuru, to direct the Shinto conversion of the main shrine. The day after Furukawa's arrival, official worship at the main shrine was converted to Shinto ritual, probably entailing the removal of a carved Buddhist image of Konpira Daigongen and the installation of a new worship object (*shintai,* literally "god-body"; in this case, a mirror). Furukawa and the now Shinto priests of Kotohira performed purification rituals and decorated each worship hall with the folded, white paper decorations (*gohei*) that now defined the buildings as Shinto. The pointed, wooden talismans for the goma ceremony, bearing the Sanskrit seed syllable of Fudō Myōō, disappeared; new, squared-off Shinto talismans prominently bore the name of Kotohira Shrine instead (figure 6.2).[43] In July 1870, the most obvious architectural alteration occurred when the pagoda—symbolizing the enshrinement of the Buddha's remains—was finally torn down.[44]

Furukawa implemented reforms of both the buildings and their ritual performances. In later years, Kotohira Shrine asserted that the site had historically been Shinto, saying that in the early Meiji period, "there were very few changes: festivals and ceremonies have remained practically the same until today."[45] This was clearly a misrepresentation. Not only had the external expert Furukawa instructed employees in elaborate Shinto dances (*kagura*) to perform for the deities, but the esoteric goma ritual to Fudō Myōō was abolished, and the entire landscape of the mountain was converted from the Shingon and shugendo worship of combinatory deities to the enshrinement of imperial and purportedly historical creator gods in their place. Moreover, two weeks after Furukawa's arrival, Kotooka dismissed all ordained Buddhist priests on Mt. Zōzu, and they either returned to lay life and were reappointed as Shinto officiants, left the mountain to establish temples in the town below (as did Fumon'in), or moved elsewhere. Evidently the changes in 1869 were significant enough to prevent the shugenja and other Buddhists from performing their accustomed roles on the mountain.

By the end of 1869, a perceptive traveler could discern the Shinto nature of the shrine. The Confucian-educated writer Narushima Ryūhoku, whose proimperial sentiments and prominence as a former lecturer to the Tokugawa shogun probably earned him an audience with the converted Kotooka Hirotsune and heightened his sensitivity to the ritual changes on the mountain, described his impressions of the shrine grounds in 1869:

> On left and right are stone lanterns donated to this shrine by people from every province: too many of them to count. I was surprised at the great numbers of them, with some dozens of stone lanterns donated reverently by generations of Takamatsu lords. The "Second Gate," built by Chōsokabe Motochika of Tosa in the Tenshō era (1573–92), is beautifully aged.
>
> There are many small shrines here and there up to the main shrine—the shrine of

✿ **6.2** Talismans from Konkōin (*left*) and Kotohira Shrine (*right*). At the top of the talisman from "Mt. Zōzu Konkōin" is the Sanskrit seed syllable for Fudō Myōō under the pointed top reminiscent of Fudō Myōō's sharp sword of enlightenment. The inscription commemorates prayers for household safety in the seventeen-day goma ceremony to Fudō Myōō, dated "an auspicious day in the first month of the third year of Kōka [1846]." The talisman from Kotohira Shrine is rectangular, with the name of the shrine at the top. It commemorates "two nights and three days" of prayers for the cure of an illness, dated "an auspicious day in September 1881." (Photo by Steve Cantley, with the permission of Kotohira Shrine.)

Homusubi no Mikoto, the Dawn Shrine (the three deities of Ise, Hachiman and Kasuga), Tsushima Shrine, the shrine of Susano'o no Mikoto Hiko (Kotoshiro Nushi), the shrine of Daigyōji (Takami Musubi no Mikoto), the Eternity Shrine (the two deities Izanagi and Izanami), the shrine of the young bride (Suseri Hime no Mikoto), the shrine of the mountain kami (celebrating Ōyamasumi)—all of which are in front of and behind the main shrine. I don't have time to record the other ones.

On the right is Konkōin, which sells amulets. The Buddhist priest has converted and is now a Shintoist. He has also changed his name from Konkōin to Kotooka, fifth rank.[46]

Although the administrative offices (as opposed to the priest) retained the name of Konkōin, for those visitors who paid attention, the mountain contained an entire new cosmology of kami and creation.

After two years of titular and ritual changes designed to prove his dedicated implementation of the nativist agenda, Kotooka finally achieved limited success in his quest for government-recognized authority. With his jurisdiction restricted to the shrine itself and no longer including any of the villages and lands that had supported his earlier position,[47] Kotooka was confirmed as the highest-ranking (but not officially the head) priest at the shrine. Between March and July 1869, with the approval of the Office of Rites, he gave 339 of his administrators and other employees Shinto occupational titles.[48] At the end of 1869, the Tosa protectorate was lifted, and the village of Konpira came under the jurisdiction of the newly created Kurashiki prefecture. Kotooka's maneuvers had been partially successful: although without the head priestship and therefore without a guarantee that his authority would last, he had been given permission to carry out orders from the central government on his own and had succeeded in evading permanent subordination to Tosa. The Tosa military leaders still held power in the town, but they were now nominally under the civil jurisdiction of Kurashiki prefecture and could not act unilaterally as before.

There is evidence that throughout the first four years of the Meiji era, Kotooka and the other men on the mountain viewed the policy of Shinto conversion as a potentially temporary measure, retaining the option to restore the old deities and rituals if the political scene changed once again. According to later testimony by Buddhist priests and sympathizers, Kotooka purportedly coordinated with still-Buddhist priests to maintain Buddhist practice—first on the mountain, and then, when that became impossible (probably around the time of Furukawa's arrival), below in the town. When the ritualist Furukawa arrived, the leaders on Mt. Zōzu locked away many of the Buddhist images, ritual implements, and sutras. They either anticipated a chance to use them again or, as the successors of the subtemple Fumon'in asserted, planned to hand them over to the priest of Fumon'in, who had not renounced his Buddhist office.[49] The only irreversible change carried out during the years of Kotooka's provisional supremacy was the destruction of the bell tower and the pagoda, both obvious symbols of Buddhism but peripheral to the combinatory worship of the site.

For Kotooka Hirotsune, the former head priest of Konkōin and administrative head of Mt. Zōzu, the conversion of the first four years of Meiji was expedient: he would do whatever necessary to protect and improve his position and that of the mountain under the new regime. Stripped of his guaranteed income from Tokugawa land grants and faced with an inevitable loss of power either to the Tosa occupiers or to central legislators, Kotooka cast his lot with the central government. In a sense, this was a recapitulation of the policy that earlier had proved successful for Konpira Daigongen under the Tokugawa shogunate, as Kotooka procured for the shrine in its new Shinto form an approximation of the site's earlier lucrative status—designation as an imperial worship shrine. After all, under the Tokugawa regime, shogunal and imperial sanction had granted Konpira an income and bolstered its claims against competitors while requiring nothing more than periodic processions and tribute to the capital. Central support had conferred relative autonomy.

Leaders of the new government, however, both interfered in the practices and circumscribed the authority of the priests. By decreeing the "separation of kami and buddhas," defining kami in exclusively nativist terms, they created sharp institutional and rhetorical divisions between Buddhism and Shinto, rending apart the complex, combinatory cosmology in which Konpira Daigongen and other popular pilgrimage sites had existed before. In priest-ruled domains such as Konpira—which enjoyed relative autonomy due to shogunal land grants—the Meiji rulers' claims of jurisdiction also redrew the lines between civil and religious authority. The priests of the shrine would no longer govern the village. In this changed religious and political context, then, Kotooka's active pursuit of imperial status would necessarily yield unintended consequences: far from earning him the autonomy he craved, it would tie him and his colleagues ever more closely to the agendas of the centralizing state.

For the State and Its Teaching
(1871–1874)

As the former samurai, administrators, nativists, and courtiers who made up the new Meiji government worked to consolidate their hold on power, they began to envision a new order. Intensely aware of the precarious position of Japan amid the imperialist powers of the West, the new Meiji leaders sought to strengthen the country militarily and economically and thereby secure the autonomy and welfare of Japan. In the early 1870s, members of the new Meiji government, public intellectuals, and entrepreneurs embarked upon a self-proclaimed age of "civilization and enlightenment" (*bunmei kaika*). They avidly worked to reshape not only the political and social order but also the scientific and cultural structures of Japan, calling upon the examples of Europe and the United States. Government and private individuals alike imported foreign experts, technologies, ideas, and even fashions (complete with top hats and hoop skirts). The courtier Iwakura Tomomi led a group of government ministers and exchange students to the United States and Europe from 1871 to 1873, intent on learning everything about law, science, religion, diplomacy, education, and anything else that might help them revise the unequal treaties the shogunate had signed with the Western powers almost two decades before. In 1873, educated men in Tokyo publicly debated the pros and cons of imported ideas in the famous Meirokusha, or Meiji Six Society. Under the slogan of "civilization and enlightenment," many of Japan's elite embarked on the wholesale adoption and adaptation of Western life.

What these people saw in the West reinforced a similar tendency in

Japan: a growing desire for a unified, centralized government that would command the dedication of all its subjects. Visiting Europe in the wake of the Franco-Prussian War of 1870–71, Japanese emissaries found a victorious, united German Empire and a fledgling French Third Republic, both bolstered by powerful nationalist sentiments. Loyalist veterans of the battles against the Tokugawa, having witnessed the apathy of Japanese peasants in 1868, especially admired the resistance of French commoners in the recent European war and emphasized the need for a more patriotic spirit in Japan.[1] Eager to broaden support for the new government and its reforms, members of the Iwakura Mission, as well as debaters in the Meiji Six Society, thus focused on adapting strategies from Europe and the United States to strengthen not just individuals or lordly domains but also the country as a whole.

The urge toward centralization grew in opposition to the West as well. Even before proponents of "civilization and enlightenment" gained sway, while members of the Iwakura mission were still abroad, leaders at home developed new structures and strategies to unite and educate the people, fostering loyalty to and identification with the imperial state while combating the threatening ideas of the West, Christianity in particular. Various intellectuals—especially Buddhists eager to prove their worth to an antagonistic administration—proposed a moralistic campaign against the Christian heresies. Nativists in the new government then built upon these proposals to transform the new Shinto shrines into an organized hierarchy of state-sponsored institutions that would not only perform rituals for the prosperity of the nation but would, they hoped, form the basis for the patriotic education of all subjects. Using the sites of gods such as Konpira (now Kotohira), they sought to foster a sense of nationalism, dedication, and loyalty to the state. In doing so, they created new structures and statuses that would entice influential men throughout the country to throw in their lot with the new regime. Both by mobilizing the elite and by educating the general populace, the system of state shrines and national teachings that they established—in effect, a Shinto version of "civilization and enlightenment"—would lay the groundwork for a sense of national identity and patriotism inextricably tied to the sites of the gods.

Shrines for the State

The crucial first step toward a unified, national government, according to which leaders in Tokyo would secure their hold over the country and ensure the implementation of their policies, was the nationalization of hitherto private domains. By obtaining the right to rule all Japan from Tokyo (formerly the shogun's capital, Edo), the new leaders set the stage not only for a new civil administration and political organization of the country, but also for its rapid industrialization and—most relevant for Kotohira—the transformation of the shrines and of Shinto into organs of the central state.

Under the Tokugawa system, the state had been familial, or private. Governments consisted of hereditary lords and their hereditary employees, whether belonging to the Tokugawa shogunate, domainal houses, or priestly lineages. The highest political value was loyalty, construed as unselfish behavior for the benefit of the lord and his family. While the lord himself swore allegiance to the shogun, his employees swore fealty to him. The shogun thus supervised a system of nested, semiautonomous hierarchies, with lords, priests, and other recognized authorities governing, in essence, their own private realms.[2]

During the Tokugawa period, large shrines and temples enjoyed relative freedom within this structure. The independent traditions of Mt. Zōzu and other sites guided everything from the format of rituals to succession of the head priestship. Through the head temple system, in which each institution was officially registered as a branch of a government-recognized denomination, shogunate officials could veto priestly appointments at the highest level, but they did not interfere with the personnel of individual worship sites.[3] Priests' relationships to domainal lords affected the economic and political welfare of each site but did not determine its inner workings.

The rhetoric trumpeted in 1868 by the new Meiji rulers, however, presaged a changed set of values. Drawing on the preexisting emphasis on service to one's lord over selfish (*shiteki,* personally oriented or private) behavior, the new rulers redefined both service and selfishness in a new, national context. Anything imperial or national—identified with the emperor, the state, and the collective interests of the realm—was good; anything private—identified with the "selfish," hereditary interest of the Tokugawa and lordly families— was bad. Whether through repeated calls for "public discussion" (*kōron*), insistence upon imperial sovereignty, or criticism of hereditary rule, the new leaders defined the Meiji state in opposition to its "private" predecessor.

In 1868, Shinto shrines, even under the revived Office of Rites, retained a large measure of autonomy within their reduced precincts. The logic of the Tokugawa religious structure remained relatively intact. Thus, although pressured by troops on the ground and by rumors of possible violence, priests such as Kotooka were still chosen locally and only confirmed in the capital; they retained the freedom to shape their immediate course of action. Those who decided to dedicate their sites to the kami in 1868 did so either voluntarily or due to violent pressure from individual extremists. No higher, recognized political institution violated their autonomy to force a conversion. Indeed, the new leaders, not yet secure in their positions, generally stayed within the established boundaries of Tokugawa authority. Accordingly, while the Office of Rites delayed recognizing Kotooka by the official title of head priest, it made no move to replace him.

In 1869, however, the leading domains of the Meiji coup articulated a new ramification of imperial rule that would override what little autonomy remained to the priests. The lords of Satsuma, Chōshū, Tosa, and Hizen "returned" their domains—both land and people—to the emperor early in that year. In a memorial justifying that return, the lords emphasized the new "sovereign authority" of the emperor in contrast to the usurpation of his rule over the centuries by domainal lords and their families. "Since the Imperial Ancestor founded this country and established a basis of government, all things in the wide expanse of heaven and all things on earth to its farthest limits have belonged to one imperial line from generation to generation, and all people therein have been its subjects," they proclaimed. "Thus no one can occupy a foot of ground or subjugate another subject [of the Emperor] for his own private gains."[4] The lords went on to reiterate the incompatibility of imperial rule and private, inherited authority. "Wherever your servants reside are Your Majesty's lands, and whomever they shepherd are Your Majesty's subjects," wrote the lords, "none of which can be privately owned by anyone of us."[5] By 25 July 1869, all domainal lords had acquiesced in this logic, and during the following eight days they "returned" their domains and census registers to the emperor, to rule their formerly private domains as governors appointed by the imperial court. The principle contrasting the "private" and the "imperial" had been accepted.

With the return of the domains, the new Meiji rulers celebrated the demise of inherited authority outside the imperial line. To recompense the lords turned governors for their "selfless" actions in the imperial interest, however, they confirmed that while authority could not be inherited, status could. On the very day of the return of the domains, they announced the merging of the former daimyo houses with the court noble families to form a new aristocracy (*kazoku*). In keeping with the identification of the imperial house as the highest authority, ranks within the new aristocracy remained contingent upon demonstrated proximity to the throne: former daimyo were generally granted the lowest ranks while imperial princes retained the highest.[6] Within days, all former samurai were designated gentry (*shizoku*), and all others commoners (*heimin*). The basic structure of the Meiji status system was thus set in place.

With the return of the domains and the creation of a new aristocracy, then, the Meiji leaders established in 1869 two new hierarchies—of values and of people—that would guide political logic under the imperial regime. First, they abolished and vilified private authority, defined as the hereditary privilege of rule by any family except the emperor's. Accordingly, any action not undertaken for the imperial state could be construed as private and therefore unacceptable. Second, because the imperial household embodied the highest authority, a hierarchy of people could be constructed, like the hierarchy of values, in which the most imperial ranked the highest. Initially, however, this hierarchy of imperial authority remained more an ideal principle and social convention than an implemented form of rule. The daimyo turned governors remained the supreme authorities of their former domains. Likewise, priests retained control over their reduced jurisdictions.

In 1871, this arrangement changed dramatically, as the Meiji leaders moved both to extend the principle of imperial sovereignty to shrines as well as domains and to apply it to the overall administration of the country. The consequences for religious policy and practice were overwhelming. Priests and shrines of the kami would no longer simply serve the state: they became part of the state. On 1 July 1871, leaders in Tokyo redefined the legal position of Shinto shrines under imperial sovereignty, creating the basis of a system that would last until 1946, with far-reaching consequences for Kotohira and other shrines.

The idea behind the 1871 reworking of the shrine system was an old one: that the performance of rites was of political importance, ensuring the peace and prosperity of each lord's domain. The new Meiji rulers had legitimized themselves not as private inheritors of Satsuma, Chōshū, Tosa, or other domains, but as representatives of "imperial" rule. By insisting on the primacy of the emperor and the state, they undercut rival claims to authority, shoring up their still precarious position. Thus, when the councilors in the Council of State, prompted by nativists in the Office of Rites, declared in 1871 that shrines are for "rites of the state" (*kokka no sōshi*), they defined the imperial state as transcending private interests and emphasized the role of shrines as sites of government-commissioned prayer rather than as places of individual or domainal worship.[7] In keeping with this political purpose, the Council of State asserted that shrines were state, not private institutions. "[Shrines] are not to be the private property of a single person or family," continued the announcement. In other words, the income of the shrine was to be used for the purpose of state worship, not for selfish gain. Consequently, the announcement forbade hereditary succession at shrines, requiring all head priests to resign and await reappointment by the central government.[8]

This proclamation, at least on paper, dealt the final blow to Kotooka and his hereditary status at Kotohira Shrine. In 1869, Kotooka's administrative jurisdiction had been reduced from the Tokugawa-granted lands to the precincts of the mountain shrine; in early 1871, the income from the land grants was confiscated as well. Now even the shrine was taken away, as the Council of State dismissed Kotooka's hereditary claims to the head priestship and claimed for the state the income of his shrine, over which he had exercised control and through which he and his predecessors had enriched the Yamashita family.[9] Indeed, the government claimed ultimate jurisdiction over the personnel of every shrine in the land, transforming the priests of these newly public shrines into government officials (*shinkan,* literally "kami officials")—a reorientation of priestly purposes that would have far-reaching effects.

Just as the Meiji leaders had simultaneously abolished hereditary rule of domains and established a new aristocratic hierarchy two years before, the Council of State in 1871 established a hierarchical system of official shrines (*kansha*) on the same day that it forbade hereditary priestship. Such systematic ranking revolutionized the relationship between government and the gods. Never before had a government dared to rank all of the gods of the land according to their importance. Sites had been sponsored by the imperial family or shogunate or placed in bureaucratic structures within separate denominations, but they (and, by inference, their gods) had not been systematically ranked in relation to every other shrine in the land.[10] As the nativists in government construed it, the purpose of the new law was to set up a version of Hirata Atsutane's system of official worship on all levels—with imperial shrines (*kanpeisha*) directed to conduct prayers for the nation, provincial shrines (*kokuheisha*) for the provinces, and domainal, prefectural, and district shrines for smaller administrative units, with each unit supporting the appropriate shrine.[11] Following the lead of Ōkuni-school nativists such as Fukuba Bisei, however, the Council of State placed Amaterasu, ancestral kami of the imperial house, at the apex of the hierarchy—not Hirata's ruler of the gods, Ōkuninushi, or even one of the earlier creator-deities mentioned in the ancient texts. Thus, the hierarchy directed ultimate attention not to the hidden mysteries of the kami (and, thus, to the moral affairs of men), but to the visible realm of the emperor and the dedication of worshippers to the emperor-centered state.

As they did with many of their initiatives, the Meiji leaders established the new hierarchy in the name of reviving ancient precedents. They determined the ranks not only of shrines, but of their priests as well, based on the system of shrines described in the tenth-century text, the *Engishiki.* Following the hierarchical principle of proximity to the imperial line that had been confirmed two years before, shrines that could claim provenance from the early age of direct imperial rule were awarded the highest ranks, followed by sites that had conducted prayer rituals for domainal governments more recently. Thus, in Sanuki province, where there were no clearly identified shrines mentioned in the *Engishiki,* there were no imperial shrines.[12] Tamura Shrine, where most of the official prayer rituals of the Takamatsu domain had been performed, was designated a middle-ranked provincial shrine. The less official Kotohira Shrine—unnamed in the ancient texts and a site for the more personal worship of domainal lords—represented an anomaly in that it received any rank at all. The Meiji leaders rewarded Kotooka's support by designating Kotohira the lowest level of provincial shrine (*kokuhei shōsha*).[13]

Like the return of the domains in 1869, the pronouncements issuing from the Council of State in 1871 seemed drastic. But in a still divided state, in which the boundaries of jurisdiction were continually in flux and former lords continued to rule their hereditary domains, there existed neither mechanism nor incentive for implementation of the edicts issuing from the central government.[14] Indeed, when originally issued in July 1871, the announcements of the national shrine system and abolition of hereditary succession stayed secret in the government offices of the Takamatsu domain, known only to a few people through uncertain rumors even more than a month later.[15] The content of the announcements did not become public knowledge even among active Shintoists in the area until almost two months after their issuance in Tokyo, when someone made a copy of the announcements in what was by then the neighboring prefecture of Tokushima and brought it back to Takamatsu on 12 September 1871.[16] Thanks to this inaction among Takamatsu officials, led by the former domainal lord turned governor, Kotooka remained the de facto head of Kotohira Shrine.

Even before Takamatsu-area nativists learned of the "shrines are for rites of the state" announcement, on 29 August, new councillors in the Council of State declared their intent to centralize not just shrines but also the administration of the entire country. The Meiji leaders summoned the former domainal lords to Tokyo, then sent to newly created districts (*ken,* known in English as prefectures) new governors appointed by, and therefore loyal to, the central government. Known as the abolition of the domains and establishment of prefectures (*haihan chiken*), this initiative replaced the last of the independent domains with prefectures subject to central control.[17] The ensuing implementation of the announcement not only centralized the civil administration of Japan; it also tightened the control of the national government over shrines throughout the country, ensuring that the priests turned officials of the new state shrines would enforce directives from the capital.

As a result of this policy, Kotohira Shrine and the town of Konpira passed from the jurisdiction of Kurashiki prefecture into the purview of a newly created Marugame prefecture, then into the large, consolidated prefecture of Kagawa (roughly analogous to the province of Sanuki)—all within a few months.[18] The new prefecture, with its capital in the city of Takamatsu, was led by Hayashi Kamekichi, a samurai from the former Tosa domain, as the newly appointed governor.

Governor Hayashi moved swiftly to standardize prefectural administration. As part of his effort to bring the area in line with central policies, he reformed the employment structure of the prefectural government, firing all former employees of the Takamatsu domain. This included, for example, firing all teachers employed by the domain, as the prefecture transferred schools to direct Ministry of Education (Monbushō) control, in effect closing them pending decisions in the capital.[19] Likewise, for the first time, the new governor and his assistants enforced in Kagawa prefecture the Council of State's orders of half a year before, abolishing hereditary succession of Shinto priests and placing official shrines such as Kotohira under governmental control.

The creation of Kagawa prefecture on 26 December 1871 and the appointment of a governor loyal to the central government definitively set in motion the comprehensive implementation of national policies at Kotohira Shrine. The governor's office appointed three men to take over management of the shrine, charging them with the task of overhauling its administration. Men of samurai status in the former Takamatsu domain, the two new senior priests (*negi*), Matsuoka Mitsugi and Ōkubo Kitaru, had held important posts in the domainal education system, while Matsuzaki Tamotsu, appointed junior priest (*gon negi*), was allied with loyalist politics in the area.[20] The three nativist and loyalist appointees arrived at Kotohira determined to reform the administration of the shrine on behalf of the new prefecture and the central government. They converted the shrine from the private institution of Kotooka and the Yamashita family to a public institution of the state and from the combinatory practices of Tokugawa "Buddhism" to the purportedly pure, stately rites of Meiji Shinto. Each of the men, having been officially appointed to a nationally determined rank, held more authority on the mountain than Kotooka, who was still limited to the simple designation of shrine officer (*shamushoku*).[21]

The employees of Kotohira Shrine greeted the arrival of the prefectural appointees with disgruntlement. Whether because a unit of the newly formed prefectural police was stationed in Konpira around the same time or because of Kotooka's avowals of Shinto reform, however, explicit protests were short-lived.[22] "Although there has been no problem with [Kotooka]," one of the new priests, Matsuoka Mitsugi, commented in his diary in March 1872, "the uproar among the employees of the former Konkōin has been very upsetting. Recently, however, it has largely subsided."[23] For three months after the arrival of Matsuoka, Ōkubo, and Matsuzaki, until Kotooka received a new appointment from the central government, the three prefectural appointees held control.

During their supremacy, they set in motion reforms to transform Kotohira fully from a private enterprise into a government institution. Having been commissioned by the governor to overhaul the administration of the shrine, they revamped the employment structure to grant rank and remuneration on the basis of performance instead of hereditary office.[24] The previous winter, economic pressures ensuing from the confiscation of shrine lands had prompted the reduction of the shrine's workforce from more than three hundred people to approximately eighty. Now, acting on directions from the prefectural office, the new priests reduced the staff to thirty—at a time when fourteen or fifteen people alone were required to sort the piles of money gathered from the shrine's donation boxes.[25] In other words, within only a few months, the staff was reduced by a factor of ten.

Since the central government had explicitly made clear that the income of shrines was to be used for state-sponsored worship, not for the personal gain of priestly families like Kotooka's, the new priests moved quickly to control the flow of money through the shrine. Matsuoka kept close track of the income gleaned from donations and the sale of amulets.[26] In his diary, he also recorded the commotion surrounding the arrival of a "foreign-made" iron safe that the reformers had ordered for the accounting office to hold the donation money, "stacked like firewood," that sometimes "reached the beams" of the storehouse. Twenty men struggled to carry it up the long steps to the shrine's accounting office, Matsuoka wrote, looking for all the world like a "centipede" pulling "a small shrine containing a buddha."[27] Ōkubo, Matsuoka, and Matsuzaki together tightened the personnel and financial administration of the shrine to conform to government directives, allowing the priests to lend ten thousand ryō to the financially strapped prefectural government only five months after taking office.[28]

The three new men, joined in April 1872 by a fourth prefectural appointee, Miyazaki Tominari, worked together to make Kotohira into a model Shinto shrine, wiping out the last vestiges of the combinatory Buddhist worship associated with the "private" Tokugawa order.[29] As part of this project, they applied to the prefecture for permission to rebuild the main hall that housed the Great Kami Kotohira. Although the buildings of the main hall were indeed three hundred years old and in need of repair, the rationale was most certainly also to rid the architecture of its Buddhist motifs and decoration.[30]

More important, the prefectural appointees oversaw the removal of the Buddhist images and implements of Konpira Daigongen. When Matsuoka arrived to take up office at the shrine in early 1872, one of his first comments concerned remaining evidence of Buddhist-style worship. "I went to the Dawn Shrine," he wrote in his diary, referring to the prominent edifice now theoretically enshrining the kami of Ise, Hachiman, and Kasuga. "This was originally the Gold Hall [Kondō], and there are still buddhas that have not been rectified," he complained. "This is extremely vexing."[31]

Matsuoka and the other appointees quickly removed the remaining images. They planned at first to burn the Buddhist objects—both those that had been hidden earlier by Kotooka and the more recent removals. As the four men wrote in a proposal submitted to the prefectural government in May 1872, "After the Restoration, all of the Buddhist images that had heretofore been in the shrine grounds were taken up and collected in a storehouse at the foot of the mountain. What shall we do with these items that were set aside? It would be no problem at all to even burn them." On 30 May, permission came back from the prefectural office: "Burn them."[32] In late May 1872, then, both the prefectural government and its appointees saw the Buddhist icons and ritual items of Mt. Zōzu as worthless and, perhaps, threatening remnants of the previous order—good only for destruction. Before the priests could carry out the prefectural directive, however, news from the capital would add a new consideration, altering the ultimate fate of the images and sutras.

Thus, amid the initial transformation from domain to prefecture, and from private shrine to state shrine, the hereditary traditions of Mt. Zōzu— whether priestly or Buddhist—had come under attack. The government-appointed priests made sure to enforce the comprehensive transformation of Konpira into a state-controlled, Shinto site, reorganizing the personnel of the shrine based on merit instead of heredity, funneling the wealth of the shrine to the prefectural government instead of to Kotooka, and planning the final destruction of Buddhist images that had been tied to hereditary rule.[33] Despite this nationalization, the role of the shrines remained unchanged from the centuries before: priests facilitated the prayers of commoners and performed rituals for the protection and prosperity of their sponsors, now for the various levels of the imperial state instead of the daimyo, the shogun, or the emperor as private individuals. The policies of 1871, however, raised new concerns among both national and local leaders. In the wake of widespread violence among people protesting the recall of the domainal lords and the imposition of new prefectural governors, the Meiji leaders would soon look to the priests of Japan—both in Buddhist temples and, especially, in the new state shrines—to pacify the populace.

Teachings of the State

Amid the unrest of 1871 and 1872, in which riots and protests highlighted the still tenuous hold of the Meiji leaders, nativists in the central government sought to take full advantage of the newly nationalized shrines. They struggled to transform the new state shrines from sites of supportive ritual to proactive agents of ideological persuasion, inculcating the values of reverence for the Shinto kami and obedience to the imperial state. Guided by the structures that the leaders set in place, Shinto would become a doctrine of the state, and Shinto priests would work increasingly for the ideological and financial goals of the government.

Meiji religious policy from 1872 onward included two initiatives, one relating to rites and one to doctrine, and both disrupted the routines at Kotohira Shrine. In 1872 the government relegated official ritual to the Bureau of Ceremonies (Shikiburyō) under the Council of State. This bureau established procedures for all imperial and provincial shrines in the country, including Kotohira, to use in performing state rites on national holidays, complete with formal presentations of offerings from the central government to the kami. Under this system, the ritual calendar of the state, virtually unrelated to preexisting practices on Mt. Zōzu, set in place a series of annual ceremonies performed by the priests in their role as government officiants. These ceremonies included Genshisai (rites for the New Year, held on 3 January), Kigensetsu (commemorating the founding of Japan by the mythical emperor Jinmu in 666 BC, held on 11 February), Kinensai (rites to pray for the harvest and the emperor, on 17 February), rites commemorating the deaths of the earliest emperor, Jinmu (3 April), and of Meiji's predecessor, Kōmei (30 January), as well as two Great Purification rituals at the end of June and December. Because of the government decree converting the calendar to coincide with Western systems on 1 January 1873, these rituals were performed according to the new dates, ensuring that even the purification ceremonies no longer corresponded to the established cycles of practice. Woodblock prints and lithographs of Kotohira from this time on regularly listed the dates of state ceremonies as well as those particular to the shrine, advertising the seasons in which representatives of the central and prefectural governments

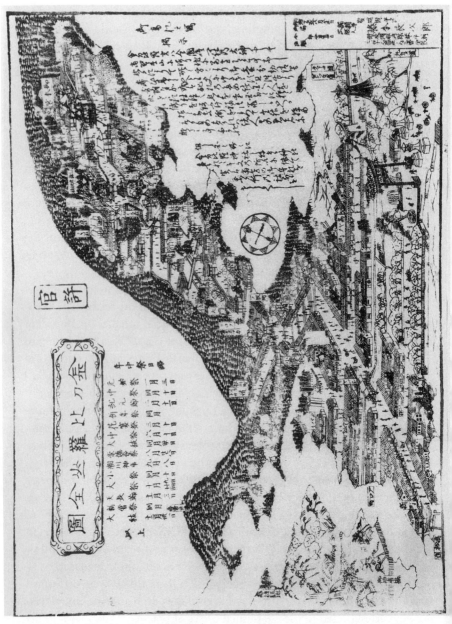

✿ **7.1** Print of Kotohira Shrine, 1882. From the mid-1870s on, the shrine supported the publication and sale of prints of the mountain that included lists of the new, state-designated holidays. Mixed among the festivals distinct to Kotohira, this print lists Genshisai (3 January), Kigensetsu (the founding of the empire, 11 February), Kinensai (a harvest festival, also in February), Great Purification (30 June), Tenchōsetsu (3 November), Niinamesai (also in November), and Great Purification (31 December). (Fujimoto Chōjirō, *Kotohirasan zenzu* [Kotohira, 1882]. From the author's collection.)

would present gold and paper offerings to the gods (figure 7.1).[34] While these ceremonies were virtually ignored by worshippers, officiating priests took them very seriously indeed, dedicating hours of effort to ensuring the accurate performance of the detailed ritual instructions sent down from Tokyo.[35]

More far reaching in its impact on priests and public, however, was the new educational project of the government. The Meiji rulers had used public religious education to combat the feared disruptive social and political impact of Christianity since 1869. At that time, persecuted Buddhists seeking to prove their worth to the new regime proposed a campaign to convert (or reconvert) Japanese Christians to the "Great Way" of both gods and buddhas— that is, the familiar practices of Japan. Not only Buddhists, but also Shinto proselytizers eagerly signed on for preaching duties, which quickly gained government support. Even as Shintoists and Buddhists vied for control of the campaign, they shifted the focus away from Christian converts alone to a preemptive educational program aimed at all Japanese.[36] With the establishment of the Ministry of Doctrine in 1872, Meiji leaders initiated the Great Teaching Campaign. Intended to fortify the populace against the expected onslaught of Christianity the next year, when, in response to diplomatic pressures, the ban on the foreign creed would be lifted, the campaign would emphasize religious, patriotic indoctrination as the guiding principle for all shrines and temples in the country.

Guided by the emperor-focused pragmatism of the Ōkuni-school nativist Fukuba Bisei, the leaders of the Ministry of Doctrine emphasized the potential usefulness of shrines and temples as stages from which to spread among the Japanese populace a message of dedication to a divinely sanctioned government, thereby maintaining social order through exhortation.[37] They directed religious policy toward civic education, and institutional arrangements served that end. Thus, shrines, temples, and priests were regulated, ranked, and paid according to their roles in propagating the national teaching. The ministry appointed doctrinal instructors (*kyōdōshoku*) from among Buddhist and Shinto priests, entertainers, storytellers, and village officials; within the year it required all Shinto priests (who were already government officials) to hold office simultaneously as such instructors.[38]

The Ministry of Doctrine dictated the substance of the proposed national teaching. In June 1872, it informed all instructors of Three Standards of Instruction (*kyōsoku sanjō*) around which they must base their sermons:

1. Comply with the commands to revere the kami and love the nation.
2. Clarify the principle of heaven and the way of man.
3. Serve the emperor and faithfully maintain the will of the court.[39]

These Three Standards formed the basis of a nationwide indoctrination campaign run by the government until 1884, albeit with decreasing intensity, and they constituted the core of lay Shinto teachings at Kotohira and other shrines for several decades thereafter.

The educational thrust of the new religious initiative magnified the importance to the government of pilgrimage centers such as Konpira, for they could potentially provide access to the minds and money of hundreds of thousands of visitors every year. For the sake of such access, nativists in Tokyo wooed Kotooka and his peers, happy to gain their cooperation. More important, however (for the Meiji leaders could always appoint someone new), Kotooka and the others saw in the wealth and popularity of their shrines an opportunity to improve their status. Such hope of advancement prompted dedication to the new regime. For Kotohira Shrine, whose absence in the ancient texts hampered its ability to rise in the classically based hierarchy of government shrines, and for Kotooka, who still sought to prove his allegiance to national Shinto policies, this emphasis on instruction provided new opportunities. The establishment in 1872 of an organized national indoctrination effort therefore added new ideological and financial priorities to policy decisions at Kotohira Shrine, determining the ultimate fate of its Buddhist assets and, more important, guiding the efforts of its priests toward moral exhortation and public outreach.

On the day it announced the Three Standards, the Ministry of Doctrine granted Kotooka Hirotsune the rank of assistant head priest (*gon gūji*) of Kotohira Shrine, raising him to the highest existing position at the shrine, although with the top place still vacant. On the next day, the ministry conferred upon Kotooka a commission as doctrinal instructor.[40] After having repeatedly denied his requests, the Ministry of Doctrine suddenly granted Kotooka advancement.

Why, at this point, did the ministry finally reward Kotooka? The basic reasons revolved around money and minds. In order to carry out its proposed indoctrination campaign nationwide, the Ministry of Doctrine required both large sums of money and prominent pulpits from which to reach as many people as possible. Kotohira Shrine could fulfill both of the ministry's needs, with the added attraction that Kotohira was now a Shinto institution.[41] Moreover, the ambitious Kotooka had quickly seized upon the opportunities presented by the indoctrination campaign to make himself indispensable to the ministry.

In order, he hoped, to secure his advancement, Kotooka wielded the wealth of Mt. Zōzu and its connections to the Toranomon Kotohira Shrine in Tokyo (formerly the popular Konpira shrine at the Marugame lord's mansion in Edo).[42] As the focus of the enthusiastic prayers of Tokyo residents, the Toranomon Shrine swarmed with worshippers during the festivals of Konpira held on the tenth day of each month. Taking advantage of both the popularity of the Toranomon Shrine and the need of the Ministry of Doctrine for effective sites to educate the populace, Kotooka arranged to build a Shinto lecture hall (*Shintō kyōkan*) on the Toranomon shrine grounds. He received official permission for the project little more than a week after receiving his appointment, suggesting that he probably proposed it before receiving his new title. Due to Kotooka's exploitation of Kotohira's resources to meet the needs of the nativists in Tokyo, Kotohira Shrine became one of only eighteen shrines around the country and the only shrine in Shikoku to merit inclusion in the initial phase of the Great Teaching Campaign.[43] Moreover, by appointing Kotooka as assistant head priest of Kotohira, the Ministry of Doctrine acquired a grateful leader at the prominent shrine intent on proving his commitment to the ministry. Kotooka would henceforth wield more influence than the four prefectural appointees, who, although nativists and loyalists themselves, owed their appointments not to the Ministry of Doctrine but to the prefectural government.

The sudden financial pressures created by Kotooka's new appointment, combined with his strategic commitment to fund the Toranomon project, prompted two shifts in the policies of the shrine. First, the financial priorities of Tokyo would take precedence over the needs of the prefecture. After all, Kotooka, now above the prefectural appointees, held his office at the whim of the Meiji leaders. The economic relevance of such interbureaucratic rivalries soon became evident. When Kotooka informed the prefecturally appointed priests at Kotohira of the financial burden of the Toranomon project (for which an initial sum of five thousand ryō was immediately required to hire carpenters and begin construction, as well as thousands more ryō later), the men panicked, reluctantly approaching the prefectural government for the return of a loan of ten thousand ryō they had extended only two days earlier.[44] Over the next two years, however, as the prefectural appointees themselves obtained designation as doctrinal instructors from the Ministry of Doctrine, studying in Tokyo to pass qualifying exams and attending instructional seminars, they too became increasingly committed to the central ministry's campaign.[45]

Second, the sudden need for money to build the Toranomon lecture hall and ultimately to support the national indoctrination campaign brought about the final disposition of the Buddhist objects at Kotohira. Overnight the priests shifted their focus from the implementing of reform to the provision of money for the national campaign. Like countless Buddhist turned Shinto priests around the country, they converted the formerly sacred symbols of Buddhism into commodities for sale. They sold the old bell to a nearby temple for more than two hundred yen. Emptying out "a two-story warehouse filled with Buddhist images and ritual implements, large and small," the priests rushed to estimate prices for each item. They held a public sale, spreading out the kimonos, paintings, calligraphy, and other objects for display. During the next three months, the shrine continued to sell paintings, mandalas, statues, and temple records to merchants, also melting down gold Buddhist items for their monetary value.[46]

Despite the need for money, however, some images were too valuable to sell. These images, which formed the center of much of the popular veneration of the mountain, were the very items that the four prefecture-appointed priests had obtained permission to burn but which were still stacked in a storehouse: the standing image of Kannon, said to have been carved by Kōbō Daishi; the standing image of Fudō Myōō, the fierce overseer of the goma ceremony, attributed to the great ninth-century priest Enchin; various ritual implements; and hanging scrolls of lesser deities.[47]

Given the powers attributed to these objects, the priests were understandably reluctant to allow them to fall into the hands of possible competitors. Indeed, as in similar redefinitions of the god in centuries before, the reinvention of Konpira Daigongen as the Shinto Kotohira had already given rise to competition away from Mt. Zōzu. After the conversion of the shrine, disgruntled shugenja and Buddhists from the mountain had moved away, claiming to continue the "true" tradition of Konpira worship elsewhere. According to an undercover investigation conducted by the shrine in October 1869 into the diversion of many pilgrims to a site across the Inland Sea in Okayama, for instance, Yūmei, the former priest of the subtemple Manpukuin, was displaying what he called the original image of Konpira Daigongen.[48] Clearly, the abolition of Konpira Daigongen on Mt. Zōzu offered an opening for competing ritualists to make money on their own. The nativist priests of Kotohira Shrine surely feared that if any outside group were to purchase the (remaining) images popularly associated with Konpira, the competition might bankrupt the shrine.

Instead of burning the most powerful images, however, the priests developed a way to preserve them on the mountain while earning money for the shrine at the same time. One day during August 1872, after most of the Buddhist items had already been sold, Matsuoka Mitsugi perused the catalog of a recent exhibition of sacred treasures at the Itsukushima Shrine on Miyajima. Suddenly, he was struck by the inclusion in the catalog of several Buddhist images and implements. "Our shrine, too, has long held many famous Buddhist images," he wrote in his diary. "There should be nothing to prevent us from preserving the most prominent of them" as shrine treasures to display in expositions and at other occasions, he continued.[49] The statues of Fudō Myōō and Kannon, as well as other items associated with famous historical figures, could be turned into capital for future profit rather than commodities for sale. In their quest to Shintoize the shrine, and now also to ensure its position as a profitable site of state ideology in the new age, Matsuoka and his colleagues agreed to preserve as cultural capital the Buddhist images that had, days before, been seen as symbols of a superstitious, alien past. They wrote an addendum to the earlier proposal to the prefectural office, requesting permission to burn the bulk of the remaining Buddhist texts and implements but to preserve the most famous images—nine wooden statues and thirteen scrolls—as shrine treasures.[50]

Matsuoka and the other priests redefined the formerly sacred images that had, in the past, garnered profits through their miracle-working reputations. The men now presented them as objects of art and craftsmanship that could potentially earn viewing fees from cultural and historical connoisseurs. They soon began distributing flyers for the first exposition to be held at the shrine, to open in the spring of 1873.[51] Instead of simply removing the Buddhist items from public view, the priests removed them from their sacralizing context of shadowy altars, glittering offerings, and the tantalizing smell of incense. Placed in plain view amid a jumble of paintings, swords, and calligraphic scrolls, the former objects of worship were equated, in this and later expositions, with other items as historical works of art: sacred images were demoted to cultural artifacts.

Because worshippers did not necessarily accept the priests' reevaluation of the Buddhist images, however, the priests' preservation of the objects not only attracted fee-paying spectators but also catered to unconverted worshippers as well. It is, after all, unlikely that overt display entirely destroyed the sacred aura of the Fudō Myōō and Kannon for all of their devotees. The attitude of a shopkeeper at Kotohira in the twentieth century provides a clue to the ways in which worshippers may have circumvented the priests' efforts. Until her death in the mid-1990s, one woman—like her mother before her—apparently insisted that there was no spiritual presence at the main shrine of Kotohira or most of the smaller shrines. She recognized an aura of power in only two places: in the small cave behind the main shrine, where the spirit of Konpira Daigongen was said to reside, and in the image of Fudō Myōō, currently housed in the shrine museum. Whenever this woman went up the mountain to worship, she would pray only at those two spots. Yet, not wanting to pay the money to enter the museum, she learned where the statue was positioned, then would stand outside the building, facing the image, and worship, placing her offerings on the ground outside.[52] Despite the recontextualization of the Buddhist images, dedicated worshippers both in the nineteenth century and in the twentieth could at times still find the miraculous aura upon which devotees relied.

The architectural, ritual, and intellectual changes implemented by the priests, however, were intended to make such independence as difficult as possible. For all but these few "cultural" masterpieces, the priests went ahead with the program of destruction. It is unclear exactly which images were taken to be burned in the back valley of Kotohira Shrine on 10 September 1872. According to Buddhist accounts and oral tradition, the "traitorous" Kamisaki Katsumi (the former Buddhist head of the subtemple Shingoin, now a Shinto priest) oversaw the bonfire in a valley behind the shrine. According to a Buddhist record published almost thirty-five years later, "When the men put the wooden image of the priest Yūsei [Kongōbō] in the fire, suddenly a rough wind blew up, the man in charge, Kamisaki, lost consciousness, and other strange things happened." The burning was then stopped, but most of the items had already gone up in flames.[53]

Such tales of the images, as well as the priests' concern for either maintaining control of them or destroying them altogether, attest to the great economic and miraculous powers believed to reside in the wood and metal of the statues. An entry in Matsuoka's diary emphasizes the reverence with which many people regarded the images. Matsuoka heard about the burning from his colleague Matsuzaki ten days after the fact, having been out of town at the time. According to Matsuzaki, the shrine handymen burned the images without any major incident and buried the ashes in no particular place. "Then a strange thing happened," continued the priest. "We don't know from whom they heard about it, but around dusk, two or three old women came, leaning on canes, and reverently gathered the scattered ashes that remained of the Buddhist images. They folded them up in some paper and took them home."[54] If the ashes of even minor Buddhist images held so much power in the eyes of worshippers that they gathered them to enshrine at home, the Fudō Myōō and other major images commanded even more veneration. Using the educational, cultural, and economic logic of the exposition at Itsukushima, Matsuoka found a rationale to preserve these images without jeopardizing the Shinto character of Kotohira Shrine. In doing so, he cleverly saved the sacred images of Mt. Zōzu, now transformed into cultural capital, simultaneously denying their use to potential competitors and retaining them as desacralized, yet profitable, assets of the shrine.

Much as the priests redefined Buddhism by lumping its images with art and culture, they simultaneously redefined Shinto by likening its shrines more to schools and lecture halls. As Kotooka signed on to the Great Teaching Campaign, he officially transformed Kotohira into a center of state indoctrination. Whereas the shrine had previously been valued for its performance of official prayer rituals that embodied the national policy of "unity of rites and rule" (*saisei itchi*), now it would focus on the spreading of a national teaching designed to bring harmony to the population through "unity of rule and doctrine" (*seikyō itchi*).[55] In the eyes of the priests, though among only a few of the worshippers, Buddhism became dead art; Shinto became living doctrine.

In addition to the activities at the Toranomon lecture hall in Tokyo, indoctrination efforts began at Kotohira Shrine in early 1873. In January of that year, the priests of Kotohira sought to ease the financial burdens on the shrine. They petitioned the Ministry of Doctrine to reduce the money required from Kotohira, thereby making more funds available for the Toranomon lecture hall in Tokyo and for indoctrination activities at the main shrine in Shikoku. The prefectural government, whose members still vividly recalled the widespread riots and destruction the previous year after the former lord of Takamatsu was recalled to Tokyo and the new governor sent in his stead, seconded this petition to the central authorities, apparently hoping that lectures at Kotohira would pacify the unsettled population.[56] "Until now, the [five hundred thousand inhabitants of Kagawa prefecture] have been deluded by the wicked teachings of villainous Buddhist priests," complained the assistant governor. "Even when revering the kami, they only pray for happiness after death. They do not know of the existence of government teachings or Japanese law." Because of the bad influence of the state-approved doctrinal instructors already preaching in the area, who were all Buddhist, he continued, it was imperative to establish a site for more appropriate instruction at Kotohira Shrine.[57] In response to this petition from the prefectural authorities, the monetary responsibilities of Kotohira Shrine were reduced, and Matsuoka Mitsugi was sent to Tokyo to undergo training and certification as a doctrinal instructor. He returned to the mountain in March of 1873, eager to begin spreading the national teachings.[58]

"In order to cause the truths of reverence for the gods, love of nation, [following] the principles of heaven and the way of man, service to the emperor and obedience of the commands of the court to penetrate among the millions of people," as Matsuoka commented, lectures on the Great Way of the Gods (*kannagara no ōmichi*) began at Kotohira Shrine in June 1873, surrounded by rules, rituals, and an altar display that emphasized the Shinto character of the content.[59] Before each lecture session, the rules required distinguished members of the audience to make offerings to the "deities of heaven and earth," beginning with the Great Kami Kotohira, and continuing through the newly enshrined kami of the indoctrination campaign, starting with the imperial ancestors Amaterasu and Amenominakanushi. Listeners were required to clap their hands and bow down, Shinto-style, in front of the deities upon entering and leaving the hall. No talk or tobacco was permitted during the lectures, and audience members were directed to applaud to demonstrate enthusiasm for the doctrinal instructor's points. Food and drink would be provided after the priest finished reciting the final prayer.[60]

A strictly defined pattern also governed the sermons themselves. First, Matsuoka or another doctrinal instructor of high rank would read out the Three Standards of Instruction.[61] Then two or three speakers would elaborate upon them, adding to the topics of the Three Standards themselves themes such as the change from the old calendar to the new, the way of husband and wife, and hidden and visible truths.[62] The sermons could also be used to publicize the power of the deity Kotohira itself, for on at least one occasion, a lecturer regaled the audience with a lively tale of Konpira protecting a worshipper from premature childbirth while on her way to the shrine.[63] With the establishment of such lectures at Kotohira Shrine, the priests began to incorporate civic education into their routine duties. Three times every month for more than a year, they conducted lecture sessions at the shrine for residents of nearby villages, who were required to attend by the local authorities.

As the national indoctrination campaign got under way, bureaucrats in the Ministry of Doctrine felt a need to train doctrinal instructors so that both Buddhists and Shintoists would convey similar (Shinto) interpretations of the national teachings. Many regional instructors wholeheartedly concurred. Some of the lectures at Kotohira in 1873 and 1874 illustrated the problem. Because the early phase of the indoctrination campaign included both Buddhists and Shintoists, Buddhist doctrinal instructors joined the priests of Kotohira in lecturing at the shrine. Matsuoka, consistently hostile to the Buddhist position, repeatedly criticized the sermons of one "fat, slovenly" True Pure Land (Jōdo Shinshū) priest for their overtly Buddhist content. As Matsuoka recorded in his diary, the Buddhist priest's interpretations of the government tenet of "respecting the gods," for instance, included the importance of praying not to the kami but to the buddhas. The sun goddess Amaterasu was actually the buddha Vairocana, he preached, and the Great Heavenly Plain mentioned in the ancient myths was actually the Buddhist Paradise.[64] In Matsuoka's eyes, the Shinshū priest had transformed the sacred symbols of the imperial state into the "degenerate" Buddhism of the Tokugawa regime. It was to ensure a reverent Shinto interpretation of the Three Standards that the Ministry of Doctrine set in place a hierarchy of nationwide institutions for the training of instructors, culminating in the Great Teaching Institute (Daikyōin) in Tokyo.[65]

As with so many of the initiatives of the early Meiji government intended to overturn centuries of established practice, the expenses of the Great Teaching Institute and the accompanying indoctrination campaign quickly overran the budget of the ministry. As soon as the institute was proposed in 1872, critics pointed out the insufficiency of government funds to support its activities. In response, the Ministry of Doctrine decreed that funding for the Great Teaching Institute would come not from the government, but from the formation of "associations of believers" (*kie shinja no kōchū kaisha*).[66] The Ministry of Doctrine, which since its creation had closely protected its authority to approve or deny the formation of new religious groups, now opened the way for the creation of thousands of new lay associations.[67] It effectively encouraged the formation of any lay religious group—whether based on pilgrimage or on a founder's revealed teachings—as long as it raised money for the state indoctrination campaign and, less crucial but still important, supported the values embodied in the Three Standards of Instruction.[68]

The dual necessities of fund-raising and indoctrination in the Great Teaching Campaign, combined with the need to create profitable lay groups, finally prompted the Ministry of Doctrine in March 1873 to fill the vacant head priestships (*gūji*) at Kotohira and other popular shrines around the country. At that time, the Ministry of Doctrine appointed head priests to several famous, nationally ranked shrines that included Ise, Suitengū (in Tokyo), and Sengen (at Mt. Fuji), as well as Kotohira. The newly appointed men were instructed to raise money and, by creating lay groups, guide popular worship into a more exclusively Shinto vein. The new head priest of Sengen Shrine at the base of Mt. Fuji, for instance, was told to encourage popular acceptance of the distinction between kami and buddhas by taking control of the mountain's lay pilgrimage group, Fujikō. The organization he established to reinvent Fujikō eventually became one of the thirteen sects of Shinto recognized by the state. The new head priest of Ise Shrine also established a lay association, the Divine Wind Association (Shinpū kōsha), to guide pilgrimage practice.[69] At other sites, money was more explicitly the top priority. The new head priest of Suitengū, for example, was told to provide one hundred yen a month to the indoctrination campaign from the shrine's income.

It was in this context that the Ministry of Doctrine appointed the new head priest of Kotohira Shrine, and thus the superior of Kotooka and the other priests, with instructions to provide money for the state's indoctrination effort. "Fukami Hayao was transferred to the head priestship of Sanuki Kotohira Shrine," recalled a central figure in the indoctrination campaign, "with the commitment to harness the monetary power of the shrine."[70] Fukami's later involvement in establishing a lay pilgrimage association at Kotohira suggests that he, too, had been involved in the discussions that linked fund-raising with the guidance of popular worship into an explicitly Shinto form supportive of the central state.

When Head Priest Fukami arrived at Kotohira in April 1873, he quickly consolidated the nativist outlook of the shrine leadership in support of Ministry of Doctrine policies. Born into a samurai family in the Satsuma domain in 1841, Fukami had served in Satsuma as a teacher of nativist studies before his summons to Tokyo and appointment at Kotohira.[71] During the years surrounding the Meiji Restoration, the Satsuma domain had been the site of the most comprehensive attacks on Buddhism and the establishment of a distinctly Shinto official religion; it was also home to many of the most influential men in the new Ministry of Doctrine and the central government.[72] Having served as an expert on nativism in one of the most nativist domains of all, Fukami clearly sympathized with the hard-line views of his fellow Satsuma Shintoists in the Ministry of Doctrine. At Kotohira, he found an enthusiastic ally in the scholar-priest Matsuoka Mitsugi. On the first two days of Fukami's tenure and frequently thereafter, the two disciples of the Hirata school discussed such topics as how to combat "heretical teachings" (i.e., Christianity) and proselytize effectively.[73] With Fukami's appointment, the leadership of Kotohira Shrine became firmly consolidated in the hands of avowed nativists, with Fukami, Matsuoka, and Kotooka all registered disciples of the school of Hirata Atsutane. Moreover, the new indoctrination policies of the Ministry of Doctrine coincided with the educational tendencies not only of the nativist teachers Fukami and Matsuoka, but also of the former school administrator Ōkubo and of Kotooka himself, whose predecessors had supported a school of Confucian studies on Mt. Zōzu since 1849.[74]

Doubtless, the commitment of these men to the campaign derived from two considerations. First, the moral teachings of reverence and obedience espoused in the Great Teaching Campaign bolstered the authority of these teachers and their peers among the landed gentry. They therefore found a meaningful place for themselves in the new order. Yet the commitment of the priests to the indoctrination campaign was also surely based on a strong underlying belief in the power of the gods and their importance in all areas of life. The tenets of nativist thought insisted that all existence derived from the gods and that sustenance of the social order relied upon their proper worship.

Indeed, at least some of the priests vividly felt the presence of the gods.

Matsuoka recorded in his diary a strange incident in which, though at first skeptical, he concluded that he had personally experienced the presence of the deity Kotohira. During the first great festival at which he officiated, in the autumn of 1872, Matsuoka recorded how he and the two priests Miyazaki and Kamisaki remained at the main shrine at midnight to perform a secret ceremony: "We entered the sanctuary again, and went about extinguishing the fire in the lantern in front of the deity and doing other tasks. As we were doing so, an awe-inspiring voice cried out from above the main hall. [I thought it was the sound of the wind,] but there was no wind. Many different thoughts came to my mind, but in the end I simply felt something press down on me from above, the hair on my body stood on end, and I prostrated myself."[75] Clearly, although Matsuoka and the other priests may seem at times to have become embroiled in the minutiae of ideological indoctrination or administrative efficiency, their actions were nevertheless undergirded with a concrete sense of the awesome presence of the gods and a divine insistence on proper service. The mobilization of the priests as lecturers for the national indoctrination campaign gave them a forum in which to convey their own convictions to thousands of people around the country.

The indoctrination campaign of the Ministry of Doctrine thus did more than increase the financial burden on Kotohira. It directed the educational and worshipful energies of the priests toward a nationally defined goal, adding to their hitherto ritualist functions a role of public, moral leadership. Before the indoctrination campaign commenced, the priests had performed rites on the mountain as commissioned by the state. Now they directed their attentions beyond the precincts of the shrine to extend the moral imperatives recently associated with the Shinto deities to the populace at large. By gaining access to the minds and money of worshippers, the priests of Kotohira Shrine hoped to fulfill their own educational role, simultaneously sustaining their deity and establishing an ideal society under the imperial state.

Rankling Priorities

The priests' commitment to their god and to their educational mission doubtless fueled much of their dedication to the Great Teaching Campaign. It was the hierarchical structures of shrine rankings and salaries set up by the central government, combined with the economic pressures of the campaign, however, that ensured not only their dedication but also the innovations and urgency that came to characterize many of the priests' efforts. In setting up a nationwide hierarchy of shrines in 1871, with the budget of shrines and the pay of their priests determined according to shrine rank, the central govern-

ment had created instant motivation for priests to cooperate with state policies in the hope of obtaining both higher rank and higher pay for their institutions and, thus, for themselves. Since the priests of Kotohira, like other
priests around the country, could obtain that advancement only through the
Ministry of Doctrine, they voluntarily carried out the ministry's indoctrination efforts. Contributing their own perspectives to the campaign, however,
the priests of Kotohira necessarily changed it as well. Indeed, in their earliest
and most ambitious involvement—the Shinto lectures at the old Toranomon
Konpira Shrine in Tokyo—the priests of Kotohira sought to raise their god to
the top of the state hierarchy.

The government's new hierarchies of shrines and gods created a sense of
unfairness at Kotohira and elsewhere that festered in the years after 1871.
From some of the highest shrines in the land to the lowest—and Kotohira
was assigned the lowest rank among the imperial and provincial shrines—
priests of countless institutions were convinced that their deities deserved
better recognition. The Office of Rites itself deliberately encouraged their aspirations. "Kotohira Shrine has been designated the rank of provincial small
shrine," the ministry notified Kotohira, as it did many other shrines. In the
next sentence, however, it explicitly held out the possibility of advancement.
"Until there is in due time communication concerning an alteration [of that
rank], you should continue as before. The cases of members of the peerage
will be answered most quickly."[76] In the very announcement that allotted
shrine ranks, therefore, the Ōkuni-school nativists who ran the Ministry of
Rites acknowledged that protests would be lodged. By emphasizing the importance of personal aristocratic rank (which, for priests, soon became linked
to shrine rank) in obtaining a hearing from the government, Fukuba Bisei
and his allies used even such protests to reinforce the focus on the imperial
house.

Wielding arguments based on history, doctrine, or popularity, many
priests protested the rankings, debating the honor and perquisites due their
god and its shrine. Such considerations fueled the so-called pantheon dispute
(*saijin ronsō*) of these years, which plagued the Great Teaching Campaign.[77]
The most prominent challenger to the emperor-centered hierarchy was Head
Priest Senge Takatomi of the Great Shrine of Izumo.[78] Senge was appalled
when his shrine was lumped with twenty-eight others in the highest rank of
imperial grand shrine (*kanpei taisha*), for it placed the deity of Izumo, Ōkuninushi, beneath Amaterasu, which stood above the rankings. As ruler of all
the gods and all hidden things, protested Senge, Ōkuninushi should stand at
the pinnacle of the shrine hierarchy; Amaterasu, after all, ruled only the visible world.[79] According to Senge's teacher, Hirata Atsutane, Ōkuninushi over-

saw the proper moral behavior of all people in both this life and the next; the emperor, descendant of Amaterasu, ruled only the present world. Thus, argued Senge, Ōkuninushi should occupy the highest place.[80]

The priests of Kotohira agreed with Senge's priorities.[81] Like other Hirata-school nativists, Kotooka, Matsuoka, and others rarely, if ever, referred to Amaterasu or the emperor unless specifically required to do so; their comments more frequently mentioned "the nation" or "the gods." Moreover, since the Great Kami Kotohira had been identified as none other than Izumo's Ōkuninushi (Ōmononushi), they shared an interest in raising the ruler of the gods to the highest prominence.

In their remonstrances to the central government, however, the priests of Kotohira phrased their objections on more practical grounds. The low ranking of Kotohira was due to its absence in the ancient texts, a deficiency that even they could not remedy.[82] In the popularity of its pilgrimage and the wealth it generated, however, Kotohira rivaled Ise, the shrine of Amaterasu. By pointing out this discrepancy in the context of support for the national indoctrination campaign (thereby attempting, perhaps, a bit of blackmail), the leadership of Kotohira sought to mobilize the main assets of the shrine—popularity and wealth—in pursuit of higher rank and privilege. In essence, they argued that the standards for ranking under the new regime should rest on two criteria: the popularity of each shrine and the amount of money it devoted to state programs. Contemporary service of the nation should count for more than historical ties to the imperial court.

The priests first tried to gain recognition of the prominence of Kotohira through the Toranomon lecture hall project. Just as Kotooka had obtained higher office through his commitment to build the hall, so too did Kotohira Shrine enhance its reputation in the Ministry of Doctrine as it fulfilled its obligations and finished construction. By the time the hall was completed and lectures ready to begin in mid 1873, Head Priest Fukami felt confident in challenging his peers in the Ministry of Doctrine to recognize the overwhelming popularity of the deity. Since the most prominent public lectures in Tokyo would be held at the Toranomon hall, Fukami hoped to use the leverage of the site to raise the profile of Kotohira (and thus of both Ōkuninushi and himself) in the indoctrination campaign as a whole. He therefore negotiated with the Ministry of Doctrine to carry out his plan.

Following the precedent of an 1872 policy to distribute amulets from Ise shrine to all Japanese subjects,[83] the Ministry of Doctrine decided to distribute amulets from Amaterasu, the ancestral deity of the imperial family, to the audiences at the Toranomon lecture hall. Fukami then visited the Ministry of Doctrine with a suggestion. In a bid for de facto recognition of Kotohira

Shrine as a pilgrimage site even more popular than Ise itself, he proposed that coin-shaped amulets from Kotohira Shrine be distributed as well (figure 7.2).[84] In this single move, Fukami apparently sought not only to confirm Kotohira's wholehearted dedication to the ministry's campaign, but also to capitalize upon the popularity of the god, not to mention the universal desire for coins, to promote Kotohira in its new guise. "When left to their own devices," Fukami told the Ministry of Doctrine, "even if some people do not receive [an amulet from Ise], no one will refuse [a Kotohira amulet] because of the brilliance of the divine power of [Kotohira] Shrine." He continued, appealing to the anti-Christian concerns of the government leaders, "Those who do not carry these amulets can definitely be identified as followers of heretical religions," that is, Christianity.[85] Apparently, according to Fukami's logic, only the strangest of people would decline to accept the amulet of the powerful and popular Konpira, shaped as it was like a coin, and bearing the encircled gold seal of the shrine, itself a symbol of gold and money. He proposed to enshrine the popular god of wealth and wonders alongside the ancestral god of the emperor as a representative of the highest values preached by the state.

The competition between Kotohira and Ise at Toranomon thus added a third dimension to the long-standing political and doctrinal split between Ise and Izumo. Nativist scholars disagreed over which deity was most important: while Hirata Atsutane had revered Ōkuninushi as the creator of the land and ruler of the gods, others often attributed ultimate importance to Amaterasu as ancestor of the imperial house.[86] This doctrinal conflict was sustained by a political rivalry between the priests of Amaterasu at Ise, site of the presumed progenitor of the imperial family, and the Senge family priests of Ōkuninushi at Izumo, who, until 1871, had governed Izumo province as purported descendants of Ōkuninushi. The rivalry continued into the Meiji period, becoming particularly intense as Shintoists in the Great Teaching Institute debated which kami to enshrine, and thus support, in their lectures not only in Tokyo but throughout the country. As the Ise faction gained power within the campaign, the tensions between Ise and Izumo grew. Senge, who waged a constant battle against the supremacy of Amaterasu, therefore supported his fellow Hirata-school adherent Fukami's attempt to outshine Ise. "The people of Tokyo particularly believe in Kotohira Shrine of Sanuki province," commented Senge. "Its amulets . . . should be conferred upon the people by the lecturers and head priests of the Great Teaching Institute."[87]

The attempt to distribute Kotohira's amulets at the Toranomon lecture hall failed, but Fukami's and Senge's efforts to advance their shrines through comparisons to Ise continued. In 1874, after acquiescing to a demand from

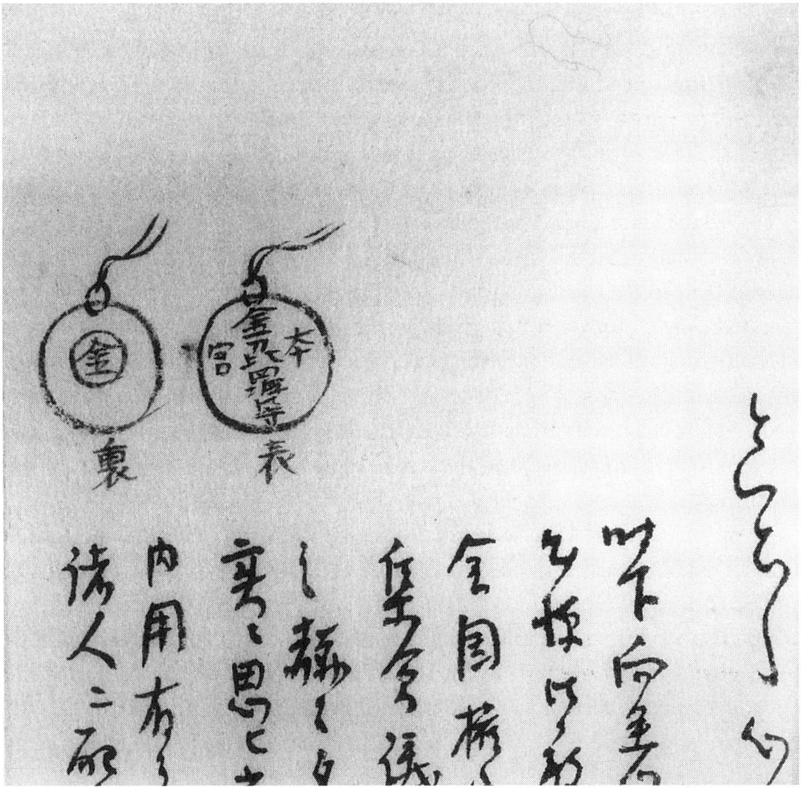

❀ 7.2 Coin-shaped amulets of Kotohira proposed by Head Priest Fukami Hayao to be distributed at the Shinto lecture hall on the grounds of the Toranomon Kotohira Shrine in Tokyo in 1873. By distributing amulets shaped like money—thereby emphasizing the tie between the god Kotohira and wealth—the priests of Kotohira apparently hoped both to publicize the shrine and to use Konpira's popularity to improve their own status in the state-supported Great Teaching Campaign. This drawing of the amulets, which were apparently never created, appears in Matsuoka Mitsugi's diary, *Nennen nikki,* 22 June 1873. (With the permission of Matsuoka Hiroyasu, Tawa Archive.)

the Ministry of Doctrine that Kotohira Shrine contribute twenty-five thousand ryō—the same amount given by Ise—to the rebuilding of the Great Teaching Institute after its destruction by fire, Fukami drafted an indisputable challenge to the hierarchy of shrine ranks. In a draft petition entitled "Concerning the Revision of the Shrine Rank of the Small Provincial Shrine, Kotohira Shrine of Sanuki Province," he wrote: "The noble, exalted, mysterious and majestic powers of the two deities enshrined here, Ōmononushi and Emperor Sutoku, are so brilliant that in times of emergency this shrine sometimes receives the prayers of the emperor and, in the consideration of myriad people in the realm, can be compared to the splendor of Ise Shrine. Therefore on this occasion . . . we respectfully hope that its rank will be revised to that of an imperial grand shrine."[88] It is unclear whether Fukami ever submitted his petition; perhaps he thought better of such blatant pressure. Indeed, to suggest that Kotohira be raised from a small provincial shrine to an imperial grand shrine could have had significant economic and political repercussions.

Under the state shrine system, such struggles for advancement were crucial to personal financial gain. If Fukami's proposed appeal had worked, his salary and Kotooka's would have doubled and the salaries of the other priests increased as well. Other funds given by the government to the shrines—for official rituals, offerings, traveling expenses, and the like—were also dependent upon shrine rank. The motivating power of the hierarchical ranking system therefore operated on many levels, turning the ambitions of the priests—for their deity, their status, and their pocketbooks—to the advantage of the government.

Senge at Izumo and Fukami at Kotohira both failed to obtain promotions for their gods in either the Great Teaching Campaign or the hierarchy of shrines. Indeed, the pantheon dispute in the Great Teaching Campaign remained intractable: for years it paralyzed and divided Shintoists throughout the country.[89] Nevertheless, by accepting the hierarchical structures of the new government, seeking to prove their credentials within the new rules instead of attacking them as a whole, Senge, Fukami, and countless other influential men—not only at shrines but in officially recognized positions of all kinds—actively dedicated their energies to the Meiji regime. Their ambitions for themselves and for their institutions both strengthened and shaped the developing structures of the centralizing state.

The early struggles over rankings, and thus the pantheon dispute itself, might even be regarded as one of the earliest debates on the priorities of the state: a debate that created general support for the government even as it highlighted participants' personal disagreements. Those who argued for the primacy of Ise, with their focus on the purported ancestor of the imperial house, suggested that the ultimate values of the state should be tied to the emperor. Proponents of Izumo, on the other hand—worshipping as they did the kami Ōkuninushi, creator of the land, ruler of the unseen world, and (at least according to Hirata Atsutane and his followers) judge of human behavior—indicated that ties to the land and moral behavior were more important. And the priests of Kotohira, who pursued their own interests, argued for the dominance of service to the state and popularity. In their opinion, since Kotohira Shrine contributed as much money to the Great Teaching Campaign as did Ise, this service to the state, made possible by the popularity of the shrine and thus its wealth from donations, should place it at the pinnacle of official worship. Each group would reiterate such arguments periodically over the years, promoting—according to their relative influence—an imperially focused state cult, an emphasis on kami and personal morality, or, in the case of Kotohira, the practical importance of money and popular influence.[90]

As only a subsidiary player in the national politics of nativist Shinto, Fukami soon ceded the stage to proponents of Ise and Izumo. Strongly influenced by his experiences in Tokyo, he turned his attention to the main shrine back in Shikoku. The Toranomon project in particular gave him an idea that would serve as the backbone of fund-raising, education, and worship at the shrine until the second half of the twentieth century, influencing the pilgrimage experience of countless worshippers over the ensuing years.

At the time of his appointment as head priest, Fukami Hayao had been instructed to raise money for the campaign and spread the state teachings. In the early months of his tenure, he did so by focusing mainly on lectures, elaborating upon the lectures that Kotohira Shrine had already been hosting before his arrival. The Toranomon experience, however, apparently reminded him of Kotohira's strength: it was the miracles and amulets of the god that attracted the attention, and thus the money, of worshippers. Inspired by the distribution of amulets (whether from Ise or from Kotohira) at the Toranomon lectures, Fukami decided to add amulets and an initiation ritual to the lecture format, thereby creating a shrine-controlled lay association. Indeed, the specific impetus for Fukami's idea came as he was developing the plan to challenge Ise at Toranomon. While itinerant priests (*oshi*) had distributed the amulets of the sun goddess around the country for centuries, Kotohira Shrine had consistently publicized a policy of only conferring amulets directly from the shrine itself. To distribute amulets at Toranomon without violating this policy, Fukami therefore proposed incorporating the amulets into some kind of ceremony. In the end, however, Kotohira's amulets were never distributed, nor such ceremonies ever performed, in the Toranomon lecture hall. Instead, Fukami took the strategy home.

In the first recorded reference to the establishment of a lay association at Kotohira, Fukami wrote a letter from Tokyo to the priests at the main shrine, suggesting a membership structure in which lecturers would "present [the amulets] to people who obey the association (*kōsha*) and undergo its initiation ceremony."[91] He instructed the priests at Kotohira to develop provisional rules for the association as well as an appropriate ceremony and oath to be required of members. This set in motion the idea of a lay association at Kotohira that would give special amulets to people who heard lectures on the Three Standards of Instruction, committed themselves through an initiation ritual to the teachings of the Ministry of Doctrine and Kotohira Shrine, and gave monetary offerings for the privilege. In this same letter, Fukami proposed the name under which the association would form: the Reverence Association (Sūkei Kōsha).[92] After months of planning, the priests of Kotohira Shrine received official permission from the Ministry of Doctrine to establish the Kotohira Shrine Reverence Association in March 1874. It still operates today.

With the establishment of the Reverence Association, Kotohira Shrine became fully incorporated into the financial, administrative, and educational structures of the Meiji state. Whereas in 1869, the hereditary priest of Kotohira had struggled to adapt his reduced domain to the preferred idiom of the new rulers, by 1874 Kotohira Shrine had been wrested from his control and its mission changed from the performance of rites to the indoctrination of the populace. In this, Kotohira shared a fate with shrines around the country. With the abolition of domains and the establishment of prefectures in 1871, the Meiji rulers finally ensured the implementation of their all-encompassing vision of state-ranked shrines and state-appointed priests as instruments of the central government. With the creation of the Ministry of Doctrine in the following year, nativists in the central government then directed those shrines—and their priests—toward reshaping the ideas and behavior of people throughout Japan. By skillfully controlling ranks and appointments while offering priests a sense of mission as well, the leaders in Tokyo secured the active participation of educated, influential priests. They created enthusiastic support for their effort to foster a sense of shrine-focused patriotism in people throughout Japan.

The Reverence Association
(1874 – 1882)

Just as, on the national level, the structures of the state enticed daimyo, priests, and other leaders to seek advancement within the new regime, the structures of the Reverence Association created new privileges associated with the shrine to attract the dedication, energies, and offerings of ambitious worshippers. Taking advantage of pilgrims' desire for access to the miracles of the god, the priests of Kotohira designed an organization that would use that demand for access, together with the civic teachings of the Great Teaching Campaign, to shape their behavior at the shrine and their attitudes toward the god. In short, the priests embedded the national teachings in modified rituals of popular worship. Merging patriotism and obedience to the emperor with the rhetoric and ritual of the gods, they began creating a model for popular participation in the emerging Shinto of the state.

As suggested by the title of the association—with its emphasis on reverence instead of petitions for miracles—the priests aimed at nothing less than the transformation of the purpose of worship: from episodes of personal petitioning to ongoing, formal expressions of respect. Yet it was the miracles and amulets of the god that formed the basis of popular interest in Konpira. Throughout the 1870s and 1880s, therefore, the priests worked to capitalize on that demand while transforming it at the same time.

Even as it promoted reverence, the association also needed to be economically viable. It was required not only to support itself but, especially, to contribute to the solvency of the dispossessed shrine. This economic imperative affected the way the priests of Kotohira translated the state-endorsed values of the Great Teaching Campaign into a format for popular, Shinto-style worship. On the one hand, they reshaped existing structures of pilgrimage to direct more money to the shrine. On the other, they added new rules and rituals to attract increased offerings while reshaping worship as a whole. The moralizing sermons of the Great Teaching Campaign, as well as new Shinto funerals offered by the priests, thus formed the core of Reverence Association activities. As they designed the rites and rules of the new association, the priests of Kotohira used them to balance the demands of their varying constituencies, appealing to the major donors to the shrine—many of them well-to-do landowners, business owners, and village headmen who supported the state's moral teachings—as well as the countless other visitors each year whose smaller donations, inconsequential on their own, filled the offering boxes with heaps of coins. Focusing on the behaviors, businesses, and beliefs associated with pilgrimage, the priests of Kotohira set forth an all-embracing vision of worship under their authority and control.

The people they targeted, in turn, incorporated the changes into their existing ideas and practices to varying degrees. The result was a veneer of formal worship, as espoused by the priests and adopted by a select few, over the continuing prayer practices of myriad worshippers. While the priests defined the rituals and beliefs of a new, civilizing Shinto, the vast majority of people maintained their interpretation of miracles at the center of Konpira pilgrimage. Despite its limited initial impact, however, the Reverence Association set new standards for belief and behavior on the mountain that would increasingly shape the meaning and experience of pilgrimage over the years to come. By aligning shrine-supported forms of pilgrimage with the procedures of the bureaucratic state and the values of educated local leaders, the association and the shrine helped create a form of everyday, popular Shinto that supported the emerging structures of the imperial regime.

Teachings of the Reverence Association

Since the early eighteenth century, well-to-do entrepreneurs, merchants, shippers, and village headmen had formed the prosperous core of Konpira's supporters. As the market economy grew, so too did their offerings. By the mid-nineteenth century, stone lanterns, fence posts, and other votive plaques at the shrine testified to the dedication of merchants, paper manufacturers, fishing-boat owners, and many others to the god on Mt. Zōzu.

Many of these people shared attitudes toward success shaped in large part by the Shingaku movement—an educational mix of Confucian and economic wisdom espoused by Ishida Baigan in 1729 that by the nineteenth century had become a dominant intellectual force throughout Japan. Shingaku teachings focused on ensuring the continuation and prosperity of one's household through frugality and diligence in one's hereditary occupation. Especially strong among merchants and other commoner households, Shingaku shaped much of their everyday morality; the values of self-restraint it espoused permeated readers studied by children as well as tales told by adults.[1]

The priests of Kotohira Shrine, themselves raised to accept these ideas, designed the Reverence Association and its rules to confirm the importance of family values and productive work. Combining what they considered to be the commonsense values of Shingaku with the principles of the Great Teaching Campaign, all in the context of the shrine's control over access to the powerful deity, the priests of Kotohira sought to make the values of self-restraint integral to the emerging Shinto style of worship. In doing so, they not only appealed to Konpira's long-standing donors, many of them influential men and women who already espoused those values. They also set up structures through which to spread this view of the world to even more people as they came to worship. Through the Reverence Association, the priests of Kotohira sought to redirect the destructive exuberance with which thousands of people had greeted falling amulets only a few years before. Instead of such drinking and dancing, common among much of the population, the priests developed and disseminated Shinto as a formal etiquette of self-restrained worship, tailored to the customs of well-to-do and influential families throughout the land.

The shrine's announcement in early 1874 of the creation of the Reverence Association set the stage for this agenda of influence, as the priests used their control over access to the deity to pressure worshippers to follow their guidelines. In April of that year, employees in the shrine office sent a circular to all kō for which they held addresses, groups that in the past had made sizable donations to the shrine or arranged special treatment for their members. Warning worshippers that a change was about to take place, the circulars acknowledged that,

> as everyone is well aware, it has traditionally been the policy of this shrine not to give permission easily for people to enter the sanctuary [*haiden*] and worship up close. However, over the years, through a verbal agreement with some believers who have formed various kō and made donations and offerings, we have come to give permission for them to enter the sanctuary two or three times a year.

The priests then juxtaposed this state of affairs with the new impetus issuing from the Ministry of Doctrine:

Since the Meiji Restoration, the Three Standards of Instruction have been issued—respect for the gods, love of country; making clear the principles of heaven and the way of man; and reverence for the emperor and obedience to the will of the court—with the intention that we should spread this Great Way of the National Teaching throughout the realm. Doctrinal instructors have been appointed so that the people will not mistake the way. In this shrine as well, we have now established rules and received permission from the Ministry of Doctrine to form an organization called the [Kotohira] Shrine Reverence Association.

Finally, they drew the connection between the state campaign and shrine policy toward kō. The priests would use access to the sanctuary as their tool to ensure conformity to the Great Way:

Formerly, kō of many different names were permitted to enter the sanctuary, but this sanctuary entry is now completely forbidden. Those believers who would like to enter the sanctuary as before must change the name of their kō to Reverence Association and follow the new rules. They will be permitted to enter the sanctuary once a year. . . . In the rare case that someone does not obey the association rules, no matter what their tradition of connection with this shrine, the privilege of sanctuary entry will no longer be permitted.

Note: Unless it is an inappropriate name, each group may retain its old kō name and be called the X kō of the Reverence Association.[2]

The shrine thus set itself up as the expert on and judge of conformity to the Great Way of the National Teaching. As the gatekeepers of the god, the priests (acting in their capacity as licensed doctrinal instructors) would now dictate the terms on which people could approach the deity—at least via the main sanctuary—instead of simply providing a service to those who arrived on their own terms.

The announcement, with its note on the "inappropriate names" of kō, reflected the nativist priests' preoccupation with Shinto symbolism. Not only had they earlier eliminated the physical evidence of esoteric or tengu worship on the mountain—redesigning amulets to avoid references to Fudō Myōō, removing tengu masks from the ema halls, and destroying almost every lantern or signpost that sported a tengu's fan or contained Buddhist language—but they now apparently used the Reverence Association to discourage such references among worshippers as well. The priests seemed to assume that readers were already thoroughly indoctrinated in nativist teachings, for they did not list the forbidden names. But such names surely included references to tengu, to Buddhist sutras (such as the Golden Light or popular Heart

Sutra), to Konpira Daigongen, and even to Mt. Zōzu (instead of Mt. Kotohira). This focus on symbolism and especially language would spread to include references to the god, the wording of prayers, and even references to
pilgrimage itself, as priests and their peers used the formal term *sanpai,* suggesting restrained obeisance, instead of the more colloquial *omairi,* with its
overtones of reckless crowds, cross-dressing, and other forms of exuberance.

In order to inculcate in pilgrims a more decorous form of worship, the
priests established the rites and rules of the Reverence Association. As the
centerpiece of the relationship between the association and its members, they
created an initiation ceremony during which they strictly controlled the actions of prospective members. From their arrival at their sponsoring inn at
the foot of the mountain, until the final ceremony in the sanctuary of the
main shrine on the following day, prospective members were guided through
the association rituals. If they had not previously performed the clapping and
bowing form of kami worship, or had not associated it with Konpira, they
were now led in clapping, bowing, and prostrating themselves before the deity. The priests introduced them to a new language of prayer aimed at a renamed god, not the popular "Konpira Daigongen," but "the Great Kami Kotohira (Kotohira Ōkami)."[3] Moreover, leaders of the groups modeled the
dress and behavior deemed appropriate for worship. As one written introduction to initiation procedures stated, when prospective members arrived
at the inns below the mountain, the guide from the inn and the leaders of the
kō "put on jackets (*haori*) and trousers (*hakama*) and reverently [led] the way
up the mountain to the teaching hall (*kyōden*)."[4] As a token of respect for the
deity above, guides encouraged proper dress, no less than proper comportment, as they led initiates up the mountain in a group, discouraging them
from wandering off on their own to inspect the lanterns or scenic views along
the way.

The process of joining the Reverence Association was filled with such details, familiar to most of the prosperous gentry, but new to many others. Village headmen and wealthy merchants, for instance, generally owned haori
and hakama; poorer peasants did not. Likewise, educated men generally carried the personal seals whose stamps the association required on the registration rosters. As less prosperous worshippers joined the association, they were
introduced to the increasing need for such seals in the growing paperwork of
"civilized" life. According to one letter written to the association in 1877, for
instance, thirty-eight prospective members arrived at their inn without seals.
Wrote the group's representative, "These people entering the association for-
got to bring seals. On this occasion, please allow the sponsor to affix his seal
on behalf of all of them."[5] The repeated use of virtually identical, crudely

carved stamps on a variety of association registers suggests that some innkeepers eventually helped many unprepared applicants circumvent the rule by lending seals from the inns.[6] In a similar lesson of the formalization of worship, the priests' insistence on following bureaucratic procedures to the letter surely reinforced among less careful worshippers the importance of following rules and regulations. One man who lost the card permitting him to enter the sanctuary for the final ceremony, for instance, was required to submit a police report, character references, an affidavit from his kō's sponsoring inn, and a written petition to the shrine office before the priests finally issued him a second card and allowed him to complete the initiation.[7]

Although they changed slightly over the years, the rules of the Reverence Association spelled out the responsibilities of members—ranging from obeying the Three Standards of Instruction of the Great Teaching Campaign to observing the shrine's festivals and promoting harmony within the kō—as well as their privileges, including not only access to the main sanctuary, but also the receipt of special amulets and prayers from the shrine.[8] The Reverence Association rules thus defined the ideal worshipper. As befitted the association's core constituency, the behavior recommended in the rules corresponded almost word for word to the teachings of Shingaku moralists. "Since simplicity and diligence are the basis of a life of household fortune received from the heavenly gods," stipulated the rules, "there should not be any hint of laziness. Luxury and indolence begin with being misled by evil spirits and are the root of bankruptcy and misfortune. This should not be forgotten for even a moment." In no uncertain terms, the Reverence Association expounded the values of diligence and hard work to its members.

The Reverence Association focused not only on guiding the behavior of individuals, but also on situating them in the larger society. The morals of Shingaku focused on the household and community; the vision of nativists encompassed the community and the nation. The rules of the Reverence Association, like the policies of the Meiji government, included all of the above. According to the association rules, membership was primarily a social commitment, not a personal endeavor: worship occurred in a group, not alone. Just as the people to be initiated into the Reverence Association were led up the mountain together, membership in the association was embedded in the community and, within it, the household as well.

The priests of Kotohira specifically designed the Reverence Association to discourage worship as an individualistic action. This is doubtless one reason that they chose to form the Reverence Association based on Konpira kō instead of appealing to individual worshippers, no matter how wealthy. During the first years of the association's existence, people could join only if all members of a kō traveled to the shrine and joined at once. This arrangement worked well as long as the association had spread only to neighboring towns and districts, but as recruiters worked farther afield, the requirement proved increasingly restrictive. In 1881, the association provisionally allowed people to undergo initiation even if they came alone to the shrine, but insisted that they formally register as part of a larger kō.[9] That is, they could join only by filling out a temporary registration form that committed them to recruiting twenty or more people at home to fill out the kō—a requirement that brought added economic benefits to the shrine as well.

Despite these later concessions to individual membership, the leaders of the Reverence Association worked from the beginning to use the existing structure of independent kō to convey their message of worship as a matter of communal action and morality. Building upon the long-standing tradition of kō as organizations of mutual self-help, the Reverence Association formalized the provisions for kō members to support each other in the community. Members "should correct each others' errors and act as close brothers," stated one association rule. Moreover, members "impoverished by fire, disaster, or being widowed or orphaned" were encouraged to apply to the association for monetary assistance. It is not clear whether anyone ever did apply to the main shrine for loans, but the association rules formally reinforced the importance of group solidarity.

Perhaps even more important than the kō, however, the Reverence Association emphasized the household as the basic unit of Konpira worship. In this, the rules of the association reinforced the social policies of the Meiji government, which shifted taxes and other burdens from entire villages, as under the Tokugawa, to household units. Indeed, the emphasis placed by the Reverence Association on the household and even some of the methods the association used to convey its importance grew out of one of the earliest policies of the Meiji government: the official population registration system, which in its initial stages was carried out through local shrines as well as the civil bureaucracy.

In 1871, the government abolished the Tokugawa-era system of temple registration in favor of a more standardized structure of population tracking, unaffiliated with the Buddhist establishment. Whereas the old temple rosters listed some people by denominational affiliation and others by address, some by birthplace and others by current residence, the new system of household registration (*koseki*) recorded all people nationwide according to the households in which they lived. Initially carried out by the lowest level of state-recognized Shinto shrines, whose role in recording births was especially valued, the new system for registering the population as the parishioners of local shrines (*ujiko shirabe*) paved the way for households to serve as the basic unit of the Meiji social order.[10]

Although the involvement of shrines in this registration work lasted less than two years, the ujiko shirabe system set forth a model of the unification of governing and ritual functions upon which shrines such as Kotohira could draw. From August 1871 until May 1873, as part of a policy to identify and thus control Christians, the Ministry of People's Affairs (Minbushō) and the Ministry of Doctrine required all Japanese residents to obtain from the shrines of their local tutelary deities (*ujigami*) amulets inscribed with their name, province of birth, address, date of birth, and father's name. The amulets were to be returned to the shrine upon death, although for people who wished to receive Shinto funerals, the priest could give the amulet, now marked with the date of death, back to the family of the deceased for use in memorial rites. Finally, the law explicitly (and, therefore, suggestively) declared that donations given to the local shrine at the time of receiving the registration amulet would be left to personal discretion.[11] The system thus strengthened the association of Shinto with the state while, during its short duration, increasing the income of the shrine.

Even after its demise, the ujiko shirabe system provided a source of inspiration to the priests of Kotohira. Although Kotohira—as a provincial, not a local, shrine—never formally participated in the shrine registration system, the priests adopted the (by then defunct) strategy in their development of the Reverence Association, providing both identifying amulets and Shinto funerary services at the same time.[12] In effect, drawing upon the example of the ujiko shirabe system, the priests on Mt. Zōzu sought to set Kotohira up as a national ujigami, registering parishioners from around the country as its supporters. In the ujiko shirabe model, they found a way to link the Reverence Association of the shrine not just to the everyday lives of devout worshippers, but to death and the many observances that followed.

The format of registration for the Reverence Association, like that of government population registration, focused on the household unit. After stating his address, the head of each household (they were almost exclusively male) appeared on association registers by name and age, designated as "household head." Then followed in status sequence the members of the household, each identified by relationship to the head (such as wife, eldest son, second son, daughter, adopted heir, father, or mother), name, and age. Each household was then tallied by gender.[13] This format suggested that only the male head of the household qualified directly as a member of the association: all others became members through him. Consistent with this attitude, the association allotted women, children, and the elderly only subsidiary responsibilities. According to the printed prayer often attached to copies of the association rules, an optional, simple line would suffice as a prayer for women and children. Moreover, such dependents were not required to go to the shrine to become members but could take the vow in front of the local association head.[14] Invariably, it was men who acted as leaders in the association. An illustration in the 1877 recruiting pamphlet *Sūkeikō no susume,* for instance, depicted worshippers at the main shrine led by men in hakama, with women only in the background (figure 8.1). Association rules reinforced the emphasis on male-headed households by stipulating that entire households, not only the individuals that composed them, could take a vacation from work or fly a flag on the god's festival day. Likewise, the priests distributed Reverence Association gate plaques only to the head of each household.

Kotohira Shrine's Reverence Association, then, like many of the institutions of the Meiji government, conveyed and reinforced the values of the educated, village elites. From diligence and frugality at home to the self-restrained comportment of male household heads abroad, the Reverence Association incorporated the mores of the nascent middle class in the emerging choreography of Shinto worship. In the eyes of Kotohira's priests, it was not the uncontrolled exuberance of petitioners on their own, but instead this well-defined behavior of reverent worshippers—inspired by the promise of access to the god and enforced by the pressure of one's fellow association members—that constituted the signs of an appropriately reverent civilization.

Reshaping Pilgrimage

Amid the economic tensions of the early Meiji era, the priests of Kotohira sought to combine this message of Shinto civilization with profit-making strategies for the shrine. Despite the popularity of the god Kotohira, the income of the institution in the early 1870s could not support both the ongoing operations of the shrine and the added expenditures associated with the Toranomon lecture hall and the Great Teaching Institute. Without its former income from shogunate-granted lands, Kotohira Shrine relied entirely on donations, the sale of amulets, the commissioning of special rituals, and other mainstays of the pilgrimage business. For the eleven months from November 1871 to September 1872, for instance, the shrine reported a net profit of less than twenty-three hundred yen, clearly insufficient to cover even the Ministry of Doctrine's annual demands of five thousand yen for support of the Great Teaching Institute.[15] Kotohira's priests thus designed the Reverence Association to reshape the experience of pilgrimage while maximizing the

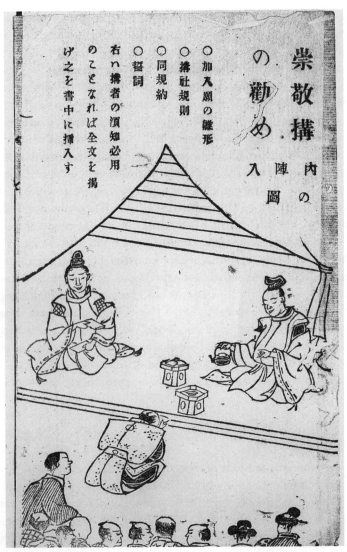

崇敬講の勧め

崇敬講内の陣図入

○加入願の雛形
○講社規則
○同規約
○誓詞
右ハ講者の須知必用のことなれば全文を掲げ之を書中に挿入す

❀ **8.1** An illustration in an 1887 pamphlet recruiting members for the Reverence Association depicted the culmination of the initiation ceremony in the main sanctuary, where members received special association amulets, gate plaques, and sanctified saké after vowing to obey the association rules. By giving association members this privilege of special access to the god, the priests of Kotohira Shrine were able to attract hithterto independent pilgrimage groups into a formal affiliation with the shrine. (From Murai Shin'ichirō, ed., *Sūkei kō no susume* [Takamatsu, 1878], 3v. Courtesy of the National Diet Library, Tokyo.)

flow of money into the shrine. They pursued a two-pronged strategy: first, re-organizing the structures of travel to direct money to the shrine; and second, working to sell even more amulets than before. These financial policies—crucial to the support of Kotohira and its priests—would both reinforce and undermine the intended messages of the association, creating new ambiguities and distinctions that would plague and profit the shrine for years to come.

As they worked to reorganize pilgrimage travel, the priests of the Reverence Association built upon existing arrangements that reinforced their teachings' message of formality. During the first half of the nineteenth century, a complex infrastructure of travel had developed that linked inns, boat services, and pilgrims throughout the country. Using the standard of the Reverence Association, the priests inserted Kotohira into that system, profiting from the exposure and income generated in the travel trade.

Travel guilds (kō) provided the pattern upon which the Reverence Association would capitalize. Guilds such as the Naniwakō, established in 1804, developed lists of inns based on the rosters of earlier pilgrimage kō, which had sought to ensure that their members could travel safely while maintaining respectable chastity on the road. In the nineteenth century, such guilds guided traveling businessmen to reliable inns where they would not be constantly importuned with prostitutes—the guilds having extracted promises from member inns not to promote prostitution blatantly on their premises. Select inns and rest stops, probably for a fee, won permission to display the names of guilds such as the Naniwakō or Isshinkō outside their establishments, thereby advertising external approval.[16]

With the establishment of the Reverence Association in 1874, the priests of Kotohira adopted the strictures and structures of such travel guilds, working to bring the private arrangements of travel establishments under the control of the shrine while expanding the network to include inns beyond the Konpira-Marugame-Osaka region. Instead of simply granting innkeepers and boat operators permission to use the encircled gold symbol in return for substantial donations, the priests of the Reverence Association placed new requirements on affiliated establishments, supporting the formal ideals of the group. The Reverence Association awarded licenses to inns selected from the four most prominent travel guilds along the main post roads of the country.[17] Each pledged to uphold a set of rules imposed by the Reverence Association, vowing to give association members directions only to another association inn. The inns, rest houses, and boat services swore neither to offer prostitutes to customers nor to direct them to expensive or unscrupulous ricksha pullers or palanquin carriers.[18] In return for these commitments, they could display

✿ **8.2** Reverence Association placard granted to a teahouse or other "rest stop." (Photo by Steve Cantley, with the permission of Kotohira Shrine.)

one of the symbols of the association: a large, wooden, talisman-like placard, a lantern, or a flag, each carrying the distinctive encircled gold insignia (figure 8.2).[19]

The arrangement proved to be mutually beneficial. Boat services and steamboat companies wrote to beg permission to display the Reverence Association logo, suggesting that the Reverence Association sign attracted many travelers.[20] Seven association inns at the junction of the Tokaido and Nakasendo post roads wrote to the association in 1876 confirming the exact pattern of the flags they were to display. They also reported that, "since August of this year, the association inns at this station have all hung up lanterns with the insignia of the association."[21] In return for its endorsement, the Reverence Association thus profited from free advertisement throughout the country. A flyer distributed by an inn in Osaka, for instance, prominently proclaimed the inn's status as "Purveyor for the Main Shrine Reverence Association" under the encircled gold insignia. The same flyer elaborated, "We provide information for people wishing to receive the initiation ceremony of entry into the sanctuary of the main shrine, in which one receives a small amulet and sacred saké, as well as a gate plaque and other items."[22]

The priests of Kotohira effectively condoned new models of travel, granting Reverence Association licenses not only to inns but to steamship operators as well.[23] Such developments in the travel infrastructure of Meiji Japan altered the experiences of people on their way to the shrine, creating dramatic contrasts between users of different modes of transport. First to change was the crossing of the Inland Sea. Until the early 1870s, this was most often accomplished on small wooden sailboats run by the Konpira boat inns of Osaka and other ports. Owing to the vagaries of wind and tides, the journey required at least one night, sometimes two, to bring the boats into port. Within the first few years of Meiji, however, steamship companies began to make inroads into the pilgrimage traffic. Offering standardized, published fares and a quicker trip, the steamships attracted more and more customers, overshadowing the Konpira boat inns.[24] As early as 1871, for instance, one traveler to Konpira recorded his journey from Osaka via Hyōgo to Tadotsu by steamship, and notations of steamship passages increasingly appeared in other diaries as well.[25] Advertisements of the boat inns in Osaka vanished after the early Meiji period, and later guidebooks mention only steamship schedules, not sailboats.[26]

Away from the crowds of Osaka, however, the small wooden boat services continued. A Tokyo newspaper, for instance, reported a case of fraud and intimidation on a Konpira boat crossing from Tadotsu to Shimotsui in 1898. Not only did the boat owners oversell the trip—taking money from fifty customers for a boat that could only hold thirty-five—but they lured passengers to extend their trip to connect with a fictitious railroad station, then told them tales of pirates and stole their money. "They are causing trouble for hundreds of Konpira pilgrims a day," reported the paper.[27]

Individuals sailed on their own as well. Farmers from Shōdoshima and other nearby islands rowed themselves in family-owned boats; owners of shipping vessels, prosperous from the booming herring trade in Hokkaido, continued to stop off at the ports; and people across the Inland Sea in Hiroshima prefecture used their own wooden boats or rented them from their fishermen neighbors.[28] Until at least the 1930s, groups of young fishermen sailed their boats to visit Konpira, then stopped off to "wait for the wind" at the brothels in the Inland Sea.[29] During the springtime height of Konpira pilgrimage, the ports of Marugame and Tadotsu were thus crowded with boats of all kinds—sailboats and rowboats as well as steamships.

People from Shikoku and around the Inland Sea thus walked or sailed to the shrine much as their parents had before them. For people from the metropolitan areas of Tokyo and Osaka, however, the increase in steamships nonetheless significantly altered the experience of travel to Konpira. On steamships, the trip across the Inland Sea, though still scenic, no longer meandered along the coastlines or afforded close-up views of coastal towns. Nor did it leave time for leisurely evenings at brothels, "waiting for the wind." Crowded "like sardines" into the lower-class cabin of a steamship from Hiroshima to Tadotsu with his pillow lined up next to his fellow passengers, one man traveling to Kotohira for the big festival in 1890 purportedly remarked, "Ahh, traveling certainly has gotten easier! In the blink of an eye, we go a distance of forty or fifty ri! And it really is very calm when there isn't any wind."[30] Travel guides of the pilgrimage no longer detailed the scenery seen on the crossing, and an entire genre of woodblock prints depicting the sea routes to the shrine disappeared after the early 1870s.[31] Steamships and new techniques in shipbuilding also made the crossing safer and more predictable. Prefectural statistics in 1890, for instance, record only two shipwrecks involving steamships, but thirty incidents in which nonmotorized boats were destroyed, sunk, or left adrift in storms.[32] Although a few ema remain to attest to the occasional dangers of the sea, the high drama of storms and capsizings increasingly receded to the pages of popular fiction.

Through the Reverence Association, Kotohira Shrine also formalized its ties to the most prestigious inns in the town of Kotohira. The inns of Konpira had played a major role in the countrywide spread and growth of the cult throughout the eighteenth and nineteenth centuries, when innkeepers and their representatives had traveled around the country recruiting pilgrims to stay in their inns and acting as intermediaries for large donations to the shrine.[33] The structure of the Reverence Association officially recognized this intermediary and income-generating role of the town's inns, encouraging them to recruit association members and donations through their relationships with regular customers. The priests and the innkeepers drew up contracts with details of incentives. The Reverence Association not only returned to inns up to 15 percent of the donations they brought in but also paid them a fixed fee for every person they recruited to enter the Reverence Association.[34] Innkeepers and their representatives therefore continued to travel around the country until the 1960s to recruit members for the Reverence Association.[35]

That the Reverence Association was based on this relationship of the

shrine to the major inns in Konpira is evident from the organizational structure of the association. No one was permitted to join the association without
registering through one of the town's inns. Hundreds of letters arrived at the
shrine over the years inquiring about joining the Reverence Association. In
every recorded case, the applicants were instructed to "submit the register of
association entrants via the designated inns at the foot of the mountain."[36]

Moreover, since the initiation ceremony of the Reverence Association occurred on two consecutive mornings, pilgrims of necessity were required to
stay one or more nights at the inn. Most Edo- and Meiji-period travel diaries
record that their writers visited the shrine for a few hours at midday or spent
only a single night, often at a cheaper lodging, for it did not take long to
climb up to the shrine and enjoy the sights.[37] In contrast, letters and diaries
testify that pilgrims who entered the Reverence Association were forced to
stay at least one night at a prominent inn. That requirement, however, limited the scope of the Reverence Association's influence. By its very structure,
the association restricted its audience to groups and individuals who could
accumulate funds for fees, rooms, and travel. Prostitutes from Inland Sea harbors, fleeing apprentices, and many other less affluent pilgrims would have
found the expenses insurmountable; staying at the many inexpensive lodg-
ings in Kotohira instead of the elite inns, they did not join the association.
From the outset, then, the Reverence Association catered to an already settled
population, excluding many of the workers and travelers whose meager donations filled the offering boxes.

In designing the Reverence Association, the priests of Kotohira also encountered another limitation. They hoped to modify miracle-oriented worship, yet without it, people would neither come to the shrine nor purchase
the amulets and prayer rituals that provided the bulk of the shrine's revenue.
For worshippers, as opposed to priests, the great attraction of Kotohira—
whether its Reverence Association or the shrine itself—lay in the miraculous
benefits of the god. Sailors told of praying to Konpira in the midst of violent
storms at sea, then being guided to safety by a mysterious bright light.
Women reported being healed from "severe illness" after seeing the god in
their dreams.[38] Most important in this physics of the miraculous was the creation of a connection between the petitioner and the deity, whether through
prayer or, even more efficaciously, through direct contact—approaching as
closely as possible to the deity or receiving an amulet blessed by the spirit of
the god.

This popular focus on amulets and access to the god formed the basis of
the shrine's wealth after its lands were confiscated in the early years of Meiji.
During the springtime pilgrimage crush in particular, worshippers clamored

around amulet booths at the shrine, overworking the priests and employees on duty. As the priest Matsuoka wrote in his diary in May 1872:

> People from every province crowded around to receive amulets. There were some who had come out of their way from Matsumae in Ezo [Hokkaido] in the east and from [the islands off Nagasaki] in the west, specifically to receive amulets and other items. By three o'clock, at least four hundred wooden talismans had changed hands, and probably more than three thousand paper ones. It was amazing: ten carpenters worked as hard as they could, with sweat pouring down their bodies, to cut and carve the boards for the wooden talismans. Then we wrote the sacred name of the deity on the talismans, and transferred the spirit to them, two or three, or even ten or twenty talismans at a time. . . . We were so busy that it seemed as if our hakama would get tangled up in our legs.[39]

In 1873, at a time when many people could not afford even a single paper amulet, the shrine sold more than 250,000 amulets of all types.[40]

The challenge for the priests, then, was to maintain the reputation and attractiveness of the god's amulets while resituating them within the "civilized" Shinto that they espoused. In designing the incentives available to Reverence Association members, the priests took care not to jeopardize the shrine's main source of income: amulet and talisman sales. Not only did the association collect donations and initiation fees to cover the conferral of the special association amulets, but it also carefully avoided giving members the more valuable large wooden talismans, thereby enhancing their desirability and, thus, their cost (figure 8.3). Although constituting only 15 percent of amulets sold in 1873, for instance, the wooden amulets made up 68 percent of the shrine's entire income from amulet sales—sales which in turn constituted between 78 and 88 percent of the shrine income.[41]

While only a minority of worshippers purchased the wooden talismans,

⊛ 8.3 (*opposite*) Collection of wooden talismans in the Minami family household, Yasuda, Kōchi prefecture. The talismans from Konpira are kept alongside enshrined amulets of other deities at the top of the entranceway to the Tokugawa-era house. On the right are visible more recent talismans from Kotohira Shrine, with older talismans from Konkōin, Tamon'in, and Hashikuraji behind. The Minami family acted as merchants and shippers from 1703 on, then focused solely on saké brewing after 1869. This shift in occupation is reflected in the talismans: for household safety, from Konkōin in 1845; for family longevity, from Tamon'in in 1848; for maritime safety, from Konkōin in 1849 and 1855; for household safety, from Konkōin in 1864; for prosperity in saké brewing, from Hashikurasan Okunoin (inner temple), undated; and for household safety, from Kotohira Shrine in 1874, 1879, 1894 and 1895 (during the Sino-Japanese War), and 1900. (Photo by the author, courtesy of the Minami family and Uchikawa Kiyosuke.)

almost all sought at least one paper one. It was the paper amulets—also renowned for their miraculous powers—that priests incorporated into the climactic ceremony of the initiation ritual. As a recruiting pamphlet described the final ritual in the main hall of the shrine,

> Two priests stand at the corridor in front of the hall and flourish white *gohei* [paper wands] and *sakaki* [sacred tree branches], using these to purify each person. Afterward, they call everyone one by one and lead them into the sanctuary. The doors above the altar are open, with gold leaf in front and an impressive curtain hung across. In the middle, the large sacred mirror is enshrined. There is no way to express its majesty, just that one naturally feels reverence within one's heart. At this point, more people enter and the person in the sanctuary moves on and prostrates himself below the altar. He makes the vow [of the association], receives sacred saké from one priest and a small amulet and the association amulet from another. Then, depending on the will of the initiate, he offers various sacred offerings, and the household head receives a gate plaque [see figure 8.1].[42]

The vow of the association, the partaking of saké, and the conferral of the amulets thus formed the culmination of the initiation.

Intimate access to the god could only be achieved in the association context; in the eyes of both priests and worshippers, it was the main perquisite of association membership. When petitioners wrote letters to the shrine or association, they repeatedly referred to Reverence Association members as "people who have received entry into the sanctuary" (*gonaijin iri ōsetsukerareni sōrō*). Many asked for details not about membership or the association as a whole, but about "procedures to enter the sanctuary" (*naijin iri no tetsuzuki*).[43]

Such sanctuary access included the amulet. In the early 1870s, the rules of the Reverence Association redefined the amulets conferred during the ceremony as evidence of membership in the association, effectively sacralizing the group affiliation:

> In regard to the amulet or association amulet received upon joining the association, each member must keep it upon his body throughout his entire life. However, he must absolutely not carry it at funerals, in the toilet, or in any impure place. It is proof of association membership.
>
> After a member's death, the association amulet may be returned to the association officials of the main shrine, who will dedicate it at the spirit shrine [*reikonsha*] in the shrine grounds and perform ceremonies each spring and fall. Alternatively, it may be enshrined in the spirit shrine [*reisha*] of the individual household.[44]

That is, both during life and after death, each member (and his surviving family) would ideally be tied to ongoing rites at, and support of, the association and the shrine.

Focusing on the worshippers' affiliation with kō, household, and shrine, the priests of the Reverence Association at first tried to sidestep the issue of miracles. Official publications of the Reverence Association during the early years of its existence in the 1870s never mentioned the miracles attributed to amulets or the wonder-working powers of the god. But the growing popularity of Christianity, Western science, and skeptical philosophy among some elements of the Meiji intelligentsia prompted a shift in strategy. In 1878, an article in a newspaper from Ibaragi prefecture, which argued that the gods did not exist, was passed around the Reverence Association headquarters at Kotohira in 1878, engendering much dismay. Three days later, Head Priest Fukami Hayao directed Matsuoka Mitsugi to begin compiling the miracle tales of Kotohira.[45] Shortly thereafter, the two priests agreed on a model for the proposed publication, choosing *Meiji Records of Filial Tales,* an illustrated collection of Confucian-inspired, moralistic stories recently published by the Imperial Household Office. It related the filial deeds of ordinary Japanese subjects, and Fukami and Matsuoka agreed that the miracle tales of Konpira, compiled and presented in a similarly appealing format, would be ideal for use in indoctrination.[46]

Such collection and publication of Konpira's miracle tales was not unprecedented. It is clear, for instance, that Matsuoka modeled his compilation after an Edo-period edition of Konpira's miracles in his personal collection.[47] But this time, Matsuoka edited and retold the tales to support the goals of the shrine and the Great Teaching Campaign, altering details to emphasize the importance of proper behavior and dedication to the god. On 2 March 1878, for example, when Matsuoka lectured to an audience of about 350 people in eastern Sanuki province, he told a tale of a large anchor donated to Kotohira, using it to illustrate the first of the Three Standards of Instruction: respect for the gods (*keishin*). As Matsuoka related the story in his collection of miracle tales, a sailor, Ushichi, refused to join his fellow crewmembers in stealing the cargo of their ship and reporting to the owner that it was lost at sea. He refused not only because he thought it would be difficult to accomplish but also because "the gods see clearly from the other world, and I am afraid." Because of this, his erstwhile companions tied him to the anchor and threw him into the sea. Ushichi, "an extremely upright [*jichōna*] fellow who had worshipped the Great Kami Kotohira for a long time," prayed with all his heart. The next thing he knew, still lashed to the large anchor, he had fallen through the roof into the living room of the ship's owner in Osaka with nary a scratch. When the case was taken before the magistrate, the villains were sentenced to death, and the shipowner and Ushichi went on pilgrimage to Kotohira, donating the anchor and several other items to the deity.[48] The dramatic tale, vividly illustrated in woodblock prints, copied in later miracle tale collections, and even performed as a play,[49] captured the imagination of listeners as it emphasized the importance of honest actions coupled with reliance upon Kotohira. "Everyone seemed impressed, saying 'Amazing!' [*kashikoki koto yo*]," Matsuoka recorded of the story's success.[50] Moreover, the story appealed to the wealthy merchants and shipowners who were Kotohira Shrine's most generous donors: Kotohira not only saved the sailor but deposited him in the owner's house, saving the property of the owner and informing him of the dangers posed to his business.

In the end, then, the priests of Kotohira, in their role as doctrinal instructors, sought to infuse the amulets and the miracles of the god—and, indeed, the structures of pilgrimage itself—with moral, behavioral lessons. By building upon existing structures and values, they succeeded in enhancing the flow of income to the shrine. At the same time, they made it possible for people simply to ignore their efforts, interpreting the new layer of Reverence Association formality in the preexisting framework of personal contact with the god and its miraculous response. The Reverence Association thus allowed the shrine to alter its official message while enhancing its financial base, adding to the vast array of interpretations already available on the sacred mountain.

Faith under the Reverence Association

To what extent did the Reverence Association fulfill the priests' goals of profit and persuasion? Economically and organizationally, the association met with modest success during its first several years. As early as 1876, when initiations into the Reverence Association had barely begun, association entry fees already constituted 2 percent of shrine income, more than the income generated from either special ceremonies or the sale of special offerings.[51] By 1880, the association could claim a membership of more than two million.[52]

The effect of the association on the thoughts and behavior of its members, however, is much less clear. Some members clearly paid attention to its teachings. Adherence to the minutiae of association rules is perhaps most evident in the adoption by some members of the Shinto funerals espoused by the association. One man, avowing his "sincerity" and "dedication to the association rules" since his initiation three years before, wrote to the shrine in 1882 requesting a mirror and prayer book to be used in memorial rites "in accordance with rule number 14" of the association handbook.[53] Other worshippers carefully returned association amulets to the shrine upon the death of family members.[54] Yet other members seem to have paid little or no attention to either the funeral rites or the other teachings. Records left by four Reverence Association members who visited the shrine in 1881 or 1882—a nativist from Kyushu, a representative of a pilgrimage kō from the Tokyo area, a pilgrim from Chiba prefecture, and a member of an association kō from Kii province—may provide a sense of the variety of ways in which members incorporated the Reverence Association into their lives.

Ogata Shōtarō (1843–1920), a Hirata-school nativist and doctrinal instructor from Kumamoto prefecture in Kyushu, for instance, arranged to take a student to Kotohira in 1882 while on a trip to visit other nativists in Shikoku. The diary of the trip he kept showed that the thirty-nine-year-old clearly hated any signs of the new, Western-inspired developments of the time. He used the old calendar, not the new, almost a decade after the official adoption of the Gregorian system. "The foreign ships I see each day singe the sky," he complained, "rowing around [our] Great Eight-Island Country just as they like. . . . How I resent it!"[55] Ogata greeted any sign of the past as better than the present. This past that Ogata revered so much, however, like the idealized past of so many of his fellow nativists, included dramatic innovations. Thus, he wrote in his journal, for instance, not of the long-familiar "Konpira" but of the newer "Kotohira no Ōkami" and adopted the nativist terminology of the priests throughout. "We visited the Great Deity," he recorded. "First, we gathered with other people at the Purification Altar [the Dawn Shrine]. After the purification was finished, we followed each other to the front of the Main Hall and worshipped from a distance. The shrine officials opened the doors [to the inner sanctum] and intoned a prayer. Everyone knelt and bowed down. Afterward, we received sanctified saké, mirror-shaped rice cakes, and other items."[56] Even recognizing the "mirror-shaped" reference of the rice cakes, Ogata saw the world through nativist eyes. Yet he never mentioned the Reverence Association. Either the shrine had begun performing the rituals for all comers, or he saw the association, its teachings, and procedures as so commonplace as not to merit mention.

Sporting the samurai topknot that had been outlawed for years, Ogata and his fellow traveling companions stood out from other pilgrims, as alien to other Japanese as the foreigners they so detested. "Along our way, on the road toward the Great Kami," Ogata wrote, "people thought our bound hair was strange. They came out of every building and called out from every gate. 'Look at that!' they said, . . . and loudly called us names."[57] Such dedicated adherents to the past clearly stood in a minority among pilgrims to Konpira.

Other pilgrims incorporated their worship of the god not into an imagined, nativist past but into the changing present. The year before Ogata's trip, in 1881, Koizumi Kakuhei (1839–1915), a representative of a kō from Tama, in present-day Tokyo, also kept a diary of his visit. Like most diaries of the time, the forty-two-year-old Koizumi's consisted less of a record of his thoughts and activities than of a list of expenses used to account for the money he received from his kō.[58]

Koizumi's trip to Konpira occurred in the context of a longer, fifty-two-day trip of sightseeing and worship. Accompanied by one or two people from another village, he stopped in Kyoto and Yokohama, worshipping at temples to Kannon and other kami and buddhas along the way. At the main shrines and temples—including Kiyomizudera, Hōryūji, and Mt. Kōya—Koizumi purchased talismans, amulets, and prints to distribute to people at home. At Konpira, he bought the most: thirty prints, at least thirty-two amulets of various types, and six boxes in which to enshrine them. Konpira—written as "Konpira," never as "Kotohira"—thus existed for Koizumi and his fellow kō members within a combinatory world of kami and buddhas. On his ride from Tadotsu to Konpira, for instance, he stopped off at Zentsūji, "the birthplace of Kōbosama [Kūkai]" and donated three sen toward the replacement of the tiles on its roof.

For Koizumi, this combinatory Konpira existed in no discernible tension with the new developments of the age. He frequently rode steamships and rickshas. He recorded the dates in his diary according to the new calendar. It is unclear, however, to what extent the new timetable influenced his worship: he prayed at Kotohira and joined the Reverence Association on 9 March, which corresponded to the tenth day of the old second month. In this respect, Koizumi may have been like many others. During 1880 and 1881, for instance, crowds of people came to the shrine to pray and buy amulets on the tenth day of the old third month, although it occurred during at a time when no shrine-sanctioned festivals were scheduled (figure 8.4).

Conveniently, Koizumi may not have needed to choose. Because of the length of the initiation procedures for the Reverence Association, he stayed over at Kotohira until the tenth day of March, as well. Indeed, Koizumi ended up staying at the Bizen'ya for three nights, spending a large amount of money on purchases for his kō. Although Koizumi, like the nativist Ogata,

⊛ 8.4 (*opposite*) Number of wooden talismans sold at Kotohira Shrine during the old third month of 1880 and 1881. Although the official calendar of both the nation and the shrine had been changed in 1873, people continued to visit Kotohira Shrine on the tenth day of the old month—although in these years it fell on Monday, 19 April, and Friday, 8 April, respectively, when no official festivities were planned at the shrine. (Data from Matsuoka Mitsugi, *Nennen nikki*, entry for 9 June 1881.)

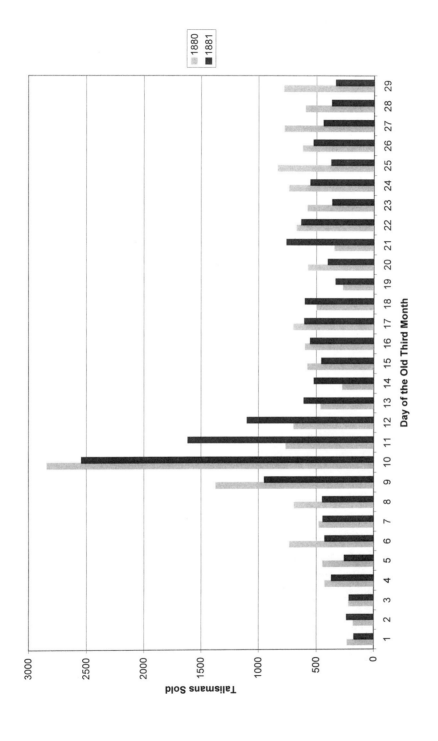

did not mention the Reverence Association explicitly, he kept his personal-ized, dated membership amulet with his journal of the pilgrimage. Evidently, his terse records of expenditures and itinerary fail to mention his attendance at the initiation sermon and sanctuary ritual.[59]

In contrast to the diaries kept by Ogata and Koizumi, the evidence of the other two pilgrims comes not from journals kept for themselves or their de-scendants, but from a letter to the shrine and a votive plaque to the god. Both demonstrate how some members of the Reverence Association incorporated the rites of the association into their own petitions for miracles.

The ritual surrounding the new association amulets, when interpreted by prospective members according to their own experience, apparently added to their magical value. The amulet, intended to be carried as identification by a member for his or her entire life, was valued far more for its long-lasting pow-ers. It became, in popular parlance, a "lifelong protection amulet." As one man, Ōmori Saburōhei, wrote to the shrine in 1882, such an amulet was in high demand:

> After wanting to [go on pilgrimage] for years, I finally had an opportune time, and last year, during the second month of 1881, I was able to go to worship and climb the mountain at the main shrine. On the way, I met and traveled with a man named Koyasu Isetarō, from the post town of Ōami in the district of Yamabe in the province of Kazusa in Chiba prefecture. He explained that he was going on a pilgrimage to the main shrine of Kotohira, and that since he was a faithful believer, he would receive a lifelong protec-tion amulet [*ichidai shugo*] and return home. So of course I also received the amulet. Upon my return home, news and rumors of this spread throughout the village, and many people wanted to join [the association]. Therefore, I beg you to please inscribe the following names in the register. Each person has contributed ten sen for the entrance fee, for a total of ten yen which I send. . . . Each person will also donate more every year. . . . Please send a receipt and confirmation of this.[60]

Thus, as Ōmori wrote, once people heard of his "lifelong protection amulet," they all wanted one too. One hundred of his fellow villagers sent money for this special, effective amulet. Since the only way to receive one was to enter the Reverence Association, Ōmori requested that the shrine inscribe them all as members. For Ōmori and his neighbors, then, the purpose of the Reverence Association was to provide amulets with concrete, magical results. Nowhere in the letter does he mention that he himself especially believes in nativist Shinto, nor does he cite the Way of the Gods, the emperor, or the state. Instead, his at-tention focuses on the especially efficacious, "lifelong protection" amulet.

Similarly, the donors of a votive plaque to the shrine in 1881 also seemed to interpret membership in the Reverence Association as either a recognition or an enhancement of a special relationship with the god that would facilitate a miraculous response to prayer. Donated by "Matsumura village, Kishū" the votive plaque stated: "On New Year's of Meiji 14 [1881], Matsu, the forty-nine-year-old mother of Hayase Katsujirō, of Matsushima village, Nakusa district, Kii province, unexpectedly began speaking in tongues, possessed by foxes. Unable to bear seeing this, we, the Reverence Association of the village—thirty-eight people beginning with Tsuda Sutenoshin—together made a vow to Kotohira Shrine, in which we believe. At that time, we received the favor of the god, and soon she recovered completely. Thankfully, with awe and rejoicing, we offer this sketch of that incident." The accompanying image showed a golden paper wand (gohei) on a cloud, with several foxes fleeing from a woman below.[61]

Belief in fox possession was surely anathema to the priests who led the Reverence Association at the shrine. In 1873, for instance, a Ministry of Doctrine edict banned the practice of fox exorcism and various other forms of possession, as well as the performance of prayer rites, such as goma ceremonies, for divination and the like. These were exactly the "superstitious" practices that the moral teachings of the association were meant to displace. And yet, in 1881, an association kō thanked the god for its help in performing just such an exorcism. Clearly, far from destroying previous beliefs and practices, the Reverence Association frequently became a part of them. Or, perhaps, it grew apart *from* them, for many worshippers donated votive plaques depicting tengu, testifying to their abstention from eel and crab, thanking the god for healings, rescues, and protection from fire—with never a mention of the Reverence Association.[62] Whether supporting a nativist preoccupation with the past, accommodating the pilgrimage practices of combinatory kō, encouraging belief in particularly efficacious amulets, or enhancing the miraculous ties between members and the god, the Reverence Association, for many people, fitted seamlessly into existing practice.

As the priests promoted their Shinto civilization, merging moralism with moneymaking in their effort to survive, they incorporated pilgrimage and amulets into the rites and rules of their new, shrine-centered pilgrimage association. In doing so, they ensured both popular interest in the association and members' interpretation of the rites according to their own frameworks. In effect, the priests overlaid the long-standing emphasis on miracles with a formal veneer of Shinto worship tailored to the values and customs of the shrine's well-to-do supporters. They provided a shared economic and ritual framework within which all worshippers—rich or poor, educated or illiterate—could continue bringing to Konpira their own meanings, hopes, and desires.

A Shrine without Religion
(1882–1892)

9

During the early years of the Meiji government, as during the founding decades of the Tokugawa shogunate and the Takamatsu domain centuries before, priests on Mt. Zōzu renamed their gods, altered long-standing rituals, and, in the Meiji case, even adopted a new educational mission—all to ensure the survival and status of their institution through support of the new regime. In each case, however, once the new rulers secured their positions and no longer worried so much about convincing people of their sacred right to rule, they shifted both their attention and their investments away from the shrine. From the 1670s on, successors to the first lord of Takamatsu reduced their support for Konpira Daigongen, focusing instead on issues of administration and economy. Likewise, in the 1880s, the priorities of leaders in Tokyo altered: the reformers in power set limits on funding for state shrines such as Kotohira, turning instead to broader military, industrial, and legal initiatives as they prepared to establish a constitutional state. The new political system that resulted would dramatically reshape the role of Kotohira and other state shrines in society as a whole.

The shift to a constitutional order posed a terrible dilemma for the priests at Kotohira and other prominent shrines. Even as they faced the prospect of dwindling financial support from the state, they also encountered new constraints on their activities that tied them ever more closely to the ideological interests of the Meiji regime. This awkward state of affairs grew out of changes and compromises within the central leadership in Tokyo. In a series of confusing religious policies, competing factions first bolstered, then limited official ties between the kami, the imperial house, and the imperial government. As rivals struggled to shape the upcoming constitutional order, they worked to reconcile their proposed religious policies with the concept of "separation of state and religion"—a separation that eventually aligned Kotohira and other major shrines with the "state," not with "religion," according to the principle soon to be set forth in the constitution of 1889.

The Meiji leaders wrote the constitution as part of their ongoing effort to strengthen Japan. During the last two decades of the nineteenth century, they established popularly elected assemblies, promoted industry, and expanded the army and navy, hoping to encourage domestic support and secure international favor. By transforming Japan into a strong, industrializing, constitutional power, government leaders hoped to demonstrate Japan's equality with the West—a crucial first step in revising the unequal treaties of the 1850s and ensuring the independence of Japan in an age of European and American imperialism.

Changes in shrine policy thus coincided with an era of official industrializing efforts supported by high taxes and other deflationary policies. These policies drastically reduced the discretionary income of people throughout Japan and therefore reduced both the number of pilgrims to Kotohira and the size of their offerings. Indeed, between 1882 and 1886, declining income forced the priests of Kotohira to dismiss 188 employees of the shrine, abolish the retirement benefits of the remaining workers, and close down both the shrine's publishing office and the stall that sold amulet boxes in the precincts.[1] For the priests of Kotohira, therefore, the 1880s proved a dismal decade, for even as it faced the constitutional ban on "religious" activity, the shrine also lost income from both state and populace.

Forced to look away from the state in their search for financial support, the priests of Kotohira focused on cultivating connections to more promising sponsors. In the eighteenth century, the priests of Konkōin had turned to the increasingly influential local administrators, merchants, and entrepreneurs eager to sponsor the prominent deity. Now, in the late nineteenth century, the men of Kotohira wooed the successors of those affluent donors—the prominent taxpayers who would soon elect and populate the prefectural and national assemblies of the constitutional regime. But, as they catered to these landlords, business owners, and other local leaders, the priests of Kotohira could, at least in theory, no longer address their "religious" needs. Instead, they would need to find new ways to serve this promising public. The resulting innovations of priests at Kotohira and around the country would shape the history of Kotohira, of Shinto, and of Japan until 1946 and, in many ways, beyond.

Rites, Religion, and Shinto

In the 1870s and 1880s, the growth of constitutional thinking in Japan dramatically altered the religious landscape. The Great Teaching Campaign, of which Kotohira Shrine's Reverence Association was a part, had been designed to combat the threat of Christianity by uniting Buddhists and priests of the kami to preach support of the imperial government. Yet, when nativists enshrined kami from the ancient histories in the Great Teaching Institute and in the Toranomon lecture hall, emphasizing through ritual and formal reverence the sacred Shinto identity of the imperial line, they began alienating the very Buddhists who had initially proposed the campaign.

It soon became clear that nativists had used the campaign to create a new set of doctrines, rituals, and gods, in effect defining a "national religion" (*kokkyō*) to be imposed upon all. Japanese studying abroad in the early 1870s criticized this development, using the importance of constitutional separation of church and state in the West to put pressure on the Meiji government to reform. "The [Ministry of Doctrine's] attempt to impose upon our people a religion of its creation cannot receive too severe condemnation, because such an attempt not only disregards our sacred liberty of conscience, but its effect is to crush the very soul of man," wrote Mori Arinori in the United States.[2] The Buddhist Shimaji Mokurai, a priest of the True Pure Land sect and one of the early proponents of the Great Teaching Campaign, complained in Paris that the Meiji leaders had "in a very short period of time, constructed a new religion with which they seek to strengthen the people."[3] Instead of bringing men of different traditions together to preach against the Christians in their own ways, the Great Teaching Campaign had served as the birthplace of a new religion: a Way of the Kami (Shintō) tied not just to the gods but explicitly to the state, its hierarchies, and its history. The institutional and doctrinal requirements of the campaign had drawn hitherto autonomous priests into a unified structure of Shinto priests, shrines, and teachings.

Protesting this increasingly inflexible structure, Shimaji's True Pure Land sect withdrew from the Great Teaching Institute in February 1875. Deprived of the support of the largest Buddhist denomination in the country, the Ministry of Doctrine abolished the Great Teaching Institute only three months later, freeing Shinto and Buddhist doctrinal instructors to spread their teachings separately. Before the end of the year, pressured by the Buddhists, the Ministry of Doctrine announced even more explicitly that doctrinal instructors' "freedom of belief [*shinkyō no jiyū*] in each Shinto or Buddhist denomination is protected by the government." Distinguishing between the teachings of the state and the beliefs of its preachers, the ministry laid the groundwork for a constitutional separation of state and religion. This distinction, however, confronted many advocates of Shinto with a dilemma: how to find a balance between Shinto as a religion (complete with gods, miracles, and even funerals) and Shinto as above religion—as a state cult or symbolic system that could transcend the battles between believers and sects while still sharing the rituals and, indeed, gods of Shinto "religion."

In the convoluted policies of the years that followed, "freedom of religious belief" increasingly implied the equality of Buddhism and the new Shinto as well as the right of people to choose between them. While the Meiji leaders continued to promote Shinto symbols and rites, they redefined the vast majority of Shinto shrines and their priests, placing them on a par with their Buddhist counterparts. In 1876, the Ministry of Doctrine created the Shinto equivalent of Buddhist denominations, rewarding the fund-raising and dedication of two lay associations (the Kurozumi kōsha and the Shūsei kōsha) by promoting them to the status of independent Shinto sects (Shintō Kurozumi *ha* and Shintō Shūsei ha). Within less than a month, the Council of State abolished the Ministry of Doctrine, with its implications of overseeing a state religion; Shinto shrines and Buddhist temples alike were placed instead under the Home Ministry. Reinforcing the emerging emphasis on personal religious choice, the Home Ministry in 1879 stripped the vast majority of Shinto shrines and priests (excluding Ise, the imperial shrines, and the provincial shrines—that is, those with recognized imperial ties, such as Kotohira) of their official, state-funded status, equating them with Buddhist temples and priests as optional sites for popular worship. Thus, while doctrinal instructors toured the country preaching reverence for the kami and obedience to the imperial court, belief in buddhas or kami (at lower shrines, at least) had become, in principle, a matter of private choice.

Ranging far beyond this issue of religious freedom, ideas of constitutional government gained popularity in Japan throughout the 1870s. In early 1874, some of the Meiji leaders left the government, proposed the establishment of a nationally elected representative assembly, and founded their own political party. Former samurai, stripped of their elite status, supported the idea. Wealthy peasants wrote their own draft constitutions, and poorer peasants saw the possibility of land or tax reform.[4] Within the central government as well, several leaders saw a connection between a constitutional government, recognized by the West, and improved prospects for revision of the unequal treaties. In the wake of a political scandal in 1881, when yet another member of the Meiji oligarchy left the government to establish a political party, the remaining leaders reluctantly succumbed to public pressure, promising to write a constitution for Japan and establish an elected national assembly in 1890.

This constitutional commitment changed the debate over religious policy. Reformers in the government—including Yamagata Aritomo, Inoue Kaoru, and Matsukata Masayoshi—argued for the importance of complete separation of church and state. They urged the abolition of all doctrinal instructors and an end to attempts to spread a government teaching. A significant group of men in the Council of State, however, insisted on the importance of reverence for the imperial house. Prominent leaders during the Restoration, these conservatives—including Yamada Akiyoshi, Sasaki Takayuki, and Ōki Takatō—insisted on the primacy of the emperor and the imperial court, and thus the promotion of widespread reverence for the sacred imperial line and the kami associated with it. They praised the value of Shinto in uniting the nation and insisted that the priests of lower shrines, at least, be permitted to remain as doctrinal instructors.[5] The unresolved tension between the two groups became evident in January 1882, when the Home Ministry announced that "from now on, the simultaneous employment of priests [*shinkan*] as doctrinal instructors is abolished, and they may not have anything to do with funerals. . . . However, the priests of metropolitan and prefectural shrines and below will continue as before." In other words, only the priests of highly ranked, state-supported shrines—Ise, imperial shrines, and provincial shrines (of which Kotohira was one)—would be prohibited from performing funerary rites or acting as doctrinal instructors.

Priests of prominent state-supported shrines were thus forced to make a choice: maintain their rank and position at the shrine or give it up to act as doctrinal instructors in the lay associations that they led. In fact, two prominent priests—from the shrines of Ise and Izumo—chose the latter option, resigning from the head priestship and instead promoting their shrine lay associations, obtaining recognition in 1882 as the heads of new Shinto "sects."[6] In effect, they joined the world of "religious" choice. When two years later, in 1884, the doctrinal instructor system was abolished entirely, both these lay association leaders and the priests of lower-ranking shrines would henceforth preach merely as representatives of their own organizations, without official government support: they would be representatives of "religion."

Most priests of state-funded shrines, however, gave up their roles as doctrinal instructors. At Kotohira, Head Priest Fukami, Kotooka, Matsuoka, and the others proved no exception. Somehow, however, Fukami and Kotooka received permission from the Home Ministry to straddle the division between shrine and "religion"; they maintained control over the Reverence Association, presumably delegating the actual performance of such "religious" matters as funerals and sermons to others.[7] Tied closely to the shrine, the Kotohira Reverence Association did not become a separate "religious" sect of Shinto. Instead, it continued as it had before, but with the priests less intimately involved and, on occasion, with formal contracts drawn up to clarify the fiscal relationship of the association to the shrine.[8]

So, if the priests of shrines such as Kotohira were forbidden the realm of "teachings" or "religion"—that is, preaching and funerals—what could they do? By separating these priests from doctrinal instructors, the Home Ministry's edict of 1882 intensified the distinction between lower, "religious" shrines and state-supported, "nonreligious" shrines. The "kami officials" (shinkan, priests) at state-funded shrines were thus left with performing the "rites of the state" (kokka no sōshi)—intoning prayers and offering donations to the kami of the imperial texts. Through their rituals, they would in effect recognize the inviolable, sacred legitimacy of the imperial government and enact the values of loyalty to the imperial state (figure 9.1).

Kotohira and other shrines thus became sites for the rituals of imperial subjecthood.[9] Much as the rite of reciting the Pledge of Allegiance in the United States today promotes respect for the flag and the republic, often tying the nation explicitly to God, the rituals at state shrines in Japan—on the day of the founding of the empire and other state holidays—promoted respect for the imperial lineage and the kami that protected it. Moreover, while shrine priests could not preach "religious" sermons, they could certainly study the texts of the nation: the ancient imperial histories (such as the *Kojiki* and *Nihon Shoki*) and other nativist-revered writings that spelled out the basis of the imperial government. Indeed, Finance Minister Matsukata Masayoshi reportedly proposed the study of such texts as the appropriate job of the priests.[10] That these nativist "classics" invariably referred to kami and were interpreted (following Motoori Norinaga and other nativists) as evidence of the unbroken sacred lineage of the imperial throne did not make them "religious" in the terminology of Meiji leaders. Instead, they testified to the centrality of the Way of the Kami in the structure of the nation (*kokutai,* commonly translated as "national polity"). In theory, the texts, like the rites, supported the imperial state as a whole, not the individual choices of divided individuals.

On 28 January 1882, the very day that the priests of Kotohira Shrine tendered their resignations as doctrinal instructors, they seized upon the edict's

❋ **9.1** (*opposite*) Print from 1881 explaining the formal Shinto process of worship in detail, complete with the proper order of clapping and bowing and the correct wording of a prayer to the Great Kami Kotohira. Avoiding any reference either to miracles or to the Reverence Association, such prints conveniently distanced the state-sponsored shrine from any ties to "religion." (Hattori Seijirō, *Sanukiguni Kotohira sanzu* [Kotohira: Kotohirasan, 1881]. From the collection of the author.)

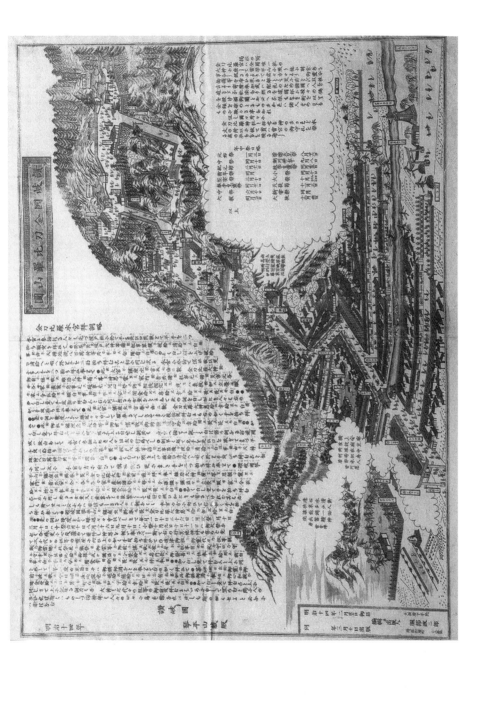

implications of a heightened, imperial importance for highly ranked shrines in an attempt, once again, to raise the stature of their shrine. Fukami, Kotooka, and the other priests submitted two memorials to the central government. In the first, they supported the proposals of several other nativists and Shinto priests, both inside and outside government, to reestablish the Office of Rites and make it the highest decision-making body in the government, thereby placing shrine worship at the center of administration.[11] In the second, they reiterated the popularity of Kotohira and the power of its miracles—rivaling those of Ise—and requested once again the designation of Kotohira Shrine as an imperial grand shrine (kanpei taisha), second only to the shrine of the sacred imperial ancestor.[12]

Within months of the edict, the priests of Kotohira also formally adopted the study and teaching of the ancient nativist texts as a primary goal, both independently and as part of a larger initiative among Shinto priests nationwide. This scholarly shift took shape in two new institutions. In July 1882, following an initiative in Tokyo to establish "sites for lecture and research on the imperial classics" (*kōten kōkyūjo*), the priests began organizing a Classics Study Group (Kōten Gakkai) intended—as Matsuoka Mitsugi remarked at the time and the founding rules of the group stated when it formally opened the next year—to "clarify the national polity and inculcate virtues."[13] Kotohira's Classics Study Group would eventually develop as a site for the education and certification of Shinto priests throughout western Kagawa prefecture.[14] Indeed, as Matsuoka commented in his journal, the Classics Study Group became the vehicle through which priests, banned from giving sermons under the "religious" Reverence Association, could still lecture on Shinto around the country. When worshippers wrote to the shrine requesting that a priest come to lecture on the classics and on the virtues of the god, Matsuoka and his peers now accommodated the requests no longer as doctrinal instructors but as representatives of the study group.[15] The effect was an intensification of the priests' role as interpreters of the texts of nativist Shinto: as Matsuoka repeatedly expressed, a sense that they brought to people interested only in spectacles and magic "the *true* Shinto" of scholarship and reverence.[16]

The nativist scholarship of the Classics Study Group also shaped a school that operated on the mountain. Known at the time as the Dawn Academy (Asahi Juku), the school had long hosted lectures twice a month, mainly on Confucian topics, but since 1881 also to "clarify the way of the kami." In June 1882, Head Priest Fukami and his fellow priests reorganized the academy as the Myōdō Gakkō, or "School of Illuminating the Way [of the kami]," a middle school catering to the sons of priests and wealthy men in the area.

Teaching science and English alongside Shinto interpretations of the historical and literary classics, the school focused on educating the children of the local elite within a context of reverence for the kami and Japanese history, serving as one of the few institutions of higher learning in the prefecture until the first public middle schools were established in 1893.[17]

As a result of the edict of 1882, then, the highest-ranked, state-supported shrines of the kami—Kotohira included—became sites not only for the rituals of the imperial state, but also for the study and explication of the historical, moral basis of the nation as well. After all, it was only through study of the classic texts that the appropriate rituals could be resurrected and performed. Moreover, by focusing on the national heritage and the imperial line, these shrines of the state could, at least in theory, avoid the divisive, private choices of more personal "religion." Legally, then, elite shrines of the kami performed the rites of the state; lower shrines of the kami catered to the prayers of the people.

Phasing Out the Shrines of the State

Soon, however, it seemed that Kotohira and other government shrines would lose their special status. Financial pressures combined with the politics of reform to threaten the position of the high-ranking shrines as institutions of the state.

As part of their attempts to secure the prosperity and independence of Japan, the Meiji leaders embarked on a concerted program of industrialization and military growth. Matsukata Masayoshi, finance minister from 1881 until 1892 (and then periodically thereafter), therefore tightened the finances of the state, raising taxes and seeking to reduce all government expenditures not immediately supportive of the strengthening policies. In early 1883, the conservative home minister, Yamada Akiyoshi, sought more money in order to promote several shrines that, like Kotohira, had requested advancement in the wake of shifting shrine policies. Matsukata, however, refused to provide the funds.[18] Instead, he eventually sought to reduce shrine expenditures as a whole, teaming up with supporters of a stronger separation between church and state to propose ending all state subsidies of the shrines.

Temporarily enjoying dominance in the newly established cabinet system, the reformers in the Meiji government won the day, albeit while giving concessions to shrine supporters. The reformers, for instance, could only phase out support for state shrines, not abandon it abruptly. On 17 March 1887, then, the Home Ministry established a system of payments, dubbed "preservation funds" (*hozonkin*), to all state-supported shrines except Ise. These funds would be distributed to each major shrine over the next fifteen years, after which government support would cease altogether. Shrine priests were directed to save a percentage of each payment to serve as the financial basis of their institution from 1902 on.[19]

The cabinet reinforced this eventual eradication of state support the very next day, in effect eliminating the two-tiered structure of funded and unfunded shrines altogether. Leaving only the priests of Ise Shrine as representatives of the state, they stripped all other priests of their titles as "kami officials" (shinkan) and relegated them to the status of private sectarians (*shinshoku,* literally "kami workers"), thereby freeing them to pursue aspects of "religion."[20] In a concession to conservatives, however—who still argued for state promotion of Shinto, including the revival of the Office of Rites and the need for Shinto ceremonies at the respected core of imperial government—the cabinet did allow that the highest priests of the (as yet) government-funded shrines would still be treated as lower nobility, acknowledging the ties of the priests to the imperial court. A plan for complete separation of shrines from the state—always excepting Ise, the shrine to the sacred, imperial ancestor—had thus been set in place. The priests of Kotohira and other imperial and provincial shrines were forced to confront the prospect of financial independence, cut off from funding by the state.

In the end, the Meiji government continued to provide support to the shrines. With the establishment of the emperor's Privy Council in 1888, the power of conservatives in government soon balanced the reformers once again, as they convinced their colleagues of the importance of ensuring peace in the nation through inculcation of reverence for the emperor. The Meiji Constitution and the ceremonies surrounding its announcement were thus filled with references to the "Imperial Ancestors," "a line of Emperors unbroken for ages eternal," and the explicit statement in article 3 that "the Emperor is sacred and inviolable." The constitution guaranteed a variety of rights but restricted them with broad conditions favorable to the state. Article 28, on religious freedom, stipulated that "Japanese subjects shall, within limits not prejudicial to peace and order, and not antagonistic to their duties as subjects, enjoy freedom of religious belief." For the increasingly nervous leaders, however, even these constitutional limitations did not suffice to guarantee the imperial preeminence. Shortly before the first elected Diet convened in the autumn of 1890, the emperor, under their direction, issued the Imperial Rescript on Education. In it, he exhorted his subjects to obedience and virtue, which he called "the teaching bequeathed by Our Imperial Ancestors, to be observed alike by Their Descendants and the subjects, infallible for all ages and true in all places." Recited in every school, the rescript brought rites of reverence for the emperor out of the shrines and into public education.[21] Yet the sacred inviolability of the imperial line, associated with the imperial ancestor Amaterasu, still relied upon the inviolability of the kami and, by extension, their shrines. Within a month of the rescript, the "preservation funds" were extended for thirty years; in 1900, elected representatives in the Diet abolished the "preservation fund" system, permanently reinstating state funding of shrines.[22]

Planning for Independence

In 1887, however, the priests of Kotohira and other high-ranking shrines could not know that their income would, after all, remain secure. Prompted by the "preservation fund" system and the projected loss of official funding in 1902, the priests sought out new sources of income—always maintaining their "nonreligious" stature in the hope of regaining state support. Closely tied to imperial prestige and well versed in the study of the nativist classics, rites, and arts, the priests of Kotohira allied themselves both socially and politically with the local educated elites. For years, the priests of Kotohira had shared the viewpoints of their social peers, the wealthy landlords and former domainal employees of the area. On his lecture tours for the Reverence Association, during which he stayed at wealthy families' homes, for instance, Matsuoka Mitsugi had preached not only on reverence for the gods but also, during a time of peasant uprisings against landlords, on "the harm of freedom and popular rights."[23] Together, priests and prominent landowners and businessmen promoted obedience to authority—a value they deemed even more important amid the rapid economic and social changes required to ensure the prosperity not only of Japan in general but of Kagawa prefecture and Kotohira town in particular. Beginning in late 1887, then, faced with the specter of disappearing funds, the priests of Kotohira wooed the prominent men of their area in earnest, capitalizing upon the imperial prestige of the shrine in order to support local initiatives and remaking the shrine of the kami into a shrine for national progress.

In 1886, Head Priest Fukami Hayao died, and the Home Ministry named Kotooka Hirotsune to take his place. Kotooka, having transformed Konpira Daigongen into the Great Kami Kotohira eighteen years earlier, was acutely aware of what needed to be done to maintain the viability of the mountain shrine, regardless of any particular interpretation of its god. He quickly moved to improve the fortunes of Kotohira by appealing to the wealthiest and most influential men in the surrounding area and in the country as a whole. To do so, he repeatedly redefined the shrine for each audience, effectively creating Kotohira as an arena for the concerns of its most generous and well-connected constitutents. Under Kotooka's pragmatic, donor-focused leadership from 1886 until his death in 1892, Kotohira became a stage for the support of progress and prosperity, tied closely to the imperial state.

Kotooka's emphasis on cultivating wealthy donors became evident shortly after Fukami's death, even before Kotooka received confirmation as head priest. The priests focused their attention on the movers and shakers of Shikoku: wealthy landlords and innovators, as well as the new elite of local military officers, bureaucrats, and other administrators. One of these was Ōkubo Jinnojō (1849–91), a village head in Saita, who had worked with his colleagues in the area to improve roads and promote new silk-raising technologies since the early 1870s. In 1886, Kotohira Shrine hosted a large ceremony commemorating the beginning of construction on the Shikoku New Road, promoted and planned by Ōkubo, at which the Saita leader intoned a blessing.[24] In 1888, the shrine hosted a similar ceremony for the beginning of construction on the Sanuki Railroad, the first leg of which would connect Marugame, Tadotsu, Zentsūji, and Kotohira, whose eighteen sponsors also included Ōkubo. Ōkubo, who arranged the emigration of impoverished peasants and fishermen from Shikoku to Hokkaido, brought more than four hundred emigrants to the shrine in that same year for a final blessing and ceremony in the sanctuary before their departure for the north. This ritual blessing of emigrants to Hokkaido would continue in subsequent years, establishing a strong tie between select communities on the northern island and the shrine in Shikoku.[25]

The shrine also cultivated ties to the military, especially at the army base nearby in Marugame. Since many soldiers at the base were recruited from Shikoku and were therefore already familiar with the deity, it was not surprising that their leaders incorporated worship at Kotohira into the rituals of military life. In September 1889, for example, officers in Marugame prevailed upon the shrine to answer a request for closer contact with the deity. "Today, Army General Kumazawa Yasusada came from the Marugame base," recorded Matsuoka Mitsugi in his diary. "He said that the soldiers whose terms are completed at this time would all like to receive a small amulet from Kotohira Shrine. . . . This is unprecedented." Four days later, on 28 September 1889, Matsuoka and the other priests conferred amulets on four officers and 107 soldiers at a ceremony in the main shrine.[26]

Kotooka's emphasis on ties to influential leaders extended far beyond responding to local elites' desires for the blessing of the god. The new head priest elevated fund-raising to an unprecedented level: instead of targeting promising donors individually or through the Reverence Association, as had been done to raise money for the rebuilding of the main shrine over the preceding decade, Kotooka established a separate fund-raising organization altogether, based on the government's "preservation fund" initiative.

In February 1888, not quite a year after the government's policy was announced, Kotooka and his colleagues established the Kotohira Shrine Preservation Society (*hozonkai*). Citing the shrine's miracles and its recognition by "generations of emperors," in particular, Emperor Momozono's conferral of the "exclusive shrine" designation in 1760, announcements of the Preservation Society urged people to donate funds for the refurbishment of buildings throughout the shrine grounds and receive special treatment in return.[27] By the end of the year, Kotooka had traveled to Tokyo and secured donations from several of the most influential men in the land, including, as one newspaper article recorded, all of the imperial princes, most of the government ministers, generals and other officers of army divisions in western Japan (including those in Osaka, Hiroshima, Kumamoto, and especially Nagoya), and the former daimyo of Shikoku, with the exception of Kōchi (the former Tosa).[28]

The loss of guaranteed government support and the subsequent establishment of "preservation societies" not just at Kotohira but also at other shrines seem to have shifted the priorities of priests throughout the country. Unable to focus only on rites, they needed to secure incomes for the shrine "business" as well. Indeed, as one anonymous priest bemoaned in a national journal for Shinto priests shortly after Kotohira's announcement of its Preservation Society had appeared in the pages of the journal, the preservation fund system was encouraging priests to focus on fund-raising, praising the culture, history, and status of their shrines instead of the virtues of the gods they worshipped.[29]

At Kotohira, at least, the Preservation Society was only the beginning. In his quest for influential official sponsorship, Kotooka shifted attention away from the god, instead presenting the shrine as a site of progress for the national good. Kotooka's final initiative placed Kotohira at the forefront of shrine innovations and won it profitable connections in the name of the nation. In 1889, in the wake of the nationalist fervor inspired by the promulgation of the Meiji Constitution and inspired by the example of a Russian maritime rescue association founded two years before, Kotooka secured a massive loan from Konpira's Reverence Association to establish the Great Japanese Imperial Maritime Rescue Association (Dai Nihon Teikoku Suinan Kyūsaikai). Designed "to rescue people and ships that encounter difficulties in Japanese seas," the Maritime Rescue Association established lookout stations and emergency crews at known danger spots, pushed for shippers' adoption of the latest in rescue technology, and assisted the families of drowned sailors and rescuers alike.[30] Drawing upon his connections in Tokyo, Kotooka gained the support of Meiji leaders for his organization. The group then recruited Prince Arisugawa Takehito as its president, the police chiefs of various prefectures as vice presidents, and governors, government ministers, and naval officers as members.[31]

The Maritime Rescue Association would at first glance seem an inspired way for Head Priest Kotooka to advertise the miracles of Kotohira as guardian of the sea. Doubtless, the association served this purpose as well, since survivors of shipwrecks were encouraged to report incidents to the association headquarters, located at the shrine until after Kotooka's death in 1892. Kotooka, however, used the association to appeal to influential men leery of religious politics. He laid out as strongly as possible a "nonreligious" position, extolling the association's support for the values and technologies of international progress. In a printed circular petitioning prospective sponsors for their support in August 1889, Kotooka repeatedly emphasized the "nonreligious" (*hishūkyōteki*) character of the group. "There are people who, upon hearing that we intend to establish a Maritime Rescue Association, believe that it is religious [*shūkyōshugi*]," he wrote. "However, this is mistaken. For the Maritime Rescue Association, there is no glory above the nation. As the world becomes civilized [*bunmei*], the charitable nature of people expands, and they establish charitable hospitals, poor houses, and nurseries. The Maritime Rescue Association is [intended as] one of these. Whether it is established or not attests to the civilization or barbarism of the country."[32] Thus, at least in fund-raising rhetoric, Kotooka vehemently asserted the nonreligious nature of the association, aligning it instead with the progress of world civilization.

Indeed, the rhetoric of the rescue association seems to have signaled the priests' latest interpretation of the god and its miracles, adding yet another layer of meaning to the already multivalent site—now in the language of secular, scientific progress. The founding rules of the Maritime Rescue Association set the tone, with Kotooka proclaiming, "It is a misunderstanding . . . to think that it is the divine will that one rely solely upon [the god] without exhausting all possible human actions."[33] Subsequent shrine publications built upon this theme, finding a role for the kami in a human-centered, scientific world. Priests and students of the shrine school wrote, published, and sold a booklet in 1892 that conveyed the dual lessons of self-reliance and the awesomeness of the deity. Articles included a biography of a famous eighteenth-century scholar and scientist from the area, Hiraga Gennai, as well as a reprint of the founding statement of the Maritime Rescue Association—both emphasizing the importance of innovation and self-help.

The anonymous author of a third article in the booklet extended the new emphasis to the logic of miracles, using the example of Konpira's expertise in saving people from shipwreck to assert that the god's miracles were in fact really inspiration for human effort:

> In an uncivilized world, people used incomplete vessels and tools. When crossing the great sea, they tried to achieve safety by single-minded faith. Therefore, when they encountered bad winds, Kotohira displayed a golden purification wand or a spark of light, fortified their spirits, and thus caused them to work to avoid danger without yielding or slackening their efforts. These were the miracles of an uncivilized world. In the age of civilization, the deity inspires people to learn astronomy and navigation, build vessels and tools, even pay attention to harbor lanterns, light signals, weather predictions, and water depths and causes the charitable people of each province to form the Maritime Rescue Association. These are the miracles of a civilized age.[34]

Having explained away the physical intervention of the god, reducing it to a psychological motivation, the author attempted to demote prayer and amulets while still allowing them a place in worship (and, thus, in the shrine economy).

> The deeper the faith, the more easily believers are led astray. . . . People mistakenly try to act today according to things long ago. Hearing that other people have received divine help—and overlooking those people's virtues and diligence—they want to receive the same divine protection. They exhaust their energy in shallow learning and devote their minds to prayers and charms. . . . Although prayers and charms are fundamentally means to seek divine protection, it is a mistake not to exhaust one's own efforts and heedlessly to rely solely upon divine protection.[35]

People should therefore rely less on the god than on themselves, for while the gods may choose to help a believer, they cannot be magically coerced through human action. The kami Kotohira, as opposed to the miracle-conferring Konpira Daigongen, thus existed far above mere mortal concerns. Civilized people should rely on themselves while acknowledging the distant superiority of the gods.

The priests of Kotohira thus redefined the god, the shrine, and themselves in support of human progress and civilization. They still acknowledged the miracles of the god—after all, in times of desperation, even the most secular-seeming bureaucrat could resort to fervent prayer. But the priests subordinated the magic of miracles to the virtues of the educated rural elites—hard work, study, and self-help—now placed, for the bureaucratic audience at least, more in the context of international progress and scientific understanding than in the communal worship of the newly "religious" Reverence Association. They represented Kotohira Shrine—now a nonreligious entity—as a symbol of national progress, whether through its charitable, semigovernmental work or as a site for rites in support of civic initiatives.

As a nonreligious, state-supported organization, the shrine was understood to stand above all social and political divisions: it represented the common good, not particular interests. Or, rather, it stood for the interests of the imperial state—a desire for peaceful obedience to the law. This was a viewpoint that the priests of Kotohira shared with the wealthy landlords and businessmen who made up the electorate in 1890: those over twenty-five years of age who paid at least fifteen yen in national taxes—that is, approximately 1 percent of the population.[36] These voters, like the bureaucrats in government, exhibited a fear of conflict, whether based on income or on "religion," and emphasized instead the moral rectitude of obedience to the state.

Thus, for instance, when a group of Tokyo politicians in 1892 established the Kokumin Kyōkai—a progovernment organization but explicitly not a "divisive" political party—the wealthiest landlord in Kotohira, the town doctor Mitsui Shōsaburō, pushed for its support. Kotooka's successor in 1892 as head priest, Count Minami Mitsutoshi, who maintained his connections among the imperial household and cabinet ministers, apparently encouraged forty or fifty priests of Kotohira Shrine to join the organization.[37] The conservative priests provided a counterbalance to the strength of the opposition Liberal Party (Jiyūtō) among merchants, innkeepers, and brothel owners in the town.[38] Indeed, with the support of Mitsui and the priests, the town of Kotohira became a stronghold for the Kokumin Kyōkai in Kagawa prefecture—an organization in which shrine priests mingled with the most influential conservative leaders of the prefecture to promote support of government policies and candidates in the upcoming elections. Whether formally, as in their support of the Kokumin Kyōkai, or informally, in lectures and conversations, the priests of Kotohira gave the sanction of the gods to government authority.

Historians have often commented on the "conservatism," "Japanization," or "ideological activity" of the 1880s, in which liberal, democratic progress and Westernization were overshadowed by a nationalist, nativist backlash.[39] Interestingly, this move coincided with the pushing of the most prominent and influential Shinto priests out of their world of theology and worship and into ever closer contact with government and business leaders, as they sought to survive as nonreligious entities. With "religion" now defined as private, divisive, and selfish, the priests—focusing more on the educated elite than on the "superstitious" masses—increasingly aligned the gods with values of unity and the public good as part of the nation, not with faith. This would change with the outbreak of war, when people of various backgrounds sought to tie the shrine to the nation on their own terms. It would require the tensions of wartime and the initiative of the very community leaders that the priests so actively wooed to remind them once again of the faith of the many, not just the funds of a few.

The Crucible of War
(1894–1895)

10

At Kotohira, the twenty-seventh year of the Meiji era (1894) began much like any other. After the customary lull during the January cold season, pilgrims arrived at the mountain around the time of the old New Year in February. Their numbers rose again during the popular springtime pilgrimage season of April and May, as travelers took advantage of the agricultural downtime to view cherry blossoms at the shrine. By June, this spring rush had ended, and the shrine entered its regular period of "summer drought"—the typical shortage of visitors during the hot, summer season. The priests at Kotohira busied themselves conferring amulets on members of the Reverence Association, lecturing around the country, and planning for the official festivities the next year, in 1895, to mark the 2,555th anniversary of the founding of the empire by the mythical first emperor, Jinmu. Worrisome reports arrived from the continent, but the troubles all seemed far away.[1] An occasional newspaper article mentioned the Tonghak rebellion in the south of Korea, but even Matsuoka Mitsugi, who was usually so diligent in recording matters of national concern in his diary, did not remark on any hint of impending Japanese involvement.

In the first week of June, however, Japan did become embroiled in the turmoil on the peninsula. The Japanese government sent a military contingent to Korea in response to Chinese involvement in the unrest. Closest to the site of conflict, the Fifth Army Division at Hiroshima was deployed and shortly found itself facing off against Chinese troops south of Seoul. As mediation efforts failed, tensions escalated until Japanese warships opened fire on Chinese troop carriers in late July. The Japanese government declared war at the beginning of August.

Like the gradual entry into full-scale war, the involvement of residents in and around Kotohira was slow to develop. A few young men of Kotohira were called to report to the Marugame base when the first troops left for Korea in early June.[2] But the shrine and town of Kotohira remained quiet in the summer pilgrimage lull. The calm was not broken until the second week of July, and then for reasons unrelated to the developing conflict. As it did every year, Konpira's traditional festival day on the tenth day of the old sixth month (in 1894 falling on 12 July) attracted people from nearby islands and mainland coastal areas, so many that the Sanuki Railroad, as it had since its inception five years before, increased the trains running from the ports to the shrine.[3]

Adding to the crowds was another factor unrelated to the war: drought. Beginning at the end of June, communities on the islands of the Inland Sea and in surrounding prefectures prayed to Konpira for rain, as they had the previous summer and in periodic droughts before that.[4] The god of Mt. Zōzu was well known throughout the Inland Sea area and Kyushu for its efficacy in summoning rain. Local governments, both the Takamatsu lord under the Tokugawa regime and the new prefectural government afterward, had repeatedly ordered the priests of the mountain to perform rain-summoning rituals during extended dry spells.[5] Agricultural communities performed their own rituals, lighting bonfires, dancing, and singing in an attempt to influence the gods. For many communities, pilgrimage to Konpira was integral to the proceedings. Sometimes this entailed sending village representatives with offerings to obtain an amulet or talisman in commemoration of the event. Frequently, however, villages suffering from drought sent a representative to obtain a flame from the fire—whether of the goma ceremony before 1868 or the everlasting fire of the shrine in the years since—and then bring it back to light a bonfire in the village and pray for rain.[6] As week after week passed without precipitation during the summer of 1894, representatives from villages throughout Kagawa and Ehime prefectures and surrounding areas visited the shrine to pray for rain well into September.[7]

Amid this increased traffic, the first hint that the heightened tensions in Korea were influencing activities at the shrine was subtle. A newspaper article written during the summer standoff reported that a prominent manufacturer of bamboo containers in Tadotsu, whose exports to China had been disrupted by the situation, led a group of fifty-odd craftsmen to Kotohira in early July. There is no suggestion, however, that the men prayed for anything unusual, probably following the long-standing tradition of manufacturers and shopkeepers praying at Konpira for prosperity in business.[8] A month after the departure of troops to Korea, the impact of the hostilities was thus apparently felt only by a few export-oriented businesses and addressed at the shrine as a personal reversal of fortune.

With the Japanese occupation of the Korean palace and the successful attack on Chinese positions in Songhwan, south of Seoul, in late July, however, a burst of patriotic fervor seized the educated elites of the town and shrine. In a pattern consistent with their roles as community leaders, the influential men of Kotohira, including the head of the amulet box sellers' guild and some of the shrine priests, began collecting money to send saké to the troops in Korea and support the activities of the Red Cross.[9] The priests, although they doubtless felt as strongly about their duties to support the nation as did the village leaders, could not afford to donate as much money as the local businessmen. While the head of the amulet box sellers' guild donated twenty yen, for instance, priests such as Miyazaki donated only sixty sen, and Matsuoka was able to offer only thirty-two sen.[10] "It's not much," Matsuoka wrote in his diary, "but I told the mayor that on the thirtieth we will hold a special prayer festival for [the efforts in] Korea at the Reverence Association headquarters."[11] Utilizing his own talent for ritual rather than business, Matsuoka carefully drafted morning and evening prayers to offer to the deity on behalf of the soldiers in Korea, asking the kami to protect all of them, regardless of rank.[12]

Local Involvement

On 29 July, the reality of war became clear to many of the people living near Kotohira. On that day, the first transport ships of the Twelfth Infantry Division, stationed in Marugame, departed for Korea. Within a week the entire division would follow; a total of 1,836 men left from Marugame alone.[13] On the thirtieth, the Reverence Association hosted a special ceremony in its headquarters outside the main gate, after which Matsuoka and Matsuzaki explained the reasons for the invasion to the assembled Reverence Association members, reiterating the official line as it appeared in newspaper coverage: that the emperor, because of his closeness to the king of Korea, and because of the official, mercantile, and personal links between the people of Japan and the peninsula, was sending troops to protect the Korean king and Japanese people in Korea. The priests then gave the worshippers saké blessed by the god and sent them home.[14]

While at first special rituals were hosted by the Reverence Association, not the "nonreligious" shrine, the priests soon found a model for larger-scale support for the war. The high-ranking ties of Kotohira's priests involved them in a world where people vied to demonstrate support of government initiatives. On the night of 30 July, imperial pageantry in Tokyo suddenly offered to Kotohira's priests the idea for a dramatic new way to demonstrate their support for the military. Kawasaki Shigetake, one of Kotohira Shrine's regular representatives in Tokyo, rushed home from the capital with an urgent idea to propose to Head Priest Minami and the other priests. "The priests in Tokyo think that one should choose a pure bit of land, hold a grand ceremony for a victorious army, make special amulets in commemoration of this festival, then send two or three people to Shimonoseki to give them to the soldiers," he related. "How about it?"[15] This idea quickly evolved a step further into a plan to send priests from Kotohira Shrine to Korea to distribute amulets to the soldiers. Everyone agreed enthusiastically.[16]

Indeed, they may have agreed a bit too enthusiastically. Leaders at the highest levels of government were becoming concerned about overzealous former samurai forming volunteer units throughout Japan, and officials at all levels started to emphasize the need for each person to fulfill his own duty instead of running off to war.[17] By 7 August, even the emperor became involved, issuing a proclamation recognizing the "patriotic loyalty" of the volunteers but insisting that "each subject must not be dilatory in working at his own personal occupation."[18]

In this atmosphere of defined responsibilities, the governor of Kagawa prefecture passed on a warning from Tokyo to control the exuberant priests of Kotohira and other shrines. As he wrote to Head Priest Minami, "I have heard that there are some people among the priests who are very enthusiastic. They want to go to war themselves and become soldiers. Although it is laudable in this crisis that people of pure heart and mind want to serve bravely in the public good, they should not just run off and be soldiers. That is why we have a national army. Priests especially have their own public service to do. They help preserve order. They pray for the nation and to avert evil. If someone abandons his duty and runs off, we cannot easily overlook such a terrible crime. I am passing on my superiors' request that you all stay and do your own work."[19] In accordance with this warning, the priests limited their direct involvement on the continent to their plans to manufacture several thousand amulets and send two priests to Korea to distribute them to the troops. This they did in the middle of September.

The amulet mission to Korea, no matter how close to the hearts of a few dedicated priests, remained peripheral to the regular activities of the shrine. The priests saw their primary ritual responsibility as prayer for the nation, befitting their role at a state-sponsored institution. After the official declaration of war on 2 August, Kotohira Shrine held a special three-day festival "for the total victory of the imperial army and the safety of the country."[20] Each morning the drums began to beat at 5:30 to announce the ceremonies, and prayers were offered every day at 5:30 a.m. and 5:30 p.m. Because of the importance of the occasion, the priests brought out swords and arrows from the treasure-house to present in front of the kami, saddled the sacred horses, and lined flags up in front of the main shrine.[21] Residents in the town decorated buildings with national flags and lit the mountain at night as they carried lanterns on their way to worship at the shrine.

Similar prayer ceremonies were held on these days in villages and towns throughout the area,[22] however, and since apparently no unusual numbers of worshippers attended, in this case Kotohira Shrine acted simply in its capacity as the main shrine for the town. The priests made no special accommodations for broader participation in these ceremonies. As the prefectural government had noted, the "public service" of priests was to "preserve order" through prayer. By displaying the mightiness of the god in rituals for the imperial military, the priests fulfilled their function as a state-supported shrine. They staged ceremonies for the national good.

Soon, however, influential leaders in nearby villages began to insist on a more personalized relationship with the shrine. Just three days after the special ceremony, on 10 August, the head of Okada village in Uta district, six kilometers northeast of the shrine on the main road to Takamatsu, visited Kotohira Shrine and consulted with Matsuoka Mitsugi. As Matsuoka recorded in his diary that night, "The village head said that twenty-six men are about to be sent from Okada to Korea as soldiers. The people of the village plan to pray for their safety at Kotohira Shrine, and hope to receive one wooden talisman for each soldier's family. There are about one thousand households in the village, and beginning tomorrow with sixteen people, they will come in groups to worship for seven days." The village head then requested that Matsuoka allow them all to worship at the main shrine and enter the sanctuary. As Matsuoka recorded, "I had no choice but to permit it and inform the attendant on duty."[23]

On the appointed day, the village head and influential citizens of Okada walked together to Kotohira, wearing formal dress. According to a newspaper report, they entered the sanctuary, prayed for national safety as well as good military fortune and long life, and received twenty-seven of the coveted large wooden talismans: one for each soldier's family as well as one for the town office. The next day, sixty people visited Kotohira, and sixty visited the shrine of their local kami to pray for the health of the soldiers in Korea.[24]

For the leaders of Okada and other villages that quickly followed their example, the grand ceremonies of the shrine did not answer their needs for more personal support of the soldiers and their families. In a steady stream, they came to Kotohira, insisting through their actions that the role of the shrine was not just to pray for the nation in the abstract, but to connect individual worshippers personally to the power of the god as the families of soldiers, as concerned groups, and as entire village units. On 18 August, Matsuoka recorded in his diary that "recently, groups of ten and twenty people from each province, district and village have come in great numbers, carrying banners with large writing proclaiming 'Long Live the Emperor,' 'Promote National Power,' 'Total Victory of the Imperial Forces,' and 'Health for the Soldiers.' These people are probably the parents or siblings of the soldiers."[25] By 20 and 21 August, one report estimated that more than one thousand people had come to the shrine in groups, carrying large banners from Tadotsu, Marugame, and elsewhere to pray for victory.[26] In announcing and commemorating these appeals with military slogans and imperial rhetoric, these worshippers, with their personal prayers, both appropriated and affirmed the aims of the state.

For their own part, the priests of Kotohira were quick to perceive the implications of such village pilgrimages. Little more than a week after the Okada pilgrimage, they had streamlined the procedure for village visits enough that representatives from the groups could be sent ahead only an hour or so to make arrangements. Eventually, the financial and logistical procedures for entry into the sanctuary could be conducted on the spot.[27]

After the offical declaration of war, the priests of Kotohira had set about planning a special prayer ceremony for victory. Initially, they were undecided whether to hold the festivities up at the main shrine or at the *jinjiba,* a broad, flat area below the mountain where large crowds of people were accommodated each year during the great autumn festival. As the number of village pilgrimages grew, Head Priest Minami decided in favor of the larger, more accessible space.[28] Advertising the ceremony so as to link the national and the personal, the priests announces rites "for the power of the country and the health of the soldiers."[29] Employing thirty priests from shrines throughout Kagawa prefecture as officiants and placing newspaper advertisements inviting "all patriotic believers" to the ceremony on 15 August, the priests of Kotohira Shrine sought to raise the profile of Kotohira as a regional site for prayer in support not just of the state but also of the soldiers. Dramatic attractions enticed large numbers of spectators. Framed by fireworks before it began at 6:00 p.m. and again at the end at midnight, the ceremony—complete with prayers and sacred dances—drew impressive numbers of people from both Kotohira town and surrounding areas.[30] Prompted by public demand for prayers for the soldiers, the shrine had transformed the ceremonies for victory from a two-way communication between priests and kami into a grand, public spectacle.

The priests also recognized that they could use public demand for wartime prayer to shore up the troubled finances of the shrine. By 22 August, the shrine office had erected a notice advertising a new service. "Now, on the occasion of the commencement of war against China," it stated, "prayers will be offered for the welfare of all imperial troops each morning at the main shrine. People who want prayers offered specifically for officers or soldiers in Korea should write the person's family name on the prayer register. . . . A fee will be charged for these prayers."[31]

The size of the pilgrimage groups varied greatly. Okada village sent sixteen notables the first day and sixty villagers on subsequent days. A week later, Matsuoka recorded groups of ten and twenty people from other villages arriving at the shrine, praying for husbands, sons, and brothers.[32] At the same time, the newspaper reported that 480 people went to Kotohira together from Marugame's Hirayamachi area, and more than sixty households traveled together from Tadotsu a few days later.[33] By then, thousands of people were taking advantage of half-price train tickets to go to the shrine, primarily from Marugame, Tadotsu, and other places in the close vicinity of Kotohira.[34]

Except for a steady trickle of people praying for rain, the number of worshippers from across the Inland Sea or even outside western Sanuki, as in most years, remained almost nonexistent during the busy summer months of the agricultural season. Local residents, however, found a way to take a few hours or a day off from work to go on this special pilgrimage. The huge, local, mainly female turnout crowded the town and shrine of Kotohira. As one newspaper article recorded: "Although usually this is the season of summer drought, . . . because of the Sino-Japanese war, people are coming in groups, carrying large banners with 'Promote National Prestige' and 'Triumphal Return of the Brocade Flags' and the like written bravely in large letters. The thin arms of the women help each other as they come to pray for the safety of husbands, brothers, and sons. There are also the wives of commissioned officers. Without any distinction between day and night, there are many worshippers. Since this unseasonable prosperity has come to the town, the people of Kotohira put out lanterns on tall poles at night to welcome the visitors."[35] The concerns of war thus turned Kotohira into the focus of mass local pilgrimage, notable for the presence of large numbers of women praying for the safety of their men.

By the end of the busy agricultural season in September, village leaders vied with each other in demonstrating support for the troops. Men in Sogisho, about seventeen kilometers east of Kotohira in the foothills of the Sanuki mountain range, planned a huge, one-thousand-person pilgrimage to pray for the health of the departed soldiers on the minor festival day of Konpira, 10 September. According to a newspaper report, they divided the entire village into fifteen groups, each making a flag proclaiming "one-thousand-person pilgrimage." The groups, with each member wearing a medal on his or her left breast, would depart by foot for Kotohira at 6:00 a.m.[36]

The day after the pilgrimage from Sogisho, the local newspaper, *Kagawa Shinpō,* carried a report from nearby Yamada village. Village leaders had collected pickled plums (*umeboshi*), sandals, and snowboots to send to the soldiers and had held lectures on the course of the war, hygiene, and similar issues. Now, apparently after learning of Sogisho's pilgrimage, they too made arrangements for pilgrimage to Konpira. Dividing the village into nine groups, they planned a pilgrimage by one group on the first, tenth, and twentieth of every month.[37]

As reports of Japanese victories began to appear, pilgrimage became an excuse for festivities that had been postponed because of wartime worries. After the occupation of Pyongyang and a naval victory in the Yellow Sea in September, people began going to Kotohira from throughout the prefecture to celebrate victory, calling the journey *oreimairi* (pilgrimage in thanks).[38] In Tokiwa village (now part of Kan'onji city), after two men returned from Korea with a report of the progress of the war, leaders organized the entire village to go on pilgrimage to Konpira on 15 December; then the next day everyone took a day off work, and the whole village held grand festivities for victory.[39]

In this way, through community pilgrimages initiated by village leaders in the area, Kotohira Shrine became redefined as a focus of support for soldiers at the front. Residents paraded to the mountain carrying large flags with slogans, which were then planted near the main shrine, to flutter in the wind and present a valiant, warlike image, almost as if the shrine were leading the way into battle. Day and night, pilgrims traveled to Kotohira, jostling one another and encountering other groups along the way. As the most powerful deity within walking distance—and conveniently accessible from towns along the railroad—Konpira attracted worshippers from a circle of about twenty kilometers in radius, eager to tap the miracles of the deity for their men in battle overseas. Collecting donations for the families and neighbors of soldiers sent to the continent was not enough: village leaders pressured everyone to display their support publicly through long marches to Kotohira Shrine. They then brought the power of Konpira back into each community, distributing amulets to families and enshrining them in village offices.[40]

The importance of pilgrimage, however, did not go undisputed, even among educated elites. For some local leaders—especially businessmen in the trade and manufacturing areas of Marugame and Tadotsu—the daily pilgrimages seemed wasteful and misguided. The *Kagawa Shinpō* began reporting on a backlash in late August, when the number of people going on group pilgrimages to Konpira had climbed to the thousands. The rationale for one of the first reported oppositions to wartime pilgrimage in western Sanuki was twofold. First, merchants reiterated an argument common among businessmen for centuries: that worship of the gods and buddhas, while acceptable under normal conditions, should not be carried to such extremes that it threatened profits.[41] Second, the businessmen capitalized on the earlier warning of the emperor to would-be warriors. Everyone should stick to his own job, they said, people to production, and priests to prayer. "Respectful of the imperial proclamation," reported the *Kagawa Shinpō* on 24 August 1894, "the townspeople of Yokomachi [in Marugame] have discussed the matter. While exerting themselves at their work, everyone has pledged to limit all unnecessary expenditures in their households and respond to the call for donations and war bonds. . . . To conduct prayers and ceremonies is the work of Buddhist and Shinto priests. Merchant families are always to devote themselves to trade."[42]

The trend spread. In early September, the people of Monzenmachi in Tadotsu concluded that the daily pilgrimages they had performed until then were too expensive: they decided to stop the practice and save the money for military expenditures instead.[43] Other communities followed suit: several enshrined an amulet from Kotohira in a small hall in the neighborhood, where people could come to worship daily without the expense in money and time needed to go to the main shrine.[44] Thus, in merchant communities in particular, the expression of support for the war through pilgrimage was self-limiting. Few business owners were likely to beggar themselves and their families for repeated trips to the shrine.

Despite this opposition, however, the massive and frequent pilgrimages to Kotohira continued not only from rural areas but from the cities as well. In late October, a newspaper report from Tadotsu was still bemoaning "the large numbers of people going from Marugame and Tadotsu to Kotohira daily, morning and evening," as a waste of time and money.[45] Yet many people clearly found in the trips a community-sanctioned escape from the mundane routine of work. Pilgrimage offered an active way to support the war. Most worshippers did not accept the argument that worship was only for priests: they saw it as something that must be done personally—by the individual or a family representative, or at the very least a village representative—if their personal prayers were to be answered. As a result, countless individuals participated in Shinto ritual supporting the war, creating direct links between themselves, the god, and the national project.

At the Front

Konpira's wartime prominence extended far beyond the villages of western Kagawa prefecture. As the protector of ships and sailors, Konpira connected soldiers to their fellow fighters and to the nation as they were sent to battle across the sea. During the Sino-Japanese war, troop ships passing through the Inland Sea appropriated the long-standing tradition of seaborne offerings to the deity, turning them into rituals to improve the morale and solidarity of soldiers on their way to the front.

For more than a century, sailors and fishermen at sea had floated kegs of saké to Konpira to pray both for the safety of themselves and their cargo and for a bountiful catch. Whoever picked up the keg, either at sea or on a beach, and took it to the shrine was believed to share in the resulting favor of the deity.[46] On military vessels during the Sino-Japanese war, these individual offerings of saké were transformed into group offerings of money. Modifying the traditional donation of floating saké, soldiers on their way to the front each contributed a bit of money that was placed into a keg or cloth bag and attached to a wooden board so it would float. On the board, they wrote the names of the donors and any prayer or additional comment. Once in sight of Mt. Zōzu, the whole crew gathered on deck to worship Kotohira from afar, then threw the offering into the sea.[47]

This new tradition of floating monetary donations from the crews of large ships apparently began during the Sino-Japanese war. A record, compiled in 1914, of extant board inscriptions from such offerings begins with donations in 1894, and the priest Matsuoka, who liked to record anything new or unusual at the shrine, first described the donations in an August 1894 entry in his diary.[48] Floating monetary donations (later formally called *nagashi hatsuho*, "floating first-fruits offerings") arrived at Kotohira from at least six military ships during the Sino-Japanese war.[49] Four of them were simply dedicated in the popular, combinatory name of the deity, "In offering to Konpira Daigongen." Matsuoka's diary and other sources provide more detail on the other two.

What may have been the first such offering—five yen attached to a pine board about sixty centimeters in length—arrived at Kotohira Shrine on 29 July, one day after having been thrown into the Tadotsu Straits. The inscription on the front of the board gave the names of ninety-four soldiers, designated as "notables" (*yūshisha*) aboard the military ship *Hanjō*, under the inscription, "In donation to Kotohira Shrine: [praying for] national safety, military fortune and long life, victory in war." On the back of the plank were written the words to "Kimigayo," which by the previous year, 1893, had come to serve as the de facto Japanese national anthem, as well as the information that it was thrown into the Tadotsu Straits "while on the way to the front" on 28 July 1894. The offering floated into the Straits of Marugame, where it was picked up the next day by the fisherman Matano Iwakichi, as also recorded on the board. Iwakichi's wife then carried the offering to the mountain and hung the board in the Ema Hall.[50]

This and other donations not only contributed to the linking of Kotohira Shrine with national, imperial ritual, such as indicated by use of "Kimigayo." They also reflected the growing monetization of offerings to the deity. Whereas during the Edo period, donations to the shrine had often been in kind—in saké, lumber (for the production of wooden talismans), or stone lanterns (to decorate and light the path up the mountain)—during the Meiji period they increasingly took the form of money. The priests themselves placed a moratorium on the erection of stone lanterns at the shrine in the 1870s, thereafter commemorating large donations with flat stone slabs that lined the steps, funneling worshippers to the shrine.[51] By the 1880s, as evident in the shrine's advertisements soliciting bids for lumber contracts in the local newspaper, Kotohira Shrine was forced to purchase wood for the amulets, no longer able to rely upon trees sent downriver by believers in the mountains.[52] And finally, starting with the Sino-Japanese war, the floating keg of saké—that last surviving trademark of Konpira worship illustrated in *Hizakurige*—was gradually replaced by a monetary version.

But the patriotic context and monetary content of the new offerings did not signify any attenuation of personal belief in miracles and omens, as the second offering recorded by Matsuoka shows:

> A similar sixty-centimeter-long pine board arrived on 13 August 1894. It had written in the middle of it "Hōnō Kotohiragū" [In offering to Kotohira Shrine] in big letters, and on the front and back 219 names. . . . A white cloth bag holding five yen, eighteen sen, and three rin was attached to the board so it floated upon the sea. It came to land on the west shore of Honjima village on the island of Ushijima. Ōkura Chōji picked it up and immediately took it to the village office, where an official wrote the date on it and sent it to the shrine. It arrived on 15 August. People are saying that because the donation arrived on the day of the big prayer ceremony, after floating for such a distance and being battered by the waves, it is a good omen for the fulfillment of people's prayers.[53]

Indeed, as a newspaper article attested after the end of the war, the offering proved to be auspicious. After recounting the donation much as in Matsuoka's account—describing the donors as Kusume Shindo, a man from Kō-chi prefecture, and his shipmates aboard the Navy ship *Kongō*—the *Kagawa Shinpō* chronicled the aftermath of the donation: "In February of this year [1895], Kusume Shindo miraculously escaped harm in the attack on Weihaiwei. And when our ship *Kongō* shot and hit the cannon [at another battle], he went ashore, took the cannon, and on the first day of this month [April], he gave it in commemoration of the divine mercy of Kotohira Shrine. It is now on display in the shrine office, where it can be seen by crowds of people."[54]

Konpira worship, although ritualized in a collective, military context, continued to display its personal character. Kusume Shindo, one among 219 worshippers on board ship who offered the donation to Konpira from the middle of the straits, attributed his survival to Konpira despite the apparent demise of his shipmates. But his offering of thanks for his personal salvation itself took the shape of a trophy of the nation: a captured cannon. Not only soldiers but also other worshippers—whether attending the prayer festival for victory during which the offering arrived, or viewing the cannon later when it stood on display as testimonial to the saving powers of the kami—came to associate the maritime miracles of Konpira not just with the rescue of individuals but also with the protection and triumph of the Japanese military and the empire.

Exactly how people envisioned Konpira and the other gods of Japan contributing to the war effort is unclear. For most people both at home and on the battlefield, the physical objects they encountered on Mt. Zōzu shaped their images of the god more than any abstract doctrinal identity. For years, horses at Konpira had attracted the attention of pilgrims, as petitioners seeking to be healed rubbed the wooden horse donated by the Takamatsu lord in 1650, then a bronze one donated almost two centuries later.[55] Pilgrims could buy prints and drawings of the shrine and its famous sites, in which the bronze horse near the Ema Hall frequently appeared.[56] They could also admire and feed the three white, living horses kept for use in the annual procession and other ceremonies. According to a British tourist in 1900, these horses were even trained to bob their heads in rapid succession when visitors approached.[57] The horses at Konpira thus captured the imagination of worshippers as symbols of the shrine and companions of the god.

The horses' popularity is evident in stories of the deity that circulated during the Sino-Japanese war. In late August of 1894, for instance, Matsuoka recorded in his diary that "these days, around Toyota district, people are saying that our Kotohira Shrine's bronze horse left the shrine, crossed to Korea, then came back. [They also say] that the reason the sacred horses are not eating their food is because, though the horses' bodies are in the stable, their spirits are being ridden by the Great Kami, headed toward Korea."[58]

Soldiers on the battlefield also envisioned the deity Konpira accompanied by a horse. At a special celebration held for the families of soldiers in Tomi-kuma village in Uta district in November 1894, for instance, village leaders read a letter from a former town hall employee then serving as a soldier at the front. The letter, written on the same day as the victorious attack on Chiu-liench'eng on 26 October, vividly described the battles of Pyongyang and Uiju. A newspaper account of the ceremony summarized the rest of the letter: "The night before the attack on Pyongyang, the spirit of Izumo Shrine appeared (it was neither a dream nor reality), saying 'If you attack suddenly, you will win without fail.' The night before the attack on Uiju, [Konpira] appeared riding on the gold horse-spirit of Kotohira Shrine. On the night of October 25th, the spirit of Kasuga appeared like Izumo's. All the soldiers felt the same: that Chiuliench'eng would fall in half a day."[59] Konpira's spirit-horse had joined the horses of the Japanese cavalry on the mainland. The deity Konpira, popularly known as one of the only gods in Japan that did not travel to Izumo each autumn for the annual gathering of the gods,[60] was now thought by everyday believers to have flown to the continent to ensure victory.

In other, more official, contexts these visions of horses and individual deities often gave way to a more formalized recognition of "the gods" (*kamigami* or *shinbutsu*) in general. Patriotic, imperial rhetoric absorbed the particularity of Konpira, Kasuga, and other individual deities, sometimes even in donations to a particular shrine. When two sailors in the navy donated a votive plaque to Kotohira Shrine in 1896, for instance, they subsumed the specifics of Konpira's favor within formal expressions of reverential, imperial rhetoric, praising "the miracles of the gods of our great country" in saving them. "On 21 December in the winter of the 2,555th year since the national founding [1894], the imperial military ship *Hiro 3* met with difficulties in the Taiwan Straits," they wrote. "The warship's ensign respectfully shouted 'Long Live the Emperor!' [*Tennō Banzai*] in a prayerful voice, and disappeared from view. At that time, the ship sank completely below the water. We finally climbed up onto other boats. . . . Exhausted after several hours, we happily, thanks to the miracles of the gods of our great country, escaped with one life out of ten thousand deaths. It was truly due to divine assistance that we were able to safely tread upon the land of our birthplace."[61]

Not just sailors but also state officials brought the prayers of the nation to Kotohira, interpreting the military efforts of the Sino-Japanese War as an integral part of the civic, state-supported progress now associated with the highly ranked shrine. After the national government, the emperor, and the wartime command moved from Tokyo to Hiroshima in September 1894, cabinet ministers, members of parliament, and other people with government business frequently included a pilgrimage to Kotohira Shrine on their trips between Hiroshima and Okayama, Kobe, or Osaka. One newspaper notice in October, for instance, described the pilgrimage of seven members of parliament and the Minister of Education, Saionji Kinmochi, who wrote in calligraphy the slogan "Defeat of the Enemy Country" and donated it to the shrine school.[62] The frequency of such semiofficial visits to the shrine included Kotohira in a ritualized recognition, not just by the state but by nationally prominent leaders, of the role of the kami in support of the war.

Priests and donors also linked the military efforts with the shrine's role of national, historical education, displaying the treasures of the shrine to illustrate not only its imperial ties and cultural prominence but its long reputation for miracles as well. For three months during the peak springtime pilgrimage season, from April through early July 1895, the shrine opened its treasures to public view in conjunction with a series of festivals celebrating the capture of Pyongyang.[63] An extended description of the temporary exhibition itemized the objects. A watercolor of the ship *Hie* in battle appeared next to the wooden horse donated by Matsudaira Yorishige and a fan attributed to Emperor Gotoba. Kusume Shindo's cannon stood in front of famous screens by Maruyama Ōkyo, next to piles of bows and arrows, a copy of the Heart Sutra supposedly written by Kōbō Daishi, and the records of the warlord Chōsokabe's construction of the Upside-Down Gate. The Buddhist images of Kannon and Fudō Myōō, saved from burning and auction some twenty-two years before, occupied positions alongside Takahashi Yūichi's Western-style oil paintings of Kotohira.[64]

The conclusion of the war in May turned these displays into an accompaniment to victory celebrations, such as the two days of festivities staged by the shrine in early June. There, framed by four large victory arches of greenery, the shrine, the Reverence Association, and local leaders sponsored shows of fireworks, sumō, and various other entertainments.[65] Even when the shrine separated its "historical" treasures from more recent donations to the shrine, displaying them in a newly built, Western-style museum, they were again surrounded with military pageantry. When the two-story museum opened a decade later, in 1905, near the end of the Russo-Japanese war, Kotohira's inns donated a large, thatched victory gate to be erected in front of the museum "patterned on the Pyongyang gate" and festooned with the flags of Japan and its allies.[66]

Throughout these activities, the educated local gentry played a pivotal role, organizing pilgrimages and insisting on the participation of priests. Moreover, formal worship during wartime seemed in many cases to mark a person's social importance. In shrine documents, newspaper articles, and the texts of the offerings themselves, it was "notables" (*yūshisha*) who led the village pilgrimages, and "notables" among the sailors who donated cash on the Inland Sea. The state shrine of Kotohira, formally separated from the selfishness and divisiveness attributed to personal religion, embodied the public-minded support of the nation attributed to such men.

During the Sino-Japanese war, concerned leaders at home and nervous soldiers at sea and in battle mobilized the god Konpira in support of the military. Whereas the priests of the shrine had originally focused on more symbolic service—sending amulets to Korea and staging ceremonies for victory—soldiers and villagers insistently attested to the relevance of the miracles of the deity (and its horse) on foreign soil. Village leaders, intent upon supporting the troops and the war effort, pressured the priests of the shrine to expand their ritual duties beyond general support of the nation to provide an arena in which villagers could personalize their prayers, calling on the assistance of the god. In the process, they created new group rituals that tied their communities together, through the god, to the military, the nation, and the empire. In doing so, they pushed the priests once again to return the miracles of the deity to the rites of the state.

Public Good, Private Gain
(1895–1898)

11

The end of the Sino-Japanese War in 1895 brought with it a return to economic reality at the shrine. Wartime profits from local pilgrimage had not reversed the more dismal long-term trend in shrine finances. Since the nationwide recession of the 1880s, when priests at Kotohira had worked to reposition the newly "nonreligious" shrine, increased expenses, reduced income, and financial mismanagement had transformed the spectacular surplus of the Tokugawa era into a devastating debt. Thus, whether the rituals of Kotohira addressed national or personal needs, they would not continue long unless the shrine could regain a sound financial footing.

Lacking the political clout and land-based resources of their Tokugawa-era predecessors, the priests of Kotohira faced a dilemma: how to increase the income of the shrine while maintaining the image of impartiality now deemed suitable to a highly ranked institution of the imperial government. That is, confronted both with the politics of their rituals—whether civic or miraculous—and with the economics of their pilgrimage, the priests of Kotohira were forced to seek out new ways to compete within the rapidly changing economy of industrializing Japan.

During the years from 1896 to 1898, influential men throughout Japan dramatically altered the economic and financial policies of the nation. From leaders in Tokyo and their handpicked prefectural governors around the country to business groups in small towns like Kotohira and the heads of individual enterprises such as the priest of Kotohira Shrine, they sought to strengthen the country and their own communities through the development of manufacture and trade. On the national level, bureaucrats and businessmen focused on building heavy industries, such as shipping and steel, and on the financial structures and regulatory legislation required to support them. Seeking to survive or, better, prosper in this changing environment, smaller entrepreneurs sought their own profitable niches amid the growing industrial conglomerates.

In and around Kotohira, this meant, in large part, promoting pilgrimage to the mountain shrine. As consumer spending revived after the war, innkeepers, brothel owners, merchants, and priests in Kotohira, as well as boat operators and ricksha pullers in Marugame and Tadotsu nearby, worked to enhance their profits from the pilgrimage business. Who would profit most from such endeavors, however, was unclear. The priests of Kotohira, desperate for funds, launched new profit-making projects that would disrupt the carefully cultivated alliances of decades, even a century, before. As the priests, their competitors, and their allies in the town adjusted to the changing conditions of the late nineteenth century, they defined a new role for Kotohira Shrine in the regional power structure—a role that had been foreshadowed during the recent war by the growing responsiveness of priests to popular demand.

The preceding decades had already diminished the lordly authority of the priests, and the trend only intensified. As they sought to survive after 1895, the priests of Kotohira confronted a new political and economic order. In the competitive context of industrializing Japan, their former glory as priestly lords brought fewer present privileges. Their word was now law only within the precincts of the mountain shrine, not on the plain below. Forced to compromise with their former subordinates, priests found themselves supporting, not dictating, the strategies of the town. The structures of local politics, and economics, had been irreversibly changed.

Crisis at the Shrine

The events that surrounded the ending of the Sino-Japanese War in April 1895 caused consternation among people at Kotohira and throughout Japan. Peace negotiations at Shimonoseki proceeded well: Japan received several concessions from China, including recognition of the independence of Korea; cession to Japan of Formosa, the Pescadores Islands, and the Liaotung Peninsula; the opening of four additional ports in China; and a large indemnity. A week after the treaty, however, on 23 April, the governments of Russia, Germany, and France intervened, insisting that Japan return the Liaotung Peninsula to China, thereby leaving it open to Russian interests. In early May, the cabinet acceded to Russia's demands but then faced sharp criticisms on the streets and in the press. Japan had won the war but had still backed down before the Western powers.

At first glance, issues of national diplomacy would seem to have little to do with the everyday life of a shrine like Kotohira. As earlier noted, the business of shrine management had proceeded apace throughout the war as priests processed incoming donations and planned initiatives to praise the god, glorify the state, and enrich the coffers of the shrine. Yet in April 1895 the mundane activities of the priests unexpectedly brought them into conflict with the changing diplomatic stance of the cabinet.

On the thirteenth of that month, Head Priest Minami Mitsutoshi hosted the third annual meeting of the head priests of state shrines in the four Inland Sea prefectures of Kagawa, Okayama, Hiroshima, and Tokushima. The long-planned meeting happened to occur during the negotiations for the Treaty of Shimonoseki, while Russia, Germany, and France were exerting pressure on Japan to refrain from claiming the Liaotung Peninsula. Like many members of the public, as well as the priests of Kotohira who had already been warned by officials to restrain their enthusiasm for the war, the head priests of the state shrines eagerly anticipated the beginning of Japan's formal empire and resented any hint of European intervention. The published agenda of the meeting reported six topics of discussion. As the record showed, after deciding to send a joint representative to Tokyo to lobby for the return to the shrines of forest lands that had been confiscated by the government in the early years of Meiji, the priests discussed their role in the new continental territories (that is, the Liaotung Peninsula) gained through the war. Among the proposals under discussion, according to the agenda, was a resolution "to rally influential men [*yūshisha*] widely, to care for soldiers in China, and to spread Shinto in the occupied areas on the continent."[1]

Even if only discussed, the possibility of such activist involvement by the priests alarmed leaders in the government. On 3 May 1895, the day before the cabinet announced its decision to return the Liaotung Peninsula to China, the Home Ministry peremptorily fired Head Priest Minami and all of the head priests of the four prefectures who had signed the agenda summary. As the governor of Kagawa prefecture informed Kotohira, "Because shrine priests are those who perform worship for the state [*kokka no sōshi*], . . . it is against their duties to interfere in government or discuss politics." The priests' plans to impede the peace agreement, continued the governor, violated the imperial rescripts that announced the peace and its acceptance by the armed forces—this despite the fact that the imperial rescripts were issued after the priests' meeting.[2] Shrine priests, it became clear, should work for the general public good (as embodied in the imperial government), not agitate for particular—even Shinto—interests.

Speculation about the sudden dismissals ran rampant. An official in the Home Ministry told one of the head priests that there would have been no problem if the record of the meeting's agenda had not appeared in print.[3] Several of the priests, as well as the author of an article in a local newspaper, suggested that the fault lay with one of the head priests from Okayama prefecture, who, because he held a grudge against another priest, had not attended the meeting. This disgruntled priest purportedly brought the record to the attention of the Home Ministry, intimating that the priests at the meeting were planning to foment riots and violence against the peace treaty.[4] Whatever the actual content of discussion, Head Priest Minami and all of the other head priests in attendance lost their jobs. Their affiliation with enthusiasm for Shinto expansionism had brought disaster.

Minami's dismissal caused consternation among the priests of Kotohira. The government order not only relieved the lower priests of their posts, but also ordered them to turn over the account books of the shrine to Nakagawa Takehiko, the new head priest appointed by the Home Ministry in May 1895. This seemingly ordinary request provoked widespread alarm among the now officially unemployed Matsuoka and his peers. Totally disorganized, the accounts of the shrine revealed years of incompetent management. The problems had apparently originated in the 1880s, after the first lucrative rush of initiations into the Reverence Association from the mid-1870s until 1881. Under Head Priest Fukami, the shrine took out loans in 1882 and 1883, hoping to recruit more people and their money into the Reverence Association. Yet few people around the economically strapped countryside were willing or able to add a new monthly expenditure to their budgets. The shrine only partially succeeded in repaying the resulting debt with the sale of branch shrine lands in 1887. Soon thereafter, Head Priest Kotooka increased the deficit by an additional one hundred thousand yen to establish the Maritime Rescue Association in 1889.[5] When Kotooka died in 1892 and the Home Ministry appointed Minami Mitsutoshi in his place, the new head priest worked to increase membership in the Reverence Association and succeeded in reducing the debt to thirty thousand yen.[6] Dealing with this debt remained a constant source of worry to the priests, but no new moneymaking strategies came to their minds.[7]

The new head priest, Nakagawa, proved to be far more concerned with reviving the profitability of the shrine than with promoting some ideal form of Shinto.[8] After the fired priests finally handed over the accounts to him in July 1895, almost two months after his arrival, Nakagawa met with the former priests, representatives of the Reverence Association, the prefectural governor, and others to discuss strategies for solving the problem. Nakagawa, with government officials in Kotohira, Takamatsu, and Tokyo, determined that the former priests of Kotohira who had overseen the accrual of debt—including former Head Priest Minami as well as Matsuoka and others—would be responsible for repaying it.[9] That is, although they had acted in their capacity as public officials, Minami and his subordinates were now held accountable as private individuals.

Understandably, this verdict seemed unfair. Priests and local businessmen called for Nakagawa's dismissal, rushing to Tokyo to press their case. While the attempt to oust Nakagawa ultimately failed, the men did secure limited concessions: the former priests would be personally responsible for only part of the thirty thousand yen, and the Reverence Association would cover the remaining amount with a forty-year loan.[10] Since the loan was to be repaid from a percentage of amulet sales and the shrine still needed to return to a stable financial footing, the problem of how to increase pilgrimage, amulet sales, and the income of the shrine in general remained. Head Priest Nakagawa would propose two solutions—one on the mountain, one off—that would challenge years of established precedent. Clearly, he thought it was time for a change.

Reviving a Hidden Power

Nakagawa's first idea was startling: to reincorporate the tengu Kongōbō into the official identity of the shrine. Kongōbō, like Konpira, had been given a Shinto name in 1868. But while Konpira (now Kotohira) remained located in the large, central shrine, Kongōbō-Yūsei disappeared from view: his image was removed, his shrine shoved aside, and his presence—as an uncivilized tengu—effectively erased from the mountain. The void thus created allowed Buddhist competitors to draw pilgrims and offerings away from the now Shinto shrine. Therefore, when Nakagawa turned to the tengu in 1896, he sought to reclaim for Kotohira a crucial element in the mountain's former glory—to reclaim the combinatory, esoteric power associated with the mountain before 1868. Using this power from the past, he hoped to increase the devotion (and the donations) of many more pilgrims in the years to come.

Despite the official conversion of Konpira Daigongen to Kotohira Ōkami, Buddhist and shugendo-style worship of Konpira Daigongen and the associated tengu had continued into the Meiji period. Yet institutional support for such worship of necessity shifted away from the now Shinto shrine. Independent practitioners staged exhibits of Konpira Daigongen in the neighboring prefectures of Tokushima and Okayama, often claiming to display the original image from Mt. Zōzu.[11] Also in Tokushima, the Buddhist temple Hashi-kuraji, which had competed with Mt. Zōzu for more than a century, contin-ued to worship Konpira Daigongen—explicitly in the form of a tengu. Ad-vertising their site as Konpira's "inner temple" (*okunoin*), the Shingon priests of Hashikuraji claimed for themselves the hidden powers long associated with the fierce, combinatory god.

The successors of Fumon'in, one of the subtemples on Mt. Zōzu during the Tokugawa era, proved particularly irksome to the shrine. In 1879, the for-mer priest of Fumon'in, Zōsan Yūon, established a Buddhist temple dedi-cated to Konpira Daigongen in the town of Kotohira itself, using the name Konkōin.[12] Each time Kotohira Shrine prevailed upon the authorities to shut the temple down, he reopened it under a new name in a neighboring com-munity, finally settling it back in Kotohira as a Shingon Buddhist temple, us-ing the Tokugawa-era name of Mt. Zōzu's Shingon temple, Matsuoji. Zōsan Yūon traveled around Japan promoting the formation of goma kō, thereby recruiting regular recipients of Matsuoji's goma ceremony talismans much as the shrine's Reverence Association organized recipients of Kotohira's amulets. Overshadowed by the prominent shrine, however, Zōsan faced an uphill bat-tle as he sought to divert attention from the now Shinto mountain.

Worshippers were frequently confused by the two competing claims of Matsuoji and Kotohira Shrine. According to a newspaper report in 1898, for instance, a man from Ehime prefecture who had joined Matsuoji's goma kō took the kō register with him on pilgrimage but mistakenly went to Kotohira Shrine instead. Unaware that he had made any mistake, he submitted the goma kō register—clearly marked "Mt. Zōzu Matsuoji"—to the priests at the shrine, who stamped it. The man also gave an offering of fifty sen and re-ceived an amulet. Upon his return home, however, his fellow kō members be-came upset that he had not received what they considered appropriate offer-ings in return; they sent a representative to Matsuoji to protest. When the temple priest insisted that he had no knowledge of the man's pilgrimage, the entire episode was revealed.[13] Clearly, the confusion engendered by the tem-ple of Konpira Daigongen and the shrine of Kotohira Ōkami, both in Koto-hira, had economic implications for all concerned.

To improve the situation, Zōsan Yūon embarked upon a new initiative early in 1890, intended to advertise that Konpira Daigongen, the object of worship at Matsuoji, was distinct from and more powerful than the kami Ko-tohira worshipped at the shrine. Zōsan traveled to Osaka and Tokyo, where he displayed the avatar's image in elaborate kaichō similar to the sacred spec-tacles of years gone by.[14] He apparently sold printed hangings of Konpira Daigongen depicted as Fudō Myōō, explaining in no uncertain terms that only the temple Matsuoji enshrined that famed performer of miracles who "protects the profit and good fortune of the people"; ever since 1868, he pointed out, Kotohira Shrine, in contrast, had worshipped Ōkuninushi and Emperor Sutoku instead (figure 11.1).[15]

Zōsan's insistence upon a distinction between Konpira Daigongen and Kotohira Ōkami provoked strident opposition in the town of Kotohira. One man wrote to the *Kagawa Shinpō* in support of the shrine, insisting that the avatar and the kami were one and the same—only the name had been changed.[16] Within weeks about two hundred people gathered at the Kotohira town hall to appeal to the Home Ministry to shut down Matsuoji's kaichō in Osaka. The meeting degenerated into a debate over whether Konpira Daigongen was the same as Ōmononushi, the kami enshrined at Kotohira. Business owners worried about the impact of the dispute on the local economy: as a reporter for the *Sanuki Nippō* commented, "If [Zōsan] really has the actual image [in Osaka], then multitudes of people will worship it. This will not only be a great inconvenience, but will be the most extreme of misfortunes for the people of [Kotohira] town."[17] At the end of the peak spring pilgrimage season in June, while Kotohira Shrine sought an injunction against the display, Zōsan brought speakers from Osaka to his temple in Kotohira, hosting lectures on Konpira Daigongen over two to three days.[18] Although the rivalry between Zōsan's Matsuoji and Kotohira Shrine subsided thereafter, it continued to simmer beneath the surface—a constant threat to the shrine's long-sought monopoly on the pilgrimage and the god.

Matsuoji's continuing insistence on a clear distinction between the kami Kotohira and the famed Konpira Daigongen (long affiliated with the miraculous Fudō Myōō and the tengu Kongōbō) undoubtedly influenced the plans of Nakagawa Takehiko, the new head priest of Kotohira, upon his arrival after the Sino-Japanese War. Drawing on a chance comment by the priest Matsuoka after his dismissal, when he recounted Kotohira's history to the new head priest, Nakagawa decided to incorporate the powerful image of Kongōbō more clearly into the Shinto shrine. He suggested elevating the spirit of Kongōbō-Yūsei to new prominence by building on Mt. Zōzu itself an "inner shrine" (*okusha*) dedicated to the spirit of Yūsei under the Shinto name given him in early Meiji: Itsutamahiko no Mikoto. Nakagawa set his plan in motion in August 1895 when, amid other efforts to put the shrine's financial house in order, he petitioned the central government to return to Kotohira the forest lands behind the main shrine, a wooded area near an old, dried-up waterfall called Uchitaki.[19]

In January 1896, as the Meiji leaders cleared the way to issue their first comprehensive forestry laws the next year, Kotohira Shrine—like other

寺尾松山頭象

⚜ 11.1 Printed image of Konpira Daigongen as Fudō Myōō distributed by the temple of Matsuoji during its kaichō in Osaka in 1890. The image was accompanied by a large scroll emphasizing the distinction between the miracle-working Konpira Daigongen, enshrined at Matsuoji, and the newer kami worshipped at Kotohira Shrine. (Courtesy of the Seto Inland Sea Folk History Museum.)

shrines and temples around the country—received permission to reincorporate into the shrine precincts forest lands that had been confiscated in early Meiji.[20] Nakagawa and the priests could thus move ahead with their plans to build the new "inner shrine." First on the agenda was to reenshrine the famous wooden image of the tengu that had protected the Kannon Hall of the old Buddhist complex and was highly revered as a powerful icon. Yet, as Matsuoka recorded in his diary, there appeared a major obstacle to the plan:

> Back in the early Meiji period, I was in charge and petitioned the prefectural office to save several Buddhist images from burning. At that time, while I was absent on shrine business, Assistant Head Priest Kotooka spoke with Head Priest Fukami, and they secretly buried the wooden image of Kongōbō-Yūsei within the taboo enclosure [*imigaki*] to the north of the main shrine, in the area of the large waterfall. Now it is Head Priest Nakagawa's idea to enshrine the image in an inner temple [*okunoin*] at Uchitaki. So we looked at the place where it had been buried, but we did not find it. Since this was twenty years ago, the people who buried it are no longer alive. We dug up everything in the area, but there is no trace of the image. This is truly strange.[21]

No matter how important the physical icon, however, the lack of the original image—or even the possibility that Zōsan or others might actually possess it—would not stop the priests from planning the shrine.

Later that month, Nakagawa followed up with the prefectural governor, proposing the construction in the returned forest lands of a large shrine to the renowned tengu. "Itsutama Shrine, a branch shrine of [Kotohira], honors Itsutamahiko no Mikoto as its object of worship," he wrote.

> He was the reviver of this shrine, with many important accomplishments, and people worshipped Kongōbō-Yūsei as second only to the main shrine. This same kami, due to the separation of kami and buddhas, was moved to a new shrine and given a kami name. But because the people do not know that Itsutamahiko no Mikoto is the spirit of Kongōbō-Yūsei, there are extremely few who revere Itsutamahiko Shrine, so that the accomplishments of this kami are well on the way to oblivion. Happily, however, within the shrine precincts that have now been returned lies an area called Uchitaki, where Itsutamahiko no Mikoto secluded himself in meditation when he was alive. Since it is a sacred trace of the kami worshipped in the main shrine, we propose moving the Itsutamahiko Shrine to that site and worshipping him alongside the deities of the main shrine, Ōmononushi and Emperor Sutoku.[22]

It suddenly became clear that Nakagawa was proposing nothing other than a radical redefinition of the deity Kotohira, a generation after its 1868 conversion. No matter how disguised in Shinto terms, he proposed to revive the esoteric tengu identity of the god—an identity that would reinvigorate the attraction of the mountain for many miracle-seeking pilgrims and their money.

Politically, the tengu identity was linked neither with the nativist myths nor with the revered imperial line, as were the two official identities of the god, Ōmononushi and Emperor Sutoku. (Indeed, the tengu form of the retired emperor Sutoku was associated more with vengeance and Buddhist magic than with the revered kami ancestry of Japan's emperors.) The image of the tengu would thus help Kotohira stake out a position independent of its standing in the hierarchy of state shrines. Moreover, by positioning Kongōbō/Itsutamahiko no Mikoto as the *inner* identity of the god, Nakagawa appealed to the esoteric logic that thereby asserted the tengu as the more powerful, *true* identity of the official god. With these strategies, Nakagawa sought to establish a renewed independent strength for the shrine through the esoteric magical powers at the base of popular pilgrimage and prayer.

Within a month, the Home Ministry forbade the elevation of Kongōbō, defending the supremacy of the imperial identity above all else. Without touching upon the magical or doctrinal aspects of the case, ministry officials argued that it was "not permitted to enshrine the spirit of a person from recent generations [*kinsei no hito*] alongside the spirit of an emperor."[23] By April 1896, however, the governor approved a counterproposal from Nakagawa allowing him to build a shrine and supporting buildings in the newly returned area of Uchitaki as long as he did not elevate Kongōbō-Yūsei through joint enshrinement with the spirit of Emperor Sutoku.[24] The way was paved for Nakagawa's "inner shrine" not to formally assert Kongōbō's identity with the imperial kami, but to imply through the layout of the mountain that the tengu was, indeed, the hidden essence of Kotohira.

Nakagawa quickly embarked upon efforts to raise money for the new "inner shrine." In May, the priests printed up an announcement of the plans for the new shrine, asking worshippers for donations and designating the perquisites awarded to donors according to the size of their offerings. Conflating the legends of Emperor Sutoku and Kongōbō without explicitly referring to their tengu forms, the shrine publicized the new site both for the aura of its natural surroundings and for the mysterious power associated with ascetic practice. "About ten *chō* [1 kilometer] to the northwest of the main shrine of Kotohira," announced the printed flyer, "at a place on the mountain called Uchitaki, there grows a luxuriant cluster of old trees. A cliff several *shaku* [feet] high rises above a spiritual site of mysterious silence. It is said that this is the ancient site where Emperor Sutoku long ago secluded himself in meditative practice. The reviver of this mountain, Kongōbō-Yūsei, who is worshipped by people to the same degree as the main shrine, also secluded himself here."

After reiterating the recent institutional history of Kongōbō on the mountain—his renaming at the time of the Meiji Restoration and the popular neglect of his small Itsutama Shrine—the announcement proclaimed the ambitious plans for the new building. "Now we have received permission to revive the sacred site of Uchitaki," it continued. "We will move the Itsutama Shrine to [Uchitaki] and build a new main hall, prayer hall, worship hall, donations hall, amulet office, ema hall, corridor, shrine office, and other buildings." This ambitious complex would be secluded, yet open to large numbers of worshippers. "For the convenience of people's pilgrimage, we will build a road three *kan* [six yards] wide from the main shrine to this site. Thus will we pass on the achievements of this kami to later generations."[25] A drawing accompanying the announcement showed the proposed road and bridges winding along the mountain to the soaring cliffs.

The politics of hidden power and priority associated with an "inner shrine" were evident not only to Nakagawa but to people throughout the area. Newspaper articles at the time repeatedly noted that while Kotohira referred to the shrine as a "branch shrine" (*massha*) in its official correspondence with the government, it called the site an "inner shrine" (*okusha*) when speaking to the public. As one writer pointed out, this is because "on the one hand, branch shrines do not receive much faith from the people; on the other hand, [Kotohira] is using the fact that inner shrines are the object of great faith of the people."[26] For this reason, perhaps, the priests referred to the new shrine as an okusha not only in fund-raising literature but on large signs on the mountain as well.[27]

Like anything related to pilgrimage, controversy surrounding the plan took both religious and economic form. As a sympathizer of the shrine's Buddhist rival Matsuoji reported in the newspaper, "Not only do the townspeople of Kotohira not agree about what effect the inner shrine will have on the future prosperity or decline of Kotohira, but many are opposed." The reason, he stated, was that "there is no inner temple at Konpira":

From the Meiji Restoration until today, it has been said that there is no inner temple at Konpira. Instead, the site has depended on the main shrine to command the faith of the people of the world. However, now suddenly it has been announced that the shrine will build something new called the inner shrine. This not only suggests that people who have heretofore made the pilgrimage to the shrine have uselessly prayed to a superficial kami [*maetachi no kami*], but suddenly to switch and say that there is an inner shrine, although it has been said since the opening of the mountain that there is no inner shrine, will make tens of thousands of pilgrims feel strange. It will decrease the value of the current main shrine. If one decreases the value, it will weaken the faith of people. This is absolutely not good for Kotohira Shrine, nor is it good for Kotohira town. This line of reasoning, however, has not been generally embraced, and the head priest and others of the mountain are going ahead wholeheartedly with the new building.

The writer went on to attack not only the superficial Shinto identity assigned to Kongōbō, but also the Shinto identity of Konpira and the mountain as a whole, reiterating in several subsequent installments the Buddhist and syncretic legends of the site.[28]

The plans for the okusha generated a debate in which opponents sought to trap the priests of Kotohira Shrine in a rhetorical snare of their own making. They pointed out the centuries-old assertion of "exclusive shrine" status by both Konkōin and Kotohira, in which the priests denied having any "inner shrine." Accepting nativists' definition of Kotohira as the pure spirits of both an emperor and a kami, they emphasized that kami of the state should be accessible to all: they should be worshipped in public, open shrines befitting the imperial state, not hidden away according to the esoteric logic of Tokugawa-era Buddhism. Hence, kami should be worshipped in "outer," not "inner" shrines. Opponents of the inner shrine also invoked the "good of the town," reinforcing the idea that Kotohira Shrine, now representing not its own lordly interests but the national government as a whole, should by all rights promote the well-being of its neighbors.

While unsuccessful in preventing the priests' project from progressing, such strategies heightened the tension between Kotohira's status as a state, "public" institution and its need to support itself, between its role promoting the benefit of all and its efforts in favor of its own funding. Even as the priests forged ahead with their plans for the inner shrine within the mountain precincts, this tension erupted on the sea lanes and at the inns surrounding the shrine, as business owners reacted violently to another proposal of the priests—this time affecting not just the layout of the shrine but the livelihoods of people throughout the surrounding area.

For the Public Good

In order to maintain the solvency of Kotohira Shrine, Nakagawa and the other priests sought not only to exploit the hidden powers of the tengu but also to profit more directly from the pilgrimage business. Nakagawa's inner shrine initiative, after all, was a long-term proposition. Unless donations for building the inner shrine were diverted to shrine finances as a whole, they would do little to address the pressing issue of the thirty-thousand-yen debt. For this purpose, Nakagawa sought more immediate income. He arranged to sell more than half of the land of Kotohira's branch shrine in Osaka.[29] He also worked in cooperation with the Reverence Association in his efforts to raise money, attracting members not with sanctuary access but with economic incentives.

Beginning in January 1896, while Nakagawa was still formulating his ideas for the inner shrine, the head priest sent out lecturers to recruit people for a new "Million-Person Kō" (*hyakumannin kō*). According to his plan, members of the new kō would pay an extra fee of thirty-six sen to the shrine and would receive in return a variety of special privileges, including steamship discounts of up to 30 percent arranged with a single company: the Kansai Steamship Corporation.[30] It was obvious, at least to current and former priests on the mountain, that the Million-Person Kō was formed for financial reasons. "This Million-Person Kō will [fulfill] our unfinished business," wrote Matsuoka in his diary, and again, "We are agreed that the Million-Person Kō is a very good thing for getting rid of the debts."[31] If successful, the incentives offered by the kō might help offset the decline in pilgrimage that was feared to have set in after the Sino-Japanese War.

However, the arrangements that Nakagawa made in order to offer such valuable discounts to members of the Million-Person Kō disrupted existing alliances in the local economy, inciting resentment against the shrine and bringing about the ultimate demise of the scheme. Over the years since the creation of the Reverence Association in 1874, the relationships among the several sectors of the local pilgrimage economy—shrine, inns, brothels, amulet box sellers, ricksha pullers, and boat companies—had become increasingly regularized and subjected to government scrutiny. Amulet box sellers and ricksha pullers, when forced to establish self-regulating trade associations under police supervision in the 1880s, had repeatedly pledged not to form exclusive alliances with specific innkeepers or boat services.[32] Although individual operators repeatedly violated the agreements, most business owners agreed that the approved relationship among businesses—enforced by the threat of losing an operating license—created an even playing field for all members of each approved trade association. Thus, members of the Kotohira town innkeepers' association, or the thirty-odd Tadotsu boat operators who shared ticket-selling arrangements as part of the Osaka Mercantile Shipping Company's Kansai League of Ships, expected business opportunities to be equally open to all within their organization.

Nakagawa's Million-Person Kō upset these delicately negotiated alliances. By arranging exclusionary agreements with a single company, indeed with a new, outside competitor that had no prior relation to the shrine, Nakagawa set off a potentially violent confrontation that contradicted the image of the shrine as an institution for the public, and especially the local, good. The ensuing conflict split the vicinity of Kotohira in two, pitting the shrine and most of the Reverence Association inns against Tadotsu boat owners and their allies. It nearly brought the business of both town and shrine to a standstill.

The immediate problem concerned steamships, now the crucial link between Honshu and Shikoku. During the Sino-Japanese War, the government had commandeered steamships of all types, reducing the number available for shipping and passenger business in the Inland Sea. Around the same time, the Ministry of Communications instituted new safety restrictions on the number of passengers permitted on each ship, reducing the average capacity by about 30 percent. At the end of the war, when the number of travelers suddenly increased en route to expositions and festivals in and around Kyoto, hundreds of people were left stranded at ports throughout the Inland Sea, waiting for space on ships.[33] The field was ripe for the entry of a new company, and Kotohira Shrine, with its Million-Person Kō, jumped into the fray. In early 1896, a competitor to the union of independent operators in Tadotsu formed in Osaka—that is, the Kansai Steamship Corporation. It was with this newcomer that Kotohira Shrine arranged the spectacular discounts it offered to members of the Million-Person Kō.

Even though conditions would seem to have favored added shipping capacity, the Tadotsu boat operators saw the new outsider company as a major threat, especially when strengthened by the economic clout of Kotohira Shrine. The Tadotsu boat owners thus mobilized against it, creating a schism that, because of the business ties between Tadotsu and Kotohira, was felt in the shrine town as well. The Bizen'ya and Yoshimaya inns, along with all twelve saké merchants in Kotohira, sided with the Tadotsu businesses. Meanwhile, the Toraya and several other Reverence Association inns in Kotohira recruited members for the Million-Person Kō, advertising the discount offered by the new Kansai Steamship Corporation. The two competing steamship lines directed passengers to stay in Kotohira only at their affiliated inns. Since the Tadotsu boat companies dominated the pilgrimage business, their passengers stayed only at Bizen'ya or Yoshimaya, opponents of the Million-Person Kō. As Matsuoka commented, "Not a single person is staying at the other inns."[34]

The conflict then intensified. The Reverence Association stopped permitting customers of Bizen'ya or Yoshimaya to join the association or to enter the sanctuary of the main shrine, and the Kinzanji brothels refused to hire out geisha and prostitutes to customers at the two inns.[35] Meanwhile, rumors flew concerning Head Priest Nakagawa's personal links to the new Osaka company. "We have heard that Head Priest Nakagawa has some connection to the Kansai Steamship Corporation that has recently formed," wrote a newspaper reporter in Tadotsu, "and he has used the good name of the shrine office to obtain the agreement of the people of Kotohira. Of course, the innkeepers and influential people of Kotohira have agreed. . . . The steamship businesses in Tadotsu have reacted violently, saying that it is not the head priest's job to propose a steamship company."[36] Tadotsu boat operators thus protested to the shrine and to local government and began agitating for Nakagawa's resignation.[37]

In the eyes of the boat owners, saké brewers, and two of the innkeepers, it was "not the head priest's job to propose a steamship company," no matter how advantageous Nakagawa may have found his ties to the Kansai Steamship Company's president, the governor of Osaka.[38] The economic impact of the Tadotsu opposition forced Nakagawa to renounce any ties with private business and to defend his record as a public servant, writing to the newspaper to deny any connection to the Kansai company.[39] Near the end of March, the governor of Kagawa prefecture and the chief of police stepped in to mediate the dispute, arranging for the discontinuation of the Million-Person Kō, the exclusion of the Kansai Steamship Company from Tadotsu, and the reincorporation of Bizen'ya and Yoshimaya into the Reverence Association structure.[40] The attempts of Nakagawa and Kotohira Shrine to raise money through an exclusionary business alliance thus came to naught. The shrine was forced back upon its other project, the building and publicizing of the shrine to Kongōbō.

The Million-Person Kō fiasco drove home to the priests new lessons about their situation. First, while they could do as they liked within their shrine precincts, they no longer set the rules for the pilgrimage business as a whole. They would be forced to accommodate their partners in pilgrimage promotion and profit making. Second, the priests dramatically learned the economic importance of maintaining a political image of disinterested openness. Special privileges could be granted on the basis of direct monetary donations or aristocratic status, but not on the basis of economic affiliations. When in later years the shrine held festivals publicizing the inner shrine, therefore, it arranged for railroad and steamship discounts on all carriers in the entire country, thereby avoiding charges of favoritism and expanding its reach throughout Japan.[41] In sum, although Nakagawa failed to wipe out the shrine's debt during his tenure,[42] his efforts highlighted the realities of regional politics that had been taking shape for years: for both economic and political purposes, the shrine needed to cooperate with former subjects and license holders. At least beyond the mountain itself, the priests of the shrine no longer ruled; they could only recommend.

Dynamics of Local Development

The people whose growing influence Kotohira now had to accommodate were business owners and landlords: the taxpayers who in the Meiji constitutional order now elected local, prefectural, and national representatives. It was the people staffing this new order—the governors, town officials, and members of voluntary business associations—who would henceforth shape the development strategies of the town.[43] The priests of Kotohira acted as just one among many such interested parties who would set the priorities for years to come.

In the years after the Sino-Japanese War, town elites and government officials turned their attention not so much to generating greater numbers of pilgrims as to extracting more money from the people who came. While innkeepers, souvenir sellers, and brothel keepers depended on the accumulated small expenditures of thousands of ordinary pilgrims, they increasingly recognized the potential of catering to the growing numbers of more prosperous, educated, and thus ostensibly more civilized, "gentlemen." In an effort to attract these elite, high-paying customers, the leading innkeepers of Kotohira—some of the wealthiest of whom sat in the elected local assembly—sought to create refined spaces conducive to the taste and behavior of this emerging middle class. They increasingly designed a Kotohira for the Westernizing, moneyed elite, even while depending for their continued prosperity on the expenditures of poorer pilgrims, who formed the overwhelming majority. Capitalizing on both constituencies, town and prefectural leaders worked to turn the profits of the popular pilgrimage into an engine for local and regional growth.

It was the governor of Kagawa prefecture, Tokuhisa Tsunenori, who set the process in motion. Whereas, in previous years, each town or business group promoted itself without outside assistance, Tokuhisa used the resources of the prefectural and national government to encourage development. After the Sino-Japanese War, expenditures on industrial promotion rose sharply throughout Japan, with the Home Ministry–appointed governors of each prefecture in charge of carrying out economic development strategies. Nowhere was this increase in government involvement more striking than in Kagawa prefecture, which in 1897, under Tokuhisa, led the country in the per capita expenditure of government money on industrial promotion. The "industrial promotion governor," as Tokuhisa came to be known, devoted 10 percent of these funds to the staging of expositions to publicize advances in industry and manufactures, and a further 12 percent to agricultural improvements. But he targeted more than half of the money—51 percent—for use in more direct incentives for trade and light manufacture.[44]

Governor Tokuhisa, who held office for only the two years between April 1896 and July 1898, is renowned in the history of Kagawa prefecture for supporting the creation of a variety of manufacturing enterprises, ranging from spinning and weaving factories to tile and lumber companies, electricity providers, and stonecutters.[45] Yet his plans for development were even more wide ranging. Shortly after his appointment, Tokuhisa toured the prefecture and spoke with a reporter about his ideas for the economy. The *Kagawa Shinpō* subsequently reported his comments about Kotohira. "When I went to Kotohira Shrine," commented the governor,

> I learned that there are no fewer than three million pilgrims every year. Now, of these three million pilgrims, each person spends on average ten sen in the area, which adds up to three hundred thousand yen. If the pilgrims increased their spending to one yen each, that would be three million yen. Even if it were only one-third of that, this would be a large amount. It is the urgent work of this area to achieve that goal.
>
> The first item of business is to get the pilgrims to spend more money. How would it be most appropriate to do so in terms of industry? At Miyajima, they make plates and other items from the local pine trees and sell them. This brings in a not insignificant amount of money. I noticed that there are some nice dishes for sale in Kotohira. But these goods are not made in Kotohira, they are brought from Miyajima. An official at Kotohira Shrine says that there are lots of pine trees in the government forest here, and they could sell hundreds of them a year for a cheap price. If dishes were made, this would be a very profitable industry. Anyway, if one produced a souvenir in Kotohira and pilgrims came, they would buy it and take it home.[46]

While amulet boxes, candy, and selected other items had been made locally in Kotohira for decades, if not centuries, the governor focused attention on new possibilities for profit.

Governor Tokuhisa backed up his words with concrete actions. During 1897, he began promoting the desirability for Kagawa prefecture of a trade school, designed to spread such important techniques in the manufacture of bowls and plates as lacquering and lathing. Competition for such a school immediately broke out, as communities vied to become the site of the proposed establishment, to be funded by the prefecture. The *Kagawa Shinpō* ran a lead article in August arguing that the school should be established in its home city, Takamatsu, to improve its lacquer industry. In Kotohira, business leaders began raising money, through a surcharge on prostitution, for a campaign to build the prefectural school in Kotohira instead. Although at the end of 1897 the governor granted the prefectural trade school to Takamatsu, the leaders of Kotohira built upon the new momentum to establish their own, town-funded trade school the following year.

A joint venture of the shrine, the government, and local businessmen, the new school focused on producing dishes and other souvenirs to sell to visitors. As supporters explained, "Since, here where travelers concentrate, the townspeople rely upon the fate of travelers, the purpose of the school is to make and sell material goods as souvenirs."[47] Town leaders established the trade school with an initial expenditure of twenty-five hundred yen, of which one thousand yen came from the shrine office, five hundred yen from town taxes, and even four hundred yen, thanks to the Ministry of Education, from the national treasury.[48] The participation of the amulet box sellers' union, which contributed another four hundred yen, highlighted the anticipated role of the school in increasing profitable employment opportunities for the townspeople. At the time, in spring 1898, the thirty or forty makers of the famous Kotohira amulet boxes—who even in a good year earned only a pittance—were out of work because of a decline in demand during the postwar recession.[49] The new school was to teach these unemployed craftsmen, as well as others, the latest techniques in lacquerwork, lathework, and wood carving. Plans were also made to expand the curriculum later to metalworking.

Part of the plan for the new school closely resembled the idea set forth by Governor Tokuhisa. Administrators of the school recruited a cadre of less advanced students to make "Mt. Zōzu Sacred Tree Chopsticks" to sell as souvenirs. They hired a teacher from Ise in the hope of emulating the economic success of Ise's sacred chopsticks, which reportedly earned craftsmen there about three hundred thousand yen a year. Nevertheless, according to newspaper reports, Kotohira's chopstick production was to be modeled more closely on that of chopsticks made at Nikkō, which would make them cheaper than those at Ise.[50]

From 1898 until 1907—when the Kotohira trade school closed its doors because of mismanagement—apprentice-made chopsticks, lacquerware, lathework, and works of sculpture were sold by local merchants, earning praise from at least one minister from the central government for increasing the local production of souvenirs.[51] Shops in Kotohira advertised the chopsticks, made from the "beautifully scented" trees on Mt Zōzu, in a variety of paper-wrapped sets designed to appeal to the broad spectrum of visitors. If a higher price suggested greater popularity, then in 1903 chopsticks adorned with either the elephant pattern symbolic of Mt. Zōzu or the five-story pagoda and new Eleventh Division army base at Zentsūji shared first place, priced at six sen for three, and eight sen for five pairs of chopsticks. Next came the Tall Lantern and Saya Bridge, prominent symbols of Kotohira, at five and seven sen, and the encircled gold pattern of Konpira at four and six sen. A Shinto headdress and sacred jewel (three and five sen) and a picture of the Kotohira trade school (two and four sen) brought up the rear, suggesting that both strict, nativist Shinto and unadorned civic institutions lacked the evocative resonances sought by visitors as gifts to take back home.[52] Members of the first graduating class of the school went on to refine their woodcarving and lathework skills, developing the distinctive *ittōbori* style of carved wood souvenirs that are sold at shops up and down the mountain at Kotohira today.[53]

The business leaders and town councilmen of Kotohira—including owners of prominent inns, the head of the brothel association, and producers and sellers of saké and souvenirs—also responded to a second initiative of Governor Tokuhisa: the building of a park. The appreciation of nature had long been a central part of pilgrimage in general, and the scenic beauty of Konpira played its part in attracting visitors to the site. Each year, pilgrimage to Konpira reached its annual peak during the blossoming of cherry trees (*sakura*), rows of which gave their name to the flat expanse of paved pathway (Sakuranobaba) inside the main gate of the compound, and clouds of which had graced screens and poems depicting Konpira's charms since the seventeenth century. Shrine and town deliberately cultivated cherry trees and spaces for entertainment as part of their attempts to attract pilgrims. Back in 1868, for instance, Yagi Hikosaburō, the head of the Tosa troops in Konpira, had overseen the planting of hundreds of cherry trees along the river and the main avenues of the town in an effort to enhance the pilgrimage business.[54]

Not only cherry blossoms in the spring, but also spectacular overlooks at any time of year provided popular attractions. The appreciation of a view, at Kotohira as elsewhere, was often integral both to the experience of pilgrimage to the shrine itself and to entertainments outside the precincts. Visitors since at least the seventeenth century had commented upon the beautiful sites on the mountain as well as the grand panorama when one overlooked the area as a whole. On a rise to the south of the shrine's festival grounds (jinjiba), as well, local businessmen had long hosted outdoor entertainment in an open space that commanded a view of the surrounding plain and out toward the Inland Sea. Located near the brothels and entertainment establishments of Kinzanji, during the Tokugawa period the site was generally crowded with visitors and the music of geisha on hot summer nights. During the first decades of Meiji, however, this space was allowed to deteriorate, and when the Shikoku New Road was constructed through the middle of town in 1888, it undercut part of the hill upon which the overlook had been situated, causing the eastern part of the area to collapse. Leaders of the town soon began to discuss plans to rebuild and enlarge the site, "taking out the bamboo and trees nearby and making one large park," following the model of the public, Western-style parks established in Tokyo and elsewhere since the early 1870s.[55] Despite much talk, however, plans for the site's refurbishment languished for nearly a decade.

The idea of investing in the park as a policy for economic promotion finally gained momentum when Governor Tokuhisa provided an opportunity in 1897. Just as he encouraged bids for a trade school in order to promote manufactures, the governor also invited bids for the establishment of a park in western Sanuki, promoting tourism. The local leaders of Kotohira rose to the occasion. Vying against the towns of Tadotsu and Kan'onji, the town assembly allotted a budget of forty-five hundred yen to lobby for the park—with the funds for the park, as for the school, coming from an added surtax on the brothels of Kinzanji.[56] The result was that for each incense stick's worth of time a geisha or prostitute worked, a surtax of five *rin* (that is, half a sen) went directly to a fund to lobby for the park as well as the trade school.[57] Although Kotohira lost its bids for prefectural funding for both the park and the school, prominent individuals, including three women in Kotohira, nevertheless made individual donations to cover the costs of park construction and improvement.[58] In March 1898, Kotohira Park was opened with an area of 24,985 *tsubo* (over eight hectares).[59]

Plans for the development of tourism continued to focus on the creation of sophisticated sights for the enjoyment of moneyed travelers. Building upon the establishment of Kotohira Park and, in Takamatsu, the renowned Ritsurin Park, formerly the retreat of the Takamatsu lord, civic leaders called for the development of Kotohira and, indeed, all of Kagawa prefecture as one great "entertainment area" (*yūenchi*) or "scenic resort" (*yūranchi*). The prominent Kotohira inn Bingo began building the Kotohira Kadan, a new luxury inn in Kotohira Park, and planned another establishment at Kotaki Springs, between Kotohira and Zentsūji, as well.

Inspired by the examples of the Kotohira Kadan and Kotaki Springs, civic leaders envisioned the development of Kotohira as a scenic site where wealthy tourists would spend money on lodging, baths, food, and entertainment. Remarking upon the growing tendency of elite visitors to value scenery over the miracles of the deity, a front-page article in the *Kagawa Shinpō* in 1897 exhorted the people of Kotohira to profit from the beauty of the town:

What is the capital [*shihon*] of Kotohira? In a word, it is the quiet, beautiful scenery of the place. Frankly, along with the spread of scientific knowledge, attitudes toward the kami must necessarily change, and are now in the process of altering rapidly. . . .

Kotohira! Use your god-given capital to make an entertainment fairyland [*yūraku no senkyō*]! You have built architecture in beautiful harmony with the natural scenery. But now, you must add to the well-known spiritual sites and advertise yourself to the world as a great paradise of entertainment. . . . You should build amenities such as restaurants, flowering bowers, a large theater, a new kabuki stage, an exhibition hall, and other things to please people's eyes. . . . When I see the Kotohira Kadan, the Kotaki Springs, or Kotohira Park, I truly think these places are capital for the development of Kotohira in the future. But the town's plans should go one step farther. If you can turn the entire area of the jinjiba into a recreation area, think how good that would be. If this were actually to happen, then a new Kotohira would arise as the most prosperous place in Shikoku.[60]

Using the new language of consumer capitalism, proponents argued that parks, upper-class inns, restaurants, and scenic nooks for picnics should attract the growing number of prosperous visitors who were attracted by natural beauty more than by miracles. As a result, improvements to Kotohira Park in the late 1890s included not only the pruning of trees and laying down of paths, but also the construction of three pavilions for enjoyment of the views.[61]

As such initiatives garnered the attention of the town council and local journalists, however, occasional voices rose to remind people of the continued importance of the majority of pilgrims. Remarked one writer in 1898, "One must pay attention: many of these people [who come to Kotohira] are middle-class, but even more are below middle class. One must make them fully satisfied with their stay by providing comfort, convenience, and a relatively cheap price. What is important is this: those so-called gentlemen who wear Western-style clothes and beards are the customers who will not appreciate Kotohira, no matter what. Kotohira's everyday prosperity is due to the people in straw raingear [*minokasa*] and leggings, the good men and women who look like pilgrims."[62] Indeed, the large, expensive inns such as Bingo and Toraya constituted only a minority of the seventy-nine inns in Kotohira in 1899, of which more than a third provided the very cheapest accommodation: a roof and firewood.[63] The great majority of visitors to the shrine stayed in these small inns, often lacking the money even for train fare, let alone for hiring a geisha or visiting the baths at Kotaki Springs.

Thus, the economic development of the town proceeded on two levels at once. Programs sponsored by the wealthiest innkeepers and the town council focused on the emerging elite, creating the park and luxury inns to cater to the growing demand for elegant, Western-style accommodations. Smaller business operators, meanwhile, continued to serve their poorer clientele, selling firewood, candy, and shelter away from the most prominent inns. Similarly, at the shrine above, priests promoted the "civilized" rites of the kami while encouraging less choreographed worship of the tengu as well.

In arguing for these innovations, priests, businessmen, and journalists alike called upon the "public" interest of the town, extolling their contributions to its economic development. In doing so, they reshaped not only the structures and rhetoric of local business, but also the place of the shrine itself. For the shrine became more supporter than shaper of local promotion policies. While still at the center of economic planning, it became in many ways the object, not the agent, of development activity. In the terminology of the new industrializing age, the shrine and its pilgrimage became capital for the future of the area as a whole: the shrine, so desperate for income of its own, was now limited by its supporting role in the welfare and development of all.

Remobilizing the God
(1898–1905)

By the turn of the twentieth century, both worshippers and entrepreneurs had seized the initiative in promoting Kotohira Shrine. Amid economic restructuring at home and military conflict abroad, they—even more than the priests—shaped public perceptions of the god. A century before, playwrights and printmakers, innkeepers and authors had expanded the image of Konpira Daigongen in directions unanticipated by the priests, establishing a prominent place for the combinatory deity in a popular culture of pilgrimage. Now, in the 1890s and early 1900s, the priests of Kotohira Shrine found themselves in a situation similar to, yet more constricted than, that of their predecessors: supporting, not themselves creating, yet another image of the god—this one taking shape in an increasingly military, imperial culture.

Japan's impressive victory in the Sino-Japanese war had intensified and, in many respects, made possible Japanese military and industrial involvement abroad. Under the terms of the Treaty of Shimonoseki, Japan gained its first formal colony, Formosa, as well as an indemnity so large that it created a budget surplus—money that could then be dedicated to the development of arms production, shipbuilding, and other heavy industries. Victory also brought recognition from the West that Japan was emerging as a military and colonial power: first the British and then others signed new treaties with Japan that excluded the earlier infringements on Japanese sovereignty.

In the years after 1895, lives and livelihoods became increasingly tied to military concerns. This rise of the military proved especially true in and around Kotohira. In 1896, the government reorganized and expanded the imperial army, drafting enough young men to staff twelve divisions instead of the previous five. Army leaders separated the forces in Shikoku from the Fifth Division at Hiroshima and, from 1898 on, placed them under a new Eleventh Division based at Zentsūji, only two miles from the shrine.[1] The Inland Sea also contributed to the military context of Kotohira. As the main water route from eastern Japan to the continent, the sea connected Tokyo and Osaka in the east to China and Korea in the west, with naval bases, ironworks, and other crucial installations in between. Kotohira thus stood in the midst of the new military, industrial economy.

This growing prominence of armies and industry undergirded a popular fascination with military themes. The decisive victory of Japan over the largest country in East Asia had, almost overnight, proved a source of great national pride. Newspapers gloated over the reversal of roles, praising the valor of Japan's modernized forces. Painters and printmakers depicted heroic Japanese soldiers routing primitive, cowering Chinese. And the gods of Japan played their own part, infusing national aspirations with the protection of the divine.

Entrepreneurs in and around Kotohira capitalized on the presence and popularity of the soldiers. With the establishment of the army base in Zentsūji, brothel owners and innkeepers in Kotohira gained a ready clientele in the many officers stationed just down the road. Sponsors of sideshows and sellers of souvenirs promoted images of national pride to extract additional money from visitors to the town. Thus, after the Russo-Japanese War broke out in 1904, when worshippers thronged to the shrine, they came to a town and a shrine already embedded in reminders of military might. Through their activities before and during the Russo-Japanese War, worshippers, entrepreneurs, and, in the end, the priests as well would create a culture at Kotohira that brought the god, the military, and the business of pilgrimage into a tighter embrace than ever before.

Between the Wars

Public enthusiasm for the victory over China in 1895 ensured that promoters of Kotohira and other sites would build upon patriotic and military themes. Even before the Sino-Japanese War, educators had begun linking Kotohira Shrine with military bases, culture, and imperial prestige. In May 1890, for instance, forty-five students in military uniform marched off with their teachers from the Takamatsu upper elementary school to witness, in the words of a reporter for the *Kagawa Shinpō,* "that praiseworthy modern convenience, the train; those defenders of the state, the army base and soldiers [at Marugame]; and the old and valuable items, art, and manufactures of Kotohira Shrine."[2] The juxtaposition of visits to the shrine and visits to the base continued. In November 1892, thirty-eight fourth-graders from Takamatsu traveled by train first to pray at Kotohira, then to tour the Marugame base—a three-day trip at the time. "Under the guidance of army infantry General Nagano," wrote one student in his diary, "we inspected each room on the base and watched the soldiers' weapons drills and exercises. Afterward, we were led to the officers' clubhouse, where portraits of the emperor, empress, and crown prince were hung. We lined up and bowed deeply in respect."[3] In the education of students, it seems, the Shinto shrine and the military base thus played complementary didactic roles, introducing young travelers to significant local landmarks in the context of the imperial family and its affiliated gods.

The popularity of Kotohira as a destination both for student groups and for pilgrims attracted entrepreneurs seeking to profit from the traffic. Shortly after the victory over China, investors built in Kotohira a diorama of war scenes, opening it to view in 1896.[4] A larger project was launched in 1900, when developers from Tokyo and Okayama prefecture recruited investors for the construction of the latest in public visual spectacles: a round panorama hall (figure 12.1).[5] Boasting a continuous 360-degree view provided by the oil paintings of Tōjō Seitarō and Goseda Shigeru II (Tokyo-based artists who had already become known for their realistic depictions of major battles), the Kotohira panorama was touted as a spur to popular interest in both historical education and the latest artistic techniques.[6]

In November 1900, while Japanese troops fought alongside European and U.S. forces to quell the Boxer Rebellion in China, local dignitaries inaugurated the panorama with great fanfare. As the *Kagawa Shinpō* described the scene,

> Firecrackers were set off from about six o'clock in the morning. An arch of pine boughs stood at the entrance to the panorama, with the characters "Panorama Hall" clearly written on it in chrysanthemum blossoms [the imperial flower], and barrels of saké stacked on either side. In front and behind, to left and right of the entrance hung red and white lanterns. National flags decorated the entrance, and small flags hung high in the air. It was just like the opening ceremony of any other building. At eleven o'clock, two priests from Kotohira Shrine came to the panorama and offered a blessing, and the dignitaries went to the shrine to pray. During this time, a military band played "Kimigayo." At noon, the ceremony ended, the panorama hall was opened, and everyone could go in.[7]

✿ **12.1** The Kotohira panorama hall, built in 1900, attracted visitors to see a painted, 360-degree view of famous scenes from the Sino-Japanese War. In ensuing years, schoolchildren on field trips, as well as adult pilgrims and visitors, frequently visited this celebration of Japan's victory on their way to or from the shrine, often combining the trip with a visit to the nearby army base in Zentsūji as well. (Courtesy of the Kotohira Ezu o Mamoru Kai.)

Militarization did not stop there. All visitors to the shrine during its first two weeks of operation received a free gift: a pamphlet of popular war songs including the national anthem ("Kimigayo"), "Marching through the Snow" ("Yuki no Shingun"), "Our Navy" ("Waga Kaigun"), and "The Trumpeter's End" ("Rappashu no Saigo"), prefaced by a newly composed song describing the Kotohira panorama.[8]

For the price of five sen (three sen for soldiers, students, or children), visitors to the panorama could see rousing scenes of famous battles of the Sino-Japanese War, especially those in which soldiers from Shikoku took part. "The paintings show the attack on Pyongyang around eight o'clock in the morning," recorded the newspaper.

> When one climbs up onto the viewing platform and looks around, it seems as if one is in the midst of mountains and rivers, grass and trees, fields and marshes, in a vast expanse of clouds and smoke. The battlefield, the explosions of gunpowder from the

firearms, and the lighting and images of houses and people are all well composed. Distant views and close-up depictions of the battle of Pyongyang follow each other as if they are real, and dozens of ri of scenery fall under a single glance. One feels as if one is physically present on the grounds of a real battle. One gets a wonderful feeling, especially when seeing the hard fighting of the Marugame troops.[9]

In the years after the opening, additional props brought the military scenes out even into the center of the hall. As one man recalled of his childhood visits to the panorama in 1910 or 1911, "They used dolls of the Japanese soldiers blown back by explosions. What especially made a lasting impression was the smoke of the cannons, made from cloth, hanging here and there from the ceiling by slender threads."[10]

Visitors viewed the life-size paintings to the sound of dramatic explanation. A newspaper report in 1903 recorded how a precocious nine-year-old boy in Kotohira informally apprenticed himself to the narrator of the panorama, eventually hiring on himself to describe the images on crowded days. "His explanation was meticulous," marveled the reporter, "describing the paintings of the Sino-Japanese War, the plight of the routed troops as they fled from the attack on Pyongyang, the field hospital, and even the smallest details of the trees that were destroyed by cannonfire."[11] A visit to the Kotohira panorama, then, was a multisensory experience, attracting people with dramatic sounds and visions elsewhere available only in the largest cities.

Newspaper items in late 1900 and early 1901 suggest that a large proportion of visitors to the shrine, especially students, stopped at the panorama. One writer reported shortly after its opening that "student groups from Ehime, Tokushima, and Kōchi prefectures all visit the panorama without fail. Every day about a thousand people see it, especially officers and soldiers from Marugame and Zentsūji as well as travelers."[12] A visit to Kotohira Shrine, juxtaposed so closely with vivid scenes of military victory and, for students at least, trips to watch the maneuvers of soldiers at nearby bases, cemented a growing tie between the shrine and the military.

The establishment of the base in nearby Zentsūji only intensified the military presence at Kotohira. The new Eleventh Division, under the leadership of General Nogi Maresuke (freshly returned from a stint as Japan's governor in Taiwan), began operation in December of 1898.[13] Unable to find sufficient amenities in Zentsūji, soldiers and especially officers descended upon the town of Kotohira, patronizing restaurants, teahouses, brothels, and inns. "The new division at Zentsūji currently has far more people than the regiment at Marugame," reported a journalist two weeks after the opening of the base. "Because there is no place for either the officers or the soldiers to stroll around on Sundays and other days, the majority of them entertain themselves in Kotohira. Therefore, Kotohira has recently prospered beyond expectations."[14] The patronage of Zentsūji's soldiers proved so important that when in 1900 new national regulations forced the town leaders of Kotohira to consolidate all of the brothels of the town within a single, strictly guarded red-light district, they built the new enclosure on the side of town nearest to Zentsūji—conveniently located near the Tall Lantern and the train station as well.[15]

Printmakers, too, prompted the growing connection of Kotohira and other prominent worship sites to the Japanese military, as is suggested by the publication in 1902 of a woodblock print of the Eleventh Division. Laying out the entire base—complete with depictions of cavalry and infantry exercises—and part of the surrounding town of Zentsūji, the print recreates the army establishment in the same artistic form as tourist prints of Kotohira and other religious sites. Prominently displayed in insets in the corners of the print are the bustling port of Tadotsu, the most famous buildings of Zentsūji temple near the base itself, and, dominating the upper-left-hand portion of the print, a profile of Mt. Zōzu and an illustration of the main shrine of Kotohira.[16] Not just on paper but also in practice, Kotohira and the Zentsūji base became drawn into the same context: just as school groups had visited both Marugame and Kotohira together, they now visited Zentsūji on the same trip.[17]

Not only the army at Zentsūji and Marugame, but also the navy across the Inland Sea at Kure and in Western Kyushu at Sasebo maintained ties to Kotohira. Upon completing classes at the Kure naval academy, new navy officers would sail their ship to Shikoku, where they would pray at Kotohira.[18] When new military ships were commissioned, they almost always stopped off at Tadotsu to pay their respects to Kotohira. When a torpedo boat was assigned from the naval shipyard in Sasebo to Yokosuka in 1903, the *Kagawa Shinpō* reported that "on the way to Yokosuka, it stopped at Tadotsu port at 3:00 p.m. The crew, twenty-three people, immediately came ashore and went on pilgrimage to Kotohira. Then the [next] morning, they left for Kobe."[19]

Recurrent military involvement on the continent during the years between 1895 and 1904 provided additional opportunities to reinforce the connection between the shrine and military endeavors. In August 1900, for example, the Kotohira Shrine office placed an ad "announcing to the concerned citizens and the families of the soldiers in China who have come on pilgrimage every day since the Boxer Rebellion" a special ceremony celebrating the entry of Japan and its allies into Beijing.[20] The continuing involvement of Japanese forces abroad supported the growth of a military culture in which Kotohira and other shrines now played an integral part. Hosting public spectacles in support of military endeavors, surrounded by national flags and glorified depictions of wartime valor, the shrine of Kotohira had become associated not just with the protection of soldiers but with the heady victories of the nation.

On the March Again

By the beginning of the Russo-Japanese War, in 1904, not only had promoters established a connection between Kotohira and military affairs, but when Japanese leaders again embroiled the country in hostilities on the continent, precedents from the Sino-Japanese War provided a still vivid model for worshippers to follow. In the more intense Russo-Japanese conflict, and the altered social and economic environment of the early twentieth century, pilgrims and priests revived and augmented the practices of a decade earlier. Building upon the shrine's growing presence in schools, the military, and public entertainments, worshippers and promoters alike used the Russo-Japanese War and the suffering it caused to transform worship into an unquestioned civic duty. They embedded Konpira and its shrine—and the gods in general—at the center of wartime thought and behavior.

People in Japan experienced the war with Russia much more intensely than they had the war with China a decade before. In the fight against the less modernized Chinese forces in 1894–95, approximately 240,000 soldiers had been mobilized nationwide, with fewer than 3 percent reported wounded or dead after less than a year of fighting.[21] During the conflict against the powerful Russian military, which lasted twice as long, more than two hundred thousand fought in a single battle, and more than 10 percent of all those mobilized never returned home. The toll affected almost every community in Japan. Not only did one out of seven soldiers from around Kotohira die on the continent or return home injured, but after six months of fighting, Kotohira Shrine converted the headquarters of the Reverence Association on Mt. Zōzu into a recuperation center for the returning wounded.[22] As if the human cost were not enough, the economic burdens of the war took a further toll. Whereas the government had financed the Sino-Japanese War through wholly domestic means, during the Russo-Japanese War it was forced to rely upon seven hundred million yen in foreign loans in addition to the more than one trillion yen raised through war bonds, taxes, and other domestic measures.[23] The resulting rise in prices and the wartime recession reinforced a widespread culture of austerity during 1904 and 1905.

The declaration of war with Russia in February 1904 was not unexpected. The press had already whipped itself into a frenzy, and political parties loudly denounced the continuing presence of Russian troops in Manchuria after their agreement to withdraw in 1902 in the wake of the Boxer Rebellion.[24] Demonstrating government leaders' growing recognition of the wartime usefulness of Shinto shrines, Meiji rulers accompanied the declaration of war with well-publicized state-mandated rituals at Kotohira and other shrines, rites that at Kotohira were attended by the prefectural governor, who brought official offerings from the central government.[25] Also to mark the announcement of war, the Sanuki Railroad ran a special train to the shrine. Railroad employees filled passenger cars with lanterns and Japanese, English, and American flags, and a band playing patriotic tunes met travelers at Kotohira station.[26] The railroad continued this festive treatment, if to a lesser degree, during later ceremonies.[27] The pageantry of pilgrimage thus combined official ritual with entertainment, all in a patriotic, military idiom.

Virtually every activity related to the shrine during the Russo-Japanese War drew upon and expanded precedents established a decade earlier. Kotohira Shrine made and distributed special amulets directly to the armed forces, sending thousands of them to every army base in Japan.[28] By this time, however, the practice of distributing amulets had caught on so widely that amulets from various shrines, lacking cases to protect them, could not be distributed and so remained stockpiled at Marugame and other bases.[29] The importance of Konpira for families on the home front also remained strong, as volunteers from military reservist associations distributed amulets to soldiers' families on their visits.[30]

Pilgrimage boomed from the very beginning of the conflict, as people headed to Konpira within days of the official declaration of hostilities. This was in part abetted by the coincidence of the calendar. February twenty-fifth, only two weeks after the declaration of war and the last day of the first wartime pilgrimage railroad discount, coincided with the tenth day of the old first month: the first day of the year dedicated to Konpira in the old calendar. According to the *Kagawa Shinpō*,

People came from east and west Sanuki and each town along the railroad line, and also arrived in Tadotsu port from Ehime, Okayama, and the Hanshin area [Osaka and Kobe]. Pilgrims swelled the ranks of railroad passengers to twice the normal number. They filled every train car, and from 10:00 a.m. to 4:00 p.m., the first- and second-class carriages were standing room only. In Kotohira, the crowds both on and below the mountain grew to twice the number of the day before. Around noon, the road was buried in people from the railroad station, along the central approach, and up the mountain. Extra police were on duty. At least several tens of thousands of people made the pilgrimage to Kotohira. This is a number rarely seen in recent years.[31]

The increase in visitors continued. "Many pilgrims are taking advantage of the large discounts on the Sanuki Railroad, and every day about a thousand people come to Kotohira from nearby regions," reported the newspaper little more than a week later. "There are more and more people making daily pilgrimage for war victory prayers, and the many banners beside the main shrine have doubled in number since a few days ago. . . . Also, the [panorama] has lowered its entry fees and is attracting many pilgrims."[32] With discounts on the railroad and at the panorama, Kotohira took on an aura of wartime festiveness, as thousands of people crowded the steps.

With thousands of people came hundreds of flags, as pilgrims followed the precedent of a decade before. "On the occasion of the Sino-Japanese War," wrote one reporter little more than a week after war was declared, "banners and national flags stood like a forest from in front of the main shrine to the corridor alongside. There were too many to count, and to see them, one was strangely moved. Now, since the beginning of war with Russia, the area in front of the main shrine has quickly redeveloped the appearance of years ago. On the far side of the kagura hall stand banners proclaiming "Defeat of the Enemy Country," "Praying for Total Victory of the Imperial Troops," or "Praying for National Peace and Tranquility," written in thick brush strokes. Most of these have been donated by farmers. When soldiers come in groups or in threes and fives, how they must rejoice."[33]

Village groups once again marched to the shrine.[34] What caught the eyes of newspaper reporters, however, were not pilgrimages by villages, which were rarely mentioned, but those organized by companies that had grown up during the previous decade of industrial promotion. Large businesses, such as railroads or factories, staged company pilgrimages and sponsored group observances open to individuals from all walks of life.[35] Five days after the declaration of war, on 15 February 1904, for instance, the Sanuki and San'yō railroads arranged a spectacular nighttime procession of about 110 people to pray for victory. Still before the fighting had begun in earnest, the lantern-lit parade provided an opportunity for revelry as well as prayer. According to newspaper reports, after gathering in front of a small Kotohira shrine in Tadotsu at nightfall, where a ceremonial benediction was read, everyone shouted "Banzai" and sang military songs about invading Russia. Then the group proceeded to the railroad station to board the 7:30 train for Kotohira. The newspaper reported the varied appearance of the worshippers: "The people included fake gentlemen wearing red paper top hats, old samurai dressed as women in wide obis and red sleeves, tradespeople, reservists wearing military uniforms and summer hats, bureaucrats, students, merchants, farmers, people of all kinds. Upon arriving at Kotohira station, they shouted "Teikoku Banzai!" (Long live the empire!) and made their way through the many other nighttime pilgrims in the center of town to climb the mountain."[36] Encouraged no doubt by memories of an unexpectedly easy victory a decade before, the euphoria accompanying Japan's entry into war with Russia thus reinforced popular attitudes of pilgrimage as a time of festivity and abandonment, far from the formal reverence officially espoused by civic leaders.

As the reality of war set in, such unruly behavior provoked a moralistic backlash. While the Sanuki Railroad used the war as an opportunity to accustom people to traveling to Konpira by train, recruiting thousands of pilgrims from the towns along the track to join a kō sponsored by the railroad,[37] others saw the railroad as an impediment, not an accessory, to appropriate worship. When workers at fan and mat factories in Marugame planned a large, joint pilgrimage, for instance, most of them planned to take advantage of the large railroad discount, riding the train both to and from the shrine. One group, however, opposed the plan on the grounds that, although the return home would not be a problem, it was disrespectful to the kami to approach the shrine by train. In the end, they all walked to the shrine and then rode home.[38]

The patriotic pageantry of wartime pilgrimage thus became a well-accepted part of home-front support for the war. If there were any objections to the practice on the basis of wasting money—as in the case of merchants a decade before—the *Kagawa Shinpō* and other publications did not record them.[39] People no longer debated whether to go on pilgrimage or to leave worship to the priest, but how best to show respect to the kami.

Eight months into the war, the contrast between exuberant pilgrims and self-restrained worshippers still troubled area leaders. Near the end of 1904, city leaders with close ties to the conservative *Kagawa Shinpō* formed the Akasaka Commemorative Association of Takamatsu, establishing their own pilgrimage kō and presenting (through ample coverage in the newspaper) their own interpretation of appropriate attitudes and behavior toward the god. "They say that everyone is doing what they can to support the troops and save money," declared the association leaders, "but there are things that human power cannot do. That is why many people go to their local kami or to Kotohira Shrine and pray for the defeat of the enemy and the health of the imperial army. Therefore, as people have suffered, sickened, and died during this past year, the Akasaka association has formed this group to pray for the defeat of the enemy, the victory of the imperial troops, and especially the health of the soldiers from the village." Organized like any other kō, with monthly fees and the designation by lottery of representatives to go on pilgrimage to Mt.

Zōzu on the first and fifteenth days of every month, the Akasaka group explicitly modeled the proper etiquette of pilgrimage. "Our pilgrims have no set costume but must not wear anything strange," announced the leaders. "They are to walk to Kotohira and ride home, or may then go around the countryside. Each group must carry the association's flag, and all pilgrims must pray especially seriously in front of the shrine for the purpose of this association."[40] In contrast to others, the members of the Akasaka kō did not readily acknowledge the leisure value of pilgrimage: according to their formal announcements, at least, worship excluded entertainment. The leaders of the association condemned the revelry of the masses—not only cross-dressing or outlandish costumes but, at least on the approach to the god, the lazy luxury of travel by train.

The ideal of solemn pilgrimage espoused by the Akasaka group and supported by the conservative *Kagawa Shinpō* became clear in a published description of its first group pilgrimage in mid-October, in which six male representatives of the kō, two wives, and another person went to Konpira:

> We were nine people in all. We left Akasaka at 4:00 a.m. We did not even notice the dew on our straw sandals. . . . Once we crossed the Purifying River and entered Enai [the village adjacent to Kotohira], we encountered people returning from praying for the soldiers. Each group held a flag bearing inscriptions for the health of the soldiers, the victory of the imperial troops, the defeat of the enemy country, and the like. On the sides of the flags were written the name of each village, or "daily pilgrimage flag." Each flag was made of simple cloth, with writing in black ink. The people holding the flags also wore simple clothes and straw sandals. They had serious expressions as they thought of the soldiers abroad. In my eyes, *this* is real Konpira pilgrimage. Around noon, we climbed the mountain, arrived in front of the main shrine, washed our hands and rinsed our mouths, and all together were serious and prayed for the association's purpose. Then we went around to worship at the various smaller shrines.[41]

That the Akasaka group, the editors of the *Kagawa Shinpō,* and other civic leaders felt it necessary not to encourage people to perform pilgrimage but to solemnize existing pilgrimage practices suggests that Konpira pilgrimage, whether serious or festive, was one of the most prominent ways in which people on the home front participated in war. Indeed, nighttime lantern processions to the shrine became such a sign of patriotic enthusiasm that one purveyor of patent medicines repeatedly ran an advertisement in the newspaper showing a lantern procession with slogans on the lanterns and banners: "Long Live the Great Imperial Navy and Army" and "Sure Military Victory" appeared alongside the name of the medicine and the stores that sold it.[42]

Pilgrimage to Konpira had become such a fixture of wartime practice that near the end of the conflict, in 1905, the *Kagawa Shinpō* reported on the unexpected economic prosperity of the town. "Business around the town of Kotohira has been extremely good since the beginning of the war," reported the paper.

> The brothels and geisha provide evidence of this. Before the war, there were about fifty prostitutes, and neither they nor the brothel owners were doing well. Since the hostilities began, that number has grown to meet the expanded demand—in fact, even with about one hundred prostitutes now, they cannot meet the demand. As for geisha, before the war, there were about thirty of them, but business was poor, and they had to give discounts. Older geisha even took younger ones along to the same appointment. Now there are about eighty and they cannot keep up with demand either. [As further evidence of this unheard-of prosperity,] people are paying national taxes and town fees without complaint and even early! Since the war started, with the coming of the severely injured [to the military recuperation center in the headquarters of the Reverence Association], the families of the wounded have come to take care of them. That also contributes to the local economy.[43]

Kotohira thus became a focal point of support for the war, one that provided both succor for the wounded and pleasure for the hale. Pilgrimage, whether festive or solemn, performed in groups or by individuals, as an excuse for entertainment or in worried prayer for an injured relative, united the home front with banners and slogans, creating a spectacle of patriotic devotion centered on the shrine.

Protection of the Gods

During the Russo-Japanese War, not only did the scope of Mt. Zōzu's pageantry expand, but so, it seems, did popular conceptions of Konpira's power. The reputation of the god rose on the battlefront in particular, where the amulets of Konpira were in high demand and greatly treasured. Shortly after the start of the war, worshippers bombarded Kotohira Shrine and the Reverence Association with requests for amulets. Whereas during the Sino-Japanese War, people had more often obtained amulets as an afterthought for the families of soldiers who had already left, they now requested amulets in advance to send along with soldiers when they were called up. As early as March 1904, letters began pouring in to the shrine's main office as well as the headquarters of the Reverence Association, requesting special prayers and amulets for sons and village recruits being sent overseas. "My oldest son, who is a soldier in the army, carried an amulet with him to China on the occasion of the Boxer Rebellion in 1900," wrote one man from Yamaguchi prefecture. "Now both he and my second son are being sent to the Russo-Japanese War. I am asking for amulets for them both."[44] Another man, after providing details of his son's name, age, and military rank and affiliation, stated, "At this time, because of the Russo-Japanese incident, [my son] was dispatched on 22 January. We would like to have prayers performed for military good fortune and long life."[45] Yet another man from the vicinity of Kobe wrote to request twenty soldiers' amulets to distribute to mobilized reservists in his village.[46]

When, in April, the Reverence Association responded to the growing number of letters by officially advertising the availability of military amulets by mail,[47] requests arrived not just for the amulets, but also for the enrollment of sons in the Reverence Association in order to obtain even greater benefits. When one man wrote to thank the association for sending the amulets he had requested, he enclosed payment (in postal stamps) for his two drafted sons to be initiated in absentia and for the performance of what he called "prayers for avoiding bullets."[48] Another man, whose sons were about to be sent abroad, mailed in 1.5 yen to enroll them in the Reverence Association, specifically requesting the association's special "lifelong protection amulet" (*ichidai mamori*) for each.[49]

Soldiers treasured these special amulets. One twenty-six-year-old conscript wrote to Kotohira Shrine from the front in 1905, describing their importance in the fight. The conscript had served in Taiwan from 1900 to 1903, then was called up again in 1904 because of the Russo-Japanese conflict. "In all that time," he wrote,

> although I participated in some ten-odd attacks, I did not receive a single injury. I believe that this is due to the kami and buddhas, and on the battlefield I wear amulets praying [for safety] hung around my neck. Since being mobilized, I have received some ten-odd amulets sent from different places. From 1 to 10 March of this year, I participated in the attack on Mukden. On the fourteenth, I sent a letter home through the military postal service, and on the day after it arrived, on the twenty-sixth, my father left to go on pilgrimage to your shrine. He requested that prayers be performed and received an amulet, which he sent to me. I received it very thankfully. But on the thirteenth of this month [June], the amulets disappeared while I was in the bath. I investigated immediately, but was unable to retrieve them, and I was extremely disappointed. . . . I intend to ask every temple and shrine for an amulet, but first I am asking you.

The soldier went on to describe the missing amulet in detail, even drawing a picture of the amulet case tied with a red string, and requesting a replacement exactly like it. "It would be a shame," he wrote, "if I came this far only to die" for the lack of an amulet.[50] For many soldiers at the front, then, amulets were not just symbols of support from people at home, but important good-luck talismans to which they attributed their continued safety in the midst of battle. Face-to-face with the prospect of death, they attributed magical powers to the small pieces of paper blessed by the god.

There are hints that Konpira became especially renowned for battlefront miracles during the Russo-Japanese War. The late Matsubara Hideaki, archivist of Kotohira Shrine, reported hearing that the popularity of the shrine increased markedly during the Russo-Japanese War because of a well-known miracle—unfortunately, a miracle unmentioned either in published accounts or in letters and records at the shrine.[51] The number of floated donations from ships on their way to the front shot up in 1905, in the midst of hostilities, suggesting not so much that offerings were sent to the shrine as a regular practice but that perhaps something happened partway through the war to encourage this sign of devotion.[52] The large number of written requests for amulets, as well as the pilgrimage to Kotohira by the winning generals to give thanks after the final victory in January 1906, also suggests that Kotohira Shrine may have become especially renowned.

Although it has not been possible to identify the basis of the growing reputation of Konpira in particular, the public announcements of military leaders enhanced the association of the gods in general with miraculous military victories. The popular admiral Tōgō Heihachirō played an especially prominent role in sacralizing the war. His well-publicized exhortations to his troops on the way to battle to "believe firmly in the grace of heaven" contributed to the attitude that worship of the kami formed an integral part of military preparation. The unexpected and overwhelming victory of the Japanese navy over Russia's Baltic Fleet in the Battle of the Japan Sea, as well as the interpretation of it offered by Admiral Tōgō in his report of the victory, intensified this connection. "Due to the grace of heaven and the help of the kami," he announced in 1905, "our united fleet fought against the enemy's Second and Third fleets in the Japan Sea on 27 and 28 May, and we were able virtually to annihilate them."[53]

Shinto priests leapt upon Tōgō's exhortations, his victory at Port Arthur, in which the weather played a large part, and later the Japan Sea battle to argue that the gods were once again protecting Japan, as they had when the "divine winds" (kamikaze) purportedly drove back the Mongol invasions in the thirteenth century. The main reason Japan won this war, one priest wrote in April 1905, was because of the power of the many kami who had created Japan. "Our Japan is a divine country (shinkoku). It is a country created by the kami, who protect that which is beyond human power. For example, in both the Mongol invasions and the attack on Port Arthur, the battles were won by a change in the weather. No matter what Admiral Tōgō may have done, it was the weather that won the battle. Therefore, the general attributed the victory to divine grace [*ten'yu*]."[54] Other writers reiterated Admiral Tōgō's assertion. "In recent naval battles, there have appeared a sacred hawk, a bisected large whale, and a captured eagle. All these were omens. And especially in the official communiqué on the great victory of Port Arthur, Admiral Tōgō said that 'one cannot but be certain that this was heaven sent.'"[55]

Many priests argued that as a result of such "heaven-sent" developments, prayer, amulets, and miracles could no longer be dismissed as useless superstitions.[56] Instead, one priest suggested, treading a fine line between theology and psychology, it was precisely because the people of Japan had flocked to obtain amulets at the shrines that Japan had won the war. "The year began with all good things," he remarked. "First was the capture of Port Arthur, second was the signing of the treaty, and third was the birth of the crown prince. All of this was due to the protection of the gods. Everyone went to the shrines and prayed. Also, since people felt that it was better to get amulets from two places than one, even those who don't usually worship went to shrines once, twice, three times, and finally daily. This reassured them—and it is this reassurance that has made us sure to win the Sino-Japanese War, Russo-Japanese War, and future wars."[57] During the Sino-Japanese War, then especially during the Russo-Japanese War, the priests of Kotohira and other shrines around the country accepted and built upon popular appreciation for the power of amulets. Owing to the circumstances of war, the disdain among many nativist Shinto priests for the "magic" and "superstition" of amulets had been replaced by their acceptance as part of public support for the war. The terror of death thus prompted renewed interest in the miracles of the gods and the importance of human effort in securing their help. While virtually all people publicly supported prayer and pilgrimage, however, they incorporated it into their lives in disparate ways. The elite conservatives of the Asakasa kō and the *Kagawa Shinpō* insisted on serious, reverent decorum during visits to the shrine, while factory workers and others combined the trip with a chance for entertainment. The priests, in public at least, simply promoted the value of amulets and pilgrimage in general, appealing to people of any outlook.

Wartime worship became a lasting, monumental presence at the shrine. As people looked back upon the Russo-Japanese War after victory, they remembered and commemorated pilgrimages undertaken during the war. In 1907, for instance, residents of Tokiwa village erected a stone inscribed "Kotohira Shrine" and "Memorial of the Russo-Japanese War," commemorating both the village residents who had gone to the front and the monthly pilgrimages performed by their families in their absence.[58] Later, in 1908, more than three hundred former soldiers received permission from Kotohira Shrine to erect on the shrine grounds a memorial stone to the Russo-Japanese War with an inscription in Admiral Tōgō's writing.[59] Communities thus built monuments to commemorate not only the war dead but also the act of wartime pilgrimage and petitioning, suggesting that the combination of fighting and prayer was what made the victory possible.

This attribution of victory at least in part to the gods was reinforced at Kotohira not only by stone monuments but also by war spoils distributed by the military to Kotohira and other shrines around the country. This, too, built on the precedent of the Sino-Japanese War. On 21 March 1896, Kotohira Shrine had received fifty-two items from the Army Ministry taken as war spoils during the Sino-Japanese War.[60] In 1907, the Army Ministry and the Eleventh Division at Zentsūji donated a much more spectacular haul: swords, guns, Qing spears, and even cannons. As the trophies were transported from Zentsūji to the shrine, hundreds of people lined the streets to watch, admiring one impressive cannon as it was dismantled at the foot of the mountain before being carried up to a place of honor in front of the new shrine museum, itself opened with great military fanfare near the end of the war, in 1905.[61] By 1907, several large cannons stood on display in front of the museum and in the large garden nearby.[62]

The offerings of individual worshippers also filled the grounds with evidence of Konpira's assistance on the battlefield. On a plaque he offered to the shrine in January 1906, one soldier from across the Inland Sea in Hyōgo prefecture testified that "when the Russo-Japanese War began, I answered a summons to join the Twentieth Infantry Regiment of the Tenth Army Division on 24 June 1904. From then on, I was moved from battleground to battleground. On 10 March 1905, at the battle of Mukden, I acquired a bayonet during the fight with the enemy. After our victorious, safe return on 4 December 1905, I offer this [bayonet] in front of Konpira Daigongen in commemoration of the victory."[63] Through the actions of worshippers, bureaucrats, entrepreneurs, and priests, then, the connection between Kotohira and the national military became illustrated for the perusal of generations to come, visible on the mountain in the form of wooden ema, metal cannon, and stone monuments alike.

Much of this activity remained very localized. Although letters requesting amulets arrived at the shrine from all over Japan, and soldiers abroad called upon Konpira in distant battles, the act of pilgrimage was limited to the areas closest to the shrine. The demands of war meant that it was difficult for people from eastern Japan or other distant areas to take a month off from work to travel to the god.[64] Trains did not run, prices rose, and people spent their spare money on necessities and war bonds, not trips around Japan.[65] Instead, most pilgrims came from within Kagawa prefecture, and sometimes from across the Inland Sea, turning the shrine into a regional center for wartime worship.

Paradoxically, it was during such limited periods of intense local pilgrimage during the Sino-Japanese and Russo-Japanese wars that the meaning of worship at Kotohira became, in a new sense, national, tied to the symbols, rhetoric, and interests of the nation's military enterprise not only in the formal rites of state observances but also in the actions of individuals, through pilgrimage and prayer. Worshippers carried banners inscribed with nationalistic slogans and shouted "Banzai" in front of the main shrine, and those who could wore their best clothes—military uniforms—for the occasion. Pilgrims, whether individuals, schoolchildren, or organized groups, stopped to see vivid depictions of battlefield heroics at the panorama, saw votive plaques and donations testifying to the miracles of the god on the front, and observed military maneuvers at nearby bases. During wartime, people converged on the shrine both to pray for their loved ones and to see the impressive fireworks and military displays staged by the shrine and town promoters. The cumulative effect was to associate the shrine and the god of Kotohira unquestioningly with the military project of empire.

During wartime, Shinto priests around the country accepted the popular emphasis on miracles. They merged the magical powers of the gods with earlier concepts of civic duty and expanded the rites of state to include the active participation of lay worshippers. War also provided priests with excellent opportunities for proselytizing among a worried populace. People sought out tales of the miraculous as they hoped against hope that their small country could defeat the large continental giant and that their sons sent to battle might, against all odds, return. Several used the opportunity to argue that the job of priests ought to be expanded. As one priest wrote to his colleagues in 1904, "Although the Home Ministry instructed priests to concentrate on their own occupations [on 19 February 1904], it is just not enough to perform victory prayers and distribute amulets to soldiers. Our job is to publicize and promote the miraculous feats of the gods."[66]

This emphasis on wartime miracles would continue as Japan became involved in military campaigns throughout the first half of the twentieth century. During the 1930s and 40s, as Japan's expansion on the continent and in the Pacific intensified, there was a surge in published testimonials to the miraculous powers of the gods.[67] In 1939, tales of Kotohira's miracles during the Russo-Japanese War were again being recycled. Ōhara Shigetsugu, a veteran of the earlier war, toured schools throughout Japan, speaking to schoolchildren of Konpira's miraculous powers and praying for his lost comrades. Ōhara repeated his tale of rescue, when he and fifty-seven of his two thousand comrades were saved by Konpira after their ship was sunk by a Russian attack, and exhorted his listeners to dedicate themselves to both the gods and the nation.[68] The lessons of the Sino- and Russo-Japanese wars thus endured. Wartime prayer had become a public spectacle as crowds of people together petitioned the gods of Japan for their miraculous protection. The resulting association between divine favor and military might would continue to shape attitudes and actions throughout the next half century.

In 1868, the priests of Kotohira had redefined the god as a native kami of the Japanese nation. Soon thereafter, government bureaucrats and local nativists incorporated the shrine into a system of rites supportive of the state. And under the Reverence Association, influential leaders in villages and towns throughout the country increasingly advocated worship of the deity as an expression of morality and respect for the public order. It was in the context of war, however, that promoters' creative evocations of victory, priests' official use of ritual, and local leaders' espousal of decorous behavior all combined with the cult of miracles at the root of the deity's continuing widespread popularity to create an image of Konpira and other gods as protectors of Japan. During the Sino-Japanese and Russo-Japanese wars, families prayed for soldiers, civic leaders enhanced their authority by organizing groups in support of the national endeavor, and railroad companies, panorama builders, the armed forces, and worshippers themselves staged visual displays of their ties to both the shrine and the imperial mission. Each for his own purpose brought prayers and products to Kotohira Shrine, fitting the god into the growing national, military structure of an expanding empire.

The Many Faces of Kotohira
(1908–1912)

13

By the end of the Russo-Japanese War, Japan had been in many ways transformed. Concerted policies of industrialization, combined with the intense demands of war, had prompted the development of new businesses, technologies, and the structures to support them. From fan factories and tobacco companies to steelmakers and shipbuilders, large-scale enterprises proliferated on the economic landscape. Roads, railroads, and ferries facilitated trade and travel, while newspapers and schools dramatically increased the flow of ideas around the country.

At Kotohira as well—with the opening of the first bank in 1895, the establishment of the trade school in 1898, and, thanks to the presence nearby of the base at Zentsūji, access to electricity in 1905[1]— there developed a growing infrastructure to support the development of business, albeit focused more on pilgrimage than production. Innkeepers planned new, electrically lighted luxury accommodations; wood-carvers used lathing technologies to add new bowls and platters to the range of souvenirs for sale; and in 1905, Kotohira Shrine finished construction and opened both its state-of-the-art, Western-style museum and the long-awaited inner shrine. In the constant struggle for survival and status, priests, businessmen, and promoters at Kotohira and throughout the land sought to guide their institutions through the rapidly changing challenges of an increasingly industrial Japan.

The greatest, continuing challenge was one that, at least in theory, the shrine of Kotohira was well qualified to address: the overwhelming heterogeneity of the population. Despite the many pronouncements of priests, statesmen, and other ideologues, the rites of emperor, nation, and kami failed to unite the populace in unquestioning reverence of the symbols of the state. Instead, these lofty ideals seemed to highlight the vast diversity that, if anything, had grown since 1868. The splits between Buddhist and Shinto, religious and nonreligious, urban and rural, wealthy and poor had become much more pronounced, with implications not only for the strategies of shrine priests and town promoters (who sought to address all audiences at once), but for attitudes about shrine and town as well. Attitudes, after all, formed the basis of Kotohira's fame and, thus, its survival. During the final years of the Meiji era, from 1908 to 1912, the priests of the shrine and the leaders of the town faced challenges in the courts both of law and of public opinion. The outcomes would affect the legal, intellectual, and cultural standing of Kotohira, both town and shrine, for decades to come.

Of Shinto and Buddhism

The success of Kotohira Shrine in maintaining, indeed building upon, its broad array of worshippers—in large part by cultivating influential patrons in Tokyo and around the country—spelled increasing disaster for its Buddhist rival in the town, Matsuoji. In the years leading up to and following the Russo-Japanese War, the struggling temple found itself increasingly isolated, its efforts to adjust to the new environment impeded by the more powerful shrine on the mountain above.

During the years 1898 to 1905, while Kotohira Shrine was building the inner shrine in its attempt to claim jurisdiction over Kongōbō-Yūsei once and for all, Matsuoji continued its struggle for survival in the town below. As the shrine solidified its claims to the seventeenth-century tengu-priest in 1898, Matsuoji's head priest, Zōsan Yūon, tried to head off the inner shrine project by wielding the authority of the Shingon Buddhist denomination, to which both the current Matsuoji and its Tokugawa-era namesake belonged. At the height of the spring pilgrimage season, in May 1898, Zōsan staged a preemptive three hundredth anniversary memorial service for Kongōbō-Yūsei. By inviting one hundred priests from the Shingon Buddhist center of Mt. Kōya to conduct the impressive esoteric rituals,[2] Yūon surrounded himself with the esteemed leaders of Shingon, situating both Matsuoji's Konpira Daigongen and Kongōbō-Yūsei within the officially recognized denominational Buddhist structures of Meiji Japan. It was a last-ditch attempt to extricate the powerful images from the Shinto categories in which Kotohira had placed them.

Despite all of his efforts, however, the priest of Matsuoji was repeatedly thwarted by the political ties and economic strength of Kotohira Shrine. In the years following Matsuoji's three hundredth anniversary celebration, the shrine was apparently able to prevent Matsuoji from raising the money it needed to renovate its temple. In 1901, for instance, when Nagahara Yūgyū, Zōsan's successor, submitted a routine request to the prefectural office for permission to raise funds for major repairs to the temple's main hall, permission was unexpectedly denied. The temple hired a lawyer to inquire into the reasons, but as journalists reported, he was told only that it was because of Matsuoji's problematic "relationship to Kotohira Shrine."[3] Matsuoji, evidently prevented by the shrine from raising money publicly, tried in 1907 to borrow funds from private lenders, only to become embroiled in a fraudulent scam and ensuing lawsuit that cost the temple hundreds of yen.[4]

Finally, unable either to seek donations from the public or to borrow money on the private market, Yūgyū turned to address the source of his problems: the relationship of the temple to Kotohira Shrine. Telling parishioners that he did so in order to force the shrine into negotiations, Yūgyū hired four lawyers from Tokyo. On 10 July 1908, he sued Head Priest Kotooka Terusato in the Takamatsu Regional Court for the return of five buildings and forty-two other items purportedly appropriated by Kotohira Shrine in the early years of Meiji. These included the Niōmon, the main gate built by Matsudaira Yorishige (valued at three thousand yen); the buildings of Konkōin, now the shrine offices (ten thousand yen); the Kondō, now the Dawn Shrine (fifteen thousand yen); the Goma Hall, now a minor subsidiary shrine (seven hundred yen); the two Ema halls (three thousand yen); the statue of Fudō Myōō that had presided over the goma ceremony; and other treasures.[5] The lawsuit set off ongoing controversies both in the town and in the courtroom over the next four years, as economic, institutional, and theological arguments eventually cohered into a veiled referendum on the legitimacy of the Meiji status quo. What began as a last-ditch effort to raise money for repairs soon led the plaintiffs down a treacherous path in which they risked challenging the entire political, social, and religious order.

The leaders of Kotohira town mobilized quickly against the Buddhist threat. In August, the wealthy members of the town assembly submitted a letter to the prefectural governor with seven hundred signatures from "the townspeople of Kotohira" arguing that the Buddhist suit impeded the future profits and development of the town. The letter, reproduced in the *Kagawa Shinpō*, asserted that "Nagahara Yūgyū's actions this time truly disturb the believers of the realm. They do not just dim the awesome powers above, but also hinder the profits of the townspeople below."[6] The Kotohira Profit Association—formed earlier in the year by prominent innkeepers, the town doctor, and other influential men seeking, among other things, to obtain telephone service in Kotohira and to calibrate time in the town with a noontime drumbeat at the shrine—held repeated meetings at the town offices, asserting that the vitality of Kotohira town depended on maintenance of the status quo.[7] Sixty prominent men from the villages that had been under Konkōin's jurisdiction during the Tokugawa period also submitted a letter to the governor in support of the shrine's position.[8]

The lawsuit brought into the open the competing pilgrimage economies of two neighboring communities—one based on Kotohira Shrine, the other on Zentsūji, an important site in the eighty-eight-temple pilgrimage circuit of Shikoku. These two centers, whose shared Shingon affiliations had supported a coherent esoteric religious landscape before 1868, now stood opposed amid competing Shinto and Buddhist claims, as innkeepers, merchants, and others who depended on pilgrimage traffic to their respective towns sought to preserve or expand their business. Zentsūji, which took its name from the Shingon Buddhist temple that marked the birthplace of Kūkai and served as the head of the Zentsūji sect of the Shingon denomination, was closely affiliated with the mainstream of Shingon—the denomination to which Matsuoji belonged. Thus, while the innkeepers and brothel owners of Kotohira supported the shrine, their competitors in nearby Zentsūji supported the temple. While the leaders of Kotohira held meetings at Kotohira town hall, the Sanuki News Company, based in Zentsūji, staged the first of several lecture meetings at a theater in the Kotohira entertainment district, attracting three hundred people to listen to speakers promoting the revival of Matsuoji.[9] The lawsuit highlighted the competing interests of these neighboring communities.

Anticipation therefore ran high when oral arguments for the Matsuoji case opened in the Takamatsu Regional Court at 10:50 a.m. on 7 October 1908. About one hundred people, supporting both sides, crowded into the courtroom to hear the lawyers' statements. After the judges called the court to order, a lawyer for Matsuoji began to outline the purposes of the case, naming the objects under dispute and their estimated value. The lawyer for Kotohira Shrine, Suzuki Atsumi, quickly rose to his feet to dispute the prices placed upon the buildings and treasures of the shrine. Matsuoji had estimated them at a total value of seventy thousand yen, he noted, but upon what basis? "It is so awesome as to be beyond speech, but these are the possessions of the Great Kami," he said, according to newspaper coverage of the trial. "From the perspective of faith, they are of a value that cannot be put into words, that can scarcely be imagined. They must be worth at least one million yen." Having explicitly evoked the sacredness of the kami, thereby implicitly invoking the unassailable superiority of another Great Kami, the imperial ancestor Amaterasu, and thus the very state in whose name the judges would rule, the lawyer for Kotohira Shrine turned to the judges to inquire, "Your Honors, what is your opinion?"[10]

By invoking the awesome, indeed transcendent powers of the state and its gods, the lawyer cleverly posed the delicate political problem of questioning a Shinto institution supported by the state. At the same time, he wielded the economic troubles of Matsuoji against the temple. For, if the court valued the objects under dispute at one million yen, Matsuoji would be forced to tender a security of more than two thousand yen to the court, when the temple had already proven unable to raise large amounts of money on its own. Although Matsuoji's lawyers tried to regain the upper hand by insisting that the court judge these objects as a matter of law, not of faith, the question of value had been raised. The judges adjourned the trial pending the submission of reports by three court-appointed evaluators concerning the value of the buildings, the Buddhist objects, and the most valuable donations: two swords. The first court appearance had lasted only ten minutes without even touching upon the substantive arguments of the case.[11]

The seemingly subsidiary matter of evaluation, however, hit upon the two central issues at stake. First, it affected the ability of Matsuoji to pursue the suit at all. Second, the issues of sacred exceptionalism hinted at the political overtones of the case: the legitimacy of the Meiji order. The sensitive question of legitimacy was addressed in more detail during the ensuing courtroom arguments, although never so directly as to explicitly challenge the ruling regime.

Regarding the issue of property value, when the court met again, the three court-appointed evaluators—one Buddhist priest who was an expert on swords and two antique sellers from Kyoto—submitted an estimate of 225,000 yen, based on the rarity of such buildings as the Kondō and such art objects as the famous tiger screens by Maruyama Ōkyo. Because the new sum exceeded Matsuoji's estimate by 146,890 yen, the court required the temple to submit an additional 444-yen security.[12] Although Yūgyū and his allies successfully raised the money at this stage, economic pressures would eventually contribute to the collapse of the Buddhist suit.

While Matsuoji secured the additional funds, the judges began hearing detailed arguments concerning the identity of the Tokugawa-era Matsuoji and its rightful successor. Scholars commenting in the popular press—in newspapers, lectures, and published monographs—used scriptural and historical sources to debate whether the god of Mt. Zōzu was originally a kami or a buddha.[13] The lawyers and judges, however, focused their argument much more closely on institutional matters. Their primary point of contention concerned the makeup of Matsuoji during the Tokugawa era. According to Yūgyū and his lawyers, the Tokugawa-era Matsuoji consisted of six subtemples: Konkōin, Shinkōin, Manpukuin, Fumon'in, Sonshōin, and Shingoin. Because Kotooka Hirotsune converted Konkōin into the Shinto shrine of Kotohira and the priests of the other four subtemples also renounced their Buddhist vows, asserted the lawyers, Fumon'in (and thus its successor, the current Matsuoji) remained the sole Buddhist heir to the temple of Matsuoji.[14]

The lawyers for Kotohira Shrine argued on a different basis entirely, trying to bypass any issues of institutional history or the Tokugawa-Meiji succession by appealing directly to the gods of the hoary past. Following nativist logic, the shrine's lawyers claimed that Kotohira Shrine had been a shrine in ancient times and only came to be called Konpira Daigongen later. The deity Konpira Daigongen was entirely distinct from its institutions, they said, both from the subtemple Konkōin, which performed combinatory prayer rituals, and from Fumon'in, which performed Buddhist funerary services. Supporting their claims with "more than three Chinese briefcases full" of documents, the lawyers for Kotohira Shrine insisted on an absolute distinction between the kami, whether the Buddhist Konpira or the nativist Kotohira, and the Buddhist-affiliated institutions of Konkōin and Fumon'in.[15]

Witnesses and experts were called on both sides. The court summoned several Shingon priests to submit briefs clarifying the complicated relationship among mountain names (e.g., Mt. Zōzu), temple names (e.g., Matsuoji), and subtemple names (e.g., Konkōin or Fumon'in). Both Matsuoji and Kotohira Shrine summoned elderly residents of Kotohira and surrounding villages to testify about the events of 1868–72. On 20 June 1909, the arguments finally ended with the concluding statement of Suzuki Atsumi, who brought up two telling analogies. The lawyer for Kotohira Shrine began by drawing a parallel between the institutional demise of the old Matsuoji and the fate of Tokugawa-era daimyo and samurai. During the Meiji Restoration, he pointed out, "the daimyo became aristocrats [*kazoku*] and their retainers became gentry [*shizoku*]. Likewise, the daimyo came to own objects as aristocrats, and samurai came to stand in the world as gentry. Despite [this change], the government of the realm was not allowed to pause for even a day. When the daimyo were abolished, they immediately became governors, and the gentry immediately became councilors or advisers and worked in government." Thus, while the people remained the same, they lost their old institutional roles and adopted new ones. Suzuki then drew a parallel between the utter transformation yet continuity of the government and the transformation yet continuation of religious institutions. "Similarly," he asserted, referring to the events of 1868, "when Matsuoji was abolished, Fumon'in was also abolished," although the priests of Fumon'in reestablished a temple to perform funerals, eventually reclaiming the name of Matsuoji. Because of the act of abolition, however, the links between the old Matsuoji and the new Matsuoji had been cut. Thus, the old Matsuoji, the old daimyo, and the old retainers had all been legitimate entities under the old system but no longer existed under the new one. People of Meiji lived in a new order.[16]

In addition to invoking the legitimacy of the new social and aristocratic hierarchy of Meiji, Suzuki drew parallels to the legitimating structure of the gods, thereby highlighting the political dangers of the temple's case. In arguing against Matsuoji's combinatory interpretation of Konpira Daigongen, Suzuki compared it to the cases of Tōshō Daigongen and, especially, Tenshō Gongen, the Tokugawa-era combinatory form of the imperial sun goddess, Amaterasu. The newspaper's summary of his speech did not elaborate, merely stating that Suzuki "painstakingly expounded upon the mistakes [of such an interpretation] as they would extend to the shrine which performs national ceremonies."[17] It was the nativist Amaterasu, after all, not the combinatory Tenshō Gongen, that formed the basis of the imperial government's claim to legitimacy. Intimating that a decision against Kotohira would undermine the nativist Shinto identity of Amaterasu as well, Suzuki compared practices at Kotohira to those of Amaterasu's shrine at Ise, highlighting the maintenance of a sacred fire and the offering of sanctified saké at both, practices which, according to Suzuki, "did not historically exist in Buddhism."[18] The case for Kotohira Shrine thus rested implicitly upon the need to uphold the legitimacy of the Meiji order, whether social or sacred. A decision for the temple would call into question not only the claims of Kotohira but more broadly the purportedly sacred, native genealogy of the imperial house, and even, he may have been hinting, the legitimacy of a structure of government based on prefectures instead of domains.

The judges' verdict issued on 6 July 1909 accepted—indeed, it virtually summarized—the shrine's position. Because the Council of State had declared in 1868 that avatars (*gongen*) such as Konpira were originally shrines and that combinatory temples such as Matsuoji should be converted to kami worship, the judge asserted that the kami and the temple had been distinct since even before the Restoration. Furthermore, Fumon'in had severed its ties to the original Matsuoji. For both reasons, the current Matsuoji could claim no right to the objects under dispute.[19] Although Matsuoji immediately appealed the decision to the Osaka Court of Appeals, the temple was unable to raise the required security money for a second suit, repeatedly failed to appear in court, and eventually lost the appeal as well. After the conclusion of the appeal in 1912, Matsuoji had become so unpopular among business owners in Kotohira that the priests were considering offers from prominent citizens in Takamatsu eager to move the temple there in an attempt to attract more pilgrims and travelers to Takamatsu and its Ritsurin Park.[20] That initiative as well came to naught, and Matsuoji has remained in Kotohira until today, a small, struggling local temple hemmed in by shrine-owned land, in a town predominantly oriented toward the shrine of the Great Kami Kotohira.

While the lawsuit brought by Matsuoji focused on the temple's institutional dispute with Kotohira Shrine, the arguments, publicity, and entrepreneurial positioning that surrounded it highlighted both the political and the economic relevance of popular faith and worship. The 1868 distinction between Buddhism and Shinto that lay at the base of the lawsuit transformed what in centuries past might have been an internal rivalry between two subtemples into a contentious competition between two clearly opposed institutions and thought systems: one legitimizing the current order, the other invoking the old. While government leaders no longer feared a resurrection of the Tokugawa order, they nevertheless took seriously the sacred foundations of the imperial house as evoked in the constitution, the Imperial Rescript on Education, and every government pronouncement in the name of the emperor. Just as Konpira Daigongen had supported the combinatory Tokugawa order, and in the sixteenth century the Thirty Deities of the Lotus Sutra had upheld the warlord Chōsokabe, the continuing existence and reputation of state-supported shrines such as Kotohira remained an important element in the authority of the Meiji state. In short, gods remained entwined in politics.

Such political considerations, however, remained peripheral to the more immediate economic concerns of the priests and supporters of both Kotohira and Matsuoji. The ongoing ugly "relationship" between the two had its base in competition for worshippers and their pocketbooks; just as Konkōin had fought before 1868 to secure and defend its "exclusive shrine" monopoly, bringing suits against competitors, the priests of Kotohira in the twentieth century used their connections in and around government to ensure their dominance as well. When hundreds of Kotohira townspeople turned out to greet the shrine's lawyers before the trial or signed a letter condemning the lawsuit as injurious to the local economy, or when people in Zentsūji and Takamatsu supported a Buddhist Konpira, they did so not out of support or antagonism for the government but to increase business in their own towns. Not only was money crucial to the continued existence of shrine and temple, but these sites that attracted worshippers were integrally connected to the economic well-being of the community as well. In the twentieth century, as in centuries before, the institutions of the gods remained inseparable from—and thus circumscribed by—both economic and political necessity.

Faith, Reverence, and Doubt

While Kotohira Shrine relied for its survival on profit and political favor, it also depended upon the minds of its constituents. Without visitors, their fees, and their donations, the shrine of Kotohira would have long since dwindled into obscurity. Only while people considered the shrine relevant to their rapidly changing lives could it continue to survive, and indeed prosper, in the years to come.

Thus, the years of Meiji brought not only legal challenges to the shrine but also intellectual challenges to the god itself. By the end of the nineteenth century, doubtless due as much to the drastic renaming and redefining of the gods in the early Meiji period as to the blossoming of new attitudes and theories in the intervening years, the gods and their powers no longer simply existed; people now consciously believed or did not believe in them and their capacity for intervention. In a world where more and more people could choose to be *either* Buddhist *or* Shinto, or indeed Christian or even atheist, belief in the abilities of whole subsets of deities became optional, not assumed. Belief became something to avow or to disavow, depending upon one's view of oneself and one's place in the world. It became a marker of identity and, at the same time, an occasion for self-questioning and doubt. The structure of pilgrimage, however, required only an outward show of respect to the deities; one's interpretation of them was still up for grabs.[21]

A votive plaque donated to Kotohira Shrine by a poultry merchant from Osaka in 1893 highlights this growing awareness of the issue of belief. Hinting at some of its donor's struggles to come to terms with the intervention of the god in his heretofore mundane world, the ema is worth quoting at length:

> Although I have never particularly believed [*shinkō*] in the kami and buddhas, neither have I been of unbelieving mind; I have simply respected [*sūkei*] them. However, I encountered something that made it impossible to contest that they help [all] equally, with no distinction between deep faith and shallow faith. It occurred on the twelfth day of June, this year. On that day, among our children was one who became three years old this year. The maid whom we usually employed was holding the small child and, thinking to make him happy, took him up to the second floor. When she let go of the child to open the sliding door looking out over the road in front, he immediately flipped over and fell to the ground.

In the end, not only was the child unharmed, but "he did not even look as if he had fallen from a high place. There was not a single speck of dirt on his clothes." The donor then commented:

> What made me think for the first time that this might be due to the help of the kami was that . . . a relative visiting us from Takamatsu in Sanuki province had unexpectedly invited my wife to go on pilgrimage to Konpira a few days before. They boarded the ferry on the eleventh, the day before the child fell from the second floor. Thus, the day that my wife would have prayed to Konpira would have been on the twelfth. Seeing that this event and my wife's worship [*sanpai*] were on the same day, I believed that this was easily the help of the Great Kami Kotohira, who ensured the safety of our child. This I could not doubt. Of course, truly, because I came to know the great powers of the kami, my wife and I came again on pilgrimage to give thanks.

Inscribed above the image of a maid dropping a child from the second floor of a building, with neighbors gathered around to exclaim, the message was dated near the end of July 1893.[22]

Clearly, before this incident, the poultry merchant had never considered faith or the gods to be of particular importance. However, he also felt it important to highlight this fact, and to publicize the powers of the god for any others who, like him, might have doubted them. Instead, not faith but the act of pilgrimage—undertaken by his wife as a sort of holiday with a relative—became the important element. It mattered not whether his wife went on a lark or as a devout pilgrim, but that she went to the mountain at all. One never knew whether a visit made for fun could pay off in unexpected ways.

The logic and structure of pilgrimage made possible a vast array of approaches to the god. Konpira, like other deities, was thought to respond to the actions, as much as the intentions, of prayer. Worship, as opposed to "religion," did not require belief. It necessitated only performance: a decided convenience in an age of rapidly changing attitudes. Pilgrims could go to Konpira in any way they chose—barefoot, fasting, in military regalia, or even drunk and in outlandish costume—and still benefit from establishing contact with the god.

Indeed, people used this diversity in approach to define their own positions in society. In 1858, as we saw in chapter 1, the wealthy peasant Nakahara Suigekka rode a horse, visited teahouses, and prayed at every shrine on the mountain. He recorded it all in his diary along with the poetry and allusions meant to demonstrate his cultivated appreciation of the pilgrimage and thus his worthiness of at least nominal samurai status. Likewise, five decades later, as seen in chapter 12, the wealthy members of the Akasaka kō set themselves up as the model for reverent, patriotic expressions during the Russo-Japanese War.

Such self-definition necessarily occurred in opposition to other visitors. Whereas in the early twentieth century, some barefoot, "naked" pilgrims intent on demonstrating their humble devotion to the god doubtless looked askance at formally dressed men proudly parading to the shrine, perhaps commenting to their neighbors on the arrogance of the elite, it was those elite who recorded their criticisms of other pilgrims on paper, disseminating their ideas of proper pilgrimage beyond their immediate peers to all who read the publications in which they were printed. Thus, not only the rites of the priests but also the print of the papers became a crucial tool in the campaign of conservative leaders to portray formal, educated etiquette as the gods' preferred form of worship.

A brief article in the *Kagawa Shinpō* in 1908 describing the encounter of two men and their attitudes on the grounds of Kotohira Shrine illustrates the dynamics of such self-definition and promotion:

> Hamaguchi Eikichi (age 23), a fisherman from Miya town in Tokushima prefecture, although from a fishing family, is quite well-to-do. Since his birth, however, he has led only the maritime life and has not known learning. A while ago, he was called up in the supply troops of Zentsūji, where he was often inconvenienced by his lack of scholarship. He therefore was drawn to study. He made a pilgrimage to Kotohira Shrine, took copies of the two reading books and one mathematics book that he was supposed to study, and buried them in the woods behind the hall in which offerings to the deity are prepared. He prayed that he would quickly learn their contents, and he studied on his own as well.
>
> Five days after [Hamaguchi's] tour of military duty was over, he came [to the shrine] and prayed dressed in civilian clothes. In commemoration of the fulfillment of his prayer, he received one fifty-sen amulet and thirty three-sen amulets. Then he dug up the books wrapped in a cloth that he had buried before. At that point, Constable Ōoka of the Mt. Kotohira police box noticed him and, not knowing all of this, thought that [the bundle] might be stolen goods. Upon investigation, the story above came to light. The constable admonished Hamaguchi, telling him that studying and the like are to be done with one's own efforts—that praying to the kami for such things is not good.[23]

This incident, as reported in the newspaper, depicts a variety of approaches to the deity and assumptions about proper worship.[24] First, the fisherman turned soldier Hamaguchi brought his work-related concerns to Konpira for help. In much the same way that ill men and prostitutes on the Inland Sea island of Mitarai donated to Kotohira sweet-bean-paste-buns (*manjū*) in shapes reminiscent of genitalia when praying to recover from syphilis and other sexually transmitted diseases,[25] or that sailors offered up fishing nets or replicas of their boats,[26] Hamaguchi incorporated a physical embodiment of his prayers into his petition to the deity. He prayed alone, not relying upon the ceremonies of the priests, although he purchased amulets—an expensive one apparently for himself and cheaper amulets for people at home. For him to have left his books on the mountain, not an inconsequential expense, Hamaguchi was clearly convinced that the power of the site would help him. Yet, as the report said, he "studied on his own as well." Both his own effort and the blessing of the deity were brought to bear on his important goal. Nor did he consider it important to stay within the expected rituals or even public spaces of the shrine: Hamaguchi forged his own path beyond even the auxiliary buildings of the shrine into the woods where others did not go.

The policeman who found him, on the other hand, held a different view of what worship to Kotohira should entail. Hamaguchi's departure from the expected route of worshippers aroused Constable Ōoka's suspicions, especially when Hamaguchi entered the forest and dug something up from the ground. In Ōoka's view, worship should neither occur outside the prescribed public spaces of the shrine nor involve prayer for something that could be acquired through human effort—in this case, learning. Constable Ōoka's attitude—that one should not rely upon the gods for something that one can do oneself, and that the uneducated do not recognize the importance of expending their own efforts—was typical of the priests and educated men of his time. As seen in chapter 9, Kotooka Hirotsune and the other priests of Kotohira, when they established the Maritime Rescue Association in the late 1880s, frequently reiterated the theme of self-help as the conduit of the deity's powers in the modern age.[27] In this way, policemen, priests, and self-consciously educated people asserted their superiority over the supposed superstitions of other worshippers even while sharing a fundamental belief that through prayers, offerings, amulets, and pilgrimage a worshipper could invite the miraculous intervention of the god in everyday affairs. The point of contention was not the existence of the god and its miracles, but the appropriate content and form of invoking them.

The writer of the article highlighted this problem of propriety. Journalists at the *Kagawa Shinpō* generally shared Constable Ōoka's attitude toward self-help, viewing it as an obvious marker of prosperous, "civilized" men. Clearly the reporter was baffled by the fact that Hamaguchi—although "quite well-to-do"—believed in what amounted to superstition. To explain Hamaguchi's backwardness, therefore, the reporter attributed it to his location in the society of fishermen, widely seen as a superstitious lot, and his lack of formal education. Having addressed this supposed contradiction to the journalist's perception of worship style as an indicator of wealth and social status, the article confronted the widespread uncertainty over the place of faith and devotion in the era of "civilization and enlightenment." By reporting the entire incident under the rubric "A Peculiar Wish," the paper suggested that while other petitions would be acceptable, prayer for learning was inappropriate in the modern age.

The editors of the *Kagawa Shinpō* often exploited the seeming irrationality of common people's prayer to elicit the superior amusement of their elite, conservative readers. In 1911, for instance, the paper reported an incident in which police apprehended a man from Okayama prefecture who insisted that Konpira had commanded him to stay on the mountain for several days, then refused to return home until he heard the voice of the deity acknowledge his prayers. Only after the police dragged the man down the mountain and the railroad stationmaster impersonated Konpira over the station's new telephone, reported the paper alongside a humorous drawing, did the man agree to return to his family.[28]

Journalists, however, did not condemn acts of faith on all fronts. Through photos of famous shrines and temples, and extensive coverage of princes' or ministers' visits to Kotohira and other sites, they promoted an ideal of formal reverence for the public good. When personal petitions coincided with patriotic duty during wartime, for instance, the *Kagawa Shinpō* held unusual acts of devotion up for praise—as when it lauded a man who bathed in the river and walked to the shrine daily to pray for the soldiers in Korea. In effect, writers and others saw in pilgrimage an expression of the either "civilized" or "uncivilized" nature of the petitioner: each person's approach to the gods became confirmation not only for himself, but also for others, of his place in the world.

The novelist Mori Ōgai neatly highlighted the pivotal role of one's relation to the gods in the construction of personal identity in twentieth-century Japan. To Ōgai, the ambivalence toward the gods fostered by the rapid changes of the Meiji era formed a central part of the myriad conflicting influences pulling people apart in the early twentieth century. How one related to the gods therefore formed an integral part of one's identity—and never more so than for Western-educated intellectuals who treasured their commitment to scientific rationalism in the face of the supposedly superstitious beliefs of everyone else. When Ōgai in 1909 chose to explore this tension, he did so in the context of pilgrimage to one of the most renowned miracle-working gods of his age: Konpira.

In the short story "Konpira," the protagonist, a professor of Western philosophy at Tokyo University, stays in the town of Kotohira while on a lecture tour. His guide, a middle-school teacher from Takamatsu, insists that the professor climb to Kotohira Shrine—if not to worship along with others on this tenth day of the month, then to admire the scenery. The professor, expressing his disdain for "superstitious" faith, refuses to climb the mountain to pay his respects. Upon returning home to Tokyo, however, he unexpectedly learns that his son has fallen ill on the very day of his insult to the god. With the son on his deathbed and his daughter ill as well, the professor's wife and neighbors pray to Konpira at the Toranomon shrine in Tokyo. The professor, staying aloof, becomes increasingly plagued by doubts of his skeptical position. The story ends with the son dead and the daughter recovering. While the professor inwardly wonders about the powers of the deity, he remains dedicated to his skeptical stance.[29] As Ōgai so vividly showed, in the final years of the Meiji era, people from all walks of life—the intellectuals who denied the importance of sacred centers, the worshippers who proclaimed it, and the people caught in between, unsure of how to interpret the world—all continued to construct their world in part through their relationships to the sites of the gods.

It was because people used pilgrimage sites to define themselves and their worlds that Konpira and other popular centers of worship remained central to the creation of social unities and differences in twentieth-century Japan. Members of Konpira kō consolidated their social ties around personal commitments of time, money, and dedication, while the founders of such groups often capitalized upon miraculous signs of divine favor to establish their credentials as social leaders. Initiates into Kotohira Shrine's Reverence Association further declared their distinctive status by wielding the markers of bureaucratic procedure and privileged worship. Groups and individuals donated monuments, publicizing their exceptional devotion to the deity and their acknowledgment of the responsibilities of social prominence. Self-styled guides and cultural connoisseurs expounded upon the history of the shrine, deciphered the architectural styles of its roofs and torii, and lauded the famed beauty of its paintings, treasures, and scenery.[30] These people, whether through private acts of devotion or public avowals of skepticism, used sites such as Konpira to construct and continually reaffirm their own self-image and position in society.

What united all of these attitudes, despite the differences, was an acceptance of the importance of Kotohira itself—even if, for the most skeptical of intellectuals such as Mori Ōgai's professor, this entailed only an acknowledgment that other people considered it a major attraction. A primary difference between the Meiji- and Tokugawa-era landscapes of the gods thus lay not in the importance of the sites, but in their interpretation. Until the mid-nineteenth century, there was a broad public consensus that the gods could intervene actively in the lives of worshippers. A few merchants might express reservations and nativist historians speculate on the specific identities of the powerful beings, but most public discourse accepted the importance of divine response in everyday life. During the Meiji period, this broad agreement disintegrated as nativists inside and outside government advocated reverence over petition, as the idea of self-help increasingly displaced the rhetoric of reliance on the gods, and as sites of popular pilgrimage were portrayed as picturesque pockets, prettily preserving a time not present, yet never completely past.

The Rural versus the Urbane

In 1912, when the priests of Kotohira staged a grand festival at the shrine, the varied interpretations of the gods erupted with a vengeance. Not only did thousands of people visit the shrine, but they also wrote of their experiences for all to read, in newspaper articles, travel contest entries, books, and more. The festival thus highlighted both the diversity and the unity of approaches to the site.

At the height of the pilgrimage season—from the beginning of March, through the blossoming of the cherry trees in April, until the rainy season in June—Head Priest Kotooka Terusato and his colleagues at Kotohira Shrine staged a commemoration of the three hundredth anniversary of the death of Kongōbō-Yūsei, now the kami Itsutamahiko, in the inner shrine. In doing so, they both sought to overshadow memories of Matsuoji's celebration in 1898 and conveniently ignored the even more recent provenance of Kotohira's inner shrine, finished only seven years before. Using this event as the catalyst, priests and promoters hoped to place Kagawa prefecture on the map as a premier tourist and pilgrimage destination. With almost a year's notice to prepare for the occasion, business leaders in Kotohira, Takamatsu, and around the area made plans to pull the region out of its persistent slump, hosting concurrent displays of treasures, decorating the streets and railway lines, and publicizing attractions to the expected onslaught of visitors.[31] Railroad and steamship companies offered discounts, the city of Marugame built a special observation tower on top of its castle ruins, and entrepreneurs in Kotohira hosted exhibition matches between famous sumō wrestlers from Osaka.[32] At a time when tourism had become big business—with many organizations, including newspapers, offering package tours of the Inland Sea and other famous pilgrimage routes[33]—the papers in Osaka, Nagoya, and farther afield covered the events with unusual attention, eager to fill their pages with attractive photographs and entertaining accounts of travel to rural areas.

To the dismay of promoters, however, the prominent coverage was not all positive. Indeed, instead of appreciating the national art treasures and historical attractions that the shrine, local boosters, and the *Kagawa Shinpō* had worked so hard to promote, journalists from the big cities depicted Kotohira as an entertaining, provincial backwater, visited by gullible idiots from the surrounding countryside.

One of the most egregious examples of this ridicule appeared in the series "Kotohira Pilgrimage" in the *Ōsaka Asahi Shinbun*, beginning the first day of the festival in March. In the fourth installment, entitled "A Bus That Wears Clogs," a writer ridiculed both the high prices and the seeming irrationality of people in the town. "A wooden talisman (the old goma talisman) that sold ten years ago for thirty-three sen now costs a dear seventy-five sen," began the article. "There are lots of people in Kotohira who are not satisfied just to make money through inns and souvenirs. They hate work and live luxuriously, in the end dabbling in the stock market and accumulating debts larger than themselves. Oh, Wind of Civilization! Please blow here just the littlest bit!"[34] The writer went on to give an example of the absurd lack of business sense in Kotohira. "Then there is the incident of Kotohira's useless bus," he wrote. "They established a bus to Kotaki Springs, north of the mountain. But, according to the talk of people in town, a salesman said that a simple bus was not interesting enough, and instead proposed the latest, best, clog-wearing bus. On each of its wheels were attached what looked like several wooden clogs [*geta*]. . . . [An operator in Kotohira] happily bought and drove it. He kept taking off his own clogs and putting them on the wheels, until after a short while, he went out of business."[35] Whether or not the tale was based on even a small grain of truth, it dramatically illustrated the viewpoint spread in much of the national coverage of the festival that Kotohira was a place of stupid entertainments left untouched by modern civilization: a site treasured only by the poor, uneducated rural population still steeped in ignorance.

If, as urban writers said, Kotohira had been left untouched by modern progress, it could still provide a window onto the past. All sorts of publications described the quaintness of Kotohira, fueling a growing nostalgia in the second decade of the nineteenth century for the purported innocence and naturalness of life under the Tokugawa.[36] Informed in part by the historical analyses that had appeared in support of Matsuoji's lawsuit a few years earlier, as well as publicity for the anniversary of the inner shrine, a visit to Kotohira as portrayed in newspapers around the country became virtually a visit to the past. Even while remarking on changes at Kotohira brought about by the convenience of modern travel, writers immediately evoked Edo-period pilgrimage in their articles. In the same *Ōsaka Asahi Shinbun* series that ridiculed the clog-wearing bus, for instance, the author conjured "the Konpira pilgrimage of the past," when "visitors came in Konpira boats, '*shu shu shu*,' tasting the sweetness of gambling and women, then opening their eyes to find their wallets empty."[37]

Needless to say, the priests and promoters of the festivities were appalled to read the widely printed public disdain shown by urban journalists. Within weeks of the festival's opening in March, the *Kagawa Shinpō* bemoaned the unforeseen effects of widespread coverage. "On the occasion of the festival commemorating the three hundredth year of the Kotohira inner shrine," reported a front-page article, "newspapers and magazines from each place are suddenly writing articles about our prefecture. The gist of most of these articles, however, is almost all the same. They do not tell of the beauty of Yashima and Ritsurin Park, but instead about the quaintness of drawings and curios. Among them, for instance, even among youths, bowing down to a *tokonoma* and praising a scroll is unknown. Some even write ridiculing [us] as something that should be entirely excluded from the world of social interaction."[38] Here appeared in print the clash between two visions of civilization and progress: the determinedly secular, yet nostalgic, view of the urban intellectuals who wrote and read the *Asahi Shinbun* and other major national dailies, and the culturally and historically embedded view more widespread outside the major urban centers. Wealthy landlords, village officials, prosperous businessmen and, yes, Shinto priests shared this focus on art, history, and literature as the sign of a civilized man—viewpoints evident as well in the newspapers that catered to them.

The local *Kagawa Shinpō*, published in Takamatsu—which not only promoted the development of tourism in its home town but had also been affiliated since its inception with the conservative Kaishintō, Kokumin Kyōkai, and other national political organizations—presented the shrine as the height of respectability. Its special commemorative edition for the festival featured articles and photographs replete with images of grandeur and solemn celebration.[39] Large photographs in other newspapers in the region featured staid views of the shrine buildings, Maruyama Ōkyo paintings, and festival processions.[40] These politically conservative newspapers[41] catered to the population of educated, devout, and generally well-to-do worshippers whose reverence for Kotohira and other shrines was based on moral teachings, wartime miracles, a national cultural heritage, and the sacralized history of the imperial house. While many urban intellectuals envisioned progress toward a universal, scientific civilization, seeing in Kotohira the backward gullibility and quaintness of a secluded country town, regional leaders often portrayed the shrine as the symbol of a morality, culture, and civilization particular to Japan.

For many people in the second decade of the twentieth century, as in centuries before, however, a trip to Konpira was their first introduction to urban amenities, linking the trip to the shrine with the attractions of railroads, electricity, and indeed progress as a whole. Many of these visitors did not come by train. People from Kyushu or around the Inland Sea sailed their own boats, and travelers from other parts of Shikoku hiked over the mountains to get to the shrine. The journal of one such boy, Kanezawa Osamu, who hiked with his father to Kotohira for the festival in 1912 during the spring vacation after his sixth year of elementary school, reflected the wide-eyed wonder of a boy on his first trip outside Tokushima prefecture—indeed, the first trip in which the normally barefoot boy even wore straw sandals.

The boy, educated in public school, was well aware of his presumed rural backwardness. As he wrote, "The many lanterns, metal torii, metal lions, and the like all surprised my countrified eyes [*inakamono no me*]." He went on to comment on the other attractions as well: "Since this year was the three hundredth anniversary festival, it was even busier than usual. There were three moving pictures, a zoo, an aquarium, and lots of other entertainments. As for sightseeing at night, there were lighted lanterns, and illuminated advertisements for [the patent medicine] Jintan. . . . We saw the Yano Zoo and listened to the lion roar. I cannot express our joy in the music that greeted the trains and the music that saw them off."[42] Whether looking at the ponds and waterfall of the brick and glass aquarium that had replaced the old panorama on the hillside[43] or admiring the impressive monuments at the shrine, Osamu absorbed the sights and sounds of Kotohira as his first view of the outside world. Combined with his first trip to the seaside, as he and his father rode the train from Kotohira on to Tadotsu and Takamatsu, this mountain boy's pilgrimage to Konpira became a memorable adventure, with the urbane attractions of Kotohira making him increasingly aware of his own lack of sophistication.

Others, as well, commented on how the town so denigrated by big-city intellectuals seemed, to many visitors, to be a big city of its own. Responding to a readers' contest held by the *Nagoya Shinbun* for the cheapest, most interesting trip within a ten-yen budget, one man, Nakao Rosan, wrote of his trip to Kotohira from the Hashikura Pass between Kagawa and Tokushima prefectures. Like Kanezawa Osamu and thousands of travelers from Shikoku to the shrine, Nakao arrived at Kotohira after a wearying hike down the mountain path. "At noon, I arrived in Kotohira," he wrote in his summary of the trip. "On the eaves of each building in town hung flags and lanterns with the encircled gold symbol. On both sides of the long, long stone steps up to Kotohira Shrine were lined inns, candy shops, drinking shops, picture postcard shops, toy shops, and the like. Shopkeepers were crying out loudly in an attempt to entice into their shops even one more country bumpkin [literally *mukudori:* gray starling] going up and down the steps. . . . Even outside the town were displays of art or dolls, zoos, and five or six small sideshows that had been hastily built. But all of these were extremely local, all of them just stupid things to deceive children."[44]

Travelers and visitors to Kotohira thus perceived the town—and the shrine—from a great variety of viewpoints. As Mori Ōgai showed, few people viewed the god in only one way. On the one extreme were big-city journalists and others, who generally avoided the god entirely, and on the other were devotees such as sailors who gave thanks for rescues or women who made offerings for health. In between, the educated rural elites—conservative landlords, teachers, military officers, bureaucrats, and priests, among others—avoided both extremes by identifying the shrine with the values of the nation: culture and civilization, progress and propriety. Thus, the shrine and town of Kotohira could be—and were—used by a variety of people to define "civilization" and to place themselves in relation to others on the scale of progress.[45]

At Kotohira, anyway, these measurements of progress rarely focused on the emperor. Although scholars have long focused on the "emperor worship" of state-supported Shinto, especially after the Russo-Japanese War, the emperor figured more in the abstract (in phrases such as "the imperial army" or "the imperial gods") than in real flesh and blood. It was in 1912, when the emperor lay dying during Kotohira's grand festival, that he finally entered the imagination of some worshippers, at least, as an individual person, not just a unifying symbol.

In late July, a group of six well-heeled men from Tokyo, ranging in age from fifty-three to seventy-seven, visited the shrine as part of a tour that included the Great Shrine of Izumo, Miyajima, Kotohira, and the headquarters of the Shinto sect Konkōkyō in Okayama. They later published an account of their journey, emphasizing its formal, Shinto character in the title—not only referring to Kotohira Shrine, instead of Konpira, but calling their journey a record of "sanpai" (formal worship), not the more informal "omairi" (pilgrimage). The formal nature of the trip, and the status of the men, can be seen from their arrangements for special treatment at the shrine office, when the dying emperor suddenly became a part of prayer at the shrine:

[At the shrine office,] Mr. Kurosawa came to speak with us. We were supposed to meet Head Priest Kotooka [Terusato], but [Mr. Kurosawa] told us that the head priest and all of the employees were secluded in prayer in the main shrine because of the illness of the emperor. Therefore we could not meet him. We talked about various things. With a telephone call, he arranged with someone at the main shrine for us to perform formal worship. He arranged a specific time, and we set off from the shrine office.

We climbed dozens of stone steps and arrived at the main shrine. We gave the person our cards and were made to wait a little while. In the precincts of the main shrine and along the road, pilgrims old and young, male and female, were carrying in their hands flags inscribed, "Prayers for the health and recovery of the emperor," and the names of people and their villages. There were thousands of people, as if gathered for a kaichō. Our formal worship was announced, and we were led to the purification site and underwent the purification ceremony. When we arrived in front of the kami, we offered up a prayer. When each of us bowed down, we ended with a prayer for the recovery of the emperor. We received sanctified saké and retreated.

The six men then climbed up to the inner, Itsutama Shrine and once again prayed for the recovery of the emperor.[46]

Thus, it was during the vigil over the emperor's deathbed that prayers for the emperor became a temporary focal point at the shrine. While schoolchildren bowed to the emperor's portrait and recited the Imperial Rescript on Education at their schools, there is no evidence that, under ordinary circumstances, the emperor himself became an object of special reverence or worship at Kotohira Shrine before 1912. Instead, as he lay dying, village leaders and devout educated men led the way in praying for the welfare of the emperor, as they had the welfare of soldiers and the nation during the Sino-Japanese and Russo-Japanese wars.

The death of the Meiji emperor in late July 1912 brought an end to both the shrine festivities and the Meiji era. By then, the shrine and town of Kotohira had acquired the broad spectrum of reputations, practices, and institutions that they would maintain until 1945 and beyond. Since the Restoration of 1868, rural notables, schoolteachers, and military officers, as well as the priests and town leaders of Kotohira, had added new dimensions to the site of the god. They focused attention on cultural attractions, building museums and publicizing historical displays. They supported the development of parks, inns, and small resorts catering to the leisure requirements of the fledgling middle class. And they reincorporated worship of the tengu Kongōbō in the more restrained context of a formal shrine building and Shinto ritual. While shopkeepers and priests since the Edo period had long promoted and profited from the cultural, scenic, and entertainment value of the site, now their entrepreneurial activities were explicitly couched in the language of capital, economic development, and the promotion of "tourism" (*kankō*). Newspapers and guidebooks—catering to their overlapping audiences of business leaders, cultural connoisseurs, and leisured elites—increasingly detached the shrine from its combinatory, miraculous context, embedding it instead in the language of imperial heritage and regional development. Building upon, yet rarely acknowledging, the solid attraction provided by the powers of Konpira, the media and local leaders resituated the mountain in a tourist's geography of commodified culture and scenic quaintness.

Yet, despite the focus of development initiatives on the preferences (and, thereby the pockets) of these consumers of middle-class tourism, the popularity of both the miracles of the god and the prostitutes of the town still drew the vast majority of pilgrims to the shrine. Thus, when outside commentators arrived in 1912 to cover the shrine's festival for the national press, they found a mixture of the respectable and the raucous, the formal and the frivolous, the pretentious and the plebeian. For those concerned with broader issues of "civilization," the combination highlighted both the strengths and the weaknesses of Shinto ideals. On the positive side, the clear linkage of formal shrine rituals to popular practices seemed to demonstrate the native roots of Shinto propriety. Thus, the dignified culture, history, and ritual of the shrine bespoke an indigenous model of civilization that maintained national traditions in an age of foreign influence. For many of the conservative rural elites who were among the shrine's major supporters, this "national" past was more civilized than the foreign present. Yet for others, many of them critics of such a sacralized order, prayers to a miraculous kami recalled a superstitious, uneducated age: the vision of a reverential, communal culture denied the modern future in favor of a backward past.

Meanwhile, the object of criticism by proponents of either sacred or scientific civilization—the vast majority of pilgrims and visitors—continued to provide most of the profits that enabled the very continuity of the institution as a whole. Intent on the present, focusing on their relationship to the god and their leisure in the brothels and sideshows, the "country bumpkins" found in Kotohira a consumer's paradise of choice, entertainment, and novel experience. Presenting different faces to different visitors, Kotohira was in 1912, among other things, a destination of devout pilgrimage, an exciting urban adventure, a cultural monument, and a rural anachronism. Embedded in the overlapping contexts of recreation and prayer, imperial reverence and national history, the attractions of Kotohira had been created, directly and indirectly, by the diversity of its visitors.

EPILOGUE
Konpira, Then and Now

In the years since 1912, much has changed. Japan gained and lost an empire, fought and lost a war. Its people transformed the Japanese economy into an industrial powerhouse and built a consumer's paradise. They created a high-tech, information society. As a consequence, people increasingly travel to Kotohira not by foot, boat, or train, but by bus or automobile, and on the Internet as well.

On a steamy morning near the end of the rainy season in early July 2003, the roads were practically deserted when I arrived by car in the town of Kotohira almost exactly a decade after my first visit there. In the midst of Kotohira's usual "summer drought," exacerbated by the continuing economic recession in Japan, attendants tried to wave me into brightly marked but almost empty parking lots. A few vehicles with license plates from Okayama and Hyogo stood scattered in the lots, having crossed over to Shikoku on one of the large new bridges that, since 1988, have transformed the island from a backwater reached only by boat into a readily accessible tourist destination. Connected by elevated tollways that bypass the town of Kotohira, the bridges have both helped the tourist business in Kagawa prefecture and encouraged countless travelers to rush beyond Kotohira and other local attractions to the relatively pristine forests and rivers of Kochi prefecture beyond.

No longer do all roads lead to Konpira; instead, the shrine and local businesses must rely on advertisements, word of mouth, and newspaper and television coverage to maintain their prominence in people's minds. On the roads of Kagawa prefecture, not just highway signs but also countless gold and red advertisements for Kyūman sweet-bean-paste buns (manjū), pasted on telephone poles or billboards, draw attention to the shrine—the twentieth-century replacement for the stone markers of the past.

While the old road posts may have disappeared, many lanterns remain, with rows of them lining a block in the former red-light district (defunct since the elimination of prostitution in the 1950s), and larger, more impressive versions now decorating the plaza in front of the train station. A driver arriving in town, however, proceeds quickly past both these lanterns and the old Tall Lantern, which stands in a small, deserted park beside Kotohira's second train station, the electric train running straight to Takamatsu. With the proliferation of cars, these prominent landmarks from the past have receded into obscurity.

Instead, the focus of visitors has narrowed. Ignoring the former entrance to the town, and barely noticing the train station, they see the path up the mountain as the defining element of pilgrimage to the shrine. When asked about their trips to Konpira, people today inevitably comment on the many, many steps: 785 to the main shrine, then an additional 1,368 to the inner shrine. In an age when people sit in offices, on trains, in cars, and at home—rarely walking more than a mile a day, and almost never uphill—the climb up Mt. Kotohira has become a physical exertion that shapes all other experiences at the site.

The approach to the steps begins with a wide, stone-paved road. On the hot and humid July morning, the broad expanse of paving stones seems cool and inviting. The dark wooden facade of the saké brewing museum and the half-open shutters of shops just opening for the day accentuate the calm quietness of the morning. On the left stands Kyūman (of the ubiquitous advertisements) as well as the large, renovated Sakuraya Inn. At the end of the broad pathway on the right, near the foot of the steps leading up, stands the old Toraya, still a Meiji-era, wooden, two-story building. It no longer houses guests. Instead, later in the day, a woman will stand at the door inviting passersby to try the renowned local specialty, noodles (*udon*). On the walls of the restaurant inside, the Toraya displays its old wooden Reverence Association plaques as scenic decorations evoking the past age of Konpira pilgrimage.

Proceeding slowly in the heat, I set off up the stone steps, shaded by awnings drawn by shopkeepers across the path. The few tour groups traveling at this time of year have already been and gone from the shrine: they stay the night at one of the large hotels down below, then make the climb around five or six o'clock in the morning, just as the dawn light hits the eastward-facing mountain, but before the heat of the day sets in. At eight o'clock, I am practically alone.

I climb several flights of steps, past a side street leading to the Kanamaruza Kabuki Theater—the oldest theater in the country and, since its renovation and the revival of periodic performances in 1985, a major attraction in the town. From a small plateau beyond several souvenir shops and the glass sliding doors of Toramaru inn, a road leads off to the left: the old route to Iyo and Tosa provinces. On each side of the steps both below and above this point, souvenir shops stand crowded against each other. During the nineteenth century, almost all of these shops had been inns, housing and feeding pilgrims to the shrine. The changes of industrialization, however, spelled their doom. As train tickets became increasingly affordable, visitors could arrive and leave on the same day; pressured by the decrease in customers, and a series of local bank failures, inns began to close their doors. Out of thirty-five Reverence Association inns in 1913, only fourteen remained in operation in 1941.[1] After the war, changes in transportation once again prompted a wave of closures in the 1960s and 1970s. Owing to a combination of factors, including the demise of officially sanctioned prostitution as well as the rise of bus tours and private automobiles, the number of overnight visitors to the shrine declined precipitously.[2]

Membership in the Reverence Association fell dramatically as well. The increased production of relatively safe fiberglass boats apparently weakened the fervent dedication of many sailors and fishermen, some of whom had also found jobs in nearby industries. As people could increasingly afford to travel on their own, they no longer needed to pool their money in kō in order to fund a trip to the shrine. The effect on both the Reverence Association and the inns was dramatic. For years, whenever a Reverence Association inn closed, it sold its kō registers to other inns staying in business: the guaranteed custom of kō pilgrims remained a valuable commodity. By the 1980s, however, membership in the Reverence Association, as well as the frequency with which remaining members came to the shrine, had declined to such an extent that retiring innkeepers, rather than selling the registers, could only ask other inns to house their affiliated associations.[3]

With the demise of the inns, the male heads of innkeeping families found jobs elsewhere while their wives or elderly parents stayed at home to mind what had become stores. Today, the steps up Mt. Kotohira are lined not with placards welcoming Reverence Association kō for the night, but with manufactured souvenirs. Glittering pictures of the Great Seto Bridge hang beside hand towels showing the Seven Lucky Gods and the encircled gold symbol of Kotohira Shrine. Boxes of candy sit with packaged, dried udon or with round red fans bearing the encircled gold logo. As a legacy of the short-lived Kotohira Trade School, almost all of the shops also offer *ittōbori*: roughly carved wooden images of the Seven Lucky Gods, Kannon, or other items of interest (figure 14.1).

After a while, past the first hundred steps or so, the shops give way to a small, stone-paved plateau on the right. At the far end stands a statue of the first Shinto priest of Kotohira, Kotooka Hiroshige, in priestly garb. First erected in 1928, then requisitioned during the Pacific War and rebuilt in 1955, the bronze statue and the area as a whole commemorate Kotooka's establishment of the Maritime Rescue Association (figure 14.2). A long wooden display case holds a life preserver, a life vest, and other tools of the lifesaving trade. Paintings on the wooden back of the display case depict Maritime Rescue Association outposts and rescue dinghies, each flying a banner bearing Kotohira's symbol for gold as the center of the Imperial Navy flag: a blazing red sun radiating lines. The plateau is deserted. Visitors, intent on climbing the next step, or looking at the shops on the left, walk on by without even noticing the spot. The monument, hidden in plain sight, seems to commemorate a forgotten moment in the history of the shrine.

Indeed, the tiny, painted flags on the Maritime Rescue Association painting constitute some of the only overt reminders of Japan's—and Kotohira's—imperial past. The few monuments to wartime dead on the mountain are located off the beaten path, accessible to those who seek them, yet virtually invisible to those who do not. In the same way, no mention remains of Kotohira's status in the hierarchy of state shrines that existed from 1871 until Japan's surrender in 1945. According to a former priest at the shrine, the priests of Kotohira quickly hid or destroyed donations and other items reminiscent of wartime nationalism during the weeks between Japan's surrender and the arrival of Occupation troops in 1945. Votive plaques depicting worshippers dressed in their best—that is, in military-style uniform—thus disappeared. Three months after the surrender, on 15 December 1945, Occupation forces announced the Shinto Directive, halting state funding of shrines. In February 1946, Kotohira Shrine helped establish the Association of Shinto Shrines (Jinja Honchō), a private, umbrella organization designed to coordinate the management of affiliated shrines. While Kotohira still receives periodic offerings from the Imperial Household Agency (Kunaichō)—for re-

❀ 14.1 (*opposite*) Display at a souvenir shop along the steps leading up to Kotohira Shrine, 2000. The boat in the middle of the picture is the treasure boat of the Seven Lucky Gods, and the hangings with two faces depict two of those gods, Ebisu and Daikoku (another reading for "Ōkuninushi," or Kotohira, according to a sign at Kotohira Shrine). To the upper right of the boat is a tengu mask. Many of the wooden items ranged below and to the left are examples of the local carving style, ittōbori; to the right, small statues of beckoning cats are used by businesses to symbolically beckon in customers. (Photo by the author.)

✿ **14.2** Statue of Kotooka Hirotsune erected in honor of his creation of the Maritime Rescue Association in 1892. This bronze statue was built in 1955 to replace the 1928 statue that had been requisitioned during the Pacific War. On a small plateau to the side of the steps leading up to the shrine precincts, this memorial to an association with strong ties to the prewar government bureaucracy and navy attracts little attention from visitors to the shrine. (Photo by the author, with the permission of Kotohira Shrine.)

building the main sanctuary in 1971,[4] for instance, and in honor of its annual festival—its official ties to state coffers and rankings have been severed.

Farther up the steps, just outside the main gate, stands yet another transformed relic of the past: the headquarters of the Reverence Association (now Kotohira Honkyō). The association has long since changed its rules. After the promulgation in 1947 of the Shōwa Constitution, patterned in many ways after the Constitution of the United States, the Reverence Association at Kotohira, like so many around the country, discarded its teachings of "reverence for the emperor" and "love of country" for principles of "fairness" and "equality," all in the context of the gods. Claiming Itsutamahiko no Mikoto (that is, Kongōbō-Yūsei) as its founder, the Honkyō provides special services and meeting places for the few affiliated kō still in existence. It supports kō that, during the annual great festival in October and especially on New Year's Day, parade to the shrine with identifying banners in order to receive a shared blessing in the sanctuary above.

Just beyond the Reverence Association headquarters towers the main gate to the shrine precincts: the gate donated in 1648 by the first Takamatsu lord, Matsudaira Yorishige, when he and Yūten together redesigned the mountain. Dark with age, the imposing structure beckons visitors under its wooden sign announcing "Mt. Kotohira" to the broad path of the Sakuranobaba beyond, where five women—representatives of the five families with hereditary rights to sell candy in the shrine precincts—sit at tables covered with their wares. They sit in the shade of large, bright red umbrellas, enjoying the breeze from electric fans plugged into outlets in the ground, encouraging passersby to sample and buy the hard candies they sell.

The Sakuranobaba evokes a sense of continuity between past and present. Along the sides of the broad walkway stand stone railings and lanterns given by donors during the Tokugawa period, now beautifully covered with moss. On the ground along the edge of the path lie old stone foundations with rectangular holes—holes that once held in place slabs erected in the early twentieth century to commemorate major donors to the shrine. The holes have stood empty since the middle of the 1940s, when the 3,396 rectangular slabs then standing were taken down to build docks and airport runways during World War II.[5]

Today, too, major donors are commemorated by tall imposing slabs inscribed with their names. Now, however, the memorials are erected behind the lanterns, encouraging visitors to admire the picturesque, older offerings (see figure 14.3). This emphasis on highlighting the Tokugawa-era monuments emerged in the last few decades under the late head priest, Kotooka Mitsushige (in office 1948–94). Taking over as head priest shortly after World War II, Kotooka, like many other people, dedicated his career to the preservation and promotion of a depoliticized Japanese culture. Focusing more on objects than ideas, more on an idealized peace before 1868 than on the conflicts and war that followed, Kotooka diverted attention away from the more recent, and more uncomfortable, military past.[6] He restaged the traditions of the ancient (and thus innocent) aristocracy, such as a courtly form of football (*kemari*), and emphasized the customs of "the people," as seen in the many lanterns, ema, and other offerings at Kotohira. In 1979, he secured the designation by the Agency for Cultural Affairs (Bunkachō) of 1,725 offerings to the shrine as Important Tangible Folk Cultural Properties (Jūyō Yūkei Minzoku Bunkazai), partaking of and adding support to a nationwide nostalgia for a popular past. Kotooka Mitsushige thereby obtained substantial government subsidies for the study and documentation of these items (ultimately publishing the three-volume *Konpira Shomin Shinkō Shiryōshū*, with photographs, transcriptions, and diagrams of the objects) as well as for the construction of an up-to-date, climate-controlled storehouse

and exhibition space to house the old ema, tengu masks, and other designated treasures. The new storehouse stands, with the old museum, up a path
to the right of the Sakuranobaba. The museum, still the original two-story
building constructed in 1905, holds not only the statue of Fudō Myōo alongside several Buddhist scrolls and sutras, but also a dark wooden pillar purportedly from the old Upside-Down Gate, some armor, and other valuable
donations.

At the end of the Sakuranobaba stands a cute, stylized statue of a small
dog. In 1993, the shrine ran a publicity campaign, "Everybody, Konpirasan,"
based on a letter in the shrine's archives that mentioned people of Edo (now
Tokyo) sending their dogs to Konpira as proxy pilgrims in the 1800s (see
chapter 5). The priests published posters and advertisements with drawings
of the "Konpira dog" surrounded by a dragon, a tengu, courtiers playing kemari, a man retrieving an offering to Konpira from the sea, and other colorful
images. They even created telephone cards and commissioned an illustrated
children's book relating the travels of the dog.[7] Amulets and votive plaques
depicting the Konpira dog are available for purchase at the shrine, evoking
cheerful images of Konpira's great popularity in the past. To the left, across
from the statue, three sacred white horses stand in an open stable, and nearby
a huge ship's propellor—donated by a shipbuilding company in Shikoku in
1994—dominates an open plateau. To the right stands the new, multistory
shrine office. In the summer of 2003, the entry to the shrine office is taken up
with an exhibit and video explaining the process of restoring the gilded ceiling of the main sanctuary—a process for which the priests are busy raising
money. The entire main shrine is currently undergoing renovation; I wonder
what I will see as I climb higher in the heat.

As I leave the shrine office and start up the steps, however, there is little
hint of any changes above. At the top of a short flight of stairs, the entrance to
the old shrine office (previously Konkōin) stands open on the right. I can go
in and admire the famous screens by Maruyama Ōkyo or Itō Jakuchū, enjoy
the beautiful garden, or view the courtyard where shrine priests periodically
perform kemari, reminding spectators of the purportedly ancient roots of
Shinto and Kotohira's ties to the imperial court.

꙰ 14.3 (*opposite*) Today, large slabs honoring major donors to the shrine stand behind Tokugawa-era
lanterns and balustrades, encouraging visitors to notice the long history of popular donations to the
shrine. This focus on commoners' donations before 1868 contributes to the image of Kotohira Shrine
as a site of popular tradition, feeding the widespread nostalgia in late twentieth- and early twenty-first-
century Japan for a peaceful, more community-minded, preindustrial past. (Photo by Steve Cantley,
with the permission of Kotohira Shrine.)

Just outside the gate, a large sign explains the identity of the Great Kami Kotohira as a joint enshrinement of Emperor Sutoku and the kami Ōkuninushi—the formal Shinto reading, the sign informs readers, of the Chinese characters for the name of the popular god of good fortune and wealth, Daikoku. It is unclear when this identification with Daikoku, one of the Seven Lucky Gods, was added. Clearly, it must have been after Konpira became linked with the kami Ōkuninushi or Ōmononushi. Yet in my researches of materials up until 1912, I have never run into the association. Perhaps it was added in the 1980s, during the nationwide popularity of the Seven Lucky Gods in general; perhaps it arose earlier. In any case, even official signs in the shrine precincts now link the nativist Shinto kami with a group of popular deities of diverse origin, associated with the quest for wealth and good fortune. Just as priests in the 1890s reincorporated the popular tengu Kongōbō into the identity of the god, so it seems their successors added the popular, Chinese-influenced Seven Lucky Gods to the mix.

I continue up the steps to the left, past more memorials to recent donors and beyond a small shelter for the wooden horse donated by Matsudaira Yorishige in 1651. As I turn to the right, I pass a group of four men in business suits carrying walking sticks and fans from a souvenir shop below: the souvenir seller clearly expects them to stop on the way down to return the sticks, then buy souvenirs for their friends at home. A young couple stands panting in the shade—the girl in three-inch-high heels, contemplating the steps extending farther and farther up toward the top.

After passing the Dawn Shrine, entering through the Sakaki Gate (the old Upside-Down Gate), and climbing the final, steep flight of steps, I finally approach the main shrine, and the reconstruction work becomes obvious. The sounds of heavy equipment and hammering ring in the air, even as preparations for a ritual in the main sanctuary begin. It is the Tsukinami, or Monthly Festival, held on Konpira's *ennichi,* the tenth day of each month.

I climb the steps up to the main sanctuary, leaving my shoes below and kneeling outside the railing at the top to watch the proceedings. Next to me kneels a youngish man, perhaps in his early thirties, bowing and reciting a Shinto prayer from a printed booklet. Every time he reaches the end, he bows, claps, and closes the folded prayer book, then opens it, bows, claps, and begins reciting again. He has apparently been there for hours, petitioning the god for something with all his efforts.

But the ceremony is beginning. Both priests and women officiants (*miko*) enter to sit in rows in front of the inner sanctuary door, with flute and drum players off to the side. Then a man in a dark business suit arrives, settling on the tatami mats closer to us at the front edge of the sanctuary, facing in. It is the current head priest, Kotooka Yasutsugu. His arrival is the signal for the offerings to start. Each priest or *miko* rises in turn, walks to the balcony surrounding the sanctuary, receives an elaborate tray of vegetables, fish, or other offerings from an assistant, and brings the tray to another priest to arrange in the inner sanctum. After a seemingly interminable number of such offerings are placed, the head priest offers up a sakaki branch, then returns to his seat. After this, the process is reversed until the entire ceremony is concluded.[8]

The current head priest, who in 1994 succeeded his father in the now once again hereditary office, has instituted several innovative reforms at the shrine. Indeed, as he had only begun his term as head priest when I first began my research, I heard repeated complaints by men of his father's generation, several of whom finally left the shrine entirely. Under Kotooka Yasutsugu, women—that is, the *miko*—are now included as full officiants in shrine ceremonies; before, they were considered too impure. It was he who first placed Kotohira Shrine on the Web in January 1996, creating the first official shrine Web site in Japan (www.konpira.or.jp).[9]

The revolutionary nature of Kotooka Yasutsugu's vision for the new Kotohira—in the words of its most recent marketing campaign, "The New Konpira of the Twenty-first Century" ("21seiki no nyū Konpirasan")—is evident in the current head priest's reinterpretation of the encircled gold symbol. The construction area around the main shrine is hidden by huge curtains inscribed with the encircled gold symbol—not in red, but in gold. Instead of invoking the Japanese flag (the *hinomaru*) with a red circle on white, or a red encircled gold marker on white, the current head priest has turned the symbol from an evocation of national pride into an even more straightforward image of wealth and prosperity, an image only reinforced by advertisements promoting a new gold-encased amulet also available at the shrine since 1999 (figure 14.4). In the recession of the 1990s and early 2000s, he is clearly seeking to position Kotohira as a site to pray for economic recovery.

At the same time, Kotooka, the first head priest of Kotohira to be educated after World War II, seems to be shifting the shrine away from his father's focus on national culture and identity toward a more inclusive international outlook. Under the old priest and in the early years of the new priest, photographs of the imperial family adorned walls in offices and at the archive; magazines emphasizing shrine and imperial ties were also displayed for sale at a tea shop inside the shrine precincts. There were displays of posters drawn by schoolchildren showing the importance of the national flag, as well as the kemari demonstrations highlighting Kotohira's ties to the imperial court. Under Kotooka Yasutsugu, such activities have not disappeared. Yet, on its Web site and in the local press, the shrine promotes a cultural and artistic identity

幸福の黄色いお守り

❀ 14.4 Poster at Kotohira Shrine advertising a special, gold amulet—intended to raise funds for the rebuilding of the main shrine from 1999 on. (Photo by the author, with the permission of Kotohira Shrine.)

that ranges beyond national borders, including even an exhibition of American modern art since Jackson Pollock.[10] By changing the color of the encircled gold mark, then, Kotooka Yasutsugu is creating yet another new image of the god for the current context. His bold initiative—cleverly changing yet preserving the encircled gold symbol as his predecessor in 1868 changed yet preserved the name of the deity—serves as a reminder of the constant dynamism of the god, its symbol, and its site.

As I turn to leave after the ceremony, I notice another ritual about to begin. Three people—a woman and two men—have apparently arranged for a special ceremony of purification and blessing. A young priest quickly places a small table in front of each person, each table with a small cup of saké and a sakaki branch upon it. Each of the worshippers has placed at his or her side a small paper bag from the shrine office (inscribed with the encircled gold symbol in gold), presumably holding a commemorative gift and perhaps some saké or an amulet from the shrine. A priest brings out a large wand (gohei) with glittering gold streamers, much like the wands depicted in century-old votive plaques or found in small neighborhood Konpira shrines around the country. He proceeds to first wave the wand over, then touch it upon, the head of each bowed petitioner (figure 14.5). Clearly, to these worshippers—as to the man kneeling next to me, still reciting the printed prayer over and over—the benefits of the god are very real: they pursue them wholeheartedly, whether through personal prayer or through the mediating offices of the priests.

I finally turn away from the main shrine to start on the long climb to the inner shrine. Passing the bronze lanterns donated in 1697 by Izumiya and the other investors in the Besshi copper mine, I head up the shallow steps into the woods (figure 14.6). A few slabs commemorating donors line the bottom of the path, but soon all I see are trees on either side. Perhaps because of the sense of adventure on this secluded trail, whenever I meet someone on the path to the inner shrine, we exchange greetings, commenting on the heat or the distance yet to go. In the end, I emerge from the trees into the sun, with the wooden shrine in front and a building with a shrine employee selling amulets to the right. Hanging high on the cliff alongside the inner shrine are two wooden masks of tengu, reminders of Kongōbō-Yūsei, the seventeenth-century priest enshrined here as the kami Itsutamahiko. There are no offerings in sight in 2003: the inner shrine seems more a goal for the energetic hiker than a destination for fervent worshippers. In the quiet seclusion, after the efforts of the climb in the humid, oppressive heat, I can certainly sense how this "inner shrine," built only a century ago, can evoke Yūsei's ascetic meditations of the seventeenth century.

After a peaceful rest, I turn to go, leaving the serenity of the closed-in forest for the spacious buildings and noisier people below. On my return down the mountain, I walk past the main shrine, where the man still chants and bows, two hours after the ceremony. I then wander past the amulet sales office, across to the Ema Hall, which is currently truncated due to the con-

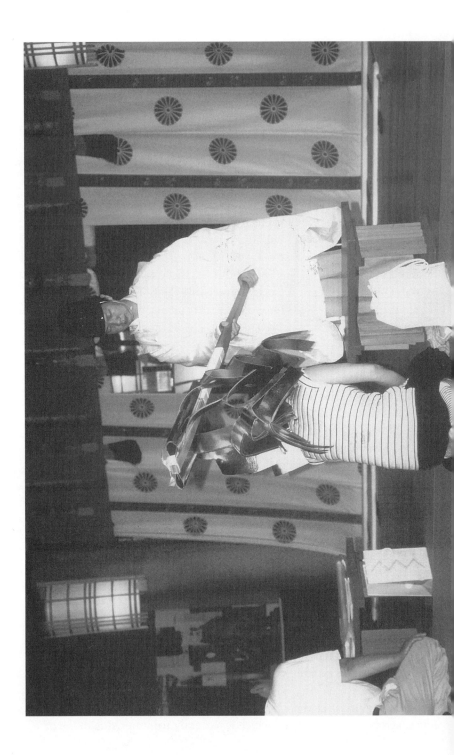

⊛ **14.6** The main shrine, with bronze lanterns on its right, 2003. Note the white paper gohei decorations indicative of its Shinto status. The encircled gold motif is repeated at the ends of beams and on the rooftop. Construction on the left is hidden behind curtains bearing the gold-colored encircled gold insignia. (Photo by Steve Cantley, with the permission of Kotohira Shrine.)

struction. There are still displayed countless offerings: mainly small wooden plaques that people purchase and upon which they inscribe their prayers— for success on college entrance examinations, for true love, for finding a good job. Among the larger offerings selected by the priests to remain visible during construction are colorful flags and ema from fishermen, a solar-powered boat, and an ema donated by Japan's first astronaut, Akiyama Toyohiro, after returning safely in 1990 from his maiden voyage in space (figures 14.7 and 14.8). The protector of shippers and fishers has become, for some people anyway, a god for the protection of long-distance travel.

Walking down into the town, I reflect upon the many changes I have seen on the mountain. Some of the additions since 1912 are startling: the astronaut and the solar boat, the encircled gold symbol transformed from red to

⊛ **14.5** (*opposite*) Purification ceremony in the main sanctuary. The priest first waves the gold wand (gohei) and its streamers over, then touches it upon, the heads of the worshippers, extending the blessing of the god to the petitioners. (Photo by Steve Cantley, with the permission of Kotohira Shrine.)

⊛ 14.7 Solar-powered boat and other donations to Kotohira Shrine at the Ema Hall, 2003. This boat highlights the continuing blessings of the deity on seafaring vessels, no matter how technology changes. (Photo by Steve Cantley, with the permission of Kotohira Shrine.)

gold, the cuteness of the new Konpira dog. Such changes highlight above all the position of Kotohira Shrine *within* history, not outside it. Far from being frozen in an ideal past, the mountain shrine is dependent for its survival upon the abilities of its priests to negotiate successfully between several groups, including rulers, worshippers, and donors, as well as owners of businesses related to the shrine. That Kotohira Shrine in the early twenty-first century is still large, prosperous, and even completing a major rebuilding project testifies to the skill of the present priest, his advisers, and his predecessors in navigating the waters of political, cultural, and economic change.

The history of the shrine can therefore be seen as a concentration of larger forces in history. Indeed, the story of Kotohira Shrine not only during its growing popularity under the Tokugawa but especially during the dramatic changes of the Meiji era can draw our attention to important aspects of those times that, while often acknowledged, are rarely emphasized in analyses of the age.

Throughout, the story of Konpira highlights the ongoing connections between politics and the gods—and the lasting impact of those connections on the physical and ritual landscape of Japan. Minor lords from the four-

✿ **14.8** Ema donated to Kotohira Shrine by Akiyama Toyohiro, Japan's first astronaut, after returning safely in 1990 from his maiden voyage in space. With this offering, prominently displayed by the priests even while the Ema Hall was being reconstructed, the god of sailors and shippers is seen to extend its protection over travel in spaceships as well. (Photo by Steve Cantley, with the permission of Kotohira Shrine.)

teenth to the sixteenth centuries sponsored the Thirty Protective Deities of the Lotus Sutra in response to outside threats, holding lectures and rituals on the tenth day of the tenth month: the day that would later become the great festival of Konpira. The conquering warlord Chōsokabe Motochika claimed the title of the universal king Mahābrahman, commemorating his short-lived dominance with the construction of a gate that, like the mountain itself, has been reinterpreted ever since. His successors—first Hideyoshi's general, Sengoku, then the Ikoma and finally the Matsudaira lords—sponsored the rites of Konpira according to the Golden Light Sutra, calling upon the protection and benefits of the fierce general of the gods in tandem with rites to Fudō Myōō and other deities of the esoteric rites. Working with local lords, the Shingon priests of Konpira developed a cult of Fudō Myōō and tengu on the mountain; then, appealing to increasingly influential members of the imperial court, identified the Indian deity with the kami Ōmononushi as well. From decade to decade, with the rise and fall of potential donors—whether rulers seeking legitimacy and benefits, entrepreneurs seeking status and wealth, or playgoers and pilgrims in the 1850s finding reassurance in the powers of the tengu once again—the concerns of sponsors, worshippers, and the priests and business owners who appealed to them became inscribed in the buildings, monuments, rhetoric, and rites of the gods.

These processes of religious and political change by no means stopped with the rise of the modern nation-state in the nineteenth and twentieth centuries. Just as successive rulers in earlier eras espoused new gods to legitimize themselves, the leaders of the Meiji government in 1868 encouraged the transformation of existing deities into exclusively nativist kami allied with the new, imperial regime. What the history of the Konpira-Kotohira conversion highlights, however, is the span of five or six years during which the new government in Tokyo seemed shaky, at best. Throughout those years, always prepared for the demise of the fledgling regime, the priests temporized between the immediate demands of nativists and the more long-standing interests of the majority of worshippers. Moreover, even after the government gained clear, national authority in 1873, divisions within the Meiji leadership produced constantly shifting policies that belie any sense of a consistent, monolithic state from 1868 on.

The contradictory policies that emerged from the central government concerning the relationship of shrines to the state, in particular, fostered the development at Kotohira not just of nativist practices but of nativist interpretations of the history, literature, and culture of Japan. Notably, however, the nation-centered attitudes fostered by the priests were not simple xenophobic, antitechnological reactions on the part of Shinto priests. Instead, through the shrine school and the Maritime Rescue Association, for instance, they disseminated and validated new ideas, technologies, and organizational forms from Europe and the United States in the name of the kami, of progress, and of the nation as a whole. Shinto priests, as much as Western-educated intellectuals, sought to support the progress of Japan: they simply legitimized their version of "civilization" with the authority of the gods and the culture of the nation, not the technological or geopolitical dominance of the West. As a result, the newly imported structures and sciences gained authority from multiple sources: they became Japanese, not foreign.

While the leaders in the Meiji government may have wavered on specific policies, directly and indirectly encouraging a merging of kami-focused and nation-focused activities at the shrine, they consistently exhibited a strong awareness of the broad, social foundation of politics. The history of Kotohira Shrine both before and after 1868 highlights the extent to which politics (and shrine survival) are inevitably social: jockeying for the ability to influence policy of necessity involves jockeying for the status that confers that ability. All societies have hierarchies, and despite the Meiji call for "men of talent," status was enormously important in the Meiji era as well as in the centuries that preceded it. In large part, this was due to the Tokugawa legacy of hereditary rank, a legacy only intensified by the emperor-centered ideology of the new regime.

The Meiji leaders skillfully exploited the desirability of titles and rank, first and foremost to entice daimyo to give up their domains, then also to construct a hierarchy of state shrines. By making aristocratic rank, no matter how low, accessible to priests, select landholders, and other leaders throughout Japanese society, the Meiji government harnessed the enthusiastic and innovative support of these influential people. This strategy of status proved effective throughout Meiji society. It was used by the priests of Kotohira, for instance, not only to attract members to the Reverence Association but also to encourage ambitious individuals to recruit even more members and donors on their own initiative. Clearly, status and hierarchy proved to be valuable tools. Indeed, it was through the creation of such hierarchies, alongside the revised aristocratic system, that the Meiji state so successfully modernized the country. The rulers did not do it themselves. Instead, they set up structures of incentives—widely recognized as desirable, because of earlier emphases on rank—that encouraged individuals throughout the country to dedicate their efforts, and their money, to the nation and its leaders.

Clearly, money was a crucial part of politics. Indeed, the priests' alliance with producers, shippers, landlords, village officials, and other members of the fledgling "middle class" that voted and filled government offices after 1890 began forming in the late seventeenth century because of money: the shrine needed donations, and the donors desired a community of similar people.[11] In large part because of the importance of these people as a source of income for the shrine, Kotohira became in many ways a shrine for this emerging middle class: the values of the Reverence Association, the art in the museum, the poetry gatherings, and the privileges extended to village leaders during wartime all supported and linked the god to the beliefs and practices of these educated local elites. Moreover, as the economy changed, so this network of privileged worshippers expanded, growing to include not only the owners of lacquer or latheworking factories, but the heads of heavy industries in shipping and manufacturing as well.

Indeed, the great variety of Kotohira's donors highlights a complexity in the Meiji economy that can often disappear from view. It was clearly not just Mitsubishi, Mitsui, and other mercantile, industrial powerhouses that shaped the economy of Meiji. Perhaps more important were the innumerable small craft businesses that benefited from new technologies. And, as the history of Kotohira's pilgrimage businesses shows very well, the service industry by no means disappeared. Instead, innkeepers and brothel owners worked alongside landlords and doctors to rule towns such as Kotohira, forging development policies often distinct from, though still coordinated with, the initiatives of shrine priests.

Not only small businesses but also small spenders shaped the economy and society more than we are often aware. Although the priests of Kotohira promoted a culture aimed at the influential, educated elite, they were also constantly forced to cater to the countless visitors who only dropped a coin or two in the offering box. Priests reinstated Kongōbō, reemphasized miracles, and even sent amulets by mail—all in response to popular demand. Through the accumulated power of myriad small expenditures, then, the commoners who could not vote in the Meiji era nevertheless influenced the role of Kotohira and similar kami in modern Japan. It is because of the great variety of worship among fishermen, farmers, prostitutes, sailors, factory workers, souvenir sellers, and countless others that the Great Kami Kotohira could not remain the exclusive, nativist deity it first appeared to be in 1868. The nativist kami, and Shinto as a whole, thus grew to encompass tengu, not just emperors, and miracles, not just reverence.[12]

The concept of Shinto—like the idea of Japan—grew into a grand, overarching category. In theory, it was well defined: as the worship of kami mentioned in the ancient texts or enshrined by the imperial government. In practice, however, this formal designation of Shinto hid a great variety. With no core "Shinto" texts, almost every aspect of shrines, sects, or lay associations remained open to interpretation and innovation. Like the skillfully constructed

encircled gold symbol, or the writing of the name of Kotohira, Shinto became a formal symbol whose conveniently and purposefully created ambiguity hid a great variety of ideas and practices.[13] For the shrine of Kotohira, like
every Shinto shrine in Japan and, indeed, many institutions around the
world, grew in large part through the power of ambiguity to unite myriad individuals for what they see as a single purpose: in this case, pilgrimage.

The processes of political maneuvering, social ranking, economic strate-
gizing, and cultural blurring at religious institutions are not unique either to
a "modern" period or to Japan. At Kotohira, they were clear for centuries before 1868. More broadly, they are evident in any organization, in any place,
that successfully survives over the changing years. As humans—constantly
seeking to survive and prosper in a world ultimately beyond our control—we
are constantly redefining our values as well as our relationships to the people
and the world around us: we are constantly rearranging the landscape of our
gods.

Head Priests of Konkōin and Kotohira Shrine

Head Priests (*bettō*) of Konkōin

Yūga (?–1579)

Yūi (1583–?)

Yūgon (1584–1600)

Yūsei (1600–1613)

Yūgen (1613–45)

Yūten (1645–66, d. 1675)

Yūei (1666–91)

Yūzan (1691–1736)

Yūben (1736–60)

Yūzon (1761–87)

Yūshō (1787–99, d. 1807)

Yūkō (1799–1811)

Yūshin (1811–13)

Yūgaku (1813–1813)

Yūji (1814–24, d. 1844)

Yūten (1824–32)

Yūnichi (1832–36)

Yūmoku (1837–57)   **Head Priests (*gūji*) of Kotohira Shrine**

Yūjō (1857–) ——————— [Kotooka Hirotsune (–1872)]*

Fukami Hayao (1873–86)

Kotooka Hirotsune (1887–92)

Minami Mitsutoshi (1892–95)

Nakagawa Takehiko (1895–98)

Kamimiya Takatoshi (Nov. 1898–Dec. 1898)

Kotooka Terusato (1898–1942)

Kuze Fuminari (1942–48)

Kotooka Mitsushige (1948–94)

Kotooka Yasutsugu (1994–present)

* From 1863 to 1872, Kotooka effectively acted as head priest, although there was no one formally appointed to that position.

Abbreviations

Chōshi Kotohira	Kotohira Chōshi Henshū Iinkai, ed. *Chōshi Kotohira.* 5 vols. Kotohira: Kotohira-chō, 1995–98.
KSSS	Nihon Kankō Bunka Kenkyūjo, ed. *Konpira shomin shinkō shiryōshū.* 3 vols. Kotohira: Kotohiragū shamusho, 1982–84.
KSSS nenpyō	Matsubara Hideaki, comp. *Konpira shomin shinkō shiryōshū nenpyōhen.* Kotohira: Kotohiragū Shamusho, 1988.
NN	Matsuoka Mitsugi. *Nennen nikki.* 141 vols. Bunkyū 4 (1864)–1904. Original at Tawa Archive, Tawa Shrine, Kagawa prefecture. Microfilm available at Kokubungaku Kenkyū Shiryōkan, Tokyo.
SBBS	Murakami Senshō, Tsuji Zennosuke, et al., eds. *Meiji ishin shinbutsu bunri shiryō.* 5 vols. Tokyo: Tōhō Shoin, 1926–29. Reprinted as *Shinpen Meiji ishin shinbutsu bunri shiryō.* 9 vols. Tokyo: Meichō Shuppan, 1984.

Notes

Introduction

1. Motoori Norinaga, *Kojikiden* (1798), vol. 3, reprinted in *Zōho Motoori Norinaga zenshū,* ed. Motoori Toyokai and Motoori Seizō (Tokyo: Yoshikawa Kōbunkan, [1902] 1926), 1:135. Translation from Daniel C. Holtom, *The National Faith of Japan: A Study of Modern Shinto* (London: Kegan Paul, Trench, Trubner and Co., 1938), 23–24. While Motoori Norinaga's interpretation of *kami* has dominated attitudes in the centuries since, not all scholars have identified *kami* in such tangible terms. See Susan L. Burns, *Before the Nation: Kokugaku and the Imagining of Community in Japan* (Durham, N.C.: Duke University Press, 2003).

2. Japanese language usage does not designate gender, so the gender of specific kami can be ambiguous at times. Amaterasu is most often referred to as female, however, both in English and in Japanese. The genders of other kami (including Konpira or Kotohira) can also be ambiguous; they will therefore be referred to as neuter.

3. Allan G. Grapard called for this kind of site-specific, politically and socially sensitive approach in his seminal work *The Protocol of the Gods: A Study of the Kasuga Cult in Japanese History* (Berkeley: University of California Press, 1992). Although Grapard focuses on an earlier time period at a site more closely tied to the imperial court, his analysis of the politics of ritual and institutional change at Kasuga is very similar to my approach in this book.

4. See, for example, Shikitei Sanba, *Ukiyoburo* (1809), cited in Moriya Takeshi, "Konpira shinkō to Konpira sankei o meguru oboegaki," in *Konpira shinkō,* ed. Moriya Takeshi, Minshū shūkyōshi sōsho, vol. 19 (Tokyo: Yūzankaku Shuppan, 1987), 181.

5. This book examines some of the combinations of deities on Mt. Zōzu. On the complicated relationships between kami, buddhas, and other gods, see Mark Teeuwen and Fabio Rambelli, eds., *Buddhas and Kami in Japan* (London: Routledge Curzon, 2003).

6. The translation of *shinbutsu bunri* as "separation of kami and buddhas" is derived from Allan G. Grapard's article "Japan's Ignored Cultural Revolution: The Separation of Shinto and Buddhist Divinities (*shinbutsu bunri*) in Meiji and a Case Study, Tōnomine," *History of Religions* 23, no. 3 (February 1984): 240–65.

7. On the study of religion in Japan, see Isomae Jun'ichi, *Kindai Nihon no shūkyō gensetsu to sono keifu: shūkyō, kokka, shintō* (Tokyo: Iwanami Shoten, 2003).

8. On translating *kami* as "god," see Norman Havens, "Immanent Legitimation: Reflections on the '*Kami* Concept,'" in *Kami*, ed. Inoue Nobutaka, Contemporary Papers on Japanese Religion 4 (Tokyo: Institute for Japanese Culture and Classics, Kokugakuin University, 1988).

9. Scholars differ on the extent to which a concept similar to "religion" existed in Japan before the Meiji period. Most scholars have focused on the newness of the concept in the mid-nineteenth century. For both references and an example of this scholarship, see Isomae, *Kindai Nihon no shūkyō gensetsu to sono keifu*, esp. 1–66. Michael Pye, in contrast, contends that the concept existed as early as the first half of the eighteenth century, more than a century before its more widespread use in the decades following 1868. "What Is 'Religion' in East Asia?" in *The Notion of 'Religion' in Comparative Research: Selected Proceedings of the XVIth Congress of the International Association for the History of Religions,* ed. Ugo Bianchi (Rome: L'Erma di Bretschneider, 1994), 115–22. I would like to thank Ian Reader for his help with these references.

Chapter 1

1. The text of Nakahara's diary has been published as Nakahara Suigekka, "Tabi no nikki," in *Chōshi Kotohira*, ed. Kotohira Chōshi Henshū Iinkai (Kotohira: Kotohirachō, 1997), 2:342–49; hereafter referred to as *Chōshi Kotohira*.

2. Nakahara does not make clear in his diary what he had prayed to Konpira for, but hints of illness in the text suggest that it might have been an issue of health.

3. Susan B. Hanley and Kozo Yamamura, *Economic and Demographic Change in Preindustrial Japan, 1600–1868* (Princeton, N.J.: Princeton University Press, 1977), 193.

4. Narushima Ryūhoku, *Kōbi nikki* (1869), in *Seto Naikai,* ed. Yoshii Isamu et al. (Tokyo: Sekkasha, 1965), 120.

5. Seto Naikai Rekishi Minzoku Shiryōkan, *Konpira sankei michi,* 2 vols., Kagawa-ken rekishi no michi chōsa hōkokusho 5 and 7 (Takamatsu: Seto Naikai Rekishi Minzoku Shiryōkan, 1991), 1:42.

6. Seto Naikai Rekishi Minzoku Shiryōkan, *Konpira sankei michi,* 1:52.

7. *Chōshi Kotohira,* 1:16–17. Prints of Mt. Zōzu up until the 1730s and 1740s clearly depict two large waterfalls close to Mt. Ōsa that disappear in later views of the mountain. Ibid., 5:32ff.

8. Nakahara, "Tabi no nikki," 344.

9. Seto Naikai Rekishi Minzoku Shiryōkan, *Konpira sankei michi,* 1:45.

10. Narushima, *Kōbi nikki,* 120.

11. Nihon Kankō Bunka Kenkyūjo, ed., *Konpira shomin shinkō shiryōshū,* 3 vols. (Ko-

tohira: Kotohiragū Shamusho, 1984), 3:62. Henceforth, this collection will be cited as *KSSS.*

12. *KSSS,* 3:12.

13. Studies of spatial perception and the construction of approaches to Japanese shrines have enunciated a principle of "interiority" (*oku*) in which the spaces of shrine approaches continually point in a single, inward vector. Ueda Atsushi, *Kūkan no enshutsuryoku* (Tokyo: Chikuma Shobō, 1985), cited in Suzuki Nobuhiro, Shimizu Hideki, and Shiota Yō, "Sandō kūkan ni okeru shikaku, kioku kōzō ni kansuru kenkyū," *Nihon kenchiku gakkai keikakuke ronbunshū,* no. 457 (March 1994): 100 n. 1. The example of Kotohira is a classic case. See, for example, Toshi Dezain Kenkyūkai, *Nihon no toshi kūkan* (Tokyo: Shōkokusha, 1971), 108–17; and Ushio Saitō, "Jinja sandō no kūkan kōsei ni kansuru kenkyū," *Nihon toshi keikaku gakkai gakujutsu kenkyū ronbunshū* 24 (November 1989): 457–62. My description of the landscape as a whole has been greatly influenced by Tony Hiss, *The Experience of Place* (New York: Knopf, 1990), especially his masterly analysis of Olmstead's Prospect Park in Brooklyn, New York, and my interpretation of the spatial hierarchy, in particular, draws upon Jonathan Z. Smith's analysis of Ezekiel's temple in *To Take Place* (Chicago: University of Chicago Press, 1987).

14. *KSSS,* 1:246.

15. Akatsuki Kanenari, *Konpira sankei meisho zue* (1847), reprinted with annotations by Kusanagi Kinshirō (Tokyo: Rekishi Toshosha, 1980), 118.

16. Akatsuki, *Konpira sankei meisho zue,* 119.

17. On the distinction between esoteric and exoteric, see Ryūichi Abe, *The Weaving of Mantra* (New York: Columbia University Press, 1999), 10–12ff.

18. Iwai Hiromi, *Ema* (Tokyo: Hōsei Daigaku Shuppankyoku, 1974), esp. 3 and 23.

19. Jippensha Ikku, *Zoku hizakurige shohen: Konpira sankei* (1810), reprinted in *Hizakurige sono ta,* vol. 1, Nihon meichō zenshū, Edo bungei no bu 22 (Tokyo: Nihon Meichō Zenshū Kankōkai, 1927), 477.

20. Akatsuki, *Konpira sankei meisho zue,* 119.

21. Muta Bunnosuke, "Shokoku kaireki nichiroku," in *Zuihitsu hyakkaen* (Tokyo: Chūō Kōronsha, 1979), 376.

22. Akatsuki, *Konpira sankei meisho zue,* 115.

23. *KSSS.* 1:250–59.

24. On the importance of practical benefits throughout Japanese religious practice, see Ian Reader and George J. Tanabe, Jr., *Practically Religious: Worldly Benefits and the Common Religion of Japan* (Honolulu: University of Hawai'i Press, 1998).

25. Nam-lin Hur, *Prayer and Play in Late Tokugawa Japan: Asakusa Sensōji and Edo Society,* Harvard East Asian Monographs 185 (Cambridge, Mass.: Harvard University Asia Center, 2000); Nelson Graburn, *To Pray, Pay, and Play: The Cultural Structure of Japanese Domestic Tourism* (Aix en Provence: Centre des Hautes Études Touristiques, 1983).

26. For the classic statements of the theory of liminality and communitas in pilgrimage, see Victor Turner, *Dramas, Fields, and Metaphors* (Ithaca, N.Y.: Cornell University Press, 1974); and Victor Turner and Edith Turner, *Image and Pilgrimage in Christian Cul-*

ture (Oxford: Blackwell, 1978). The primary tension in pilgrimage studies during the 1990s was the debate over whether pilgrimage brings people together (either through the shared experience of communitas or by using shared symbols to disguise conflicting religious discourses) or keeps them apart (by emphasizing the diversity of practices and confirming social, economic, and political divisions). On more unifying tendencies, see Simon Coleman and John Elsner, *Pilgrimage: Past and Present in the World Religions* (Cambridge, Mass.: Harvard University Press, 1995), esp. 208; in Japan, in particular, see James Foard, "The Boundaries of Compassion: Buddhism and National Tradition in Japanese Pilgrimage," *Journal of Asian Studies* 41, no. 2 (February 1982), 231–51; Winston Davis, "Pilgrimage and World Renewal," in *Japanese Religion and Society: Paradigms of Structure and Change* (Albany: State University of New York Press, 1992); and Karen A. Smyers, *The Fox and the Jewel: Shared and Private Meanings in Contemporary Japanese Inari Worship* (Honolulu: University of Hawai'i Press, 1999). On more diverse and divisive dynamics in pilgrimage, see the essays in John Eade and Michael J. Sallnow, eds, *Contesting the Sacred: The Anthropology of Christian Pilgrimage* (London: Routledge, 1991); and Susan Naquin and Chün-fang Yü, eds., *Pilgrims and Sacred Sites in China* (Berkeley: University of California Press, 1992); and, in Japan, Sarah Thal, "Sacred Sites and the Dynamics of Identity," *Early Modern Japan* 8, no. 2 (November 2000): 28–37.

27. The phrase *reigen arataka* is used in countless works to describe Konpira. See, for example, Akatsuki, *Konpira sankei meisho zue,* 4; and Jippensha, *Zoku hizakurige shohen: Konpira sankei,* 477.

Chapter 2

1. For a translation of the relevant section of the *History of the Kingdom of Wei* [Wei Zhi] (ca. 297 CE), see *Japan in the Chinese Dynastic Histories,* trans. Ryusaku Tsunuda (South Pasadena, Calif.: Perkins, 1951), 8–21.

2. Russell Kirkland, "The Sun and the Throne: The Origins of the Royal Descent Myth in Ancient Japan," *Numen* 44, no. 2 (May 1997): 109–52; Matsumae Takeshi, "Early Kami Worship," in *The Cambridge History of Japan,* vol. 1, ed. Delmer M. Brown (Cambridge: Cambridge University Press, 1993), 347–49.

3. Tim Barrett, "Shinto and Taoism in Early Japan," in *Shinto in History: Ways of the Kami,* ed. John Breen and Mark Teeuwen (Surrey: Curzon Press, 2000), 13–31.

4. *Taishō shinshū daizōkyō,* ed. Takakusu Junjirō, Watanabe Kaikyoku, et al., 85 vols. (Tokyo, 1914–22), vol. 16, no. 663 (p. 350), and vol. 16, no. 664 (p. 446). For English translation, see *The Sutra of Golden Light,* trans. R. E. Emmerick (Oxford: Pali Text Society, 1990), 74. In the Golden Light Sutra, as in the handful of other sutras in which Kumbhīra appears, the god is only one of many—a very minor figure. Why this minor deity was then selected for worship in Japan is an intriguing question, related perhaps to divinatory practices or a focus on protective deities in preparation for rituals.

5. Shanti Devi, *Hospitality for the Gods: Popular Religion in Edo, Japan: An Example* (Ann Arbor, Mich.: University Microfilms International, 1986), 25–42.

6. On Fotudeng's work for the emperor of the Later Chao, for instance, see Arthur F. Wright, *Studies in Chinese Buddhism,* ed. Robert M. Somers (New Haven, Conn.: Yale

University Press, 1990), 37–38, 130 n. 14. I would like to thank Timothy Barrett for drawing my attention to this reference.

7. *Nihongi,* trans. W. G. Aston (1972; reprint, Rutland, Vt.: Charles E. Tuttle Company, 1998), 2:65–66.

8. Translation in Wm. Theodore De Bary, Donald Keene, George Tanabe, and Paul Varley, comps., *Sources of Japanese Tradition,* 2d ed., vol. 1 (New York: Columbia University Press, 2001), 107.

9. This interpretation of the innovations of Kūkai's esoteric teachings draws heavily upon Abe, *The Weaving of Mantra.*

10. Ibid., chapter 8, esp. 344–57. For excerpts and analysis of the Golden Light Sutra and its use in early imperial Japan, see Mimi Hall Yiengpruksawan, *Hiraizumi* (Cambridge, Mass.: Harvard University Asia Center, 1998). Three Chinese versions of the sutra appear in the *Taishō shinshū daizōkyō,* vol. 16, nos. 663–65.

11. *Taishō shinshū daizōkyō,* vol. 9, no. 262. For English translations, see *The Lotus Sutra,* trans. Burton Watson (New York: Columbia University Press, 1993); and *Scripture of the Lotus Blossom of the Fine Dharma,* trans. Leon Hurvitz (New York: Columbia University Press, 1976).

12. *The Lotus Sutra,* 188.

13. Murakami Bōryū, *Shugendō no hattatsu* (1943; reprint, Tokyo: Meichō Shuppan, 1978), 71; Enjōji, ed., *Chishō Daishi zenshū* (Saga-ken, Ōtsu-shi: Enjōji Jimusho, 1918), 1118–19.

14. Willa Jane Tanabe, "The Lotus Lectures: *Hokke Hakkō* in the Heian Period," *Monumenta Nipponica* 39, no. 4 (Winter 1984): 393–407. On the political implications of such lecture and debate rituals, see Neil McMullin, "The Sutra Lecture and Doctrinal Debate Traditions in Early and Medieval Japan," in *Tendai shisō to higashi Ajia bunka no kenkyū* (Tokyo: Sankibō, 1991), 77–95.

15. On Kannon and the wish-fulfilling jewel, see Brian Ruppert, "Pearl in the Shrine: A Genealogy of the Buddhist Jewel of the Japanese Sovereign," *Japanese Journal of Religious Studies* 29, nos. 1–2 (Spring 2002), 1–33.

16. On the localization of universal buddhas, see Satō Hiroo, "Wrathful Deities and Saving Deities," in Teeuwen and Rambelli, *Buddhas and Kami in Japan,* 95–114.

17. Ichirō Hori, "Mountains and Their Importance for the Idea of the Other World," in *Folk Religion in Japan,* ed. Joseph Kittagawa and Alan L. Miller (Chicago: University of Chicago Press, 1968), 141–79.

18. *Chōshi Kotohira,* 1:108–9.

19. Dōhan Ajari, "Nankai Rurōki," in *Gunsho Ruijū,* rev. 3rd ed., vol. 18 (1932; reprint, Tokyo: Zoku Gunsho Ruijū Kanseikai, 1977), 474.

20. *Chōshi Kotohira,* 1:111, 179–80.

21. Ichihara Terushi and Yamamoto Takeshi, *Kagawa-ken no rekishi* (Tokyo: Yamakawa Shuppansha, 1971), 60–61.

22. Dōhan, "Nankai Rurōki," 175. On the identification of Kannon with the daugh-

ter of the dragon king, see Ruppert, "Pearl in the Shrine," 7, 10. The presence of Kannon (attendant of Amida) may also help explain the presence of Shōmyōin in the forest below.

23. Ruppert, "Pearl in the Shrine," 7.

24. Murayama Shūichi, *Miwaryū shintō no kenkyū* (Tokyo: Meichō Shuppan, 1983), 32–38; Ruppert, "Pearl in the Shrine," 10.

25. Mark Teeuwen and Fabio Rambelli provide an excellent introduction to these confusing relationships in "Introduction: Combinatory Religion and the *honji suijaku* Paradigm in Pre-modern Japan," in Teeuwen and Rambelli, *Buddhas and Kami in Japan,* 153.

26. Grapard, *Protocol of the Gods,* 75. Grapard, 74–97, examines several strategies for such associations at Kasuga Shrine. Iyanaga Nobumi, "*Honji suijaku* and the Logic of Combinatory Deities: Two Case Studies," in Teeuwen and Rambelli, *Buddhas and Kami in Japan,* 145–76, argues convincingly that religious experts in Japan may have identified local kami with Hindu deities mentioned in the sutras because they saw the Hindu gods as most analagous to kami in Japan.

27. On the relation of Yoshida Shinto to the Hokke cult, especially as concerns the Thirty Protective Deities, see Lucia Dolce, "Hokke Shinto: Kami in the Nichiren Tradition," in Teeuwen and Rambelli, *Buddhas and Kami in Japan,* 222–54.

28. Teeuwen and Rambelli, "Introduction," 47–48; Iyanaga, "*Honji suijaku* and the Logic of Combinatory Deities," 145–76.

29. *Chōshi Kotohira,* 1:200; Ichihara Terushi and Yamamoto Takeshi cite notations on sutras and the sponsorship of special protective rituals against the Mongols at Zentsūji and other temples in Sanuki province. *Kagawa-ken no rekishi,* 69–70.

30. *Chōshi Kotohira,* 1:200 and 3:53. On the promotion of the Thirty Protecting Deities by Nichiren's youngest disciple, Nichizō (1269–1342), in his work around the capital in the 1330s, see Dolce, "Hokke Shintō: Kami in the Nichiren Tradition," 228.

31. Thomas Conlan, *In Little Need of Divine Intervention* (Ithaca, N.Y.: Cornell University East Asia Program, 2001), 254–75.

32. *Chōshi Kotohira,* 1:187–88.

33. The ridge placard (*munafuda*) of this first Konpira Hall is now a secret treasure of Kotohira Shrine and cannot be viewed. The recorded text is reproduced in *Chōshi Kotohira,* 1:187. While the priests of Konpira claimed that this 1573 ceremony marked only the *rebuilding* of a shrine to the god, not its establishment, evidence for an earlier date is not conclusive. Matsubara Hideaki, "Tenshō zengo no Zōzusan," in Moriya, *Konpira shinkō,* 73. On Yūga's relationship to Nishi Nagao, see Keihan et al., "Korōden kyūki," in *Shinpen Kagawa sōsho,* shiryōhen 1, ed. Kagawa-ken Kyōiku Iinkai (Takamatsu: Shinpen Kagawa Sōsho Kankō Kiga Iinkai, 1979), 227–28; and *Chōshi Kotohira,* 1:189, which cites an 1825 genealogy of the priests of Mt. Zōzu.

34. Nisshū, *Chinju kanjō gakugo yō* (1552 or 1588), cited by Dolce, "Hokke Shintō: Kami in the Nichiren Tradition," 241–42.

35. Matsubara, "Tenshō zengo no Zōzusan," 73–75. On this ambiguity of the term *kami* or *shin* in Buddhist contexts as it relates to the term Shinto in particular, see Mark Teeuwen, "From *Jindō* to Shinto: A Concept Takes Shape," *Japanese Journal of Religious Studies* 29, nos. 3–4 (Fall 2002): 233–64.

36. Indeed, Yūga at some point copied a fifteenth-century record of Yūhan's life, inserting passages asserting not only that Yūhan had prayed and spoken to the god Konpira, but also that Yūhan had even founded a "Konpira temple" on "Mt. Matsuo." *Chōshi Kotohira,* 1:181, 190–91. Yūga's evocation of Yūhan would later form the basis for Zentsūji's claim of jurisdiction over Konpira. See chapter 4.

37. *Chōshi Kotohira,* 3:42. Thus, the only record remaining on the mountain from before 1576 is the ridge placard of the Konpira hall cited above.

38. Matsubara Hideaki, "Konpira shinkō to shugendō," in Moriya, *Konpira shinkō,* 63.

39. Miyake Hitoshi, *Shugendō: Essays on the Structure of Japanese Folk Religion* (Ann Arbor: Center for Japanese Studies, University of Michigan, 2001).

40. The text of the ridge placard of Chōsokabe's gate is partially reproduced in *Chōshi Kotohira,* 3:38. Matsubara, 'Konpira shinkō to shugendō," 60–61. Magakishima Kenshūshi, author of *Chūgoku meisho zue* in the early nineteenth century, commented that Chōsokabe built the gate "as an overall protective deity for the four provinces upon his pacification of Shikoku." Cited by Matsubara, "Konpira shinkō to shugendō," 63. On the associations of Mahābrahma in medieval Japanese texts, see Iyanaga, "*Honji Suijaku* and the Logic of Combinatory Deities," 159–73. I would like to thank David Gray for his assistance with this connection in particular and issues concerning the Golden Light Sutra in general.

41. The text is reproduced in Kagawa-ken Kyōiku Iinkai, ed, *Shinpen Kagawa sōsho,* shiryōhen 2 (Takamatsu: Shinpen Kagawa Sōsho Kankō Kikaku Iinkai, 1981), 649; and *Chōshi Kotohira,* 3:42.

42. *Chōshi Kotohira,* 3:42. Texts appear in Kagawa-ken Kyōiku Iinkai, *Shinpen Kagawa sōsho,* 2:649–51.

43. This and the following evidence is based on a lawsuit brought by Yūga against Yūgon's successor, Yūsei, in 1607. *Chōshi Kotohira,* 3:38–39.

44. Ibid., 2:31.

45. On the struggles of competing priests to obtain control over the cults to deify Hideyoshi and Ieyasu, for instance, see Herman Ooms, *Tokugawa Ideology: Early Constructs, 1570–1680* (Princeton, N.J.: Princeton University Press, 1985), chapters 1–5; and Bernhard Scheid, "Schlachtenlärm in den Gefilden der *kami,*" in *Wandel zwischen den Welten,* ed. Hannelore Eisenhofer-Halim (Munich: Peter Lang Verlag, 2003).

Chapter 3

1. *Chōshi Kotohira,* 3:48.

2. Ibid., 3:127.

3. Matsubara, "Konpira shinkō to shugendō," 64–65.

4. Nagaya Tadahide, "Goshichinichihō," *Misshū Gakuhō,* no. 234 (January 1934): 9; Abe, *The Weaving of Mantra,* 347.

5. Abe, *The Weaving of Mantra,* 348–49.

6. *Kōbō Daishi zenshū,* ed. Hase Hōshū (Tokyo, 1909–11; reprint, Wakayama-ken Ito-gun Kōya chō: Mikkyō Bunka Kenkyūjo, 1966), 1:821, cited in Abe, *The Weaving of*

Mantra, 350. On the relationship of the wish-fulfilling jewel to esoteric rites concerning sovereignty and the imperial regalia in Japan, see Ruppert, "Pearl in the Shrine."

7. On identification with Fudō Myōō as a central practice of shugendo, see Murakami Bōryū, *Shugendō no hattatsu*, 186–93. On more general Shingon visualization techniques, see Taikō Yamasaki, *Shingon: Japanese Esoteric Buddhism* (Boston: Shambala, 1988), esp. 154–59.

8. Cf. Abe, *The Weaving of Mantra*, 356.

9. He also defended himself against a challenge brought once again by the persistent Yūga. By the time Yūga presented his suit to the Ikoma lord in 1607, Yūsei had already consolidated his economic, political, and ritual hold on the mountain. He was able to exploit his connections to the Ikoma family against Yūga's accusations. Countering Yūga's charges of intimidation, Yūsei in turn charged Yūga with everything from selling fake Konpira amulets in the guise of a shugenja to raping women in Awa and fomenting unrest among shugenja in nearby Iyo province. Yūsei finally triumphed, and Yūga's suit was permanently laid to rest. Two years later, in 1609, Ikoma Kazumasa confirmed Konkōin's (and thus Yūsei's) acquisition of the lands of Shōmyōin, one of the issues that Yūga had originally raised in the suit. Matsubara, "Konpira shinkō to shugendō," 60; *Chōshi Kotohira*, 3:101–2, 127; 2:31.

10. *Chōshi Kotohira*, 3:47–48; Keihan et al., "Korōden kyūki," 234.

11. "Ikomasama onkawari no toki kokuchū jisharyō daka," in Kagawa-ken, *Kagawa sōsho*, 2:57–59.

12. Matsubara, "Konpira shinkō to shugendō," 65. Matsubara, however, accepts this inscription as written by Yūsei himself.

13. On the enshrining of Tokugawa Ieyasu at Nikkō, see, for instance, Ooms, *Tokugawa Ideology*, 173–86.

14. Iemitsu also established the *terauke* system around the same time, requiring residents to register with Buddhist temples in order to prove they were not Christian. At Konpira, such registrations apparently were handled by funerary and other temples in the town below; there are no records of Konkōin or the other subtemples within the precincts of Matsuoji performing this function.

15. *Konpira shomin shinkō shiryōshū nenpyōhen*, comp. Matsubara Hideaki (Kotohira: Kotohiragū Shamusho, 1988), 6; hereafter referred to as *KSSS nenpyō*.

16. On the structure and processes of Shingon rank in the Tokugawa era as well as the fees paid to monzeki for ranks and advancements, see Takano Toshihiko, *Kinsei Nihon no kokka kenryoku to shūkyō* (Tokyo: Tokyo Daigaku Shuppankai, 1989), 117–68.

17. Nishida Nagao, "Jisha no shuinjō aratame to sono kakikae," *Shintō shūkyō*, nos. 97 and 98 (December 1979): 1–35.

18. Keihan et al., "Korōden kyūki," 234.

19. Due to an unusual circumstance, Yorishige, the eldest son of the first Mito lord (Tokugawa Ieyasu's son), did not succeed his father as lord of the Mito domain. Yorishige had been born before his father's older brothers had produced heirs. In order to avoid upstaging his brothers, then, the lord of Mito sent his son to a temple to be raised in the priesthood. Therefore, it was the Mito lord's second son, born after his cousins, who suc-

ceeded to the leadership of the Mito domain. At age seventeen, Yorishige was then summoned from the monastic life by his uncle, the shogun Iemitsu, to become first the trusted lord of the Shimodate domain in present-day Ibaraki prefecture, and later the daimyo of Takamatsu. Ichihara and Yamamoto, *Kagawa-ken no rekishi,* 124–25.

20. At this time, Saita—the home of the Yamashita family—was placed under the Marugame domain. While the branches of the Yamashita family most directly involved with Mt. Zōzu moved to Konpira, they continued to draw on relatives—whether those still in Saita or others who had moved on to Uwajima or elsewhere—to provide heirs to the priesthood or political favors for Konkōin. *Chōshi Kotohira,* 3:50, 136–37. As evident here, and in chapter 4 below, religious institutions and personal ties bridged domainal boundaries.

21. Ichihara and Yamamoto, *Kagawa-ken no rekishi,* 125; Kagawa-ken, ed., *Kagawa kenshi,* beppen 2: nenpyō (Takamatsu: Kagawa-ken, 1991), 125–38; *Chōshi Kotohira,* 3:52–53.

22. *Chōshi Kotohira,* 3:48–50.

23. Ōsaki Teiichi, "Kotohiragū no enkaku," in *KSSS,* 1:18–21.

24. The imperial prince was, at the time, a monzeki of the Tendai denomination. Keihan et al., "Korōden kyūki," 243.

25. *KSSS nenpyō,* 6.

26. An undated copy of the *Konpira Daigongen Reigenki* is in the Tawa Archive at Tawa Shrine in Kagawa prefecture, accessible on microfilm at the Kokubungaku Kenkyū Shiryōkan in Tokyo.

27. Matsudaira Yorishige [attributed], "Sanshū michi Zōzusan engi" (1656), reprinted in *Kagawa-ken, Kagawa sōsho,* 1:434–35.

28. The scenes, in two scrolls, are reproduced in *Chōshi Kotohira,* 5:8–9.

29. Matsubara, "Konpira shinkō to shugendō," 57–59; *Chōshi Kotohira,* 3:377.

30. *Chōshi Kotohira,* 3:53–54; Keihan et al., "Korōden kyūki," 246–50.

31. *Chōshi Kotohira,* 3:48, 136.

32. Ibid., 3:56, 65.

Chapter 4

1. A surge in the number of theaters elsewhere around the country finally led to a decline in theater attendance at Konpira in the 1750s. Ibid., 3:163–64.

2. *KSSS nenpyō,* 7–8. Konkōin continued to issue periodic bans until 1824. *Chōshi Kotohira,* 3:166.

3. Nam-lin Hur, *Prayer and Play in Late Tokugawa Japan,* emphasizes this "culture of prayer and play" in the urban setting of Sensōji in Edo; Nelson Graburn earlier emphasized not only prayer and entertainment but also their inextricable connection to consumption in contemporary Japan in *To Pray, Pay, and Play.*

4. Matsubara Hideaki, "Konpira shinkō no rekishiteki tenkai," *Yūkyū* 44 (January 1991): 2.

5. The two screens have been reproduced in their entirety in the front of Kotohirachō Kigaka, ed., *Kotohirachō: chōsei shikō hyakushūnen* (Kotohira: Kotohirachō, 1990).

6. Cecilia Segawa Seigle, *Yoshiwara: The Glittering World of the Japanese Courtesan* (Honolulu: University of Hawaii Press, 1993), 48–54.

7. Nam-lin Hur, *Prayer and Play in Late Tokugawa Japan.*

8. Ibid.; Kasahara Kazuo, *Nihon shūkyōshi nenpyō* (Tokyo: Hyōronsha, 1974), passim.

9. *Chōshi Kotohira*, 3:64.

10. Matsubara Hideaki, "Kotohiragū no shozō shiryō ni tsuite," in *KSSS nenpyō*, 74–75; *Chōshi Kotohira*, 3:77.

11. *Chōshi Kotohira*, 3:65–67.

12. Marugame Shishi Hensan Iinkai, *Shinpen Marugame shishi*, vol. 2 (Marugame: Marugame-shi, 1994), 293–94.

13. *KSSS nenpyō*, 8.

14. *Chōshi Kotohira*, 3:76.

15. Ibid., 3:72.

16. Kondō Yoshihiro, "Sanchō no ayame: Kotohira shinkō no kentō," in Moriya, *Konpira shinkō*, 11–31.

17. Conrad Totman, *Early Modern Japan* (Berkeley: University of California Press, 1993), 145–46.

18. Iyomishima Shishi Hensan Iinkai, ed., *Iyomishima shishi*, vol. 1 (Ehime-ken, Iyo-mishimashi: Iyomishimashi, 1984), 361–63.

19. Ibid., 1:363.

20. *KSSS nenpyō*, 9; *KSSS*, 3:346.

21. *KSSS*, 3:205; Innami Toshihide, "Keidai no tōrō," in *KSSS*, 3:268.

22. *KSSS*, 3:238.

23. Ibid., 3:204.

24. Matsubara, "Konpira shinkō to shugendō," 55; and *Kadokawa Nihon chimei daijiten*, vol. 42, *Nagasaki-ken* (Tokyo: Kadokawa Shoten, 1987), 423.

25. See, for example, Ishizu Ryōchō, *Konpirasan meisho zue* (ca. 1804–17), in Kagawa-ken, *Kagawa sōsho*, 3:377.

26. *KSSS nenpyō*, 10.

27. Donations from people connected to copper mines continued. In 1737, for instance, investors in the Tachikawa copper mine, a competitor to Besshi, donated a pair of stone lanterns to the shrine. *KSSS*, 3:169.

28. Innami, "Keidai no tōrō," 268.

29. Iyomishima Shishi Hensan Iinkai, *Iyomishima shishi*, 1:346–51, 354.

30. Ibid., 1:346–47.

31. Ibid., 1:354.

32. Donald Keene, *World within Walls: Japanese Literature of the Pre-modern Era, 1600–1867* (New York: Columbia University Press, 1999), 11–148, esp. 24.

33. Yakuwa Tomohiro, "Kinsei ni okeru moji bunka no chiikiteki shintō—jūhasseiki zenpan ni okeru Echigo no haikai bunka to kanren shite," *Kokuritsu rekishi minzoku hakubutsukan kenkyū hōkoku* 97 (March 2002): 1–18.

34. *Chōshi Kotohira,* 5:9–10. The first set of scrolls was painted between 1658 and 1660; the second set was commissioned in 1671. The poems were commissioned and added later.

35. *KSSS nenpyō,* 10–11.

36. Uemura Masahiro, "Kinsei Seto Naikai un kinō no ikkōsatsu—Sanshū Shiwaku kaisen o chūshin ni," *Ōsaka Daigaku Keizaigaku* 33, nos. 1–2 (September 1983): 59–64.

37. *KSSS,* 3:164.

38. Uemura, "Kinsei Seto Naikai un kinō no ikkōsatsu," 64–65; Kihara Hirosaki, "Kinsei ni okeru Sanuki no kaisen ni tsuite," in *Naikai chiiki shakai no shiteki kenkyū,* ed. Matsuoka Hisato (Yamaguchi-ken, Tokushima-shi: Matsuno Shoten, 1978), 163.

39. *KSSS nenpyō,* 12.

40. Totman, *Early Modern Japan,* 157–59.

41. Amano Sadakage, *Shiojiri,* quoted in Moriya, "Konpira shinkō to Konpira sankei o meguru oboegaki," 185. For other examples, see *Zōzusan Konpira Daigongen reigenki* (undated).

42. Yunoki Manabu, *Nihon suijō kōtsūshiron,* vol. 6 (Tokyo: Bunken Shuppan, 1996), 94.

43. Matsubara, "Kotohiragū no shozō shiryō ni tsuite," 77–78.

44. Keihan et al., "Korōden kyūki," 249.

45. Ibid., 250–52. On a dispute with Zentsūji from 1648 to 1651 that may have contributed to this emphasis, see Marugame Shishi Hensan Iinkai, *Shinpen Marugame shishi,* 2:954–59.

46. Keihan et al., "Korōden kyūki," 249, 252. Tamon'in, located outside the temple precincts in the town of Konpira, was more than just another subtemple of Mt. Zōzu. Founded by a vassal of the Tosa warlord Chōsokabe Motochika who became a disciple of the ascetic Yūsei, Tamon'in retained strong ties to the subsequent lords and people of the Tosa domain, from whom it received significant support. Thus, at Konpira, Konkōin stood at the peak of the administrative hierarchy, but Tamon'in—with its own power base—retained a measure of independence, managing relations with shugendo institutions and overseeing many affairs in the town on behalf of Konkōin on the mountain above. Matsubara, "Konpira shinkō to shugendō," 66–68.

47. Keihan et al., "Korōden kyūki," 250–51.

48. Ibid., 252.

49. Teeuwen, "From *Jindō* to Shinto." See also chapter 2 above.

50. Teeuwen, "From *Jindō* to Shinto," 242–43.

51. On Yoshida's creation of "Shinto" rituals out of Shingon traditions and the relation of his Shinto to India, see Allan G. Grapard, "The Shinto of Yoshida Kanetomo," *Monumenta Nipponica* 47, no. 1 (Spring 1992): 27–58.

52. Nishida Nagao, ed., *Urabe Shintō,* Shintō taikei ronsetsuhen 8 (Tokyo: Shinto Taikei Hensankai, 1985), 28. I would like to thank Bernhard Scheid for pointing out this passage.

53. On Yoshikawa Koretaru and Yamazaki Ansai, see, for example, Ooms, *Tokugawa Ideology,* 194ff.

54. Onishi Kashun, *Tamamoshū,* reproduced in Kagawa-ken, *Kagawa sōsho,* 3:26.

55. Yoshikawa Koretaru, "Nihon shoki shindai maku kaden bunsho," no. 6, in Shintō taikei ronsetsu hen 10 Yoshikawa Shintō, ed. Shintō Taikei Hensankai (Tokyo: Shintō Taikei Hensankai, 1983), 241. For the ease of readers unfamiliar with the long names of Japanese deities, such as Ōnamuchi no mikoto, they will be referred to by their single iden-tifying name, for example, Ōnamuchi.

56. This fourth Mito lord, Tokugawa Munetaka, was also the lord who presented the (yet incomplete) *Dai Nihonshi* to the bakufu in 1720.

57. *KSSS nenpyō,* 9.

58. Kikuchi Taketsune, "Sanukishū Nakagun Zōzusan Konpira kami shinshi ki," in Kagawa-ken, ed., *Kagawa sōsho,* 1:436.

59. Ibid.

60. Ibid.

61. Ibid., 437–39.

62. Matsubara, "Konpira shinkō to shugendō," 57.

63. *KSSS nenpyō,* 11–13.

64. Takano, *Kinsei Nihon no kokka kenryoku to shūkyō,* 123–24.

65. Kotohiragū, ed., *Kotohiragū sūkeishi,* 4 vols. (Kotohira: Kotohiragū, 1933), vol. 4; *KSSS nenpyō,* 11–17.

66. *Chōshi Kotohira,* 3:203.

67. Ibid., 3:85, 136.

68. Ibid., 3:203. Such imperial appointments still required religious conferment. Yūben thus received his new Buddhist investiture from the monzeki of Kaizuishin'in, a young priest who would soon return to lay life as Kujō Naozane, later to become Minister of the Left and, eventually, regent. It is not implausible that his connections to the Kujō family played a role in this development.

69. Ibid., 3:202–3. Indeed, such gifts and fees—for adoption, for rank, for induction into flower-arranging or poetic lineages of knowledge, and the like—served as a major source of income for the aristocratic houses. Fujita Satoru, *Bakumatsu no tennō* (Tokyo: Kōdansha, 1994), 34. Takano, *Kinsei Nihon no kokka kenryoku to shūkyō,* 116–43.

70. Tokutomi Iichirō, *Hōreki Meiwa hen* (Tokyo: Min'yūsha, 1926), 124–33.

71. *Chōshi Kotohira,* 3:86.

72. Ibid., 3:87. The continuing designation of Konpira as Daigongen perhaps re-flected the discomfort of the sekkanke with the Suika teachings so enthusiastically adopted by members of the lesser aristocracy. This tension had resulted in the Hōreki Incident of 1758–59, in which men who taught Takenouchi Shikibu's Suika Shinto interpretations of the *Nihon Shoki* to the young emperor Momozono were punished and Takenouchi was ex-iled from Kyoto. Tokutomi Iichirō, *Hōreki Meiwa hen.*

73. Thus, in 1762, for instance, Hashikuraji in the mountains of nearby Awa Prov-ince sent a delegation to Konkōin to secure recognition of its enshrinement of Konpira Daigongen. Matsubara, "Konpira shinkō to shugendō," 68. This relationship would cause problems in later years as the shugendo site Hashikuraji, allied with Tamon'in, promoted itself as the "inner temple" (*okunoin*) of Konpira. See chapter 11, below.

74. Matsubara, "Konpira shinkō to shugendō," 70.

75. See, for instance, Ueda Akinari's 1776 *Ugetsu monogatari* (Tokyo: Iwanami Shoten, 1934); and Takizawa Bakin's 1807 *Chinsetsu yumiharizuki,* Nihon koten bungaku taikei 60–61 (Tokyo: Iwanami Shoten, 1958–62).

Chapter 5

1. *KSSS,* 3:180.
2. *Chōshi Kotohira,* 5:66.
3. *KSSS,* 3:186.
4. *KSSS,* 2:46–47.
5. Matsubara, "Konpira shinkō no rekishiteki tenkai," 3.
6. See the photograph of "Sanuki Konpira Aki no Miyajima sankei kaijō hitori annai," in *Chōshi Kotohira,* 5:66.
7. Matsubara, "Konpira shinkō no rekishiteki tenkai," 3.
8. For examples of such prints featuring Yamatoya, Kōchiya, and Hiranoya in particular, see *Chōshi Kotohira,* 5:74–81. On the continuing importance of Tadaya and other such businesses in fund-raising for Konpira, especially for the construction of the Kondō in 1846, see Tanaka Tomohiko, "'Kondō Kishinchō' ni okeru Ōsaka no Kishinsha," *Kotohira,* no. 50 (1995): 186–88.
9. See, for example, Barbara Ambros, "Mountain of Great Prosperity: The Ōyama Cult in Early Modern Japan" (PhD diss., Harvard University, 2002), 115–64.
10. From the 1780s on, Konkōin received approximately 150 ryō a year in donations forwarded from the Toranomon shrine. In 1808, when the Toranomon shrine forwarded 14 *kan* 474 *monme* to Konkōin, that income constituted 4.6% of Konkōin's total income—compared to less than 1% derived from annual land taxes in Konpira itself, and a whopping 93% (291 kan 809 monme) from donations and fees on Mt. Zōzu. *Chōshi Kotohira,* 3:59, 73–75.
11. Onodera Atsushi, "Dōchū nikki ni miru Ise sangū ruuto no henkan: kantō chihō kara no baai," *Jinbun chirigaku kenkyū* 14 (1990): 231–55.
12. *Konpira reigenki* (Marugame,1819), cited in Kusanagi Kinshirō, "Bunka, Bunseiki no Konpira miyage," *Kotohira* 24 (1969): 31–34.
13. Innami Toshihide, "Konpira shinkō to tabi: Kotohiragū sūkei kōsha shiryō o chūshin ni," in *Gyomin no seikatsu to sono shūzoku,* Kanagawa Daigaku Nihon Jōmin Bunka Kenkyūjo chōsa hōkoku 18 (Tokyo: Heibonsha, 1995), 2:5–86; and personal interview with Ochi Kantarō, 30 October 1996. On innkeepers acting as *oshi* at Ōyama, for instance, see Ambros, *Mountain of Great Prosperity,* 115–64.
14. This original tale has been translated into English by Thomas Satchell as *Shanks' Mare* (Tokyo and Rutland, Vt.: C. E. Tuttle Co., 1960).
15. Jippensha, *Zoku hizakurige shohen: Konpira sankei* (1810).
16. "Shakutori onna yatoiire chaya dōshuku ichidō e mōshiwatashitomo seisho katsu dōnen jūgatsu tsuigan koikomi" (Bunsei 7.2), reproduced in *Chōshi Kotohira,* 2:312–18; 3:166, 198.
17. These hanegin amounted annually to as much as seventy thousand ryō in the

1820s and twenty thousand ryō during the recession of the 1830s. Kusanagi Kinshirō, "Konpira ōshibai kensetsu no genryō," in *Konpira ōshibai no subete,* Kusanagi Kinshirō senshū 15 (Takamatsu: Takemoto bukku sentaa, 1985), 15.

18. *Chōshi Kotohira,* 3:199–200.

19. Ibid., 3:166.

20. Takeda Kuninori, in conversation (Kōchi-ken, Hata-gun, Nishi Tosa-mura, Nishigahō, 5 December 1995). I would like to thank Mr. Takeda for his kindness and generosity in providing a personal tour of the area.

21. "Kotohira Jinja Yuisho Ryakki," recorded by Endō Haku. I would like to thank the Endō family and Mr. Kotō Shigeno of the Hirose-chō Kyōiku Iinkai for providing a copy of this information.

22. Anne Walthall refers to such lanterns and other local monuments as efforts toward local history writing by the nonintellectual peasants. Walthall, "Peripheries: Rural Culture in Tokugawa Japan," *Monumenta Nipponica* 39, no. 4 (Winter 1984): 387.

23. For swallowing an amulet, see the miracle tale related by Matsuoka Mitsugi in *Kotohira kokin reigenki* (1892), reprinted in "Shintoku monogatari yori," *Kotohirasan,* no. 4 (1932): 16. For amulet boxes, see "Omamoribako no shūnyū," *Kagawa Shinpō,* 24 January 1899, 2. Also personal interviews with former sellers of amulet boxes in Kotohira: Matsuura Ryōichi, Matsuura Kazumi, Orita Yaeko, Wada Yoshi, and Wada Masahide in Kotohira, 30 October 1996.

24. Miyata Noboru provides many examples of these individualized worship practices in *Kinsei no hayarigami,* Nihonjin no kōtō to shisō 17 (Tokyo: Hyōronsha, 1976). For an analysis of this kind of personalized practice in contemporary Inari worship, see Karen A. Smyers, *The Fox and the Jewel,* esp. 150–83.

25. Kotohiragū, ed., *Kotohiragū shiryō,* 90 vols. (Kotohira: Kotohiragū, 1911–44), vol. 32. Chart 3.1 has also been reproduced in Kanda Hideo, "Shinjin no sekai no hen'yō to aratana sukui," in *Minshū no kokoro,* ed. Hirota Masaki, Nihon no kinsei 16 (Tokyo: Chūō Kōronsha, 1994), 223.

26. Reader and Tanabe, *Practically Religious.*

27. On the dangers of ships and ema donated to Konpira in particular, see Mizobuchi Kazuyuki, "Ema," in *KSSS,* 1:97–104; on ema depicting boats more generally, see Ishii Kenji, "Senpakuga toshite no funa ema to sono ryūha," in *Umi to Nihonjin,* ed. Tōkai Daigaku Kaijō Gakubu (Sapporo: Tōkai Daigaku Shuppankyoku, 1977), 101–25.

28. Masaharu [pseud.], "Konpirasama," *Kagawa Shinpō,* 28 September 1907, 5.

29. Tanizawa Akira, "Sekihi ga kataru misaki no Konpira shinkō," *Kotohira* 45 (1990): 154–60.

30. On the late eighteenth- and early nineteenth-century origins of large numbers of this increasingly important rural elite in silk, cotton, tea, and saké production, see Edward E. Pratt, *Japan's Proto-industrial Elite: The Economic Foundations of the Gōnō* (Cambridge, Mass.: Harvard University Asia Center, 1999).

31. The Minami family still produces a highly respected local saké in its brewery, Tamanoi. The old house (and those of its neighbors, who stayed in the shipping buisness well into the twentieth century) shows evidence of continuing Konpira worship through-

out the years, including banners, amulets, and a small wooden shrine at the corner of the property still maintained for neighborhood worship of the deity. I would like to thank both the Minami family and Mr. Uchikawa Kiyosuke and his wife, Fumi, for the introduction and for assistance in examining the talismans on 11 November 1995. On the Minami family house, see also "Hansei makki no shuya," Tosa no minka 39, *Kōchi Shinbun,* 7 August 1995, 5. Tanaka Tomohiko has identified saké brewers as one of the most identifiable constituencies who donated funds for the building of the Kondō (Gold Hall) on Mt. Zōzu in 1846. "Kotohiragū shozō 'Kondō Kishinchō' ni miru Settsukuni no Kishinsha," *Ōsaka Joshi Tanki Daigaku Kiyō,* no. 20 (December 1995): 71–81.

32. See, for instance, the Konpira lantern erected in 1857 in Hasumi village, Shimane prefecture, not far from the river down which Zuhama Koichi, a wealthy landowner of the area who later donated a stone lantern to Konpira on Mt. Zōzu, sent the coal mined from his lands to the sea and thence to market. Interviews with Katō Shigezō and Zuhama Eitatsu (Zuhama Koichi's grandson, now a representative in the prefectural assembly, as was his father before him), June 1996. I would like to thank Katō Shigezō of the Shimane-ken Hasumi-mura Kyōiku Iinkai for arranging the visit and providing a tour of the area.

33. See, for instance, "Sanmei no sōfu hitoho no tōka ni jūri o hasu," *Kagawa Shinpō,* 1 July 1891, 3. Also Ichihara Terushi Sensei Kiju Kinen Ronbunshū Henshū Iinkai, ed., *Rekishi to minzoku denshō* (Tokyo: Maruyama Yoshio, 1992), 131–33.

34. One young man was able to raise funds for his pilgrimage after the elimination of samurai status in the early Meiji era by selling his short sword. Terada Den'ichirō, "Hachijūō danwa," *Tabi to densetsu* 108 (December 1936): 14–15.

35. Konpira kō were formed on the same model as *tanomoshi* kō, money-saving groups designed for general use. On various kinds of kō, see Sakurai Tokutarō, *Kō shūdan no kenkyū,* Sakurai Tokutarō chōsakushū, vol. 1. (Tokyo: Yoshikawa Kōbunkan, 1988).

36. Constantine Nomikos Vaporis, *Breaking Barriers: Travel and the State in Early Modern Japan,* Harvard East Asian Monographs 163 (Cambridge, Mass.: Council on East Asian Studies, Harvard University, 1994), 238.

37. Miyamoto Tsuneichi, *Ise sangū,* Tabi no minzoku to rekishi 5 (Tokyo: Yasaka Shobō, 1987), 142–44.

38. Kanda Hideo, "Shinjin no sekai no hen'yō to aratana sukui," 209–52.

39. Interview with members of the Konpira kō of Igisue village on Shōdoshima, Kagawa prefecture, 23 July 1996. I would like to thank Ishikawa Taeko and her son Nobuaki for introducing me to this kō.

40. Personal interview with Ishikawa Taeko and Nobuaki, 26 September 1995.

41. Hashida Zankyū, "Tōmyōdai to Konpira shinkō," *Susaki shidan,* no. 29 (November 1977): 26. On a visit to the local shrine before returning to one's house, see Hakoyama Kitarō, "Ise sangūshi: ryochū no nisshi," *Naganoken Minzoku no Kai Tsūshin,* no. 71 (10 January 1986): 4. On the construction of a small hut in which to serve sweet saké and celebrate, see Okazawa Shukei, "Meiji nijūhachinen sangū dōchūki," *Nagano* 56 (July 1974): 58.

42. Shinjō Tsunezō, *Shaji sankei no shakai keizai shiteki kenkyū* (Tokyo: Hanawa Shobō, 1964), 970–78.

43. This seems a classic illustration of Victor Turner's ideas of liminality and communitas. *The Ritual Process: Structure and Anti-structure* (Chicago: Aldine Publishing Co., 1969).

44. For a detailed discussion of the styles, prices, and skills of female entertainers at Konpira in 1869, see Narushima Ryūhoku's comments on his night at Konpira, *Kōbi nikki,* 121–22. On Narushima Ryūhoku's writing and his interest in entertainment, see Maeda Ai, *Narushima Ryūhoku,* reprinted in *Bakumatsu Ishinki no bungaku: Narushima Ryūhoku,* Maeda Ai chōsakushū 1 (Tokyo: Chikuma Shobō, 1989): 281–474.

45. This is the title of a study of Japanese domestic travel by Nelson Graburn, *To Pray, Pay, and Play.* The title of Nam-lin Hur's study of Asakusa Sensōji also makes the connection: *Prayer and Play in Late Tokugawa Japan.*

46. Whereas Nam-lin Hur emphasizes the importance of escape from the everyday, the approach here insists that such escape always occurs within broader structures that inevitably still link the "escapee" to reminders of his or her political, economic, or social position.

47. Terada Den'ichirō, "Hachijūō danwa," 24.

48. Foard, "The Boundaries of Compassion," 246–48.

49. Mark McNally, "Phantom History: Hirata Atsutane and Tokugawa Nativism" (PhD diss., University of California, Los Angeles, 1998).

50. H. D. Harootunian, in *Things Seen and Unseen: Discourse and Ideology in Tokugawa Nativism* (Chicago: University of Chicago Press, 1988), focuses on Hirata's validation of worship and work as one such solution especially popular among rural notables. In contrast, the elements of Hirata's work that were adopted by rural notables in and around Konpira suggest that priests and ritualists, at least, were more attracted to Hirata's ideas of the purification of kami worship and his identification of local deities with kami in the ancient texts. See below.

51. Motoori Norinaga, *Tamakushige,* cited in Hara Takeshi, *"Izumo" toiu shisō: kindai Nihon no massatsu sareta kamigami* (Tokyo: Kōninsha, 1996), 26–27. On the relationship of Motoori's interpretations to the classic myths, see Isomae Jun'ichi, "Reappropriating the Japanese Myths: Motoori Norinaga and the Creation Myths of the *Kojiki* and *Nihon Shoki," Japanese Journal of Religious Studies* 27, nos. 1–2 (Spring 2000): 15–39.

52. The Christian overtones of Hirata's theology have frequently been noted. See, for example, Richard Devine, "Hirata Atsutane and Christian Sources," *Monumenta Nipponica* 36 (Spring 1981): 37–54.

53. On the pilgrimage of dogs, see the letter to the Kotohira Shrine Office from Hara Tadao (2 December 1936), in Kotohiragū, *Kotohiragū shiryō,* vol. 74.

54. Hirata records that he heard the story from a visitor, then confirmed details with a priest in the area. Hirata Atsutane, *Tamadasuki,* reprinted in *Hirata Atsutane zenshū,* vol. 4 (Tokyo: Hirata Gakkai, 1912), 225–29. On the dating of the text, see Tahara Tsuguo, Seki Akira, Saeki Arikiyo, and Haga Noboru, eds., *Hirata Atsutane, Ban Nobutomo, Ōkuni Takamasa,* Nihon shisō taikei 50 (Tokyo: Iwanami Shoten, 1973), 663, 666. I would like to thank Mark McNally for his assistance.

55. Hirata Atsutane, *Tamadasuki sōron tsuika* (1819), reprinted in *Hirata Atsutane zenshū,* vol. 4.

56. Hirata, *Tamadasuki sōron tsuika,* 11.

57. *KSSS,* 3:206.

58. On the intellectual background and later activities of the Tengutō, albeit without a focus on tengu, see J. Victor Koschmann, *The Mito Ideology: Discourse, Reform, and Insurrection in Late Tokugawa Japan, 1790–1864* (Berkeley: University of California Press, 1987).

59. *KSSS nenpyō,* 40. Building on precedents from the reign of Emperor Kōkaku (r. 1779–1817), in particular, Kōmei used his ability to grant titles, confer ranks, and send representatives to worship at temples and shrines throughout the country in his campaign to assert the authority of the imperial court. Fujita, *Bakumatsu no tennō,* esp. 54ff. Also Fukuchi Shigetaka, *Kōmei tennō* (Tokyo: Akita Shoten, 1974), 11–15, 176–78, 229–40.

60. Reproductions of these prints, which all include both the Tall Lantern and the Gold Gate (and can therefore be dated after 1859), can be found in *Chōshi Kotohira,* 5:126, 133–35.

61. Citation by Matsuoka Mitsugi in "Tengu kanbun," reproduced in his diary, *Nennen nikki* (hereafter referred to as *NN*), 141 vols., Bunkyū 4 (1864)–1904, on microfilm at Kokubungaku Kenkyū Shiryōkan, Tokyo, entry for Keiō 2 (1866).7.30. W. G. Aston follows Chinese sources in identifying "tengu" as the constellation "Celestial Dog." *Nihongi,* 2:167.

62. Nakamura Kazumoto, *Motooriha kokugaku no tenkai* (Tokyo: Yūzankaku, 1993), 23–25.

63. Watanabe Shichimi, "Kotohiragū ni okeru shinbutsu bunri ni tsuite," *Kagawa shigaku* 1, no. 1 (January 1972): 25.

64. Arai Tomizō, ed., *Sanuki kyōdo kenkyū,* vol. 8 (Takamatsu: Sanuki Kyōdō Kenkyūkai, 1964), 3.

65. *Chōshi Kotohira,* 3:50. On Yano and Hirata, see Kageura Naotaka, *Iyoshi seigi* (Tokyo: Meichō Shuppan), 661–64, 691–93.

66. Yamashita Moriyoshi held much of the administrative authority on Mt. Zōzu. Matsubara Hideaki, "Kotohiragū toshokan zōhon bekkenki: Komatsu bunko ni tsuite," *Kotohira* 16 (1961): 98–99.

67. *NN,* Genji 1.2.24. Matsuoka's diary, *Nennen nikki* (*NN*), extends to more than 150 volumes, covering the years from 1864, when he was thirty years old, to near his death in 1904. Virtually untouched in studies of Konpira except for excerpts copied in the collection of shrine records, *Kotohiragū shiryō,* the diary provides detailed records of Matsuoka's interests: from the geographic distribution of amulet buyers at Konpira and copies of prayers, government edicts, and newspaper reports to students' grades in the shrine school and sacred texts and treasures. The original diaries are still in Tawa Bunko, the archive Matsuoka founded at Tawa Shrine in Kagawa prefecture. They are also available on microfilm at the Kokubungaku Kenkyū Shiryōkan in Tokyo.

68. *NN,* Genji 1.3.13–14, Keiō 1.4.27, Keiō 1.5.1, Keiō 2.1.12. Also *KSSS nenpyō,* 42–43.

69. For an overview of membership procedures of the Ibukinoya, see Anne Walthall, "Off with Their Heads! The Hirata Disciples and the Ashikaga Shoguns," *Monumenta Nipponica* 50, no. 2 (Summer 1995): 141.

70. After skimming the first eight chapters of *Koshiden* on Genji 1.9.4, for instance, Matsuoka commented on the "auspicious" (*medetaki*) nature of Hirata's teachings on Izanagi. Almost a year later, when Matsuoka had a chance to read the entire work more closely, he commented merely on the "novelty" (*mezurashiki*) of Hirata's ideas about Susano'o and other deities. *NN,* entry for Keiō 1.7.10.

71. Ibid., Genji 1.11.14.

72. Ibid., Keiō 1.9.20.

73. The name of the group also suggests that its members may have advocated reviving the Office of Rites (Jingikan) and establishing the primacy of worship in a new government structure, but I have been unable to locate further information on the agenda or membership of the association.

74. *NN,* Keiō 3.3.7. After this, Matsuoka consistently referred to the site as a shrine. See, for example, ibid., Keiō 4.2.18.

75. On the creation of a common identity through informal networks such as the Ibukinoya, see Walthall, "Off with Their Heads!" For the fascinating story of one woman's involvement with a Hirata school study group, see Anne Walthall, *The Weak Body of a Useless Woman: Matsuo Taseko and the Meiji Restoration* (Chicago: University of Chicago Press, 1998).

76. No mention of the Hirata school appears in histories of the prefecture, for instance.

77. *KSSS nenpyō,* 41.

78. *NN,* Keiō 4.3.1.

79. Ibid., Meiji 1.9.6.

Chapter 6

1. Administrative record of Konkōin, twelfth month of Keiō 3 (January 1868). One of the priests of Konkōin kept this administrative record, "Toriatsukai kiroku" (Keiō 3.12), reproduced in Kotohiragū, *Kotohiragū shiryō,* vol. 9.

2. Keiō 4.1.15 entry (miscopied as Keiō 4.4.15) of "Omote yakusho goyō todome," in Kotohiragū, *Kotohiragū shiryō,* vol. 32.

3. Hirao Michio, *Kaientai shimatsu ki* (Tokyo: Daidō Shobō, 1941), 316. For the same reason, Tosa also attacked the Matsuyama domain in Iyo province.

4. "Sharyō minsei kakiage danpen," in Kotohiragū, *Kotohiragū shiryō,* vol. 31.

5. "Yano Enzō naigansho," in Kotohiragū, *Kotohiragū shiryō,* vol. 29.

6. The text of "Saisei itchi no sei ni fukushi . . ." may be found in Umeda Yoshihiko, *Kaitei zōho Nihon shūkyō seidoshi,* 3 vols. (Tokyo: Tōsen Shuppan, 1971), 3:340–41.

7. The text of "Shinbutsu bunri rei" may be found in Umeda, *Kaitei zōho Nihon shūkyō seidoshi,* 3:341.

8. Haga Shōji, *Meiji ishin to shūkyō* (Tokyo: Chikuma Shobō, 1994), 40–42. In English, John L. Breen has emphasized most forcefully the importance of the Ōkuni faction in early Meiji Shinto. "Shintoists in Restoration Japan (1868–1872): Towards a Reassessment," *Modern Asian Studies* 24, no. 3 (1990):579–602.

9. Yasumaru Yoshio, Tamamuro Fumio, and other writers explain much of the force

behind the separation as a rivalry for dominance between disgruntled Shinto priests and the more powerful Buddhists who under Tokugawa policies had controlled the institutions and wealth of most religious sites (Yasumaru Yoshio, *Kamigami no Meiji ishin: shinbutsu bunri to haibutsu kishaku,* Iwanami shinsho, no. 103 [Tokyo: Iwanami Shoten, 1979], 53–57; Tamamuro Fumio, *Shinbutsu bunri* [Tokyo: Kyōikusha, 1977], 14–15.) On the most notorious such incident—Jūge Shigekuni's attack at Hie Shrine—see James Edward Ketelaar, *Of Heretics and Martyrs in Meiji Japan: Buddhism and Its Persecution* (Princeton, N.J.: Princeton University Press, 1990), 9–10; and Martin Collcutt, "Buddhism: The Threat of Eradication," in *Japan in Transition,* ed. Marius B. Jansen and Gilbert Rozman (Princeton, N.J.: Princeton University Press, 1986), 156.

10. Ketelaar, in *Of Heretics and Martyrs,* examines the strategies by which Buddhists transformed their religion in order to survive and prosper under the initially hostile Meiji regime.

11. See chapters 11 and 13, below.

12. See, for example, his letter to the accounting division of Konkōin informing them of his pledge of ten thousand ryō for the expenses of the Restoration on 6 July 1868 (Keiō 4.5.17), in "Keiō yonen gojōkyō nikki," in Kotohiragū, *Kotohiragū shiryō,* vol. 30. Later Buddhist accounts of the transition compiled in Murakami Senshō, Tsuji Zennosuke, et al., eds., *Meiji ishin shinbutsu bunri shiryō,* 5 vols. (Tokyo: Tōhō Shoin, 1926–29), reprinted as *Shinpen Meiji ishin shinbutsu bunri shiryō,* 9 vols. (Tokyo: Meichō Shuppan, 1984), 9:462–63 reproduced a document that Yūjō purportedly submitted to the government, reasserting the Buddhist origin and nomenclature of Konpira Daigongen. Subsequent references to this work will appear in the notes as *SBBS.*

13. "Sanuki Konpira no enkaku" (1912), in *SBBS,* 9:462–65.

14. By identifying Kotohira with Ōkuninushi—according to Hirata, the ruler of the hidden world of the gods—Yūjō in effect aligned himself with the Hirata faction of nativists, as opposed to the more influential Ōkuni faction that focused on Amaterasu and the imperial line. It seems unlikely that Yūjō was aware of these nuances at the time, or that he had much choice: Hirata's interpretation of Konpira as both kami and emperor was the most promising nativist identification of Konpira available. Kotohira's alignment with the Hirata faction, however, would prove important in the shrine's struggles for status in the early 1870s. See chapter 7, below.

15. The writing of the name of the shrine changed four times between 1868 and 1890. In 1868, the shrine, first called Kotohira Jinja (following Hirata Atsutane's orthography), was promoted one month later, after Yūjō's petition, to Kotohiragū, written with the character for gold. In 1871, the government began referring to it as Kotohira Jinja once again, this time combining the two writings, with "koto" from Hirata's version and "hira" from "Kon*pira.*" It was not until 1889 that the Home Ministry finally approved the return to "Kotohiragū," complete with "gold." The ambiguity of Konpira/Kotohira further makes transliteration in English problematic. I refer to the formal Shinto institution on the mountain, the mountain itself, and, after its official change of name in 1873, the town, as "Kotohira." More general, popular, or informal references to the shrine and deity will be rendered as "Konpira." Printed sources will be transliterated according to the actual characters used, even when clearly condensed to suggest the alternate reading. Any glossing in the original, however, will be followed.

16. "Kotooka," read alternately as "Kinryō," also denoted the old Chinese capital of Nanjing—an evocation frequently exploited by priests and poets both before and after 1868. I would like to thank Nanxiu Qian for bringing this reference to my attention.

17. *Chokusai no yashiro* would be the Shinto equivalent of the site's Tokugawa-era status of *chokusaisho.* "Kinchiken," in Kotohiragū, *Kotohiragū shiryō,* vol. 85.

18. "Toriatsukai kiroku, entry for Keiō 4.7, quoted in *SBBS,* 9:411–12.

19. See, for example, "Toriatsukai kiroku: kō no bu," entry for Meiji 1–2, in Kotohiragū, *Kotohiragū shiryō,* vol. 9. Michael Lewis vividly depicts the comparable arrival in Etchū of loyalist forces, likewise referred to by their domainal name. *Becoming Apart: National Power and Local Politics in Toyama, 1868–1945* (Cambridge, Mass.: Harvard University Asia Center, 2000), 1–2.

20. For example, see references to the "Tosa officials" (*Toshū yakunin*) setting up headquarters in Konpira, in "Gonaigan ni tsuki onjōkyō goyō todome yonban," in Kotohiragū, *Kotohiragū shiryō,* vol. 31.

21. Luke Roberts, "Tosa to ishin—'kokka' no soshitsu to 'chihō' no tanjo," *Nenpō kindai Nihon kenkyū* 20 (November 1997): 211–35. On han nationalism more generally, see Albert Craig, *Chōshū and the Meiji Restoration* (Cambridge, Mass.: Harvard University Press, 1967). In contrast, the innovative influence of nativist thinkers was due in large part to their formulation of a Japanese identity that cut across political and social boundaries.

22. Ishizu, *Konpirasan meisho zue,* 383. See, for example, Ōnishi Hyōjirō, *Konpiragū goreigenki* (Tadotsu: Taikyokukan, 1903), 11; Andō Ichirō, *Konpira daigongen goreigen jikki* (Kan'onji: Miyoshi Gisaburō, 1911), 10–11; Ikoma Hōshō, *Kotohira monogatari* (Takamatsu: Shikoku Shinbunsha, 1949), 13; Ōsaki Teiichi, *Konpira monogatari* (1959; reprint, Kotohira: Kotohiragū Shamusho, 1988), 63–64; Tasaka Eiki, *Konpirasan no mukashi banashi* (Marugame: Taniguchi Kurafuto, undated), 16–17.

23. "Yano Enzō naigansho," in Kotohiragū, *Kotohiragū shiryō,* vol. 29. Luke Roberts examines the Tosa idea of and commitment to petition boxes in his article "The Petition Box in Eighteenth-Century Tosa," *Journal of Japanese Studies* 20, no. 2 (1994): 423–58.

24. Sanaki Nobuo, "Miyaji Hikosaburō to Kotohira," *Kotohira* 3, no. 7 (10 July 1936): 5–7. Also "Yano Enzō naigansho," in Kotohiragū, *Kotohiragū shiryō,* vol. 29. Miyaji was Yagi's hereditary surname, abandoned while he was hiding from shogunate authorities during his years of loyalist activism.

25. Sanaki, "Miyaji Hikosaburō to Kotohira," 7. An internal shrine report asserted that Yagi and his assistants used only one thousand ryō for helping the needy and repairing bridges and riverbanks ruined by flooding and squandered the remaining four thousand ryō on their own entertainment in special brothels that they set up. "Yano Enzō naigansho," in Kotohiragū, *Kotohiragū shiryō,* vol. 29.

26. Sakamoto Koremaru, *Kokka shintō keisei katei no kenkyū* (Tokyo: Iwanami Shoten, 1994), 23. Exceptions were also granted to Ise Shrine and other "Great Shrines" (*taisha*), but these options were not available to Kotohira.

27. See the reproduction of Kotooka's 1868.8.13 petition in "Gonaigan ni tsuki onjōkyō goyō todome yonban," in Kotohiragū, *Kotohiragū shiryō,* vol. 31; it can also be found as an excerpt from the *Dajō ruiten,* vol. 122, in *SBBS,* 9:375–77.

28. "Toriatsukai kiroku: kō no bu," entry for Meiji 2.3, in Kotohiragū, *Kotohiragū*

shiryō, vol. 9; *SBBS,* 9:383–84; and "Gonaigan ni tsuki onjōkyō goyō todome yonban," entry for Keiō 4.9.14 in Kotohiragū, *Kotohiragū shiryō,* vol. 31. For documentation in the central government, see "Sanuki Kotohiragū o motte chokusai jinja to nasu" (Keiō 4.9.13), in *Dajō ruiten,* vol. 1.

29. This supports Sakamoto Koremaru's conclusion, in his study of the development of the state shrine system, that the Office of Rites did not decide issues of *chokusai* status until approached individually by each shrine. By 1870, there were thirty *chokusaisha,* to which official envoys were periodically sent with offerings from the imperial household. Sakamoto, *Kokka shintō keisei katei no kenkyū,* 52 and 69 n. 21.

30. Yamashita Sakae, "Hirata Atsutane, Rai San'yō, Yoshida Shōin no Konpira sanjōsange ni ataeta eikyō ni tsuite," *Kotohira* 39 (1984): 216.

31. "Tangan tatematsuru sōrō kōjō no oboe," in *Kotohiragū shiryō hoi,* ed. Kotohiragū, 8 vols. (Kotohira: Kotohiragū, 1913–19), vol. 5.

32. "Gonaigan ni tsuki onjōkyō goyō todome yonban," in Kotohiragū, *Kotohiragū shiryō,* vol. 31.

33. *KSSS nenpyō,* 44.

34. Ibid., 44; "Kinchiken," in Kotohiragū, *Kotohiragū shiryō,* vol. 85; "Gonaigan ni tsuki onjōkyō goyōtodome goban," entry for September 23, in Kotohiragū, *Kotohiragū shiryō,* vol. 28. Kotooka's donations were not unique. Much of the budget of the early Meiji government was covered by gifts and loans from wealthy temples, merchants, lords, and the like. Ketelaar, *Of Heretics and Martyrs,* 71.

35. Kotohiragū, *Kotohiragū shiryō hoi,* vol. 5.

36. "Tenchō goishin ni tsuki gotōsha go henkaku . . . ," in Kotohiragū, *Kotohiragū shiryō,* vol. 41.

37. Ibid.

38. "Kinchiken," in Kotohiragū, *Kotohiragū shiryō,* vol. 85.

39. *SBBS,* 9:390–92.

40. See, for instance, *Kotohiragū doku annaiki* (Konpira: Mitamadō, 1869).

41. This was delineated in Kotooka's first set of petitions on 2 August 1868 (Keiō 4.6.14). "Kinchiken," in Kotohiragū, *Kotohiragū shiryō,* vol. 85.

42. *NN,* Meiji 1.10.11.

43. "Toriatsukai kiroku: kō no bu," entry for Meiji 2.2, in Kotohiragū, *Kotohiragū shiryō,* vol. 9.

44. "Kotohiragū shinbutsu bunri shirabegaki," in *SBBS* 9:408.

45. Ibid., 9:395.

46. Narushima, *Kōbi nikki,* 121.

47. Although Kotooka lost administrative jurisdiction over the bulk of Konkōin's lands, it is common opinion in the town of Kotohira that he registered much of the land within the village as his own personal property. Land ownership records in Kotohira list Kotooka as the first owner on many early deeds.

48. "Omoteyakusho goyōtodome," in Kotohiragū, *Kotohiragū shiryō,* vol. 32, and "Sashiage tatematsuru issatsu," in Kotohiragū, *Kotohiragū shiryō,* vol. 47.

49. *SBBS,* 9:421–22; *NN,* Meiji 5.7.20. Arrangements for some priests to don Shinto

robes while entrusting the Buddhist ritual items to priests who retained their sectarian affiliation also occurred at Haguro Gongen and other sites at this time. See, for example, Ketelaar, *Of Heretics and Martyrs,* 74.

Chapter 7

1. Marius B. Jansen, *Sakamoto Ryōma and the Meiji Restoration* (New York: Columbia University Press, 1961), 357.

2. For lordly equivalents who ruled people but not land, see David L. Howell, "Territoriality and Collective Identity in Tokugawa Japan," *Daedalus* 127, no. 3 (Summer 1998): 105–32.

3. Umeda, *Kaitei zōho Nihon shūkyō seidoshi,* 3:29. While Konpira no longer answered to a specific head temple after 1739, it still belonged to the Shingon denomination as a whole and thus found itself subject more directly to the imperial court and the approval of the shogunate.

4. Ōkubo Toshiaki, et al., *Kindaishi shiryō* (Tokyo: Yoshikawa Kōbunkan, 1965), 56–57, translated in David J. Lu, *Japan: A Documentary History* (Armonk, N.Y.: M.E. Sharpe, 1997), 311–12.

5. Lu, *Japan,* 312.

6. Takie Sugiyama Lebra, *Above the Clouds: Status Culture of the Modern Japanese Nobility* (Berkeley: University of California Press, 1993), 46–47.

7. This proclamation has also been translated as declaring shrines as "sites for the performance of state ritual" (John L. Breen, "Beyond the Prohibition: Christianity in Restoration Japan," in *Japan and Christianity: Impacts and Responses,* ed. John Breen and Mark Williams [London: Macmillan, 1996], 88) or as "national establishments of rites" (Sakamoto Koremaru, "Religion and State in the Early Meiji Period [1868–1912]," *Acta Asiatica* 51 [1987]: 48), likewise emphasizing the premium placed on state ritual. Helen Hardacre translates *kokka no sōshi* as "the nation's rites and creed" (*Shintō and the State, 1868–1988* [Princeton, N.J.: Princeton University Press, 1989], 33) but is referring to a later time period.

8. Miyachi Masato emphasizes that this reduced and in some cases destroyed the local, communal nature of major shrines. Miyachi, "Kokka shintō keisei katei no mondai ten," in *Shūkyō to kokka,* ed. Yasumaru Yoshio and Miyachi Masato, Nihon kindai shisō taikei 5 (Tokyo: Iwanami Shoten, 1988), 570–71.

9. It is indicative of the strong history of autonomy on Mt. Zōzu that this ban on hereditary succession was not accepted by the priesthood. Whenever Kotooka was summoned to Takamatsu or Tokyo in 1872 and 1873, the priests on the mountain assumed he was to be appointed head priest. (See, for instance, *NN,* Meiji 5.4.7.) The idea that the priestship would be removed from the hereditary succession was unthinkable. Miyachi Masato describes the shock given to hereditary priests by the significant loss of income that this change entailed. "Kokka shintō keisei katei no mondai ten," 571.

10. The tenth-century *Engishiki* ranked only shrines affiliated with the imperial house. The Meiji system, in contrast, ranked imperial and provincial shrines, eventually extending the hierarchy down to village and even "unranked" shrines. Miyachi Masato emphasizes the drastic nature of these actions and their radical departure from earlier prece-

dent. "Kokka shintō no kakuritsu katei," in *Kindai tennōsei to shūkyōteki ken'i,* ed. Kokugakuin Daigaku Nihon Bunka Kenkyūjo (Tokyo: Dōmeisha Shuppan, 1992), 136–39.

11. "Kansha ika teikaku, shinkan shokusei nado ni kansuru ken," Dajōkan fukoku 235, Meiji 4.5.14. Unless otherwise noted, all laws cited are reproduced in Yasumaru and Miyachi, *Shūkyō to kokka.* Sakamoto Koremaru emphasizes that at the time of this pronouncement, *kanpeisha* were intended for worship by the state and *kokuheisha* were for worship by the province, the *kuni* or *koku* (Sakamoto Koremaru, *Kokka shintō keisei katei no kenkyū,* 80–81 nn. 1–2). As the central government gained power over the prefectures, *kokuheisha* were increasingly treated as national, not prefectural, shrines. From 1874, for example, they received funds for the performance of rites from the central Finance Ministry (Sakamoto Ken'ichi, *Meiji ikō jinja kankei hōrei shiryō,* Meiji ishin hyakunen kinen sōsho [Tokyo: Jinja Honchō Meiji Ishin Hyakunen Kinen Jigyō Iinkai, 1968], 80). For this reason, Hardacre and others translate *kokuheisha* as "national shrine." *Shintō and the State,* 28.

12. The one shrine of Sanuki province listed in the *Engishiki,* the Kumoke Shrine, has never been convincingly located and was not identified with any certainty in 1871, either.

13. "Tenpo jūninen yori Meiji rokunen ichigatsu itaru toriatsukai kiroku kō no bu," in Kotohiragū, *Kotohiragū shiryō,* vol. 9, reproduced in *Chōshi Kotohira,* 2:582.

14. On the lack of enforcement of directives from the central government in the new prefectures, still headed by the former domainal lords and their advisers, see, for instance, Kagawa-ken Kyōiku Iinkai, ed., *Shinshū Kagawa kenshi* (Takamatsu: Kagawa-ken Kyōiku Iinkai, 1953), 638.

15. *NN,* Meiji 4.6.24.

16. Ibid., Meiji 4.7.28.

17. For a general study of *haihan chiken* in English, see Michio Umegaki, *After the Restoration: The Beginning of Japan's Modern State* (New York: New York University Press, 1988).

18. The creation of Kagawa prefecture on 26 December 1871 was part of a nationwide consolidation of administrative units from 302 to 72 prefectures. This first Kagawa prefecture lasted until June 1873. Kotohira then fell under the jurisdiction of Meitō prefecture, then a second Kagawa prefecture in 1875, then Ehime prefecture in 1876, until finally settling as part of the third Kagawa prefecture in 1888, where it remains today. The town of Konpira was renamed Kotohira in December 1873.

19. Kagawa-ken, *Kagawa kenshi,* beppen 2: nenpyō, 238; and *NN,* Meiji 4.12.23 and 28.

20. Matsuoka Mitsugi taught nativist studies in the official school of the Takamatsu domain and during the brief existence of Takamatsu prefecture. A roster of domain employees dated Meiji 3.10.23 records Ōkubo Kitaru as the highest ranking person in the domainal educational system. See Kagawa-ken, ed., *Kagawa kenshi,* vol. 5 (Takamatsu: Shikoku Shinbunsha, 1987), 33. Matsuzaki Tamotsu was the younger brother of the locally renowned xenophobic loyalist Matsuzaki Shibuuemon, whose assassination by retainers of the former Takamatsu lord in 1869 prompted punitive actions by the Meiji government against the Takamatsu domain. Kotooka Mitsushige, *Kotohiragū* (Tokyo: Gakuseisha, 1970), 202. On Matsuzaki Shibuuemon, see Shikoku Shinbunsha, ed., *Sanuki jinbutsu*

fūkei (Tokyo: Maruyama Gakugei Tosho, 1984), 10:39–60. Matsuoka, the oldest of the three men and the most well versed in Shinto ritual and shrine administration, served as the expert on ritual and liturgical matters. See, for example, *NN,* Meiji 5.1.25 and Meiji 5.2.19. In 1872, Matsuoka was forty-two years old, Ōkubo thirty-nine, Matsuzaki thirty-five, and Kotooka thirty-two. Of the later appointees (see below), Miyazaki would have been forty-one in 1872, and Fukami thirty-one. The birth dates are recorded in *NN,* 30 April 1873.

21. This de facto demotion of Kotooka was characteristic of the treatment of formerly hereditary head priests around the country. Miyachi Masato, "Kokka shintō keisei katei no mondai ten," 571.

22. On the appointment of police, see Kagawa-ken, *Kagawa kenshi,* 5:98.

23. Report from Matsuzaki Tamotsu to Matsuoka Mitsugi, recorded in *NN,* Meiji 5.2.19.

24. Ibid., Meiji 5.2.19.

25. Ibid., Meiji 5.3.21 and Meiji 5.3.22. During the early years of the Meiji period, various forms of coin and paper money issued by the shogunate and different domains were still in circulation. The money had to be sorted before being converted into a single currency on the Osaka exchange. *NN,* Meiji 5.4.5 and passim.

26. Matsuoka's occasional records in his diary are virtually the only records of amulet sales and shrine income until the appearance of sporadic newspaper items in the 1890s. Since shrines in Japan have been private institutions since 1946, they guard even historical information about their income very closely. Personal interview with Shinano Itsuki.

27. *NN,* Meiji 5.3.9 and Meiji 5.4.27.

28. Ibid., Meiji 5.5.16 and Meiji 5.5.18.

29. Miyazaki was appointed by the governor on 29 April 1872 (Meiji 5.3.22) and was also ranked above Kotooka. He was born in 1831 as a samurai of the Tosa domain.

30. *NN,* Meiji 5.4.12. The main shrine would finally be rebuilt beginning in 1877.

31. Ibid., Meiji 5.3.9.

32. A copy of the proposal with the prefecture's responses appended can be found in "Kotohiragū shinbutsu bunri shirabekaki," in *SBBS,* 409–10, as well as in *NN,* Meiji 5.4.24, and Kotohiragū, *Kotohiragū shiryō hoi,* vol. 7. The copy in *SBBS* is unattributed; Matsuoka's *Nennen nikki* attributes the document to the four prefectural appointees; the shrine's copy attributes it to Miyazaki and Kotooka. Since Matsuoka's diary was written contemporaneously with the events, later Buddhists gave evidence that Kotooka promised the images to them, and the shrine has a continuing interest in attributing significant events on the mountain to members of the Kotooka family, I find attribution to the prefectural appointees most plausible. Indeed, the shrine's collection of documents has a history of altering texts to conform to its desired image. Just as, in this case, the shrine attributed every major change at the shrine during the modern period to members of the Kotooka family, so did copies made by Konkōin of a 1668 letter delete the references to mountain practitioners (*shugenja*) that had apparently been included. Matsubara Hideaki, "Konpira shinkō to shugendō," 67.

33. Historians have attributed the conversion of popular syncretic sites such as Konpira primarily to policies and appointments made by the Ministry of Doctrine after its es-

tablishment in 1872. As seen both at Ise Shrine (Yasumaru, *Kamigami no Meiji ishin,* 124–28) and at Kotohira, however, the abolition of the domains and establishment of prefectures was a crucial, if not determining, factor in such conversions, for the new centrally appointed governors in turn hired men committed to carrying out the central government policy. Miyachi Masato cites similar examples. Miyachi, "Kokka Shintō keisei katei no mondai ten," 567, and "Kokka shintō no kakuritsu katei," 136.

34. See, for instance, Yamaguchi Ichitarō, *Kotohirasan zenzu* (Kyoto, 1879); Fujimoto Chōjirō, *Kotohirasan zenzu* (Kotohira, 1882), and others.

35. *NN,* passim.

36. Sakamoto Koremaru, "Religion and State," 45–58; Yasumaru, *Kamigami no Meiji ishin,* 72 and 121–22; Breen, "Beyond the Prohibition," 75–93.

37. Sakamoto Koremaru points out the controversial nature of this shift, suggesting that the policy change did not reflect the majority view of the Meiji oligarchs. "Religion and State." On the importance of treaty revision and the diplomatic problem of the ban on Christianity, see also Miyachi, "Kokka shintō no kakuritsu katei," 144–45.

38. The translation of *kyōdōshoku* as "doctrinal instructors" is taken from James Ketelaar, *Of Heretics and Martyrs.* Helen Hardacre (*Shintō and the State*) refers to the *kyōdōshoku* as "National Evangelists," which suggests an emphasis on conversion that is more appropriate to the missionizing efforts that characterized efforts before the establishment of the Ministry of Doctrine.

39. This translation of the ministry's announcement on 3 June 1872 (Meiji 5.4.28) is based on Ketelaar, *Of Heretics and Martyrs,* 106.

40. *NN,* Meiji 5.5.18. The other government-appointed priests at Kotohira obtained appointment as doctrinal instructors within a year. Ibid., Meiji 6.4.30.

41. Since the indoctrination campaign was in large part the product of Buddhist proposals, Buddhist temples occupied a prominent role and provided large sums of money. This troubled the Shintoists in the movement. See, for example, ibid., Meiji 5.6.6.

42. *KSSS nenpyō,* 46. The connection of the Toranomon Kotohira Shrine with Kotohira Shrine in Kagawa prefecture during the early years of the Meiji era is unclear. The Ministry of Doctrine officially recognized Toranomon as a branch shrine of Kotohira Shrine in Kagawa in Meiji 5.10 but within less than three months separated the two (ibid., 47). The building of the lecture hall and the activities of priests from Kagawa's Kotohira Shrine at Toranomon, however, suggests that during the first half of 1872, at least, there still existed a close relationship between the two shrines.

43. The eighteen Shinto shrines stood in contrast to more than forty Buddhist temples included in the program. See *NN,* Meiji 5.5.18. Less than four months later, all Shinto priests and shrines were included in the campaign, and by the eleventh month of 1872, every shrine and temple in the nation was designated a site for sermons on the national teaching.

44. Ibid., Meiji 5.5.18. It is unclear whether the loan was returned or not.

45. The decline of prefectural authority over provincial shrines such as Kotohira contributed to the change in loyalty, as did the rapidly changing prefectural affiliation of Kotohira and the concomitant retirement of Governor Hayashi, the man who had appointed them in the first place.

46. *NN,* Meiji 5.6.5, Meiji 5.7.9–5.8.18. The sale of records at this time resulted in the loss of many of the Edo-period documents of the shrine: although shrine leaders later tried to buy them back, half of them had already disappeared. Matsubara, "Kotohiragū no shozō shiryō ni tsuite," 70. Such sales of Buddhist images eventually made possible some of the large collections of Japanese Buddhist art in museums around the world.

47. The wooden image of Kongōbō-Yūsei and any images of Konpira Daigongen that may have existed were apparently stolen, buried, or destroyed: they disappear from the official shrine documents entirely. See chapter 11, below.

48. Kotohira Shrine successfully sued for the removal of the image. See "Toriatsukai kiroku: kō no bu," entries for Meiji 2.11, Meiji 3.1–2, in Kotohiragū, *Kotohiragū shiryō,* vol. 9.

49. *NN,* Meiji 5.7.20.

50. Ibid., Meiji 5.7.20.

51. *KSSS nenpyō,* 47. Kotohira town and shrine held expositions in 1873, 1879, and 1880. *NN,* 17 June 1879 and 18 June 1880. On the relationship between kaichō and expositions, see P. F. Kornicki, "Public Display and Changing Values: Early Meiji's Exhibitions and Their Precursors," *Monumenta Nipponica* 49, no. 2 (Summer 1994): 167–96.

52. Conversation with Hashikata Toshiko, Kotohira-chō, 10 August 1995.

53. Kawaguchi Kyūdō, "Zōzusan Matsuoji to Kotohiragū no soshō ni tsuite," *Rokudai shinpō,* Meiji 41.12.20, excerpted in *SBBS,* 9:422. This account was published as part of a legal campaign to claim the assets of Kotohira Shrine for the Buddhist temple, Matsuoji. (See chapter 13, below.)

A taxi driver in Kotohira told a similar story in 1995. When the image of Fudō Myōō was put on the fire, he said, one of the men who was burning the statues heard a commanding voice demanding, "Do you dare to burn me?" (Ware o yaku no ka?) At that instant, the man realized that the deity Fudō Myōō really existed. He left household life and eventually retired to a life of meditation in a small hovel in the nearby village of Enai. (Conversation in Kotohira-chō, 9 August 1995.) As mentioned above, it seems that the Fudō Myōō image was never taken to be burned. However, the marks of smoke and fire left on the statue from years of presiding over the fire ceremony in the Goma Hall may have contributed to the taxi driver's pinpointing of Fudō Myōō as the image in the legend instead of the image of Kongōbō mentioned above. A later entry in Matsuoka's diary suggests that the Kongōbō image may not have been burned either. (See chapter 11.)

54. *NN,* Meiji 5.8.18.

55. Ketelaar emphasizes this shift in *Of Heretics and Martyrs,* 96–97.

56. On these riots, which spread to include more than ten thousand people throughout the prefecture, including some five thousand who burned down prominent inns, government offices and the homes of wealthy families in Konpira, see Kagawa-ken, *Kagawa kenshi* 5, 133–36; and *KSSS nenpyō,* 46.

57. "Kotohira kansha shanyū no kenshi," 8 February 1873, in *Shaji torishirabe ruisan,* documents in the National Diet Library.

58. *NN,* 3 March 1873.

59. "Kyōden no kisoku," in *NN,* 30 May 1873.

60. *NN,* 30 May 1873.

61. Ibid., 20 June 1873.

62. See, for example, ibid., 20 July, 1 and 20 August, 20 September, and 20 October 1873. Only the subjects, not the specific content, of the lectures at Kotohira are recorded. On the themes of the indoctrination campaign in general, see Ketelaar, *Of Heretics and Martyrs,* 105–21: and Haga, *Meiji ishin to shūkyō,* 283–323.

63. *NN,* 20 August 1873. Even Matsuoka inadvertently wrote "Konpira" instead of "Kotohira" when transcribing this tale, suggesting that priests and instructors often referred to the deity by its popular name.

64. Ibid., 1 March 1874.

65. The relationship of the Great Teaching Institute to the Toranomon Shinto lecture hall is unclear. It seems that the Institute taught instructors while lectures at the Toranomon hall, housed as it was in the popular Toranomon Kotohira Shrine, were aimed at lay worshippers.

66. "Shihi o motte Daikyōin kenchiku o yurusu," Kyōbushō futatsu, 20.1.1873, in *Dajō Ruiten.* Also reproduced as cited in the diary of Hanazono Sesshin, in Ikeda Eishun, *Meiji bukkyō kyōkai kesshashi no kenkyū* (Tokyo: Tōsui Shobō, 1994), 27. The prominence of Buddhists in instigating and funding the institute in the first months of its existence is reflected in the term used for "believers": *kie* specifically refers to Buddhist lay adherents.

67. Ketelaar, *Of Heretics and Martyrs,* 99.

68. Ikeda, *Meiji bukkyō kyōkai kesshashi no kenkyū,* 27. Quickest to respond to the call were the ever-innovative head of Izumo Shrine, Senge Takatomi, and some of the new religions, for this proclamation offered a direct path to government recognition. Indeed, Nitta Kuniteru, who founded the lay association Shūsei Kōsha in August 1873, raised so much money through the association that his was one of the first movements to be recognized as an independent sect of Shinto. Helen Hardacre discusses how involvement in the indoctrination campaign affected the doctrine and development of some of the new religions in *Shintō and the State,* 51–58, and "Creating State Shintō: The Great Promulgation Campaign and the New Religions," *Journal of Japanese Studies* 12, no. 1 (1986): 29–63.

69. Yasumaru, *Kamigami no Meiji ishin,* 193–95.

70. For the instructions given to each of these new head priests, see Tokoyo Nagatane, *Shinkyō soshiki monogatari,* in Yasumaru and Miyachi, *Shūkyō to kokka,* 386–87, 421. I am indebted to Umezawa Fumiko for pinpointing this reference.

71. Kotooka, *Kotohiragū,* 195.

72. Ketelaar, *Of Heretics and Martyrs,* 54–65; Sakamoto Koremaru, *Kokka shintō keisei katei no kenkyū,* 199.

73. *NN,* 21 and 22 April 1873 and passim.

74. *Chōshi Kotohira,* 3:512.

75. *NN,* Meiji 5.10.11.

76. "Tenpō jūninen yori Meiji rokunen ichigatsu itaru toriatsukai kiroku, kō no bu," entry for Meiji 4.8, in Kotohiragū, *Kotohiragū shiryō,* vol. 9, reprinted in *Chōshi Kotohira,* 2:582.

77. This translation of *saijin ronsō* is taken from Helen Hardacre, who provides a suc-

cinct overview of the movement and its relation to the Great Teaching Campaign in *Shintō and the State,* 48–51.

78. Senge Takatomi was a powerful figure in the world of Meiji Shinto. Like other hereditary priests, Takatomi was stripped of his position as head priest of Izumo, but he was reappointed in 1872. He was one of the most active leaders of the Great Teaching Campaign and eventually quit his position as head priest in 1882 to focus on broader Shinto proselytization activities. After his retirement, he entered politics in 1888, serving successively in the Genrōin; as governor of Saitama prefecture, Shizuoka prefecture, and Tokyo; and as minister of law.

79. Hara, *"Izumo" toiu shisō,* 114.

80. Fujii Sadafumi has reproduced Senge Takatomi's letters as well as many other key documents in the pantheon dispute in *Meiji kokugaku hasseishi no kenkyū* (Tokyo: Yoshikawa Kōbunkan, 1977).

81. See, for instance, the later support of Fukami and Kotooka for Senge's position. Ibid., 157–60.

82. In later years, Matsuoka Mitsugi and then again Kotooka Mitsushige in fact attempted to solve this problem. They marshaled evidence to support the hypothesis that Kotohira was actually the same as the Kumoke Shrine mentioned in the *Engishiki* as existing in Sanuki province. See, for instance, Muramatsu Sūei, ed., *Kotohira miyage,* no. 1 (Kotohira: Kyokuō Gakusha, 1892), iii. This theory did not result in an advancement for the shrine.

83. The distribution of amulets was part of a short-lived policy by which all people were required to register with and receive amulets from local shrines, in part to demonstrate their faith in "native" gods, not Christianity. See below, chapter 8.

84. The following information is contained in a letter from Fukami and Matsuzaki, then in Tokyo, to the priests at home at Kotohira Shrine. The letter, dated 13 June 1873, is copied in *NN,* 22 June 1873. The idea of metal, coin-shaped amulets was apparently an innovation by Fukami or Matsuzaki. The inclusion of a drawing of the proposed amulets in the letter suggests that no such amulet had been produced before.

85. *NN,* 22 June 1873.

86. Some even attributed the creation of the land to Amaterasu. A third faction favored the three creator deities who appear in the opening passages of the myths. Hara Takeshi provides a concise summary of these various positions in *"Izumo" toiu shisō,* 108–13.

87. *NN,* 22 June 1873.

88. The draft, line-edited by Matsuoka, appears in *NN,* 27 April 1874.

89. Hardacre, *Shintō and the State,* 48–49.

90. On the political overtones of the Ise-Izumo split, see, for example, Harootunian, *Things Seen and Unseen,* 411–12; and Breen, "Shintoists in Restoration Japan," 588–93.

91. Summary of a letter from Fukami and Matsuzaki in Tokyo to Matsuoka, Kotooka, and the other priests at the main shrine, reproduced in *NN,* 22 June 1873.

92. Ibid., 22 June 1873.

Chapter 8

1. Eiji Takemura, *The Perception of Work in Tokugawa Japan: A study of Ishida Baigan and Ninomiya Sontoku* (Lanham, Md.: University Press of America, 1997); and Janine Anderson Sawada, *Confucian Values and Popular Zen: Sekimon Shingaku in Eighteenth Century Japan* (Honolulu: University of Hawaii Press, 1993).

2. "Konpan Konpira hongū sūkei kōsha aimusubi sōrō ni tsuki jūzen naninani kōchū to tonae sōrō muki e kaibun," in *NN*, 3 April 1874. Also reproduced in Innami, "Konpira shinkō to tabi," 51. That the shrine did not plan to lose any money from this new policy was made clear by the additional stipulation in the text that some large donors would be given special access even if they did not join the association.

3. See, for example, Ishikawa Wasuke, ed., *Sanuki kuni Kotohira jinja sūkei kōsha kisoku utsushi* (Osaka: Ishikawa Wasuke, 1882), 1.

4. Murai Shin'ichirō, ed., *Sūkeikō no susume* (Takamatsu: Murai Shin'ichirō, 1878), 3v.

5. "Gonangan" (1877) in *Ōfuku todome,* compiled by Kotohiragū Sūkei Kōsha Honbu (bound collection of letters and replies). All subsequent letters are taken from this source.

6. The registers are in the collection of the Kotohiragū Sūkei Kyōkai Honbu. I would like to thank Mr. Yorimitsu Kanji for suggesting this possibility concerning the seals, and Professor Tamamuro Fumio and the late Matsubara Hideaki for making the registers available for study.

7. See documents concerning Fujidō Eikichi (6 May 1877), in Kotohiragū Sūkei Kōsha Honbu, *Ōfuku todome.*

8. See, for example, Murai, *Sūkeikō no susume;* Ishikawa, *Sanuki kuni Kotohira jinja sūkei kōsha kisoku utsushi; Kotohira hongū sūkei kōsha kisoku* (anonymous, undated). Unless noted, all citations of the Reverence Association rules refer to Murai, *Sūkeikō no susume,* 3v–5v.

9. Innami, "Konpira shinkō to tabi," 56–57.

10. Sakamoto Koremaru, *Kokka shintō keisei katei no kenkyū,* 183. My treatment of the ujiko shirabe system generally follows Sakamoto's discussion, 172–90.

11. On the Shinto funeral movement, see Andrew Bernstein, *Modern Passings: Death, Politics, and Social Change in Imperial Japan* (Honolulu: University of Hawai'i Press, forthcoming).

12. This may have been due to the influence of Matsuoka and Fukami. Matsuoka had issued registration amulets under the system at Tawa Shrine before his arrival at Kotohira. *NN,* Meiji 4.12.19ff.

13. Indeed, there were only two major differences between the Reverence Association registration lists and those of the government: membership in the association was optional, and status (noble, commoner, or outcast) was not included in Kotohira's lists.

14. This attitude is dramatically evident in a collection of miracle tales compiled and edited in the 1880s by Matsuoka Mitsugi, who, in succeeding drafts of the work, deliberately elided the agency of women. See the various drafts of Matsuoka's *Kokin Reigenki,* unpublished, in the Tawa Archives, on microfilm at Kokubungaku Kenkyū Shiryōkan, Tokyo.

15. *NN,* 17 July 1876. The request for twenty-five thousand yen (in five installments) came in April 1874 to fund the rebuilding of the Great Teaching Institute after it had been destroyed by fire.

16. Imai Kongo, "Naniwakō tanjō no kushin o kataru shiryō," Kosho no tanoshimi 4, *Nihon kosho tsūshin* 760 (November 1992): 4; and Innami, "Konpira shinkō to tabi," 27.

17. *Sūkei kōsha onjōyado,* preface. Excerpts of the text have been published in Shirakawa Satoru, "Dōchū anzen: Meiji shoki no Konpira mairi," *Kotohira* 32 (1977): 27–31.

18. "Meiji hachinen hachigatsu yori sūkei kōsha jōyado keisho," cited in Innami, "Konpira shinkō to tabi," 61.

19. Each style of sign apparently also signified the rank of the establishment within the association, for the list of licensed inns kept by the shrine included annotations on who was permitted a flag and who a placard. See excerpts from "Kakkoku jōyado todomari," reproduced in the appendix to Innami, "Konpira shinkō to tabi," 77–86.

20. Letter from Takeuchi Junji, 7 November 1880.

21. Letter from Nakasendō Sekigahara shuku Shisshiya Gihei, 29 October 1876.

22. *Chōshi Kotohira,* 5:86.

23. Several printed flyers advertising "Konpira steamship" operators, including one specifically licensed by the Reverence Association, are reproduced in *Chōshi Kotohira,* 5:86–87.

24. For fares and routes, see, for instance, the 1873 advertising flyer for the steamship *Kotohira Maru,* reproduced in color on the first page of Kagawa-ken, *Kagawa kenshi,* vol. 5, kindai 1.

25. Enoki Gakusui, "Enoki Gakusui nikki 2" (Meiji 4), in *Dai Nihon Kokiroku,* ed. Tōkyō Daigaku Shiryō Hensanjo (Tokyo: Iwanami Shoten, 1956), 68.

26. See, for instance, Nagata Soreji, *Kotohira annaiki* (Osaka: Nagata Soreji, 1902).

27. "Konpira fune," *Kagawa Shinpō,* 29 January 1898, 3.

28. In April 1907, for example, two men from an island in Hiroshima prefecture, ages fifty-two and forty-five, rescued a man fallen overboard from a steamship as they returned from a pilgrimage to Konpira in their own wooden boat ("Suikyaku fune yori otsu," *Kagawa Shinpō,* 5 April 1907, 5). See also an ema from Kusadochō, Fukuyama-shi, Hiroshima-ken (1900), in *KSSS,* 1:75. Interview with Kondō Matsuno, Kusadochō (31 October 1995).

29. Personal interview with Sakata Yoshinobu, Ehime-ken, Kita-gun, Futami-chō, Kaminada (22 October 1996).

30. The newspaper article reports how his fellow passenger continued the acquaintanceship, traveling with him to Kotohira, then stealing his possessions while he prayed at the shrine. "Goma no hai," *Kagawa Shinpō,* 11 October 1890, 3–4.

31. *Chōshi Kotohira,* 5:77, 82, shows two undated prints modified to include the Meiji title of the shrine. For a compilation of prints clearly showing this progression, see Matsubara Hideaki, "Konpira shinkō to sankei gaidōzu," *Chizu Jōhō* 13, no. 3 (1993): 1–5.

32. Kagawa-ken, *Meiji nijūsannen Kagawa-ken tōkeisho* (Takamatsu: Kagawa-ken, 1890), 60.

33. See chapter 5 above.

34. The Reverence Association's administrative diary for 1882 records the rotation of innkeepers who would oversee relations between the inns and the association, then records having calculated the monthly bonus to be distributed to the inns. Kotohiragū, *Nisshi* (unpublished shrine record), entry for 19 August 1882. See also the revised 1913 contract between association inns and the Reverence Association, reproduced in Innami, "Konpira shinkō to tabi," 62–64. The rebate to inns for recruitment continued at least until the early 1960s. Interview with Satō Yoshitake, 31 October 1996; and "Jōyado gesshō shirabe (shūnyū gesshō uchiwakegaki)," cited in Innami, "Konpira shinkō to tabi," 69.

35. An entry in the Reverence Association's administrative diary for 3 February 1884, for example, confirmed for the police in Fukui prefecture that the Reverence Association innkeeper Yamashita Magoichi's representative was legitimately representing the association in his recruitment activities there. Kotohiragū, *Nisshi*. The former priest Satō Yoshitake commented that during the early postwar period, employees of the inns would recruit association members on the buses between Takamatsu and Kotohira. Interview, 31 October 1996. See also Innami, "Konpira shinkō to tabi," 64.

36. See, for example, the draft response to Takeo Yoshinobu, 2 December 1912. Once registered through a particular inn, each kō within the Reverence Association was committed to staying at that inn in perpetuity. Yet not only did inns try to steal each other's customers and reregister them as new kō to earn the registration fees, but disgruntled kō members also occasionally insisted on changing inns of their own accord. In 1906, one man, infuriated by what he perceived as either disrespect for his generosity or outright embezzlement of his donation by the inn Yoshimaya, informed the main office of the Reverence Association that he had switched his kō's affiliation to Toraya. (Letter from Kadobayashi Hiroomi, Osaka metropolitan area, Izumi province, Izumi Kita district, Minami Ikeda village, 16 May 1906.) The association registers thus became legal proof of each inn's claim on a particular kō, a valuable form of capital for their business.

37. For example, "Meiji shichinen Isegū Konpira Jinja Kōyasan Dōchūki," in *Ise sangū nikki kō 2: shiryōhen sono 2,* ed. Kawasaki Yoshio (Ibaragi-ken, Tsuchiura-shi: Chikuma Shorin, 1987), 109–10; "Dōchū Nikki," in Kawasaki, *Ise sangū nikki kō 2,* 131; and "Dōchūki," in *Ise sangū dōchūki,* ed. Isa Gohei (Fukuoka-shi, undated), 7.

38. Records of plaques offered to the god contain countless such examples. Kotohiragū, *Kotohiragū shiryō,* vols. 67 and 75.

39. *NN,* Meiji 5.4.9.

40. Ibid., 22 January 1874.

41. Ibid., 22 January 1874. On the particular popularity of the wooden amulets, see Innami, "Konpira shinkō to tabi," 12–13.

42. Murai, *Sūkei kō no susume,* 6r, 7r.

43. See, for example, letter from Takimoto Keisaku, ca. 1886, and letter from Kadobayashi Hiroomi (16 May 1906) of Osaka.

44. The rules of the Reverence Association were printed in innumerable flyers distributed throughout Japan. These in 1878 are taken from Murai, *Sūkei kō no susume,* 3v-5v.

45. Matsuoka records the article as appearing in the *Ibaragi Shinpō,* copies of which are no longer extant from this time. *NN,* 12 January 1878. As early as 1874, when he first started serving as a doctrinal instructor in the government's indoctrination campaign, Ma-

tsuoka commented in his diary that he should write down tales that he heard or read in order to show people that Konpira's miracles happen every day. *NN,* 15 September 1874. Arguments against the existence of the god remained controversial. When the *Kōchi Shinbun* published an article entitled "An Essay on Atheism" [Mushinron] in 1882, it deemed it necessary to disavow that the essay represented the editor's opinion. *Kōchi Shinbun,* 5–7 January 1882.

46. *NN,* 12 January and 21 February 1878; Kondō Shigeki, *Meiji kōsetsu roku* (Tokyo: Kunaishō, 1877).

47. *Zōzusan Konpira Daigongen reigenki,* undated, in the collection of Tawa Bunko.

48. Matsuoka, *Kotohiragū kokin reigenki,* 20–21.

49. For the prints, see *Kotohira reigen kōkoku,* numbers 1–3 (1879), in the collection of Kyūman Bijutsukan, reproduced in *Chōshi Kotohira,* 5:29–30, 167. The later miracle tales include Ōnishi, *Konpiragū goreigenki;* and Andō, *Konpira daigongen goreigen jikki.* For "Konpira Daigongen Reigen Jikki Hōnō Ōikari no Yurai," performed at the theater in Kotohira's red-light district, see *Kagawa Shinpō,* 11 May 1912, 5.

50. *NN,* 2 March 1878.

51. Ibid., 17 July 1876.

52. "Kyōkai onchokkatsu no gi ni tsuki gan" (1880), in Kotohiragū, *Kotohiragū shiryō,* vol. 11. Given the large number of Reverence Association kō registers still extant at the association headquarters in Kotohira, this number—counting all formally registered members, and not just those who personally experienced the initiation ceremony—is quite plausible. See the partial index of kō registers compiled by Tamamuro Fumio and his students, *Kotohiragū sūkei kōsha kōchō mokuroku* (Kotohira: Kotohiragū Shamusho, 1995).

53. Letter from Ichimaru Kanji, Saga-ken, Higashi Matsuura-gun (23 October 1896).

54. Letter from Hirose Daikichi of Kōchi prefecture, returning his wife's association amulet upon her death on 23 May 1881. Two sponsors of another association kō in Saga prefecture wrote in 1896 to complain that their kō's designated inn, the Toraya, had neglected to remove the names of deceased members of the kō from the association lists. "This lack of reverence for the divine spirit of the main shrine, from which we receive eternal blessings," they warned, "is sure to incur a dire punishment." Letter from Ichimaru Kanji of Kagami-mura, Higashi Matsuura-gun, Saga-ken, 23 October 1896.

55. Ogata Shōtarō, "Kotohira keiki" (1882), transcribed and annotated by Minota Katsuhiko (Kumamoto-ken: Yachio Kobunsho no Kai, 1987), 10–11.

56. Ibid., 12.

57. Ibid.

58. Koizumi Kakuhei, "Meiji jūyonen dōchū mankakuchō" (1881), in *Ise dōchūki shiryō,* ed. Tōkyō-to Setagaya-ku Kyōiku Iinkai (Tokyo: Tōkyō-to Setagaya-ku Kyōiku Iinkai, 1984), 74–88.

59. See Koizumi, "Meiji jūyonen dōchū mankakuchō," 83, for a reproduction of the membership amulet.

60. Letter from Ōmori Saburōhei (Chiba-ken, 1 July 1882).

61. Kotohiragū, *Kotohiragū shiryō,* vol. 67.

62. Ibid., vols. 67, 75.

Chapter 9

1. Kotohiragū, *Kotohiragū shiryō*, vol. 9.

2. Mori Arinori, *Religious Freedom in Japan: A Memorial and Draft of Charter* (Washington, D.C.: privately printed, 1872), 4; quoted in Ketelaar, *Of Heretics and Martyrs*, 127.

3. Shimaji Mokurai, cited in Ketelaar, *Of Heretics and Martyrs*, 127.

4. Irokawa Daikichi, *The Culture of the Meiji Period* (Princeton, N.J.: Princeton University Press, 1985), 76–122.

5. Sakamoto Koremaru, *Kokka shintō keisei katei no kenkyū*, 295ff. On the conservative-reformer lineup as it affected debates on shrine-related issues at the highest levels of government, see also Yamaguchi Teruomi, *Meiji kokka to shūkyō* (Tokyo: Tōkyō Daigaku Shuppankai, 1999), 124 and passim.

6. Inoue Nobutaka, *Kyōha shintō no keisei* (Tokyo: Kōbundō, 1991), 33.

7. "Sūkei kōsha honbu sūkei kyōkai honbu hitsuyō shorui," in Kotohiragū, *Kotohiragū shiryō*, vol. 14. In keeping with its "religious" functions, the Reverence Association (*sūkei kōsha*) was renamed *sūkei kyōkai* at this point.

8. Matsuoka suggests, however, that its leaders did, in fact, consider seeking such special designation. See *NN*, 21 May 1882. See also the contract of 10 February 1883, which focuses on the division between the two entities of income from amulet sales to association members. Kotohiragū, *Kotohiragū shiryō*, vols. 11, 14.

9. Takashi Fujitani's study of imperial pageantry provides an excellent sense of the style and significance of such rituals on a national level. *Splendid History: Power and Pageantry in Modern Japan* (Berkeley: University of California Press, 1996).

10. Sakamoto Koremaru, *Kokka shintō keisei katei no kenkyū*, 291.

11. *NN*, 6 February 1882.

12. Letter dated 28 January 1882, reproduced in *NN*, Meiji 15.2.14; ibid., Meiji 15.4.19.

13. Ibid., Meiji 15.7.12.

14. See, for example, *Kagawa Shinpō*, 2 September 1892, 1. The Kōten Kōkyūjo in Tokyo was reorganized as Kokugakuin University in 1890.

15. *NN*, Meiji 15.9.30.

16. See, for instance, Matsuoka's comments on a lecture trip to Kyushu in 1893. *NN*, 23 May 1893.

17. *Chōshi Kotohira*, 3:512–13; "Myōdō Gakkō no koto," *Kotohira* (Spring 1958): 28–30.

18. Sakamoto Koremaru, *Kokka shintō keisei katei no kenkyū*, 296.

19. Hardacre, *Shinto and the State*, 33–34; Nitta Hitoshi, "Shinto as a 'Non-religion': The Origins and Development of an Idea," in *Shinto in History: Ways of the Kami*, ed. John Breen and Mark Teeuwen (Surrey: Curzon Press, 2000), 252–71.

20. Copies of these two edicts may be found in Yasumaru and Miyachi, eds., *Shūkyō to kokka*, 483–84.

21. On such rites and rhetoric in the broader ideological context, see Carol Gluck, *Japan's Modern Myths: Ideology in the Late Meiji Period* (Princeton, N.J.: Princeton University Press, 1985).

22. Sakamoto Koremaru, *Kokka shintō keisei katei no kenkyū,* 382.

23. *NN,* Meiji 15.2.6.

24. Ibid., Meiji 19.4.7–10.

25. See letters from worshippers in Hokkaido to the Reverence Association (for instance, from Yamado Asajirō and others on 28 April 1901, or Tazawa Inoshirō, 12 October 1909), as well as ema donated by the settlers and their descendants (*KSSS,* 1:96); and Ōkubo Shin'ichi, *Sanuki imin no Hokkaidō kaitaku shiryō* (Tadotsu: Tadotsu Bunkazai Hozonkai, 1981), ii–vii, 84–85.

26. *NN,* 24 and 28 September 1889.

27. Kotohiragū Hozonkai Jimusho, "Kotohiragū hozonkai kōkoku," *Kaitsū Zasshi,* no. 74 (25 March 1888): 15.

28. "Kotohiragū hozonkai," *Yosan Shinpō,* 2 November 1888, 2.

29. Kotohiragū Hozonkai Jimusho, "Kotohiragū hozonkai kōkoku," *Kaitsū Zasshi,* no. 74 (25 March 1888): 15.

30. "Dai Nihon Teikoku Suinan Kyūsaikai kisoku," reproduced in Teikoku Suinan Kyūsaikai, *Teikoku Suinan Kyūsaikai gojūnenshi* (Tokyo: Teikoku Suinan Kyūsaikai, 1939), 5–10.

31. *NN,* 25 February 1890.

32. Kotooka Hirotsune, "Suinan kyūsaikai o sansei seraremu koto o nozomu ni tsukite" (August 1889), 1. A copy of this printed circular can be found in the Miyake family collection in the Seto Inland Sea Folk History Museum.

33. Reproduced in Muramatsu, *Kotohira miyage,* 13.

34. "Yo no keishinsha ni hitogotosu," in Muramatsu, *Kotohira miyage,* no. 1:11.

35. Ibid., 10.

36. In 1891, that meant 5,510 people in Kagawa prefecture and 824 in Kotohira's Nakatado district. *Chōshi Kotohira,* 3:438.

37. Minami Mitsutoshi, born into the highly ranked aristocratic Hirohashi family, was the younger brother of Hirohashi Mitsuru, a prominent bureaucrat in the Home Ministry. He was later adopted into the Minami family of the temple Kōfukuji. Ōue Shirō, ed., *Meiji kakochō* (Tokyo: Tōkyō Bijutsu, 1971), 1155; Ōta Akira, *Seishi kakei daijiten* (Tokyo: Seishi Kakei Daijiten Kankōkai, 1936), 5847. I would like to thank Mr. Uchikawa Koresuke for drawing the Hirohashi family connection.

38. *Chōshi Kotohira,* 3:438.

39. See, for instance, Kenneth B. Pyle, "Meiji Conservatism," in *The Cambridge History of Japan,* vol. 5, ed. Marius B. Jansen (Cambridge: Cambridge University Press, 1989), 674–720; Donald H. Shively, "The Japanization of the Middle Meiji," in *Tradition and Modernization in Japanese Culture,* ed. Donald H. Shively (Princeton, N.J.: Princeton University Press, 1971); and Gluck, *Japan's Modern Myths,* 18.

Chapter 10

1. *NN,* Meiji 27.4–5.

2. Kotohiragū, *Nisshi,* entry for 6 June 1894.

3. *Kagawa Shinpō,* 14 July 1894, 3.

4. Ibid.

5. *KSSS nenpyō,* passim. For orders from the prefectural government in Takamatsu, see *Kagawa Shinpō,* 5 July 1894, 3, and 11 August 1894, 5.

6. Ichihara Terushi Sensei Kiju Kinen Ronbunshū Henshū Iinkai, *Rekishi to minzoku denshō,* 132–33.

7. See, for example, *Kagawa Shinpō,* 11 September 1894, 3.

8. Ibid., 5 July 1894, 3, and 11 August 1894, 5.

9. Ibid., 26 July 1894, 3, and 28 July 1894, 2.

10. Ibid., 7 August 1894, 3. Similar donations had begun appearing elsewhere, especially in the larger cities, more than a month earlier. Harada Keiichi, "Nihon kokumin no sansen netsu," in *Nisshin sensō no shakaishi: "bunmei sensō" to minshū,* ed. Ōtani Tadashi and Harada Keiichi (Osaka: Fuooramu A, 1994), 14. There were one hundred sen in a yen.

11. *NN,* 28 July 1894. This festival was apparently not ordered by the government since it was held at the Reverence Association headquarters, not the shrine.

12. Ibid., 27 July 1894.

13. Kagawa-ken, *Kagawa kenshi,* beppen 2: nenpyō, 308, and *Kagawa kenshi,* 5:743.

14. *NN,* 30 and 31 July 1894.

15. Ibid., 30 July 1894.

16. Ibid., 30 July 1894.

17. Harada Keiichi, "Nihon kokumin no sansen netsu," 15–18.

18. The text of the imperial proclamation, "Giyūhei o todome tamau chokuyu" (7 August 1894) can be found in Meiji Jingū, ed., *Meiji tennō shōchoku kinkai* (Tokyo: Kōdansha, 1973), 1017–18.

19. *NN,* 2 August 1894.

20. Advertisement in *Kagawa Shinpō,* 7 August 1894, 4.

21. *NN,* 5–7 August 1894.

22. *Kagawa Shinpō,* 7 August 1894, 3.

23. *NN,* 10 August 1894.

24. *Kagawa Shinpō,* 14 August 1894, 3.

25. *NN,* 18 August 1894.

26. *Kagawa Shinpō,* 23 August 1894, 3.

27. Ibid., 24 August 1894, 3.

28. *NN,* 4 and 14 August 1894.

29. Kotohiragū, *Nisshi,* entry for 15 August 1897. *Kagawa Shinpō,* 11 August 1894, 6.

30. *NN,* 14–15 August 1894; Kotohiragū, *Nisshi,* 15 August 1894.

31. Kotohiragū, *Nisshi,* 22 August 1894.

32. *NN,* 17 August 1894.

33. *Kagawa Shinpō,* 18 and 23 August 1894, 3.

34. Ibid., 22 August 1894, 2.

35. Ibid., 23 August 1894, 3. This "unseasonable prosperity," however, deriving as it

did from nearby pilgrims who arrived and left Kotohira in a single day, did not extend to the innkeepers.

36. Ibid., 9 September 1894, 4.

37. Ibid., 11 September 1894, 3. Later, near the end of the war, the families of soldiers from this town were also the guests of honor at ceremonies at the local Matsukuma Shrine, where they attended a reading of the Imperial Rescript on Education, heard an explanation with maps of the war situation in Korea, and received both booklets of the "wise sayings of the emperor" and amulets from Kotohira Shrine. Ibid., 11 January 1895, 3.

38. Ibid., 22 September 1894, 1 and 25 September 1894, 5.

39. Ibid., 20 December 1894, 1.

40. Families made sure to tell sons and brothers in letters that they had prayed to Konpira and received large wooden amulets on their behalf. Communities also included Konpira amulets in care packages sent to the front. Ibid., 16 October 1894, 4, and 19 October 1894, 3.

41. See, for example, Mitsui Takafusa's (1653–1737) exhortation to his descendants to "never waste your attention on matters which have nothing to do with your work," such as worship of the gods. Mitsui Takafusa, *Some Observations on Merchants,* trans. E. S. Crawcour (London: Japan Society London, 1960), 115.

42. *Kagawa Shinpō,* August 24, 1894, 3. For similar comments in Tadotsu, see also *Kagawa Shinpō,* 23 October 1894, 5.

43. Ibid., 7 September 1894, 3.

44. Ibid., 29 November 1894, 3.

45. Ibid., 23 October 1894, 5.

46. Kotohiragū, *Kotohiragū sūkeishi,* 3:16.

47. Kotooka Mitsushige, "Kotohiragū to umi," *Kotohira* 22 (1967):15. See also Kotooka's interview with Watanabe Yukio, "Kaijō anzen to Konpira shinkō," reprinted from the Ministry of Transportation's publication, *Toransupootu,* in *Kotohira* 39 (1984):18.

48. *NN,* 17 Auugst 1894. See also Matsubara, "Konpira shinkō no rekishiteki tenkai," 9. The record in Kotohiragū, *Kotohiragū shiryō,* vol. 7, lists a donation from the military ship *Hanjō* in 1887, but it seems to be a miscopy of 1897. See below in this chapter.

49. Several of the offerings were undated, making it difficult to assess exact numbers.

50. *NN,* 17 August 1894, and Kotohiragū, *Kotohiragū shiryō,* vol. 7. This inscription provides a clear example of how the formal record erases the participation of women in worship. No hint of Iwakichi's wife appears on the board; her involvement can only be known because of the notation in Matsuoka's diary.

51. Innami, "Keidai no tōrō," 263.

52. See the shrine's advertisements soliciting bids for lumber contracts in *Kagawa Shinpō.*

53. *NN,* 17 August 1894.

54. *Kagawa Shinpō,* 27 April 1894, 3.

55. "Konpirasan meisho zue," in Kagawa-ken, *Kagawa sōsho,* 3:386. Innami Toshihide, "Ippan hōnōbutsu," in *KSSS,* 1:236–37. On the common practice of touching the part of the horse analogous to the place the petitioner wishes to be healed, see Kotohiragū,

Kotohiragū sūkeishi, 3:164–65; and Ian Reader, *Religion in Contemporary Japan* (London: Macmillan Press, 1991), 172.

56. The prints, entitled *Sanuki Zōzusan Kotohira keidai shinzu,* and published on 2 November 1888, can be found bound into the back of the travel diary Ame no Ie Shujin (pseud.), "Yume no matsu" (1889), a manuscript in the archive of Kotohira Shrine.

57. Richard Gordon Smith, *Travels in the Land of the Gods (1898–1907): The Japan Diaries of Richard Gordon Smith,* ed. Victoria Manthorpe (New York: Prentice Hall Press, 1986), 78. Feeding the horses was a popular activity for many years. See, for instance, references in an early nineteenth-century diary (Kuriyama Bunsuke, "Kamigata, Konpira sankei oboegaki" (ca. 1804–18), reprinted in *Ise sangū nikkikō,* vol. 1, ed. Kawasaki Yoshio (Ibaragi-ken, Tsuchiura-shi: Chikuwa Shorin, 1987), 14; and Yamakawa Maki's reminiscences in "Oumasan no mame," *Kotohira,* no. 18 (1963): 49–52.

58. Matsuoka went on to bemoan the heterodoxy of these ideas, commenting, "It is because newspaper reporters do not understand the world of the spirits that they record this kind of thing." *NN,* 26 August 1894.

59. "Shukugashiki," *Kagawa Shinpō,* 8 November 1894, 3.

60. Takeda Akira, "Konpira shinkō to minzoku," in Moriya, *Konpira shinkō,* 49–51. It is unclear when or why this belief developed, although it is probably connected to the association of Kotohira with Ōkuninushi, the kami of Izumo Shrine.

61. Ema donated by Hanada Kunimatsu, sailor first class of the Great Japanese Imperial Navy, and Ōtani Genkichi, sailor third class. Text reproduced in Kotohiragū, *Kotohiragū shiryō,* vol. 67.

62. "Tadotsu tsūshin," *Kagawa Shinpō,* 26 October 1894, 1.

63. *Kagawa Shinpō,* 5 and 24 March 1895, 3.

64. "Kotohiragū hōmotsu tenranjō annai," *Kagawa Shinpō,* 15–24 May 1895, 3.

65. *Kagawa Shinpō,* 26 May 1895, 3.

66. "Hōmotsukan rakusei shikikyō," *Kagawa Shinpō,* 18 July 1905, 2. See also a photograph of the gate and museum in *Chōshi Kotohira,* 5:202.

Chapter 11

1. *NN,* 13 April 1895.

2. Notice to Kotohira Shrine from Kagawa prefecture Governor Kobatake, hodai 7, 1 gō, dated 21 May 1895, reproduced in *NN,* 19 June 1895. The two rescripts were issued on 21 April and 13 May.

3. Letter from the head priest of Ani Jinja to Head Priest Minami, reproduced in *NN,* 28 May 1895.

4. *NN,* 28 May 1895. See also "Gūji menshoku ni kansuru zengo no kiji ni tsuki," *Kagawa Shinpō,* 1 June 1895, 3. See also the newspaper clipping labeled from the *Sanuki Shinbun,* 31 May 1895, in *NN,* preceding the 1 June 1895 entry.

5. *NN,* 5 June, 26 June, and 29 August 1895.

6. Ibid., 26 June 1895.

7. Rumors of the shrine debt occasionally appeared in the local newspaper. See for instance, "Kotohiragū no zen'yo," *Kagawa Shinpō,* 5 July 1892, 1.

8. Nakagawa, born in Kyoto in 1846, had worked at the Imperial Kyoto Museum in 1890 and then was appointed head priest of Yasaka Shrine in Kyoto in 1891, where he served until his appointment to the head priestship of Kotohira in 1895. Kotooka Mitsushige, *Kotohiragū,* 196.

9. Because of their financial responsibilities, the dismissed priests were required to stay on at the mountain. Many, for the time being, still retained their offices in the Reverence Association. In addition, if they ever hoped to obtain appointment from the Home Ministry again either as shrine priests or in another capacity, they needed to clear their names. Thus, other than the ritual duties from which they had been dismissed, the fired priests continued to remain involved in shrine activities.

10. *NN,* 26 October 1895.

11. Kotohiragū, *Kotohiragū shiryō hoi,* vol. 7.

12. Ibid., vol. 8.

13. *Kagawa Shinpō,* 16 July 1898, 3.

14. Ibid., 23 February 1890, 3.

15. Copies of two such printed scrolls are preserved in the Seto Inland Sea Folk History Museum.

16. *Kagawa Shinpō,* 28 February 1890, 3.

17. "Konpira Daigongen no kaihi," *Sanuki Nippō,* 27 March 1890, 3. For an article sympathetic to the display, see "Shinbutsu kondō," *Kagawa Shinpō,* 23 February 1890, 3.

18. *Kagawa Shinpō,* 1 June 1890, 2.

19. *NN,* 10 August 1895.

20. Ibid., 11 January 1896. On the politics in the Diet and government leading up to this wholesale return of forests, see Yamaguchi Teruomi, *Meiji kokka to shūkyō,* 203–39, esp. 223–25. I would like to thank Conrad Totman for emphasizing the national scope of this forestry policy.

21. *NN,* 1 February 1896.

22. "Massha idengan," 23 February 1896, reproduced in Kotohiragū, *Kotohiragū shiryō hoi,* vol. 8.

23. Reply of 16 March 1896 from Kagawa prefecture, reproduced in Kotohiragū, *Kotohiragū shiryō hoi,* vol. 8.

24. "Massha iden saigan," 19 March 1896, and approval from Kagawa governor Tokuhisa, 20 April 1896, reproduced in Kotohiragū, *Kotohiragū shiryō hoi,* vol. 8.

25. "Kotohiragū okusha kenritsu shuisho," May 1896, photocopy at Kotohira Shrine and in the Kusanagi collection, Seto Inland Sea Folk History Museum.

26. *Kagawa Shinpō,* 27 February 1898, 4.

27. "Okusha ka massha ka," *Kagawa Shinpō,* 24 March 1897, 3.

28. "Kotohira okusha shinsetsu ni tsuite," *Kagawa Shinpō,* 31 October 1896, 3.

29. Kotohiragū Gūjishitsu Shoki, ed., *Kotohiragū sessuisha baishishi* (1921; unpublished record in the archives of Kotohira Shrine), 3:123–25.

30. "Kisen kyōsō no fungi," *Kagawa Shinpō,* 11 March 1896, 2. This was apparently a geometric expansion upon the Edo-period "hyakunin kō" (hundred-person kō) and "man-

nin kō" (ten-thousand-person kō), unrelated donors whose money was gathered at the shrine or ports to underwrite major improvements. Inoki Kazuichi, "Konpira tōrō no kōtsū chiriteki igi," *Jinbun chiri* 11, no. 3 (1959): 1–21, reprinted in Moriya, *Konpira shinkō,* 263–64. See chapter 5 above.

31. *NN,* 4 March 1896 and 6 March 1896. See also *NN,* 13 January 1896 and 18 March 1896.

32. Kagawa kenrei 84, printed in *Kagawa Shinpō,* 15 October 1892, 1, and Kagawa kenrei 68, in *Kagawa Shinpō,* 19 August 1893, 1.

33. "Kansai kakkō no konzatsu," *Kagawa Shinpō,* 18 April 1895, 4.

34. *NN,* 4 March 1896.

35. *Kagawa Shinpō,* 11 March 1896, 3; and *Kagawa Shinpō,* 19 March 1896, 3.

36. "Tadotsu Kotohira ryōchōkan daifungi," *Kagawa Shinpō,* 10 March 1896, 3.

37. "Kisen kyōsō no funjō," *Kagawa Shinpō,* 11 March 1896.

38. "Kansai kisen kaisha," *Kagawa Shinpō,* 25 March 1896, 3.

39. *Kagawa Shinpō,* 13 March 1896, 3.

40. Ibid., 28 March 1896, 3. See also an advertisement from the Reverence Association headquarters announcing the termination of the Million-Person Kō, in *Kagawa Shinpō,* 1 April 1896, 4.

41. See, for example, the advertisment for the Kotohira festival in the first half of 1898, *Kagawa Shinpō,* 24 December 1897. Matsuoka pasted the special discount pilgrimage tickets into his diary, *NN,* 16 April 1898.

42. Indeed, according to rumors in the newspapers, Nakagawa added another ten thousand yen to the debt with the spectacular failure of a six-month-long festival he arranged in honor of the beginning of construction of the inner shrine in 1898. "Hōshukusai no shuppai," *Kagawa Shinpō,* 10 November 1898, 3.

43. Kären Wigen, in *The Making of a Japanese Periphery, 1750–1920* (Berkeley: University of California Press, 1995), has highlighted a similar shift from independent business networks to rural elites and the Tokyo-based administrative hierarchy as major players in regional development. See esp. 274–78.

44. Figures from Saitō Osamu, "Meiji goki no fuken kangyō seisaku," *Keizai kenkyū* 35, no. 3 (July 1984): 243 (compiled from *Nōshōmu tōkeihyō*).

45. Kagawa-ken, *Kagawa kenshi* 5, 544.

46. "Tokuhisa chiji no monogatari," *Kagawa Shinpō,* 23 July 1896, 3.

47. "Kotohira totei gakkō no hōshin," *Kagawa Shinpō,* 6 May 1898, 3.

48. Sangawa Hiroshi, *Sanuki no ittōbori: Konpira no ittōbori o kigen toshite* (1983), 35; personal interview with Yamanaka Zōdō.

49. "Mamoribako shokkō no konnan," *Kagawa Shinpō,* 4 May 1898, 3.

50. "Hashi no seizō," *Kagawa Shinpō,* 4 June 1898, 3.

51. See, for example, comments by the minister of education in *Kagawa Shinpō,* 10 May 1899, 3; and 7 April 1900, 3. On the closing of the school, see "Kotohira kōgyōkō haishisetsu," *Kagawa Shinpō,* 27 February 1907, 2, and "Kotohira kōgyō gakkō shizen no haikō," *Kagawa Shinpō,* 10 March 1907, 2.

52. Advertisement in *Sanuki Jitsugyō Shinbun,* 2 April 1903.

53. On the history of *ittōbori* in Kotohira, see *Sanuki no ittōbori.*

54. Sanaki, "Miyaji Hikosaburō to Kotohira," 5–7.

55. "Kōen o sekken to su," *Kainan Shinbun,* 15 March 1888, 3. The first public parks (*kōen*) were established in 1873 in Tokyo on grounds confiscated from temples and shrines that had historically been used for public gatherings and entertainment. Tanaka Seidai, *Nihon no kōen* (Tokyo: Kajima Shuppankai, 1974), 47–49.

56. "Kotohira no undōhi," *Kagawa Shinpō,* 13 April 1897, 3. See also *Kagawa Shinpō,* 20 March 1897, 3; 18 April 1897, 4; and 30 April 1897, 3.

57. "Kotohira zasshin: geishōgi no jintōzei," *Kagawa Shinpō,* 21 June 1898, 3.

58. An article in the *Kagawa Shinpō* (26 June 1901, 2) reported that three women of Kotohira received commemorative plaques for their donations of over ten yen each for the construction of a road up the hill to the park.

59. *KSSS nenpyō,* 53. Between December 1897 and March 1898, Ritsurin Park in Takamatsu, Kotozensan Park in Kan'onji, and Kotohira Park in Kotohira were all officially granted land by the government. It is unclear whether the prefecture ever funded park construction under Governor Tokuhisa's plan, or whether his proposal simply prompted local leaders to go ahead with their own development strategies. Kagawa-ken, *Kagawa kenshi,* beppen 2: nenpyō, 316–18.

60. "Shin Kotohira (rekishi to shin hatten saku)," *Kagawa Shinpō,* 15 August 1897, 1.

61. "Kōen," *Kagawa Shinpō,* 7 June 1899, 3.

62. Ezawa Shō, "Kotohirachō no shūeki," *Kagawa Shinpō,* 22 October 1898, 5.

63. "Kotohirakan," *Kagawa Shinpō,* 5 July 1899, 5.

Chapter 12

1. *Chōshi Kotohira,* 3:563.

2. "Shūgaku ryokō no kenbunki," *Kagawa Shinpō,* 30 May 1890, 3.

3. "Shūgaku ryokō nikki," *Kagawa Shinpō,* 22 November 1892, 2. For other descriptions of school trips combining a visit to Kotohira with a tour of Marugame base, see, for instance, *Kagawa Shinpō,* 12 April 1891, 2; 28 May 1891, 1; 25 October 1892, 3; 21 May 1893, 3; 9 May 1895, 3.

4. Rumors of its establishment circulated as early as February 1895, while fighting was still going on. *Kagawa Shinpō,* 26 February 1895, 3, and 15 March 1895, 3.

5. The first panoramas in Japan were built in 1890 in Ueno and Asakusa parks in Tokyo, both featuring war scenes. During the Sino-Japanese War, these panoramas were changed to scenes of Port Arthur and Pyongyang. Panoramas were one of the most prominent ways in which the Japanese public became exposed to Western techniques of oil painting. Tan'o Yasunori and Kawada Akihisa, *Imeeji no naka no sensō: Nisshin Nichiro kara reisen made,* Iwanami kindai Nihon no bijutsu, no. 1 (Tokyo: Iwanami Shoten, 1996), 23–24.

6. "Kabushiki kaisha Sanuki Kotohira panoramakan shuisho," reproduced in "Panoramakan no keikaku," *Kagawa Shinpō,* 16 March 1900, 3; and Sanuki Kotohira

Panoramakan, *Teikoku gunka,* 10–23 November 1900, 1–2. I would like to thank Professor Tan'o Yasunori for making available his copy of this pamphlet in his private collection. For an example of Tōjō Seitarō's work and the style of the images that would have appeared in Kotohira's panorama, see, for instance, Tan'o and Kawada, *Imeeji no naka no sensō,* 26.

7. "Kotohira panorama no kaikan," *Kagawa Shinpō,* 11 November 1900, 2.

8. Sanuki Kotohira Panoramakan, *Teikoku gunka,* 5–16.

9. "Kotohira panorama no kaikan," 2. For the price of admission, see an advertisement in *Kagawa Shinpō,* 8 November 1900, 4, and the back matter of Sanuki Kotohira Panoramakan, *Teikoku gunka.*

10. Gōda Chōjirō, "Monzenmachi no panoramakan to sono ato," *Kotohira* 54:73. Gōda was born in 1906, and the panorama was torn down in 1912.

11. "Shinmyō naru shōgakusei," *Kagawa Shinpō,* 24 June 1903, 5.

12. *Kagawa Shinpō,* 25 November 1900, 3.

13. Kagawa-ken, *Kagawa kenshi* 5 (tsūshi hen kindai 1), 746.

14. *Kagawa Shinpō,* 16 December 1898, 3.

15. On national regulations, see Sheldon Garon, *Molding Japanese Minds* (Princeton, N.J.: Princeton University Press, 1997), 92, 94. On the creation of the red-light district of Fujimichō on land mostly owned by Kotohira Shrine, see "Kotohira yūkaku no koto," *Kagawa Shinpō,* 15 February 1900, 3; and on the required movement of several stone lanterns to make way for the district, see *Chōshi Kotohira,* 3:476.

16. Tsutsui Tōru, *Dai jūichi shidan no zu* (Zentsūji: Kawaguchi Kiyoshi, 1902). I would like to thank Mr. Ono Yasuo of Kotohira-chō Ezu o Mamoru Kai for providing me with a reproduction of this print.

17. See, for instance, *Kagawa Shinpō,* 10 November 1899, 3; 22 May 1906, 2; and 25 April 1912, 2. Also "Yogaku seito no shūgaku ryokō," in *Sanuki gakuseikai zasshi* 18 (28 February 1903): 82.

18. Kotohiragū, *Kotohiragū sūkeishi* (unpublished manuscript available at the Kotohira Shrine archives), 3:48–49.

19. *Kagawa Shinpō,* 3 December 1903, 2. See also, for example, ibid., 11 December 1903, 5.

20. Ibid., 21 August 1900, 6.

21. Kuwada Etsu, "Ryōkoku no senryoku, sakusen kōsō to daihon'ei," 176; and Yamada Ichirō, "Nisshin sensō ni okeru iryō, eisei," 243. Both in *Kindai Nihon sensōshi 1 Nisshin Nichiro sensō,* ed. Kuwada Etsu (Tokyo: Tōkyōdō Shuppan, 1995).

22. *Chōshi Kotohira,* 3:564.

23. Kanda Norio, "Senhi to sono chōtatsu," in *Kindai Nihon sensōshi 1 Nisshin Nichiro sensō,* ed. Kuwada Etsu (Tokyo: Tōkyōdō Shuppan, 1995), 579, 585. The foreign loans were to be repaid by customs duties as well as heightened taxes on tobacco and other goods, further burdening consumers.

24. James L. Huffman, *Creating a Public: People and Press in Meiji Japan* (Honolulu: University of Hawai'i Press, 1997), 271–77.

25. *KSSS nenpyō,* 54; *Kagawa Shinpō,* 14 and 23 February 1904.

26. *Kagawa Shinpō,* 24 February 1904, 5. The flags celebrated Japan's formal alliance with England (in the Anglo-Japanese Alliance of 1902) and its informal ties to the United States.

27. For the celebration of the victory of Port Arthur, for example, see *Kagawa Shinpō,* 16 March 1904, 2.

28. Kotohiragū, *Nisshi,* entries for 27 February and 2–4 March 1904. See also *Kagawa Shinpō,* 28 February 1904, 4.

29. Ibid., 4 March 1904, 2.

30. Ibid., 1 April 1905, 5.

31. Ibid., 26 February 1904, 2.

32. Ibid., 4 March 1904, 2.

33. Ibid., 19 February 1904, 5.

34. See, for example, *Kagawa Shinpō,* 19 February 1904, 5.

35. While groups of firefighters or business leaders had occasionally visited Konpira to obtain amulets for the families of soldiers during the Sino-Japanese War, for the most part the groups seem to have corresponded to village or hamlet units, not occupational associations. Ibid., 25 August 1904, 3, and 5 September 1904, 5.

36. Ibid., 16 and 17 February 1904.

37. *Kagawa Shinpō,* 11 March 1904, 2.

38. Ibid., 18 and 20 February 1904.

39. Unfortunately, few issues of the trade-oriented newspaper *Sanuki Jitsugyō Shinbun* are extant, and none from the time of the Russo-Japanese War.

40. Ibid., 15 October and 9–11 November 1904.

41. Ibid., 12 November 1904, 1.

42. Ibid., 10 January 1905, 6.

43. "Jikyokuchū no Kotohirachō," *Kagawa Shinpō,* 17 August 1905, 5.

44. Letter from Arisue Kagonoshin, March 1904. As mentioned above, all letters, as well as the Reverence Association's replies, are bound together in Kotohiragū Sūkei Kōsha Honbu, *Ōfuku todome.*

45. Letter from Nagano Masaaki, 7 April 1904.

46. Letter from Ōya Hachio, 18 April 1904.

47. *Kagawa Shinpō,* 28 April 1904, 6.

48. Letter from Arisue, 26 May 1904.

49. Letter from Maruyama Shinjūrō, 2 June 1904.

50. Letter from Hayashi Torazō, 15 June 1905.

51. Matsubara Hideaki, personal communication.

52. Kotohiragū, *Kotohiragū shiryō,* vol. 7. It is a sign of the acceptance of the practice of floating military donations as commonplace, however, that it was mentioned in the newspaper only once. *Kagawa Shinpō,* 10 February 1905, 5.

53. Ogasawara Chōsei, ed., *Seishō Tōgō zenden* (Tokyo: Seishō Tōgō Zenden Kankōkai, 1941), 3:27–28.

54. Ōtsubo Isamu, "Nichiro sensō to jinja to no kankei," *Jinja kyōkai zasshi* 4, no. 4 (April 1905): 25.

55. Nakagawa Yūjirō, "Gunjin ni taisuru mamorifuda juyo ni tsuite," *Jinja kyōkai zasshi,* no. 28 (June 1904), 7.

56. Ibid., 7.

57. Ōtsubo, "Nichiro sensō to jinja to no kankei," 26.

58. Seto Kengo, "Kotohiragū to Nichiro sensō," *Kotohira,* no. 46 (1991): 172–73.

59. *Kagawa Shinpō,* 30 July 1908, 5.

60. Kotohiragū, *Kotohiragū sūkeishi,* 3:43.

61. Kotohiragū, *Kotohiragū shiryō,* vol. 5; and *Kagawa Shinpō,* 2 June 1907, 5. On the opening ceremony, see "Hōmotsukan rakusei shikikyō," *Kagawa Shinpō,* 18 July 1905, 2. See also a photograph of the two-story, Western-style museum, and the thatched victory gate in front of it, in *Chōshi Kotohira,* 5:202.

62. "Kotohiragū Aobaoka zakken," *Kagawa Shinpō,* 29 June 1907, 5.

63. Ema donated by Kataoka Tokutarō of Takeda village, Asago district, Tajima province (present-day Hyōgo prefecture). Text reproduced in Kotohiragū, *Kotohiragū shiryō,* vol. 67.

64. See, for example, the letter from Udaka Yasaburō in Aichi prefecture, explaining that his kō is unable to go on pilgrimage to the shrine this year [1904] "because of the Russo-Japanese War and the inconvenience of the trains." Letter dated 15 April 1904.

65. See, for example, the letter from Udaka Yasaburō, 15 April 1904.

66. Kubo Shinri, "Senji ni okeru shinshoku no honbun," *Jinja kyōkai zasshi,* no. 28 (June 1904): 8–9.

67. See, for instance, Imazawa Jikai, *Fudōson no reigen* (Tokyo: Fudō Zenshū Kankōkai, 1941); Murakami Yutaka, *(Shin shintō) Kurozumikyō no shintai tsuki reigendan* (Okayama: Fujita Chōyōdō, 1936); and Yamamoto Seiichirō, *Shinbutsu no sonzai to kiseki* (Tokyo: Shōyōsha, 1935). Kotohira Shrine, for instance, republished Matsuoka's miracle tales in its newly inaugurated shrine journal during the Pacific War.

68. "Kotohirasan no goshintoku aogi," *Kagawa Shinpō,* 31 October 1939, 3.

Chapter 13

1. *Chōshi Kotohira,* 3:553–54.

2. *Kagawa Shinpō,* 26 May 1898, 3.

3. Ibid., 2 June 1901, 3.

4. Ibid., 30 August 1907, 5; and 19 and 21 September 1905, 5.

5. Ibid., 11 July 1908, 5; and 17 July 1908, 5. The full list also appears in the official court records of the case, Takamatsu Chihō Saibansho, *Meiji 45 nen—Taishō gannen dai is-shin hanketsu genpon,* Records of the Takamatsu Regional Court, 515–16. I would like to thank Professor Matsumoto Tami and the members of the Kagawa Minji Hanketsu Gen-pon Kenkyūkai in the Kagawa University Faculty of Law for their assistance in finding and interpreting these records.

6. *Kagawa Shinpō,* 7 August 1908, 2; and 22 August 1908, 2.

7. Ibid., 15 August 1908, 2; and 8 September 1908, 2; on the formation of the association, see *Kagawa Shinpō,* 18 February 1908, 2.

8. Ibid., 25 September 1908, 2.

9. For example, ibid., 6 September 1908, 1; and 25 October 1908, 2. Unfortunately, very few issues of the *Sanuki Nippō* are extant, and none from this time.

10. "Shaji jiken no soshō benron," *Kagawa Shinpō,* 8 October 1908, 5.

11. "Shaji jiken," *Kagawa Shinpō,* 8 October 1908, 5.

12. *Kagawa Shinpō,* 23 December 1908, 5; and 16 January 1909, 5.

13. "Kotohiragū sōron jiken no kihyō montō," *Kagawa Shinpō,* 22 January 1909, 3; and 24 January 1909, 4; Itō Ichirō, "Sanuki Konpira Daigongen ni tsuite," *Kagawa Shinpō,* 25–31 March 1909, 4. Itō's articles reiterated the arguments in his twenty-page book *Kotohiragū jiken no hyōron* (Kotohira: Ono Hideya, 1909). The Buddhist side was represented by Kawaguchi Akitsugi's sixty-page study *Zōzusan Konpira Daigongen no shintai* (Kotohira: Ozaki Saburō, 1908).

14. Takamatsu Chihō Saibansho, *Meiji 45 nen,* 515–16.

15. *Kagawa Shinpō,* 16 January 1909, 5. These briefcases of documents, collected by Kotohira Shrine for this occasion, formed the core of the unpublished collection *Kotohiragū shiryō,* used extensively throughout this book.

16. "Matsuoji tai Kotohiragū," *Kagawa Shinpō,* 30 June 1909, 5. The official records of the trial do not include speeches by the lawyers.

17. "Matsuoji tai Kotohiragū," *Kagawa Shinpō,* 30 June 1909, 5.

18. "Matsuoji tai Kotohiragū," *Kagawa Shinpō,* 30 June 1909, 5.

19. Takamatsu Chihō Saibansho, *Meiji 45 nen,* 522–27; "Kotohira jiken ketsuhan riyūsho," *Kagawa Shinpō,* 21 July 1909, 5.

20. *Kagawa Shinpō,* 20 July 1912, 5.

21. Karen Smyers vividly illustrates this dynamic in *The Fox and the Jewel.*

22. The text of the ema appears in Kotohiragū, *Kotohiragū shiryō,* vol. 67.

23. "Kimyō no shingan," *Kagawa Shinpō,* 7 February 1908, 5.

24. I have been unable to locate any police records for Kotohira during this time period, or any corroborating evidence. The attitudes expressed, however, appear time and again in sources of the period.

25. I would like to thank Morikawa Iemitsu for sharing his recollections of Mitarai from the 1930s on. Mr. Morikawa explained that at that time both men and women offered the manjū because of their similarity to male genitalia. The association between manjū and Konpira worship for the healing of sexual diseases was so strong in this town of brothels serving the countless men sailing to Konpira each year that before the Second World War there was a specialty shop that made only these particular manjū to be offered to Konpira, not actually eaten. Interview in Kinoe-chō, Hiroshima-ken, 23 October 1996.

26. See, for instance, the record of an ema donated in the early 1930s mentioning the donation of a net in 1929. Kotohiragū, *Kotohiragū shiryō,* vol. 53. See also photographs of boat models, anchors, and other items in *KSSS,* vol. 1.

27. See, for example, Muramatsu, *Kotohira miyage.*

28. "Denwa o kakeru Konpirasan," *Kagawa Shinpō,* 10 June 1911. Because the police records of Kotohira during that period have been destroyed, it is not possible to corroborate either this story or that of Hamaguchi. The newspaper cites names, hometowns, and dates, which suggests that the tales were based on actual incidents. Whether the actual events took place or not, the articles demonstrated and reinforced the attitudes of superiority among the writers and the educated elites of the area while depicting acts of faith that may have been extreme but were not wholly unthinkable at the time.

29. Mori Ōgai, "Konpira" (1909), reprinted in *Ōgai senshū,* vol. 1, ed. Mori Rintarō (Tokyo: Iwanami Shoten, 1978), 293–337. Mori Ōgai's tale has been translated into English by James M. Vardaman, Jr., as "Konpira," in *"Youth" and Other Stories: Mori Ōgai,* ed. J. Thomas Rimer (Honolulu: University of Hawaii Press, 1994), 102–35.

30. See, for example, the poetry in an anonymous sixty-seven-year-old's "Kotohira Miyajima kikō" (1900), reprinted in "Honkoku 'Kotohira Miyajima kikō,'" by Sakurai Takejirō, *Kotohira,* no. 39 (1984): 59–63; the descriptions of scenery in the third-year middle-school student Asaya Sōkichi's article "Kotohirayuki," in *Sanuki Gakuseikai Zasshi,* no. 38 (12 December 1909): 39–40; and countless other earlier writings cited throughout this book.

31. "Kokuhō honzon kaibi junbi," *Kagawa Shinpō,* 20 December 1911, 5. It was clear by this time that Kotohira and Sanuki, previously so centrally located in a maritime economy, were increasingly on the economic periphery. See Wigen, *The Making of a Japanese Periphery.*

32. See, for instance, "Kotohira okusha sanbyakunen taisai ihō," *Takamatsu Shohō,* 15 February 1912, 8; and "Kotohira okusha taisai," *Kagawa Shinpō,* 8 March 1912, 5.

33. See, for example, *Kagawa Shinpō,* 9 August 1898, 5; 21 August 1898, 2; 12 August 1899, 2.

34. "Geta haki no jidōsha," Kotohira mairi 4, *Ōsaka Asahi Shinbun,* 4 March 1912, 9.

35. Ibid., 9.

36. On the link between nostalgia and travel, and the contributions of the foklorist Yanagita Kunio to this constellation of sentiments in Japan in the second decade of the twentieth century, see Marilyn Ivy, *Discourses of the Vanishing: Modernity, Phantasm, Japan* (Chicago: University of Chicago Press, 1995).

37. "Ame to senburi," Kotohira mairi 1, *Ōsaka Asahi Shinbun,* 1 March 1912, 11. The "shu, shu, shu" sound of the boats appeared in a renowned drinking song that had become popular by the 1880s. Nukata Roppuku, "Konpira fune fune," *Kotohira* 2, no. 12 (1935): 10–11.

38. "Manzoku suruya ikan," *Kagawa Shinpō,* 17 March 1912, 1.

39. *Kagawa Shinpō,* Kotohiragū okusha sanbyakunensai kinengō, 1 March 1912.

40. See, for instance, photographs, usually on the first page, in *San'yō Shinbun,* 1–9 March 1912.

41. Both the *Kagawa Shinpō* in Takamatsu and the *San'yō Shinbun* in Okayama, which featured these displays of photographs and cultural, historical narration, acted as party organs of the conservative Kaishintō in the 1880s. It seems likely that, in many areas of rural Japan, conservative newspapers dominated the markets, spreading respectful images and

rhetoric of Shinto shrines and cultural sites throughout the nation. Kagawa-ken, *Kagawa kenshi* 5, 528–29; "Kokumin kyōkai no naijō," *Kagawa Shinpō,* 12 November 1892, 2; and "Mitsui Shōsaburōshi kokumin kyōkai e nyūkai no riyū," *Kagawa Shinpō,* 11 November 1892, 3; Huffman, *Creating a Public,* 128–29.

42. Kanezawa Osamu, "Gojūnen mae no shōgakusei ga nikkichō ni shirushita Kotohira mairi," *Kotohira* 16 (1961): 69–70.

43. "Kotohira Suizokukan," *Kainan Shinbun,* 5 March 1912, 5. Gōda, "Monzenmachi no panoramakan to sono ato," 73.

44. Nakao Rosan, "Kotohira sankei," part of the series "Jūen ryokō" in *Nagoya Shinbun,* 25 March 1912, 3.

45. In his seminal work, *The Tourist: A New Theory of the Leisure Class* (New York: Shocken Books, 1976), Dean MacCannell examined the ways in which both sightseers and promoters used sites to define themselves and their worlds, especially since the rise of modern mass tourism around 1900.

46. Hashikawa Hoki, ed., *Izumo Taisha Kotohiragū Sanpaiki* (Tokyo: Kaitsūsha, 1912), 63–68.

Epilogue

1. Innami, "Konpira shinkō to tabi," 63–67.

2. Innami, "Konpira shinkō to tabi," 70.

3. Personal interviews with Yamanaka Atsushi, 17 June 1996; and Ochi Kantarō, 30 October 1996. See also Innami, "Konpira shinkō to tabi," 64.

4. *Chōshi Kotohira,* 3:815.

5. Innami, "Keidai no tōrō," 263.

6. On the tendency to idealize the Tokugawa-era past while eliding the years of imperialism and militarism since, see Carol Gluck "The Invention of Edo," in *Mirror of Modernity: Invented Traditions of Modern Japan,* ed. Stephen Vlastos (Berkeley: University of California Press, 1998), 262–84.

7. For color reproductions of the materials as well as responses from viewers, see "Eburibadi, Konpirasan tokushū," *Kotohira* 48 (1993): 10–12, 216–73. The children's book was written by Tada Toshiko and illustrated by Yumura Teruhiko. *Hashiregon: Konpira inu monogatari* (Tokyo: Arai Kennosuke, 1994).

8. For descriptions of several such rituals, as well as of the atmosphere and politics of a contemporary shrine, see John K. Nelson, *A Year in the Life of a Shinto Shrine* (Seattle: University of Washington Press, 1996).

9. "Jōhō manzai!! Hankyō yobu hōmupēji," *Kotohira* 52 (1997): 10–11.

10. A link to a series of weekly essays, running from 6 April 2003 until 25 July 2004, called "Kotohiragū bi no sekai" [Kotohira Shrine: The World of Beauty] in the *Shikoku Shinbun* (successor to the *Kagawa Shinpō*) can be found on the Web site of either the shrine or the newspaper (http://www.shikoku-np.co.jp/feature/kotohira/index.htm).

11. David R. Ambaras focuses on the emergence of this "middle class" as an urban phenomenon. However, the rural "middle class" was just as important in the social, economic, and political developments at the turn of the century. "Social Knowledge, Cultural

Capital, and the New Middle Class in Japan, 1895–1912," *Journal of Japanese Studies* 24, no. 1 (Winter 1998): 1–34.

12. Sarah Thal, "Redefining the Gods: Politics and Survival in the Creation of Modern Kami," *Japanese Journal of Religious Studies* 29, nos. 3–4 (Fall 2003): 379–404.

13. John K. Nelson makes this point—concerning both the "virtuosity" of priests and the multiple approaches of worshippers—in relation to contemporary Shinto. *Enduring Identities: The Guise of Shinto in Contemporary Japan* (Honolulu: University of Hawai'i Press, 2000).

amagoi—prayers for rain

Amaterasu—the sun goddess; the kami enshrined at Ise Shrine, purportedly the ancestor of the imperial line

Amida—buddha of the Western Pure Land Paradise, to which he is thought to welcome those who call upon his name at death

bakufu—shogunal government; shogunate

bettō—administrative priest of the Buddhist temple of a kami (whether Indian or Japanese) and thus, at Konkōin, the head priest

bodhisattva—enlightened being, according to Buddhist thought, who stays in this world to help others attain enlightenment

buddha—"enlightened one" in Buddhist thought, for example, Śākyamuni, the historical Buddha, or Amida, buddha of the Western Pure Land

bunmei kaika—"civilization and enlightenment," a slogan during the early years of the Meiji era promoting the adoption of Western thought and technology

cakravartin—Buddhist king or world ruler, a concept prominent in the Golden Light Sutra

chokugansho—imperial prayer site

chokusaisha—shrine performing imperial rituals

Chōsokabe Motochika (1538–99)—warlord of Tosa province who briefly controlled the entire island of Shikoku in the early 1580s

daimyō—lord of a major domain, one of 260-odd such lords under the Tokugawa system

Daoism—loosely related schools of Chinese thought and popular worship associated with the search for immortality, theories of yin and yang, nonaction, dragons, and supernatural powers

doctrinal instructor—*kyōdōshoku,* a lecturer initially licensed by the Great Teaching Institute to preach the state teachings as part of the Great Teaching Campaign

Edo—site of the Tokugawa shogun's castle; precursor of present-day Tokyo

ema—votive plaque

Enchin (814–91)—Tendai priest and esoteric practitioner, born in Sanuki province

encircled gold—the character for gold (*kon*) with a circle around it, a shorthand symbol for Konpira, Konkōin, and Kongōbō that became the official seal of Konkōin (see figure 6.1)

engi—origin tale

ennichi—"day of connection" of a deity, on which it is considered particularly responsive to petitioners' prayers; Konpira's ennichi is the tenth day of each month

Ezo—present-day northern island of Hokkaido

fuda—talisman or amulet, usually made of wood

Fudō Myōō—fierce guardian deity of the Golden Light Sutra; he stands amid the flames of ignorance, holding a sword that cuts through illusions and a rope with which to drag people to enlightenment, and is closely associated with Konpira Daigongen and Kongōbō

Fukuba Bisei (1831–1907)—Ōkuni-school nativist from the Tsuwano domain, prominent in the early Meiji government, who emphasized the political utility of emperor-centered Shinto

Fumon'in—subtemple of Matsuoji, under Konkōin

geisha—female entertainer

gohei—purifying streamers, usually made of folded white paper, often on a wand

Golden Light Sutra—Japanese *Konkōmyō saishōō kyō*, Sanskrit *Suvarṇa-prabhāsa-uttama-sūtra*, one of the most influential sutras in early Japan; it promised protection and benefits to rulers who sponsored Buddhism in general and this sutra in particular; the guiding sutra of the Shingon Mishuhō ritual in the imperial court

goma—Sanskrit *homa*, an esoteric fire ritual in which prayers are offered—at Konkōin, to Fudō Myōō in a ceremony strongly influenced by the Golden Light Sutra

Great Teaching Institute—*Daikyōin* (1872–75), the central educational and licensing organization for doctrinal instructors in the Great Teaching Campaign

gyōja—an ascetic, usually a shugenja

Hachiman—kami of war

haikai—linked verse

hakama—formal split skirt for men

hanegin—percentage taken from fees charged by prostitutes and geisha, used in Konpira to fund the construction of a kabuki theater or, later, a park and trade school

haori—formal jacket

Hashikuraji—Shingon Buddhist temple in the mountains of Awa province that advertised itself as the "inner temple" (*okunoin*) of Konpira Daigongen

Hirata Atsutane (1776–1843)—nativist scholar and self-proclaimed successor to Motoori Norinaga; he identified Konpira as the native kami Kotohira—a joint enshrinement of Ōmononushi and the spirit of Emperor Sutoku

Hokke Hakkō—lectures on the Lotus Sutra

Hōnen (1133–1212)—Buddhist priest and founder of the Pure Land sect in Japan; he lived in exile in Sanuki province from 1207 to 1211

hozonkin—system, begun in 1887, of "preservation funds," payments given to state-supported shrines as part of a plan to phase out state support

Ibukinoya—nativist school of Hirata Atsutane

Iemitsu—see Tokugawa Iemitsu

Ikoma Chikamasa (1526–1603)—first Ikoma lord of Sanuki, appointed by Toyotomi Hideyoshi to replace Sengoku Hidehisa in 1587

Ise Shrine—shrine of the kami Amaterasu, the sun goddess, purportedly the ancestor of the imperial line

Itsutamahiko no Mikoto—kami name for Kongōbō-Yūsei

ittōbori—rough wood-carving technique distinctive to Sanuki province

Izumo—location of the shrine to the kami Ōkuninushi in Shimane province

Jingikō—nativist organization active in Sanuki province in 1867, presumably promoting the reestablishment of the ancient Office of Rites and, thus, the re-creation of an emperor- and kami-centered government

jinjiba—large, flat site used for festivals of Kotohira Shrine in the town below

Jinmu—mythical first emperor of Japan, supposed to have established the empire in 666 BCE

Jippensha Ikku (1765–1831)—author of the humorous travel tale *Hizakurige*

Kagawa—present-day prefecture corresponding to Sanuki province, in which Mt. Zōzu stands

kagura—sacred dance performed for the kami

kaichō—periodic "opening of curtains" to display a hidden image of worship—an event usually used by Buddhist temples to raise money

Kaientai—Tosa-led navy active during the Meiji Restoration

kami—Japanese "god" or "deity," denoting some spirit or being of particular power; Japanese translation for Indian *deva,* or god

Kanetomo—see Yoshida Kanetomo

Kannon—Sanskrit *Avalokiteśvara,* the bodhisattva of compassion

Khumbīra—Japanese *Konpira,* a fierce, crocodile-like god associated with a mountain in northern India

Kimigayo—poem from the eighth-century *Manyōshū* that became the de facto Japanese national anthem in 1893

Kinzanji—theater and entertainment area of the town of Konpira

kō—confraternity or confraternities formed by several members who donate some money each month, often formed to fund pilgrimage or offerings to shrines or temples

Kōbō Daishi—"Great Teacher who Spreads the Buddhist Law," posthumous title granted to the Buddhist priest Kūkai, founder of what became the Shingon sect of esoteric Buddhism in Japan

Kōchi prefecture—formerly Tosa province

Kojiki—history of Japan commissioned by the imperial house, completed ca. 712; the early chapters became the main source for Motoori Norinaga's interpretations of the kami

kokuheisha—provincial or national shrines, part of the hierarchy of state-supported shrines

Kokumin Kyōkai—organization established to support the government under the parliamentary system, although explicitly not a political party, from 1892 to 1899

Kongōbō—tengu form of Yūsei, head priest of Konkōin from 1600 until 1613

Konkōin—subtemple of the Golden Light, a subtemple of Matsuoji, focused on Konpira, whose priests generally functioned as the head priests of the mountain

Konpira—Japanese pronunciation of the Sanskrit *Khumbīra*, the name of the deity enshrined on Mt. Zōzu during the Tokugawa era—a name still in popular use to refer to the deity today

Konpira Daigongen—Great Avatar Konpira; Konpira as a manifestation of Fudō Myōō

koseki—household register

Kotohira—name identified by Hirata Atsutane as the original, Japanese name of Konpira; the Shinto name given to the kami in 1868; the name given to the town of Konpira from 1873 on

Kotooka Hirotsune (1839–92)—lay name adopted by Yūjō, head priest of Konkōin at the time of the Meiji Restoration, when he renounced his Buddhist affiliation and became a priest of the kami

Kujō—one of the highest aristocratic families in Japan, which held an estate in the area of Mt. Zōzu during the thirteenth century and sponsored a lottery at Konpira in the nineteenth

Kūkai (774–835)—priest who brought esoteric Buddhism to Japan from China and founded what became the Shingon denomination of Buddhism; posthumously Kōbō Daishi

Kyōgoku—lords of the Marugame and Tadotsu domains

Lotus Sutra—Japanese *Myōhō rengekyō,* Sanskrit *Saddharma-puṇḍarīka-sūtra,* one of the most influential Buddhist sutras in Japan, the central sutra of the Tendai and Nichiren Buddhist denominations

mandala—visual aid for meditation in the esoteric Shingon Buddhist tradition

Marugame—port of entry to Shikoku for pilgrims to Konpira; the second-largest domain in Sanuki province, ruled by the Kyōgoku lords

Matsudaira Yorishige (1622–95)—first lord of the Takamatsu domain; appointed by Tokugawa Ieyasu, he worked closely with the priest Yūten to promote Konpira Daigongen as a manifestation of Fudō Myōō tied closely to the priest-tengu Kongōbō-Yūsei

Matsukata Masayoshi (1835–1924)—finance minister in the Meiji government from 1881 until 1892

Matsuoji—temple name of the institution on Mt. Zōzu during the Tokugawa era; the temple name adopted by Zōsan Yūon and his successors from the mid-Meiji era on

Matsuoka Mitsugi (1834–1904)—head priest of Tawa Shrine and, from 1872, a priest at Kotohira Shrine; author of the diary *Nennen nikki* and founder of Tawa Archive

mikoshi—sacred palanquin used to carry the kami during festivals

Mishuhō—ritual performance for the protection and empowerment of the ruler, based on the Golden Light Sutra, promoted by Kūkai, performed by Shingon priests in the ancient imperial court, and revived in the court in the early seventeenth century

miso—soybean paste

Mito—domain whose scholars compiled the *Great History of Japan,* begun by Tokugawa Mitsukuni (father of the first Takamatsu lord, Matsudaira Yorishige), which traced the history of the imperial house

Miyajima—island site of Itsukushima, the renowned coastal shrine in present-day Hiroshima prefecture

Motoori Norinaga (1730–1801)—nativist literary scholar whose studies of the chapters on the Age of the Gods in the *Kojiki* inspired an increased focus on native kami

Mt. Besshi—site of a copper mine in Iyo province that in the eighteenth century was one of the largest copper mines in the world

Mt. Hiei—site of the headquarters of the Tendai Buddhist sect

Mt. Kōya—headquarters of Kūkai's Shingon Buddhist sect

Mt. Zōzu—"Mt. Elephant Head," the mountain on the plains of Sanuki where Konpira was enshrined

mudra—esoteric Buddhist gesture used to identify a practitioner with a particular buddha as an aid to meditation

Myōdō Gakkō—middle school at Kotohira Shrine in the mid-Meiji era

Naniwakō—travel guild guiding customers to reputable inns in the nineteenth century

nativist—scholar of explicitly Japanese, not Chinese, literature and history; many nativists became ardent proponents of an exclusively Japanese Way of the Kami (Shinto) in the mid-nineteenth century

nenbutsu—recitation of the name of the buddha, usually Amida, in order to be reborn in his Pure Land after death

Nichiren—school of Buddhism based on worship of the Lotus Sutra, founded by the Buddhist priest Nichiren (1222–82)

Nihon Shoki—history of Japan commissioned by the imperial house, completed ca. 720; written in classical Chinese, its early chapters became the preeminent source for study of the Japanese kami until the late eighteenth century

Niōmon—"Gate of Two Guardian Kings," the main gate to the precincts of a Buddhist temple

Nitenmon—"Gate of Two Heavenly Kings," a temple gate subsidiary to the Niōmon

Office of Rites—Jingikan, the highest bureaucratic department under the ancient, emperor-centered government, which nativists in the 1860s hoped to revive; a bureaucratic office dominated by nativists in the early Meiji government until its abolition in 1871

Ōkuninushi—literally "Great-Country-Master," alternative name for Ōmononushi, identified by Motoori Norinaga and Hirata Atsutane as the ruler of the hidden world of the gods

okunoin—"inner temple"

okusha—"inner shrine"

omairi—"pilgrimage," a popular term

Ōmononushi—snake-shaped kami appearing in the *Nihon Shoki*

Ōnamuchi—alternative name for Ōmononushi

pantheon dispute—*saijin ronsō,* controversy over which kami should be enshrined in the Great Teaching Institute, generally pitting supporters of Ise and Amaterasu against supporters of Izumo and Ōkuninushi

prefecture—administrative unit created to replace the domains in 1871; Takamatsu, Marugame, and Tadotsu domains together eventually became Kagawa prefecture

Reverence Association—*sūkei kōsha,* shrine-controlled pilgrimage organization created by the priests of Kotohira Shrine in 1873 to tie independent worshippers and pilgrimage kō to the shrine

ricksha—small, two-wheeled carriage drawn by a person

Ryūkyū Islands—islands south of Kyushu; present-day Okinawa prefecture

Saichō (766–822)—founder of what became the Tendai school of Japanese Buddhism

Saijō—domain in Iyo province, near Konpira

saisei itchi—"unity of rites and rule" declared during the Meiji Restoration in 1868, identifying worship of the nativist kami as an essential part of government

Saita—village in Iyo province, home to the Yamashita family, whose younger sons became priests of Konkōin

sakaki—sacred tree in Shinto ritual

saké—rice wine

sakura—cherry trees

Sakuranobaba—broad, straight walkway just inside the main gate of Konpira or Kotohira Shrine, lined on both sides by cherry trees

Śākyamuni—the historical Buddha, Gautama Siddharta

Sanjūbanjin—the Thirty Protecting Deities of the Lotus Sutra

sanpai—"pilgrimage," or "worship," a term most often used by and about well-educated, decorous, formal Shinto worshippers

Sanuki—province on the island of Shikoku in which Mt. Zōzu stands

Sayabashi—covered bridge in the town of Konpira

sekkanke—the five highest aristocratic families in Japan, among whom the Kujō was one, qualified to act as regents to the emperor

Senge Takatomi (1845–1918)—head priest of Izumo Shrine and active leader in the Great Teaching Campaign

Sengoku Hidehisa (1552–1614)—general under Toyotomi Hideyoshi who defeated Chōsokabe Motochika and was appointed as lord of Sanuki province in his place

shamisen—three-stringed instrument, somewhat like a banjo, played most often by geisha to accompany singing

Shikoku—smallest of the four main islands of Japan, on which Mt. Zōzu stands

shinbutsu—kami and buddhas

shinbutsu bunri—"separation of kami and buddhas" in 1868

Shingaku—movement based on teachings promoted by Ishida Baigan in 1729, which emphasized a focus on one's household occupation

Shingon—school of Japanese esoteric Buddhism that developed out of the teachings of Kūkai

shinkan—Shinto priest, literally "kami official"

shinkoku—land of the kami, divine country

shinshoku—Shinto priest, literally "kami worker"

shintai—body of the kami

Shintō—Way of the Kami

Shiwaku Islands—islands in the Inland Sea, between Marugame and Kurashiki, home to international shippers and pirates in the sixteenth century

shōen—privately owned estate

shogun—head of the hereditary Tokugawa administration, to whom local lords (daimyo) swore fealty

shogunate—the Tokugawa government

Shōmyōin—"subtemple for the recitation of the name," apparently the hermitage of a Pure Land Buddhist monk on or near Mt. Zōzu in the thirteenth century

shugendo—mountain asceticism

shugenja—one who practices shugendo; a mountain ascetic

stupa—Buddhist marker built to commemorate the dead

Suika Shinto—Way of the Kami promoted by Yamazaki Ansai in the seventeenth century, espousing loyalty to the emperor as the descendant of the sun goddess Amaterasu

sumō—Japanese wrestling

Susano'o—kami, brother of Amaterasu, mentioned in the *Kojiki* and *Nihon Shoki*

Sutoku (1119–64, r. 1123–41)—emperor who, after the Hōgen War in 1156, was exiled to Sanuki province; according to legend, the retired emperor vowed vengeance against the imperial house and became a tengu

sutra—Buddhist scripture

Tadotsu—port of entry on Shikoku for pilgrims to Konpira; ruled by a branch house of the Marugame Kyōgoku lords

Takamatsu—domain and castle town of the Matsudaira lords in eastern Sanuki

Takenouchi Shikibu (1712–67)—teacher of Suika Shinto influential among lesser aristocrats in the imperial court, including the tutor of Emperor Momozono

Takidera—"Waterfall Temple," enshrining Kannon on Mt. Zōzu in the thirteenth century

Tamon'in—shugendo subtemple of Matsuoji that acted as an administrative arm of Konkōin and was sponsored by donors in Tosa province

tatami—straw mats used as a floor covering

Tendai—school of Buddhism, including both esoteric and exoteric elements, that developed out of the teachings of Saichō

tengu—long-nosed, winged, goblinlike spirit generally thought to reside in the mountains, often associated with mountain ascetics (shugenja)

tennō—emperor

Thirty Protecting Deities—Japanese kami identified as guardians of the Lotus Sutra and worshipped in Nichiren Buddhism and Yoshida/Yoshikawa Shinto

Tokugawa Iemitsu (1604–51)—third Tokugawa shogun, 1623–51, who restricted foreign trade, established the temple-branch system to control temples, and expanded the system of alternate attendance to control daimyo

Tokugawa Ieyasu (1542–1616)—founder of the Tokugawa shogunate after his victory at Sekigahara in 1600; enshrined at Nikkō Tōshōgū after his death as Tōshō Daigongen according to Tendai rituals

Tokuhisa Tsunenori (1843–1910)—governor of Kagawa prefecture from April 1896 to July 1898

Toranomon—site of the Marugame daimyo's mansion and its shrine to Konpira in Edo; after 1868, the site of the Toranomon Kotohira Shrine

torii—simple, gatelike structure considered a marker of Shinto shrines after 1868

Tosa—large province on the Pacific side of Shikoku; home of the warlord Chōsokabe Motochika; one of the major loyalist domains in the Meiji Restoration; present-day Kōchi prefecture

Toyotomi Hideyoshi (1536–98)—warlord who continued Oda Nobunaga's subjugation of lesser lords throughout Japan; regent of Japan from 1585 until 1598

Uchimachi—"inner town" of Konpira, the area in which many of the main inns stood on the main route to the shrine

Uchitaki—wooded area at the base of a cliff to the northwest of the main shrine of Konpira, in which the shrine to Itsutamahiko no Mikoto was built from 1898 on

ujigami—local tutelary kami

ujiko shirabe—system of population registration in the early Meiji period in which births, deaths, and changes of residence were recorded at Shinto shrines

yaksha—Indian demon appearing in the sutras; according to some sutras, Konpira was a king of the yakshas

Yakushi—the buddha Medicine Master; according to some sutras, Konpira was a servant of Yakushi

Yamashita—family from which head priests of Konkōin came from 1613 on

Yamazaki Ansai (1618–82)—Confucian scholar influenced by Yoshikawa Koretaru who promoted Suika Shinto, emphasizing loyalty to the emperor as a descendant of the sun goddess Amaterasu

Yano Harumichi (1823–87)—nativist promoter of the revival of the Office of Rites in 1867

Yoshida Kanetomo (1435–1511)—proponent of the idea that kami are original, that buddhas are manifestations of Japanese kami; founder of Yoshida Shinto

Yoshida (Yuiitsu) Shinto—One and Only Way of the Kami, promoted by Yoshida Kanetomo, asserting that kami were primary and buddhas only secondary; under the Tokugawa shoguns, the Yoshida school controlled the qualifications of Shinto priests at smaller shrines around the country

Yoshikawa Koretaru (1616–94)—heir to the lineage of Yoshida Shinto whose Shinto teachings became influential in Confucian circles

Yūsei—reviver and head priest of Konkōin, 1600–1613, a Shingon Buddhist priest and shugenja known posthumously as the tengu Kongōbō

yūshisha—"notables," generally educated and propertied men

Yūten—head priest of Konkōin (1645–66, d. 1675) who worked closely with the first Takamatsu lord, Matsudaira Yorishige, to develop a cult of Konpira Daigongen and Fudō Myōō around the tengu image of Kongōbō-Yūsei

Zentsūji—birthplace of the Buddhist priest Kūkai and, from 1900, the base of the Eleventh Division of the army

Zōsan Yūon—former priest of Fumon'in who during the Meiji period established a series of temples dedicated to Konpira Daigongen, eventually claiming the name Matsuoji for his establishment

BIBLIOGRAPHY

Abe, Ryūichi. *The Weaving of Mantra*. New York: Columbia University Press, 1999.

Akatsuki Kanenari. *Konpira sankei meisho zue*. 1847. Reprinted with annotations by Kusanagi Kinshirō. Tokyo: Rekishi Toshosha, 1980.

Ambaras, David R. "Social Knowledge, Cultural Capital, and the New Middle Class in Japan, 1895–1912." *Journal of Japanese Studies* 24, no. 1 (Winter 1998): 1–34.

Ambros, Barbara. "Mountain of Great Prosperity: The Ōyama Cult in Early Modern Japan." PhD diss., Harvard University, 2002.

Ame no Ie Shujin (pseud.). "Yume no Matsu." 1889. Unpublished manuscript in the collection of the Kotohira Shrine library.

Andō Ichirō. *Konpira Daigongen goreigen jikki*. Kan'onji: Miyoshi Gisaburō, 1911.

Arai Tomizō, ed. *Sanuki kyōdo kenkyū*. Vol. 8. Takamatsu: Sanuki Kyōdo Kenkyūkai, 1964.

Asaya Sōkichi. "Kotohirayuki." *Sanuki Gakuseikai Zasshi,* no. 38 (12 December 1909): 39–40.

Barrett, Tim. "Shinto and Taoism in Early Japan." In *Shinto in History: Ways of the Kami,* edited by John Breen and Mark Teeuwen, 13–31. Surrey: Curzon Press, 2000.

Bernstein, Andrew. *Modern Passings: Death Rites, Politics, and Social Change in Imperial Japan*. Honolulu: University of Hawai'i Press, forthcoming.

Breen, J. L. "Beyond the Prohibition: Christianity in Restoration Japan." In *Japan and Christianity: Impacts and Responses,* edited by John Breen and Mark Williams. London: MacMillan, 1996.

———. "Shintoists in Restoration Japan (1868–1872): Towards a Reassessment." *Modern Asian Studies* 24, no. 3 (1990): 579–602.

Burns, Susan L. *Before the Nation: Kokugaku and the Imagining of Community in Early Modern Japan*. Durham, N.C.: Duke University Press, 2003.

Coleman, Simon, and John Elsner. *Pilgrimage: Past and Present in the World Religions*. Cambridge, Mass.: Harvard University Press, 1995.

Collcutt, Martin. "Buddhism: The Threat of Eradication." In *Japan in Transition*, edited by Marius B. Jansen and Gilbert Rozman, 143–67. Princeton, N.J.: Princeton University Press, 1986.

Conlan, Thomas. *In Little Need of Divine Intervention*. Ithaca, N.Y.: Cornell University East Asia Program, 2001.

Craig, Albert. *Chōshū and the Meiji Restoration*. Cambridge, Mass.: Harvard University Press, 1967.

"Dai Nihon Teikoku Suinan Kyūsaikai Kisoku." Reproduced in *Teikoku Suinan Kyūsaikai gojūnenshi*, by Teikoku Suinan Kyūsaikai, 5–10. Tokyo: Teikoku Suinan Kyūsaikai, 1939.

Davis, Winston. *Japanese Religion and Society: Paradigms of Structure and Change*. Albany: State University of New York Press, 1992.

De Bary, Wm. Theodore, Donald Keene, George Tanabe, and Paul Varley, comps. *Sources of Japanese Tradition*. Vol. 1. 2nd ed. New York: Columbia University Press, 2001.

Devi, Shanti. *Hospitality for the Gods: Popular Religion in Edo, Japan: An Example*. Ann Arbor, Mich.: University Microfilms International, 1986.

Devine, Richard. "Hirata Atsutane and Christian Sources." *Monumenta Nipponica* 36 (Spring 1981): 37–54.

Dōhan Ajari. "Nankai Rurōki." In *Gunsho Ruijū*, 18:468–76. 1932. Reprint, Tokyo: Zoku Gunsho Ruijū Kanseikai, 1977.

Dolce, Lucia. "Hokke Shinto: Kami in the Nichiren Tradition." In *Buddhas and Kami in Japan*, edited by Mark Teeuwen and Fabio Rambelli, 222–54. London: Routledge Curzon, 2003.

Eade, John, and Michael J. Sallnow, eds. *Contesting the Sacred: The Anthropology of Christian Pilgrimage*. London: Routledge, 1991.

Enjōji, ed. *Chishō Daishi zenshū*. Saga-ken, Ōtsu-shi: Enjōji Jimusho, 1918.

Enoki Gakusui. "Enoki Gakusui nikki 2." 1871. Reprinted in *Dai Nihon Kokiroku*, edited by Tōkyō Daigaku Shiryō Hensanjo. Tokyo: Iwanami Shoten, 1956.

Figal, Gerald A. *Civilization and Monsters: Spirits of Modernity in Meiji Japan*. Durham, N.C.: Duke University Press, 1999.

Foard, James. "The Boundaries of Compassion: Buddhism and National Tradition in Japanese Pilgrimage," *Journal of Asian Studies* 41, no. 2 (February 1982): 231–51.

Fujimoto Chōjirō. *Kotohirasan zenzu*. Kotohira, 1882.

Fujita Satoru. *Bakumatsu no tennō*. Tokyo: Kōdansha, 1994.

Fujitani, T. *Splendid Monarchy: Power and Pageantry in Modern Japan*. Berkeley: University of California Press, 1996.

Fukuchi Shigetaka. *Kōmei tennō*. Tokyo: Akita Shoten, 1974.

Garon, Sheldon. *Molding Japanese Minds*. Princeton, N.J.: Princeton University Press, 1997.

Gluck, Carol. "The Invention of Edo." In *Mirror of Modernity: Invented Traditions of Modern Japan,* edited by Stephen Vlastos, 262–84. Berkeley: University of California Press, 1998.

———. *Japan's Modern Myths: Ideology in the Late Meiji Period.* Princeton, N.J.: Princeton University Press, 1985.

Gōda Chōjirō. "Monzenmachi no panoramakan to sono ato." *Kotohira,* no. 54.

Graburn, Nelson. *To Pray, Pay, and Play: The Cultural Structure of Japanese Domestic Tourism.* Aix en Provence: Centre des Hautes Études Touristiques, 1983.

Grapard, Allan G. "Japan's Ignored Cultural Revolution: The Separation of Shinto and Buddhist Divinities (*shimbutsu bunri*) in Meiji and a Case Study, Tōnomine." *History of Religions* 23, no. 3 (1984): 240–65.

———. *The Protocol of the Gods: A Study of the Kasuga Cult in Japanese History.* Berkeley: University of California Press, 1992.

———. "The Shinto of Yoshida Kanetomo." *Monument Nipponica* 47, no. 1 (Spring 1992): 27–58

Haga Shōji. *Meiji ishin to shūkyō.* Tokyo: Chikuma Shobō, 1994.

Hakoyama Kitarō. "Ise sangūshi: ryochū no nisshi." *Naganoken Minzoku no Kai Tsūshin,* no. 71 (January 1986).

Hanley, Susan B., and Kozo Yamamura. *Economic and Demographic Change in Preindustrial Japan, 1600–1868.* Princeton, N.J.: Princeton University Press, 1977.

Hara Takeshi. *"Izumo" toiu shisō: kindai Nihon no massatsu sareta kamigami.* Tokyo: Kōninsha, 1996.

Harada Keiichi. "Nihon kokumin no sansen netsu." In *Nisshin senso no shakaishi: "bunmei senso" to minshū,* edited by Ōtani Tadashi and Harada Keiichi, 11–40. Osaka: Fuooramu A, 1994.

Hardacre, Helen. "Creating State Shintō: The Great Promulgation Campaign and the New Religions." *Journal of Japanese Studies* 12, no. 1 (1986): 29–63.

———. *Shintō and the State, 1868–1988.* Princeton, N.J.: Princeton University Press, 1989.

Harootunian, H. D. *Things Seen and Unseen: Discourse and Ideology in Tokugawa Nativism.* Chicago: University of Chicago Press, 1988.

Hashida Zankyū. "Tōmyōdai to Konpira shinkō." *Susaki shidan,* no. 29 (November 1977).

Hashikawa Hoki, ed. *Izumo Taisha Kotohiragū Sanpaiki.* Tokyo: Kaitsūsha, 1912.

Havens, Norman. "Immanent Legitimation: Reflections on the 'Kami Concept.'" In *Kami,* ed. Inoue Nobutaka, Contemporary Papers on Japanese Religion 4. Tokyo: Institute for Japanese Culture and Classics, Kokugakuin University, 1988.

Hirao Michio. *Kaientai shimatsu ki.* Tokyo: Daidō Shobō, 1941.

Hirata Atsutane. *Tamadasuki.* 1815. Reprinted in *Hirata Atsutane zenshū,* vol. 4. Tokyo: Hirata Gakkai, 1912.

———. *Tamadasuki sōron tsuika.* 1819. Reprinted in *Hirata Atsutane zenshū,* vol. 4. Tokyo: Hirata Gakkai, 1912.

Hiss, Tony. *The Experience of Place.* New York: Knopf, 1990.

Hori, Ichiro. *Folk Religion in Japan.* Edited by Joseph Kitagawa and Alan L. Miller. Chicago: University of Chicago Press, 1968.

Holtom, Daniel C. *The National Faith of Japan: A Study in Modern Shinto.* London: Kegan Paul, Trench, Trubner and Co., 1938.

Howell, David L. "Territoriality and Collective Identity in Tokugawa Japan." *Daedalus* 127, no. 3 (Summer 1998): 105–32.

Huffman, James L. *Creating a Public: People and Press in Meiji Japan.* Honolulu: University of Hawai'i Press, 1997.

Hur, Nam-lin. *Prayer and Play in Late Tokugawa Japan: Asakusa Sensōji and Edo Society.* Harvard East Asian Monographs 185. Cambridge, Mass.: Harvard University Asia Center, 2000.

Ichihara Terushi Sensei Kiju Kinen Ronbunshū Henshū Iinkai, ed. *Rekishi to minzoku denshō.* Tokyo: Maruyama Yoshio, 1992.

Ichihara Terushi and Yamamoto Takeshi. *Kagawa-ken no rekishi.* Kenshi shiriizu, no. 37. Tokyo: Yamakawa Shuppansha, 1971.

Ikeda Eishun. *Meiji bukkyō kyōkai kesshashi no kenkyū.* Tokyo: Tōsui Shobō, 1994.

Ikoma Hōshō. *Kotohira monogatari.* Takamatsu: Shikoku Shinbunsha, 1949.

Imai Kongo. "Naniwakō tanjō no kushin o kataru shiryō." Kosho no tanoshimi 4. *Nihon kosho tsūshin* 760 (November 1992).

Imazawa Jikai. *Fudōson no reigen.* Tokyo: Fudō Zenshū Kankōkai, 1941.

Innami Toshihide. "Ippan hōnōbutsu." In *KSSS,* 1:236–38.

———. "Keidai no tōrō." In *KSSS,* 3:263–84.

———. "Konpira shinkō to tabi: Kotohiragū sūkei kōsha shiryō o chūshin ni." In *Gyomin no seikatsu to sono shūzoku* 2:5–86. Kanagawa Daigaku Nihon Jōmin Bunka Kenkyūjo chōsa hōkoku 18. Tokyo: Heibonsha, 1995.

Inoki Kazuichi. "Konpira tōrō no kōtsū chiriteki igi." *Jinbun chiri* 11, no. 3 (1959): 1–21. Reprinted in *Konpira shinkō,* edited by Moriya Takeshi, 245–69. Tokyo: Yūzankaku Shuppan, 1987.

Inoue Nobutaka. *Kyōha shintō no keisei.* Tokyo: Kōbundō, 1991.

Isa Jin'uemon. *Dōchūki.* 1885. Reprinted in *Ise sangū dōchūki,* edited by Isa Gohei with annotations by Takemoto Kōichi. Fukuoka-shi, 1989.

Ishii Kenji. "Senpakuga toshite no funa ema to sono ryūha." In *Umi to Nihonjin,* edited by Tōkai Daigaku Kaiyō Gakubu, 101–25. Sapporo: Tōkai Daigaku Shuppankyoku, 1977.

Ishikawa Wasuke, ed. *Sanuki kuni Kotohira jinja sūkei kōsha kisoku utsushi.* Osaka: Ishikawa Wasuke, 1882.

Ishizu Ryōchō. *Konpirasan meisho zue.* Ca.1804–17. Reprinted in *Kagawa sōsho,* edited by Kagawa-ken, 3:352–422. Takamatsu: Kagawa-ken, 1943.

Isomae Jun'ichi. *Kindai Nihon no shūkyō gensetsu to sono keifu: shūkyō, kokka, shintō.* Tokyo: Iwanami Shoten, 2003.

———. "Reappropriating the Japanese Myths: Motoori Norinaga and the Creation Myths of the *Kojiki* and *Nihon Shoki.*" *Japanese Journal of Religious Studies* 27, nos. 1–2 (Spring 2000): 15–39.

Itō Ichirō. *Kotohiragū jiken no hyōron.* Kotohira: Ono Hideya, 1909.

Ivy, Marilyn. *Discourses of the Vanishing: Modernity, Phantasm, Japan.* Chicago: University of Chicago Press, 1995.

Iwai Hiromi. *Ema.* Tokyo: Hōsei Daigaku Shuppankyoku, 1974.

Iyanaga Nobumi. "*Honji suijaku* and the Logic of Combinatory Deities: Two Case Studies." In *Buddhas and Kami in Japan,* edited by Mark Teeuwen and Fabio Rambelli, 145–76. London: Routledge Curzon, 2003.

Iyomishima Shishi Hensan Iinkai, ed. *Iyomishima shishi.* Vol. 1. Ehime-ken, Iyomishimashi: Iyomishimashi, 1984.

Jansen, Marius B. *Sakamoto Ryōma and the Meiji Restoration.* New York: Columbia University Press, 1961.

Japan in the Chinese Dynastic Histories. Translated by Ryusaku Tsunoda. South Pasadena, Calif.: Perkins, 1951.

Jippensha Ikku. *Shank's Mare.* Translated by Thomas Satchell. Tokyo and Rutland, Vt.: C. E. Tuttle Co., 1960.

———. *Zoku hizakurige shohen: Konpira sankei.* 1810. Reprinted in *Hizakurige sono ta,* vol. 1. Nihon meichō zenshū, Edo bungei no bu, no. 22, 465–514. Tokyo: Nihon Meichō Zenshū Kankōkai, 1927.

Kadokawa Nihon chimei daijiten. Vol. 42, *Nagasaki-ken.* Tokyo: Kadokawa Shoten, 1987.

Kagawa-ken. *Meiji nijūsannen Kagawa-ken tōkeisho.* Takamatsu: Kagawa-ken, 1890.

———, ed. *Kagawa kenshi.* 15 vols. Takamatsu: Shikoku Shinbunsha, 1985–90.

———, ed. *Kagawa sōsho.* 3 vols. Takamatsu: Kagawa-ken, 1939, 1941, 1943.

Kagawa-ken Kyōiku Iinkai, ed. *Shinpen Kagawa sōsho.* 6 vols. Takamatsu: Shinpen Kagawa Sōsho Kankō Kikaku Iinkai, 1979–84.

———, ed. *Shinshū Kagawa kenshi.* Takamatsu: Kagawa-ken Kyōiku Iinkai, 1953.

Kageura Naotaka. *Iyoshi seigi.* Tokyo: Meichō Shuppan, 1972.

Kanda Hideo. "Shinjin no sekai no hen'yō to aratakana sukui." In *Minshū no kokoro,* edited by Hirota Masaki, Nihon no kinsei 16, 209–52. Tokyo: Chūō Kōronsha, 1994.

Kanda Norio. "Senhi to sono chōtatsu." In *Kindai Nihon sensōshi 1 Nisshin Nichiro sensō,* edited by Kuwada Etsu, 578–93. Tokyo: Tōkyōdō Shuppan, 1995.

Kasahara Kazuo. *Nihon shūkyōshi nenpyō.* Tokyo: Hyōronsha, 1974.

Kawaguchi Akitsugi. *Zōzusan Konpira Daigongen no shintai.* Kotohira: Ozaki Saburō, 1908.

Kawasaki Yoshio. "Ise sangū nikki kō: Meiji shichinen." In *Ise sangū nikki kō 2: shiryōhen sono 2,* edited by Kawasaki Yoshio, 1–5. Ibaragi-ken, Tsuchiura-shi: Chikuwa Shorin, 1987.

Keene, Donald. *World within Walls: Japanese Literature of the Pre-modern Era, 1600–1867.* New York: Columbia University Press, 1999.

Keihan et al. "Korōden kyūki." In *Shinpen Kagawa sōsho,* shiryōhen 1, edited by Kagawa-ken Kyōiku Iinkai, 225–37. Takamatsu: Shinpen Kagawa Sōsho Kankō Kiga Iinkai, 1979.

Ketelaar, James Edward. *Of Heretics and Martyrs in Meiji Japan: Buddhism and Its Persecution.* Princeton, N.J.: Princeton University Press, 1990.

Kihara Hirosaki. "Kinsei ni okeru Sanuki no kaisen ni tsuite." In *Naikai chiiki shakai no shiteki kenkyū*, edited by Matsuoka Hisato. Yamaguchi-ken, Tokushima-shi: Matsuno Shoten, 1978.

Kikuchi Taketsune. "Sanukishū Nakagun Zōzusan Konpira kami shinshi ki." In *Kagawa sōsho*, edited by Kagawa-ken, 1:436–42. Takamatsu: Kagawa-ken, 1939.

Kirkland, Russell. "The Sun and the Throne: The Origins of the Royal Descent Myth in Ancient Japan," *Numen* 44, no. 2 (May 1997): 109–52.

Kōbō Daishi zenshū. Edited by Hase Hōshū. 6 vols. Tokyo, 1909–11. Reprint, Wakayama-ken Ito-gun Kōya-chō: Mikkyō Bunka Kenkyūjo, 1966.

Koizumi Kakuhei. "Meiji jūyonen dōchū mankakuchō." 1881. Reprinted in *Ise dōchūki shiryō*, edited by Tōkyō-to Setagaya-ku Kyōiku Iinkai, 74–88. Tokyo: Tōkyō-to Setagaya-ku Kyōiku Iinkai, 1984.

Kondō Shigeki. *Meiji kōsetsu roku*. Tokyo: Kunaishō, 1887.

Kondō Yoshihiro. "Sanchō no ayame: Kotohira shinkō no kentō." In *Konpira shinkō*, edited by Moriya Takeshi, 11–31. Tokyo: Yūzankaku Shuppan, 1987.

Konpira Daigongen Reigenki. Undated. In Tawa Archive. Available on microfilm at the Kokubungaku Kenkyū Shiryōkan in Tokyo.

Kornicki, P. F. "Public Display and Changing Values: Early Meiji Exhibitions and Their Precursors." *Monumenta Nipponica* 49, no. 2 (Summer 1994): 167–96.

Koschmann, J. Victor. *The Mito Ideology: Discourse, Reform, and Insurrection in Late Tokugawa Japan, 1790–1864*. Berkeley: University of California Press, 1987.

Kotohira Chōshi Henshū Iinkai, ed. *Chōshi Kotohira*. 5 vols. Kotohira: Kotohira-chō, 1995–98.

Kotohirachō Kigaka, ed. *Kotohirachō: chōsei shikō hyakushūnen*. Kotohira: Kotohirachō, 1990.

Kotohiragū, ed. *Kotohiragū shiryō*. 90 vols. Kotohira: Kotohiragū, 1911–44.

———, ed. *Kotohiragū shiryō hoi*. 8 vols. Kotohira: Kotohiragū, 1913–19.

———, ed. *Kotohiragū sūkeishi*. 4 vols. Kotohira: Kotohiragū, 1933.

———, ed. *Nisshi*. Unpublished shrine record.

———, ed. *Nōkensha*. Unpublished list of donors, 1877–1944.

Kotohiragū doku annaiki. Konpira: Mitamadō, 1869.

Kotohiragū Gūjishitsu Shoki, ed. *Kotohiragū sessuisha baishishi*. 6 vols. (1921). Unpublished record at Kotohira Shrine.

Kotohiragū Hozonkai Jimusho. "Kotohiragū hozonkai kōkoku." *Kaitsū Zasshi*, no. 74 (25 March 1888): 15.

"Kotohiragū okusha kenritsu shuisho." May 1896. Photocopy at Kotohira Shrine and in the Kusanagi collection of Seto Inland Sea Folk History Museum.

Kotohiragū Sūkei Kōsha Honbu, comp. *Ōfuku todome*. Letters to and replies from the Reverence Association.

"Kotohira Jinja Yuisho Ryakki." Recorded by Endō Haku. Hirose-chō.

Kotooka Hirotsune. "Suinan kyūsaikai o sansei seraremu koto o nozomu ni tsukite." August 1889. Printed circular available in the Miyake family collection at the Seto Inland Sea Folk History Museum.

Kotooka Mitsushige. Interview with Watanabe Yukio. "Kaijō anzen to Konpira shinkō." *Kotohira,* no. 39 (1984).

———. *Kotohiragū.* Tokyo: Gakuseisha, 1970.

———. "Kotohiragū to umi." *Kotohira,* no. 22 (1967).

Kubo Shinri. "Senji ni okeru shinshoku no honbun." *Jinja kyōkai zasshi,* no. 28 (June 1904): 8–10.

Kuriyama Bunsuke. "Kamigata, Konpira sankei oboegaki." (Ca. 1804–18). Reprinted in *Ise sangū nikkikō,* vol. 1, edited by Kawasaki Yoshio, 1–15. Ibaragi-ken, Tsuchiura-shi: Chikuwa Shorin, 1987.

Kusanagi Kinshirō. "Bunka, Bunseiki no Konpira miyage." *Kotohira* 24 (1969): 31–34.

———. *Konpira ōshibai no subete.* Kusanagi Kinshirō senshū 15. Takamatsu: Takamatsu bukku sentaa, 1985.

Kuwada Etsu. "Ryōkoku no senryoku, sakusen kōsō to daihon'ei." In *Kindai Nihon sensōshi 1 Nisshin Nichiro sensō,* edited by Kuwada Etsu, 174–92. Tokyo: Tōkyōdō Shuppan, 1995.

Lebra, Takie Sugiyama. *Above the Clouds: Status Culture of the Modern Japanese Nobility.* Berkeley: University of California Press, 1993.

Lewis, Michael. *Becoming Apart: National Power and Local Politics in Toyama, 1868–1945.* Cambridge, Mass.: Harvard University Asia Center, 2000.

The Lotus Sutra, trans. Burton Watson. New York: Columbia University Press, 1993.

Lu, David J. *Japan: A Documentary History.* Armonk, N.Y.: M. E. Sharpe, 1997.

MacCannell, Dean. *The Tourist: A New Theory of the Leisure Class.* New York: Schocken Books, 1976.

Maeda Ai. *Narushima Ryūhoku.* In *Bakumatsu ishinki no bungaku: Narushima Ryūhoku,* Maeda Ai chōsakushū 1, 281–474. Tokyo: Chikuma Shobō, 1989.

Marugame Shishi Hensan Iinkai. *Shinpen Marugame shishi.* 5 vols. Marugame: Marugame-shi, 1994–96.

Matsubara Hideaki. "Konpira shinkō no rekishiteki tenkai." *Yūkyū,* no. 44 (January 1991): 1–9.

———. "Konpira shinkō to sankei gaidōzu." *Chizu Jōhō* 13, no. 3 (1993): 1–5.

———. "Konpira shinkō to shugendō." In *Konpira shinkō,* edited by Moriya Takeshi, 53–71. Tokyo: Yūzankaku Shuppan, 1987.

———. "Kotohiragū no shozō shiryō ni tsuite." In *KSSS nenpyō,* 68–80.

———. "Kotohiragū toshokan zōhon bekkenki: Komatsu bunko ni tsuite." *Kotohira,* no. 16 (1961): 94–104.

———. "Tenshō zengo no Zōzusan." In *Konpira shinkō,* edited by Moriya Takeshi, 73–80. Tokyo: Yūzankaku Shuppan, 1987.

———, comp. *Konpira shomin shinkō shiryōshū nenpyōhen.* Kotohira: Kotohiragū Shamusho, 1988.

Matsudaira Yorishige [attributed]. "Sanshū michi Zōzusan engi." 1656. Reprinted in *Kagawa sōsho,* vol. 1, edited by Kagawa-ken, 434–35. Takamatsu: Kagawa-ken, 1939.

Matsui Masakore. *Kotohira keiki.* 1882. Transcribed and annotated by Minota Katsuhiko. Kumamoto-ken: Yachio Kobunsho no Kai, 1987.

Matsumae Takeshi. "Early Kami Worship." In *The Cambridge History of Japan,* vol. 1, edited by Delmer M. Brown, 347–49. Cambridge: Cambridge University Press, 1993.

Matsuoka Mitsugi. *Kotohiragū kokin reigenki tsuika.* Two unpublished, undated drafts of Matsuoka's second collection of miracle tales. Original in the Tawa Archive; microfilm at Kokubungaku Kenkyū Shiryōkan.

———. *Kotohiragū reigenki.* Vol. 2. Unpublished, undated draft of Matsuoka's first collection of miracle tales. Original in the Tawa Archive; microfilm at Kokubungaku Kenkyū Shiryōkan.

———. *Kotohira kokin reigenki.* 1892. Reprinted in *Kotohirasan,* nos. 1–7 (1929–35).

———. *Nennen nikki.* 141 vols. Bunkyū 4 (1864)–1904. On microfilm at Kokubungaku Kenkyū Shiryōkan, Tokyo.

McMullin, Neil. "The Sutra Lecture and Doctrinal Debate Traditions in Early and Medieval Japan." In *Tendai shisō to higashi Ajia bunka no kenkyū,* 77–95. Tokyo: Sankibō, 1991.

McNally, Mark. "Phantom History: Hirata Atsutane and Tokugawa Nativism." PhD diss., University of California, Los Angeles, 1998.

Meiji Jingū, ed. *Meiji tennō shōchoku kinkai.* Tokyo: Kōdansha, 1973.

Mitsui Takafusa. *Some Observations on Merchants.* Translated by E. S. Crawcour. London: Japan Society London, 1960.

Miyachi Masato. "Kokka shintō keisei katei no mondai ten." In *Shūkyō to kokka,* edited by Yasumaru Yoshio and Miyachi Masato, Nihon kindai shisō taikei 5, 565–93. Tokyo: Iwanami Shoten,1988.

———. "Kokka shintō no kakuritsu katei." In *Kindai tennōsei to shūkyōteki ken'i,* edited by Kokugakuin Daigaku Nihon Bunka Kenkyūjo, 119–48. Tokyo: Dōmeisha Shuppan, 1992.

Miyake Hitoshi. *Shugendō: Essays on the Structure of Japanese Folk Religion.* Edited by H. Byron Earhart. Ann Arbor: Center for Japanese Studies, University of Michigan, 2001.

Miyamoto Tsuneichi. *Ise sangū.* Tabi no minzoku to rekishi 5. Tokyo: Yasaka Shobō, 1987.

Miyata Noboru. *Kinsei no hayarigami.* Nihonjin no kōtō to shisō 17. Tokyo: Hyōronsha, 1976.

Mizobuchi Kazuyuki. "Ema." In *KSSS,* 1:97–104.

Mori, Arinori. *Religious Freedom in Japan: A Memorial and Draft of Charter.* Washington, D.C.: privately printed, 1872.

Mori Ōgai. "Konpira." 1909. In *Ōgai senshū,* vol. 1, edited by Mori Rintarō, 293–337. Tokyo: Iwanami Shoten, 1978.

———. "Konpira." Translated by James M. Vardaman, Jr. In *"Youth" and Other Stories: Mori Ōgai,* edited by J. Thomas Rimer, 102–35. Honolulu: University of Hawaii Press, 1994.

Moriya Takeshi. "Konpira shinkō to Konpira sankei o meguru oboegaki." In *Konpira shinkō,* edited by Moriya Takeshi, Minshū shūkyōshi sōsho 19, pp. 181–216. Tokyo: Yūzankaku, 1987.

———, ed. *Konpira shinkō.* Minshū shūkyōshi sōsho, vol. 19. Tokyo: Yūzankaku Shuppan, 1987.

Motoori Norinaga. *Kojikiden.* 1798. 44 vols. Reprinted in *Zōho Motoori Norinaga zenshū,* edited by Motoori Toyokai and Motoori Seizō, vols. 1–4. Tokyo: Yoshikawa Kōbunkan, [1902] 1926.

Murai Shin'ichirō, ed. *Sūkeikō no susume.* Takamatsu: Murai Shin'ichirō, 1878.

Murakami Bōryū. *Shugendō no hattatsu.* 1943. Reprint, Tokyo: Meichō Shuppan, 1978.

Murakami Senshō, Tsuji Zennosuke, et al., eds. *Meiji ishin shinbutsu bunri shiryō.* 5 vols. Tokyo: Tōhō Shoin, 1926–29. Reprinted as *Shinpen Meiji ishin shinbutsu bunri shiryō.* 9 vols. Tokyo: Meichō Shuppan, 1984.

Murakami Shigeyoshi. *Kokka shintō.* Tokyo: Iwanami Shoten, 1970.

Murakami Yutaka. *(Shin shintō) Kurozumikyō no shintai tsuki reigendan.* Okayama: Fujita Chōyōdō, 1936.

Muramatsu Sūei, ed. *Kotohira miyage.* No. 1. Kotohira: Kyokuō Gakusha, 1892.

Murayama Shūichi. *Miwaryū shintō no kenkyū.* Tokyo: Meichō Shuppan, 1983.

Muta Bunnosuke. "Shokoku kaireki nichiroku." 1855. In *Zuihitsu hyakkaen,* vol. 13, edited by Mori Senzō et al. Tokyo: Chūō Kōronsha, 1979.

"Myōdō Gakkō no koto." *Kotohira* (Spring 1958): 28–30.

Nagata Soreji. *Kotohira annaiki.* Osaka: Nagata Soreji, 1902.

Nagaya Tadahide. "Goshichinichihō." *Misshū Gakuhō,* no. 234 (1934): 1–19.

Nakagawa Yūjirō. "Gunjin ni taisuru mamorifuda juyo ni tsuite." *Jinja kyōkai zasshi,* no. 28 (June 1904).

Nakahara Suigekka. "Tabi no nikki." 1858. In *Chōshi Kotohira,* 2:342–49.

Nakamura Kazumoto. *Motooriha kokugaku no tenkai.* Tokyo: Yūzankaku, 1993.

Nakao Yasutarō. *Kotohira sankei doku annai.* Kotohira: Nakao Yasutarō, 1892.

Naquin, Susan, and Chün-fang Yü, eds. *Pilgrims and Sacred Sites in China.* Berkeley: University of California Press, 1992.

Narushima Ryūhoku. *Kōbi nikki.* 1869. Reprinted in *Seto Naikai,* edited by Yoshii Isamu et al. Tokyo: Sekkasha, 1965.

Nelson, John K. *Enduring Identities: The Guise of Shinto in Contemporary Japan.* Honolulu: University of Hawai'i Press, 2000.

———. *A Year in the Life of a Shinto Shrine.* Seattle: University of Washington Press, 1996.

Nihongi. Translated by W. G. Aston. 1972. Reprint, Rutland, Vt.: Charles E. Tuttle Company, 1998.

Nihon Kankō Bunka Kenkyūjo, ed. *Konpira shomin shinkō shiryōshū.* 3 vols. Kotohira: Kotohiragū Shamusho, 1982–84.

Nishida Nagao. "Jisha no shuinjō aratame to sono kakikae." *Shintō Shūkyō,* nos. 97 and 98 (December 1979 and March 1980): 1–35.

————, ed. *Urabe Shintō.* Shintō taikei ronsetsuhen 8. Tokyo: Shintō Taikei Hensankai, 1985.

Nitta Hitoshi. "Shinto as a 'Non-religion': The Origins and Development of an Idea." In *Shinto in History: Ways of the Kami,* edited by John Breen and Mark Teeuwen, 252–71. Richmond, Surrey: Curzon Press, 2000.

Nukata Roppuku. "Konpira fune fune." *Kotohira* 2, no. 12 (1935): 10–11.

Ogasawara Chōsei, ed. *Seishō Tōgō zenden.* Vol. 3. Tokyo: Seishō Tōgō Zenden Kankōkai, 1941.

Ogata Shōtarō. "Kotohira keiki." 1882. Transcribed and annotated by Minota Katsuhiko. Kumamoto-ken: Yachio Kobunsho no Kai, 1987.

Okazawa Shukei. "Meiji nijūhachinen sangū dōchūki." *Nagano* 56 (July 1974): 57–61.

Ōkubo Shin'ichi. *Sanuki imin no Hokkaidō kaitaku shiryō.* Tadotsu: Tadotsu Bunkazai Hozonkai, 1981.

Ōkubo Toshiaki et al. *Kindaishi shiryō.* Tokyo: Yoshikawa Kōbunkan, 1965.

Ōnishi Hyōjirō. *Konpiragū goreigenki.* Tadotsu: Taikyokukan, 1903.

Onishi Kashun. *Tamamoshū.* 1677. Reprinted in *Kagawa sōsho,* edited by Kagawa-ken, 3:1–131. Takamatsu: Kagawa-ken, 1943.

Onodera Atsushi. "Dōchū nikki ni miru Ise sangū ruuto no henkan: kantō chihō kara no baai." *Jinbun chirigaku kenyū* 14 (1990): 231–55.

Ooms, Herman. *Tokugawa Ideology: Early Constructs, 1570–1680.* Princeton, N.J.: Princeton University Press, 1985.

Ōsaki Teiichi. *Konpira monogatari.* 1959. Reprint, Kotohira: Kotohiragū Shamusho, 1988.

Ōta Akira. *Seishi kakei daijiten.* Tokyo: Seishi Kakei Daijiten Kankōkai, 1936.

Ōtsubo Isamu. "Nichiro sensō to jinja to no kankei." *Jinja kyōkai zasshi* 4, no. 4 (April 1905): 26–29.

Ōue Shirō, ed. *Meiji kakochō.* Tokyo: Tokyo Bijutsu, 1971.

Pratt, Edward E. *Japan's Proto-industrial Elite: The Economic Foundations of the Gōnō.* Cambridge, Mass.: Harvard University Asia Center, 1999.

Pyle, Kenneth B. "Meiji conservatism." In *The Cambridge History of Japan,* vol. 5, edited by Marius B. Jansen, 674–720. Cambridge: Cambridge University Press, 1989.

Reader, Ian. *Religion in Contemporary Japan.* London: Macmillan Press, 1991.

Reader, Ian, and George J. Tanabe, Jr. *Practically Religious: Worldly Benefits and the Common Religion of Japan.* Honolulu: University of Hawai'i Press, 1998.

Roberts, Luke. "The Petition Box in Eighteenth-Century Tosa." *Journal of Japanese Studies* 20, no. 2 (1994): 423–58.

————. "Tosa to ishin—'kokka' no soshitsu to 'chihō' no tanjo." *Nenpō kindai Nihon kenkyū* 20 (November 1997): 211–35.

Ruppert, Brian. "Pearl in the Shrine: A Genealogy of the Buddhist Jewel of the Japanese Sovereign." *Japanese Journal of Religious Studies* 29, nos. 1–2 (Spring 2002): 1–33.

Saitō Osamu. "Meiji goki no fuken kangyō seisaku." *Keizai kenkyū* 35, no. 3 (July 1984): 236–48.

Sakamoto Ken'ichi. *Meiji ikō jinja kankei hōrei shiryō.* Tokyo: Jinja Honchō Meiji Ishin Hyakunen Kinen Jigyō Iinkai, 1968.

Sakamoto Koremaru. *Kokka shintō keisei katei no kenkyū.* Tokyo: Iwanami Shoten, 1994.

———. "Religion and State in the Early Meiji Period (1868–1912)." *Acta Asiatica* 51 (1987): 42–61.

Sakurai Takejirō. "Honkoku 'Kotohira Miyajima kikō.'" *Kotohira,* no. 39 (1984): 59–63.

Sakurai Tokutarō. *Kō shūdan no kenkyū.* Sakurai Tokutarō chōsakushū, vol. 1. Tokyo: Yoshikawa Kōbunkan, 1988.

Sanaki Nobuo. "Miyaji Hikosaburō to Kotohira." *Kotohira* 3, no. 7 (10 July 1936): 2–11.

Sangawa Hiroshi. *Sanuki ittōbori: Konpira no ittōbori o kigen toshite.* 1983.

Sanuki Kotohira Panoramakan. *Teikoku gunka,* 10–23 November 1900. In the private collection of Tan'o Yasunori.

Satō Hiroo. "Wrathful Deities and Saving Deities." In *Buddhas and Kami in Japan:* Honji Suijaku *as a Combinatory Paradigm,* edited by Mark Teeuwen and Fabio Rambelli, 95–114. New York: RoutledgeCurzon, 2003.

Sawada, Janine Anderson. *Confucian Values and Popular Zen: Sekimon Shingaku in Eighteenth Century Japan.* Honolulu: University of Hawaii Press, 1993.

Scheid, Bernhard. "Schlachtenlärm in den Gefilden der *kami.*" In *Wandel zwischen den Welten,* edited by Hannelore Eisenhofer-Halim. Munich: Peter Lang Verlag, 2003.

Scripture of the Lotus Blossom of the Fine Dharma. Translated by Leon Hurvitz. New York: Columbia University Press, 1976.

Seigle, Cecilia Segawa. *Yoshiwara: The Glittering World of the Japanese Courtesan.* Honolulu: University of Hawaii Press, 1993.

Seto Kengo. "Kotohiragū to Nichiro sensō." *Kotohira,* no. 46 (1991): 172–73.

Seto Naikai Rekishi Minzoku Shiryōkan. *Konpira sankei michi.* 2 vols. Kagawa-ken rekishi no michi chōsa hōkokusho 5 and 7. Takamatsu: Seto Naikai Rekishi Minzoku Shiryōkan, 1991–92.

Shikoku Shinbunsha, ed. *Sanuki jinbutsu fūkei.* Vol. 10. Tokyo: Maruyama Gakugei Tosho, 1984.

Shinjō Tsunezō. *Shaji sankei no shakai keizai shiteki kenkyū.* Tokyo: Hanawa Shobō, 1964.

Shirakawa Satoru. "Dōchū anzen: Meiji shoki no Konpira mairi." *Kotohira* 32 (1977): 27–31.

Shively, Donald H. "The Japanization of the Middle Meiji." In *Tradition and Modernization in Japanese Culture,* edited by Donald H. Shively, 77–119. Princeton, N.J.: Princeton University Press, 1971.

Smith, Jonathan Z. *To Take Place.* Chicago: University of Chicago Press, 1987.

Smith, Richard Gordon. *Travels in the Land of the Gods (1898–1907): The Japan Diaries of Richard Gordon Smith.* Edited by Victoria Manthorpe. New York: Prentice Hall Press, 1986.

Smyers, Karen A. *The Fox and the Jewel: Shared and Private Meanings in Contemporary Japanese Inari Worship.* Honolulu: University of Hawai'i Press, 1999.

The Sutra of Golden Light. Translated by R. E. Emmerick. Oxford: Pali Text Society, 1990.

Suzuki Nobuhiro, Shimizu Hideki, and Shiota Yō. "Sandō kūkan ni okeru shikaku, kioku kōzō ni kansuru kenkyū." *Nihon kenchiku gakkai keikakuke ronbunshū,* no. 457 (March 1994): 93–100.

Tada Toshiko and Yumura Teruhiko. *Hashiregon: Konpira inu monogatari.* Tokyo: Arai Kennosuke, 1994.

Tahara Tsuguo, Seki Akira, Saeki Arikiyo, and Haga Noboru, eds. *Hirata Atsutane, Ban Nobutomo, Ōkuni Takamasa.* Nihon shisō taikei 50. Tokyo: Iwanami Shoten, 1973.

Taishō shinshū daizōkyō. Edited by Takakusu Junjirō, Watanabe Kaikyoku, et al. 85 vols. Tokyo, 1914–22.

Takada Zenbei et al. "Dōchū nikki." 1880. Reprinted in *Ise sangū nikki kō 2: shiryōhen sono 2,* edited by Kawasaki Yoshio, 118–44. Ibaragi-ken, Tsuchiura-shi: Chikuwa Shorin, 1987.

Takamatsu Chihō Saibansho. *Meiji 45 nen–Taishō gannen dai isshin hanketsu genpon.* 1912. Records of the Takamatsu Regional Court.

Takano Toshihiko. *Kinsei Nihon no kokka kenryoku to shūkyō.* Tokyo: Tōkyō Daigaku Shuppankai, 1989.

Takeda Akira. "Konpira shinkō to minzoku." In *Konpira shinkō,* edited by Moriya Takeshi, 33–51. Tokyo: Yūzankaku Shuppan, 1987.

Takemura, Eiji. *The Perception of Work in Tokugawa Japan: A Study of Ishida Baigan and Ninomiya Sontoku.* Lanham, Md.: University Press of America, 1997.

Takizawa Bakin. *Chinsetsu yumiharizuki.* Nihon koten bungaku taikei 60–61. Tokyo: Iwanami Shoten, 1958–62.

Tamamuro Fumio. *Shinbutsu bunri.* Tokyo: Kyōikusha, 1977.

Tamamuro Fumio et al., eds. *Kotohiragū sūkei kōsha kōchō mokuroku.* Kotohira: Kotohiragū shamusho, 1995.

Tanabe, Willa Jane. "The Lotus Lectures: *Hokke Hakkō* in the Heian Period." *Monumenta Nipponica* 39, no. 4 (Winter 1984): 393–407.

Tanaka Seidai. *Nihon no kōen.* Tokyo: Kajima Shuppankai, 1974.

Tanaka Tomohiko. "'Kondō kishinchō' ni miru Ōsaka no kishinsha." *Kotohira,* no. 50 (1995): 186–88.

———. "Kotohiragū shozō 'Kondō kishinchō' ni miru Setsukuni no kishinsha." *Ōsaka joshi tanki daigaku kiyō,* no. 20 (December 1995): 71–81.

Tanizawa Akira. "Sekihi ga kataru misaki no Konpira shinkō." *Kotohira* 45 (1990): 154–60.

Tan'o Yasunori and Kawada Akihisa. *Imeeji no naka no sensō: Nisshin Nichiro kara reisen made.* Iwanami kindai Nihon no bijutsu, no. 1. Tokyo: Iwanami Shoten, 1996.

Tasaka Eiki. *Konpirasan no mukashi banashi.* Marugame: Taniguchi Kurafuto, undated.

Teeuwen, Mark. "From *Jindō* to Shinto: A Concept Takes Shape." *Japanese Journal of Religious Studies* 29, nos. 3–4 (Fall 2002): 233–64.

Teeuwen, Mark, and Fabio Rambelli, eds. *Buddhas and Kami in Japan.* London: Routledge Curzon, 2003.

Terada Den'ichirō. "Hachijūō danwa." *Tabi to densetsu,* no. 108 (December 1936): 14–24.

Thal, Sarah. "Redefining the Gods: Politics and Survival in the Creation of Modern Kami." *Japanese Journal of Religious Studies* 29, nos. 3–4 (Fall 2002): 379–404.

———. "Sacred Sites and the Dynamics of Identity." *Early Modern Japan* 8, no. 2 (November 2000): 28–37.

Tokoyo Nagatane. *Shinkyō soshiki monogatari.* In *Shūkyō to kokka,* edited by Yasumaru Yoshio and Miyachi Masato, Nihon kindai shisō taikei 5, 361–422. Tokyo: Iwanami Shoten, 1988.

Tokutomi Iichirō. *Hōreki Meiwa hen.* Tokyo: Min'yūsha, 1926.

Toshi Dezain Kenkyūkai. *Nihon no toshi kūkan.* Tokyo: Shōkokusha, 1971.

Totman, Conrad. *Early Modern Japan.* Berkeley: University of California Press, 1993.

Turner, Victor. *Dramas, Fields, and Metaphors.* Ithaca, N.Y.: Cornell University Press, 1974.

———. *The Ritual Process: Structure and Anti-structure.* Chicago: Aldine Publishing Co., 1969.

Turner, Victor, and Edith Turner. *Image and Pilgrimage in Christian Culture.* Oxford: Blackwell, 1978.

Ueda Akinari. *Ugetsu monogatari.* Tokyo: Iwanami Shoten, 1934.

Uemura Masahiro. "Kinsei Seto Naikai un kinō no ikkōsatsu—Sanshū Shiwaku kaisen o chūshin ni." *Ōsaka Daigaku Keizaigaku* 33, nos. 1–2 (September 1983): 59–64.

Umeda Yoshihiko. *Kaitei sōho Nihon shūkyō seidoshi,* 3 vols. Tokyo: Tōsen Shuppan, 1971.

Umegaki, Michio. *After the Restoration: The Beginning of Japan's Modern State.* New York: New York University Press, 1988.

Ushio Saitō. "Jinja sandō no kūkan kōsei ni kansuru kenkyū." *Nihon toshi keikaku gakkai gakujutsu kenkyū ronbunshū* 24 (November 1989): 457–62.

Vaporis, Constantine Nomikos. *Breaking Barriers: Travel and the State in Early Modern Japan.* Harvard East Asian Monographs 163. Cambridge, Mass.: Council on East Asian Studies, Harvard University, 1994.

Walthall, Anne. "Off with Their Heads! The Hirata Disciples and the Ashikaga Shoguns." *Monumenta Nipponica* 50, no. 2 (Summer 1995): 137–70.

———. "Peripheries: Rural Culture in Tokugawa Japan." *Monumenta Nipponica* 39, no. 4 (Winter 1984): 371–92.

———. *The Weak Body of a Useless Woman: Matsuo Taseko and the Meiji Restoration.* Chicago: University of Chicago Press, 1998.

Watanabe Shichimi. "Kotohiragū ni okeru shinbutsu bunri ni tsuite." *Kagawa shigaku* 1, no. 1 (January 1972).

Wigen, Kären. *The Making of a Japanese Periphery, 1750–1920.* Berkeley: University of California Press, 1995.

Wright, Arthur F. *Studies in Chinese Buddhism.* Edited by Robert M. Somers. New Haven, Conn.: Yale University Press, 1990.

Yakuwa Tomohiro. "Kinsei ni okeru moji bunka no chiikiteki shintō—jūhasseiki zenpan ni okeru Echigo no haikai bunka to kenren shite." *Kokuritsu rekishi minzoku hakubutsukan kenkyū hōkoku* 97 (March 2002): 1–18.

Yamada Ichirō. "Nisshin sensō ni okeru iryō, eisei." In *Kindai Nihon sensōshi 1 Nisshin Nichiro sensō*, edited by Kuwada Etsu, 232–50. Tokyo: Tōkyōdō Shuppan, 1995.

Yamaguchi Ichitarō. *Kotohirasan zenzu*. Kyoto, 1879.

Yamaguchi Teruomi. *Meiji kokka to shūkyō*. Tokyo: Tōkyō Daigaku Shuppankai, 1999.

Yamakawa Maki. "Oumasan no mame." *Kotohira*, no. 18 (1963): 49–52.

Yamamoto Seiichirō. *Shinbutsu no sonzai to kiseki*. Tokyo: Shōyōsha, 1935.

Yamasaki, Taikō. *Shingon: Japanese Esoteric Buddhism*. Boston: Shambhala, 1988.

Yamashita Sakae. "Hirata Atsutane, Rai San'yō, Yoshida Shōin no Konpira sanjōsange ni ataeta eikyō ni tsuite." *Kotohira* 39 (1984).

Yasumaru Yoshio. *Kamigami no Meiji ishin: shinbutsu bunri to haibutsu kishaku*. Iwanami shinsho, no. 103. Tokyo: Iwanami Shoten, 1979.

Yasumaru Yoshio and Miyachi Masato, eds. *Shūkyō to kokka*. Nihon kindai shisō taikei 5. Tokyo: Iwanami Shoten, 1988.

Yiengpruksawan, Mimi Hall. *Hiraizumi*. Cambridge, Mass.: Harvard University Asia Center, 1998.

"Yogaku seito no shūgaku ryokō." *Sanuki gakuseikai zasshi*, vol. 18 (28 February 1903).

Yoshikawa Koretaru. "Nihon shoki shindai maku kaden bunsho." In *Shintō taikei ronsetsu hen 10 Yoshikawa Shintō*, edited by Shintō Taikei Hensankai, 115–335. Tokyo: Shintō Taikei Hensankai, 1983.

Yunoki Manabu. *Nihon suijō kōtsūshiron*. Vol. 6. Tokyo: Bunken Shuppan, 1996.

Zōzusan Konpira Daigongen reigenki. Undated. In the collection of Tawa Bunko.

Newspapers

Kagawa Shinpō
Kainan Shinbun
Kōchi Shinbun
Nagoya Shinbun
Ōsaka Asahi Shinbun
Sanuki Jitsugyō Shinbun
Sanuki Nippō
Sanuki Shinbun
San'yō Shinbun
Takamatsu Shōhō
Yosan Shinpō

STUDIES OF THE WEATHERHEAD EAST ASIAN INSTITUTE
COLUMBIA UNIVERSITY

Selected Titles

Japan's Colonization of Korea: Discourse and Power, by Alexis Dudden. University of Hawai'i Press, 2004.

Divorce in Japan: Family, Gender, and the State, 1600–2000, by Harald Fuess. Stanford University Press, 2004.

The Communist Takeover of Hangzhou: The Transformation of City and Cadre, 1948–54, by James Gao. University of Hawai'i Press, 2004.

Gutenberg in Shanghai: Chinese Print Capitalism, 1876–1937, by Christopher A. Reed. UBC Press, 2004.

The North Korean Revolution: 1945–50, by Charles Armstrong. Cornell University Press, 2002.

Taxation without Representation in Rural China, by Thomas P. Bernstein and Xiaobo Lü. Modern China Series, Cambridge University Press, 2003.

Korea between Empires, 1895–1919, by Andre Schmid. Columbia University Press, 2002.

Limits to Power: Asymmetric Dependence and Japan's Foreign Aid, by Akitoshi Miyashita. Lexington Books, 2003.

The Dawn That Never Comes: Shimazaki Toson and Japanese Nationalism, by Michael Bourdaghs. Columbia University Press, 2003.

Spanning Japan's Modern Century: The Memoirs of Hugh Borton, by Hugh Borton. Lexington Books, 2002.

Consumer Politics in Postwar Japan: Institutional Boundaries of Citizen Activism, by Patricia Maclachlan. Columbia University Press, 2001.

Abortion before Birth Control: The Politics of Reproduction in Postwar Japan, by Tiana Norgren. Princeton University Press, 2001.

Japan's Imperial Diplomacy: Consuls, Treaty Ports, and War with China, 1895–1938, by Barbara Brooks. University of Hawai'i Press, 2000.

Japan's Budget Politics: Balancing Domestic and International Interests, by Takaaki Suzuki. Lynne Rienner Publishers, 2000.

Assembled in Japan: Electrical Goods and the Making of the Japanese Consumer, by Simon Partner. University of California Press, 1999.

Civilization and Monsters: Spirits of Modernity in Meiji Japan, by Gerald Figal. Duke University Press, 1999.

The Logic of Japanese Politics: Leaders, Institutions, and the Limits of Change, by Gerald L. Curtis. Columbia University Press, 1999.

Trans-Pacific Racisms and the U.S. Occupation of Japan, by Yukiko Koshiro. Columbia University Press, 1999.

Bicycle Citizens: The Political World of the Japanese Housewife, by Robin LeBlanc. University of California Press, 1999.

Alignment despite Antagonism: The United States, Japan, and Korea, by Victor Cha. Stanford University Press, 1999.